A Violent Peace

Post 45 Loren Glass and Kate Marshall, Editors
Post•45 Group, Editorial Committee

A Violent Peace

Race, U.S. Militarism, and Cultures of Democratization
in Cold War Asia and the Pacific

Christine Hong

Stanford University Press
Stanford, California

STANFORD UNIVERSITY PRESS
Stanford, California

©2020 by the Board of Trustees of the Leland Stanford Junior University. All rights reserved.

No part of this book may be reproduced or transmitted in any form or by any means, electronic or mechanical, including photocopying and recording, or in any information storage or retrieval system without the prior written permission of Stanford University Press.

Printed in the United States of America on acid-free, archival-quality paper

Library of Congress Cataloging-in-Publication Data
Names: Hong, Christine, author.
Title: A violent peace : race, U.S. militarism, and cultures of democratization in Cold War Asia and the Pacific / Christine Hong.
Other titles: Post 45.
Description: Stanford : Stanford University Press, 2020. | Series: Post*45 | Includes bibliographical references and index.
Identifiers: LCCN 2019048061 (print) | LCCN 2019048062 (ebook) | ISBN 9781503603134 (cloth) | ISBN 9781503612914 (paperback) | ISBN 9781503612921 (ebook)
Subjects: LCSH: War and literature—History—20th century. | Politics and literature—History—20th century. | Racism—United States—History—20th century. | Militarism—United States—History—20th century. | Anti-imperialist movements—History—20th century. | United States—Armed Forces—East Asia—History. | United States—Armed Forces—Southeast Asia—History. | United States—Race relations—Political aspects—History. | United States—Politics and government—1945–1989.
Classification: LCC PN56.W3 H64 2020 (print) | LCC PN56.W3 (ebook) | DDC 809/.93358—dc23
LC record available at https://lccn.loc.gov/2019048061
LC ebook record available at https://lccn.loc.gov/2019048062

Cover art: "We Are Here to Stop You," Nan Young Lee, 2013

Cover design: Rob Ehle

Typeset by Kevin Barrett Kane in 10/15 Minion Pro

to 별

Contents

Acknowledgments ix

INTRODUCTION 1

1 "Democracy within the Teeth of Fascism":
The Black POW and the Invisible War at Home
in Ralph Ellison's War Writings 23

2 Revolution from Above: Ōe Kenzaburō,
the Black Airman, and Occupied Japan 54

3 A Blueprint for Occupied Japan: Miné Okubo and the
American Concentration Camp 79

4 Possessive Investment in Ruin: The Target, the Proving
Ground, and the U.S. War Machine in the Nuclear Pacific 107

5 People's War, People's Democracy, People's Epic:
Carlos Bulosan, U.S. Counterintelligence, and
Cold War Unreliable Narration 137

6 The Enemy at Home: Urban Warfare and
the Russell Tribunal on Vietnam 165

7 Militarized Queerness: Racial Masking and the
Korean War Mascot 195

EPILOGUE 219

Notes 227

Index 285

Acknowledgments

Joe O'Wren, Monica Kim, Karen Tei Yamashita, Gautam Premnath, Neda Atanasoski, Nick Mitchell, and Jasmine Syedullah, all treasured people to me, have been closest to this project in its current form. At moments along the way, they gave me the fullness of their time, attention, and care. Joe supported me in every imaginable way. He, Monica, and Gautam offered discerning feedback. KT read nearly every chapter. While burning the midnight oil on opposite coasts, Monica and I grounded each other as we labored on our respective projects.

Early on, Colleen Lye, Dori Hale, and Saidiya Hartman offered important mentorship and guidance. Conversations at Berkeley with Chris Berry, Lorna Hudson, Abdul JanMohamed, Samera Esmeir, Donna Jones, Leti Volpp, Scott Saul, and Lyn Hejinian enlivened my research. Sue Schweik was a source of wisdom and great kindness throughout. A vital interlocutor, Elaine Kim offered a ready ear and an incisive critical perspective. In the context of campus organizing, she and Ling-chi Wang stood alongside students and workers, modeling activist-scholarly engagement. Since meeting them at Berkeley, I have drawn on the warmth, love, and constancy of Amy Lee, Kasturi Ray, Katherine Lee, and Audrey Wu Clark, who have become lifelong friends. Discussions about future collaborative projects with Amy, my coimaginator, have brought levity to hard times. I am grateful to Judy Han and Jenny Chun for creating a space for critical Korean studies where there was none. I thank Miryam Sas for her courage and clarity. Jeff Santa Ana, Mary Melinn, Sharon Goetz, Victor Mendoza, Snehal Shingavi, and Gail Offen-Brown fostered a rare sense of community in Wheeler Hall. Discussions with Nigel Hatton about James Baldwin, human rights, and race have stayed with me, as have conversations with Rudy Guevarra about overlapping empires and diaspora.

At UC Santa Cruz I have been anchored by many good friends and colleagues, including Nick, Neda, KT, Alice Yang, Ronaldo Wilson, Marcia Ochoa, Neel Ahuja,

Jenny Kelly, Eric Porter, Felicity Schaeffer, Taylor Ainslie, Shauntay Larkins, and the inspiring faculty in the vibrant hub that is Critical Race and Ethnic Studies (CRES), as well as Amy Lonetree, Loisa Nygaard, Micah Perks, Karen Bassi, Rob Wilson, Gina Langhout, Gail Hershatter, Bettina Aptheker, Judy Scott, Amanda Smith, Deanna Shemek, Nancy Kim, Pam Lawson, Anne Callahan, Amy Tessier, Julie Krueger, Amy Bruinooge, Jay Olson, and Kim Hwe. I have worked with talented and imaginative graduate students, including Sherwin Mendoza, Steph Chan, Melissa Poulsen, Calvin McMillin, Tim Yamamura, Tsering Wangmo Dhompa, Sarah Papazoglakis, Kara Hisatake, Trung Nguyen, Yuki Obayashi, Ka-eul Yoo, Steph Padilla, Danielle Crawford, Melanie Ho, Noya Kansky, Jane Komori, Darline Kim, Talib Jabbar, Kiley McLaughlin, Xindi Li, and Anny Mogollón. Discussions in graduate seminars on race, militarism, and empire in Asia and the Pacific; the nuclear Pacific; race, labor, and migration; and human rights, decolonization, and racial justice have bolstered this book. Johanna Isaacson and Dustin Wright furnished valuable research support. I have also been fortunate to teach, mentor, and organize alongside stellar undergraduates, including Veronica Mayeda, Maryela Perez, Tem Ismael, Alli Mayorga, Nadine Brennan, Anna Louie, Mariana Jimenez, Anney Traymany, Farrah Safari, Pilipinx Historical Dialogue coordinators, local Anakbayan members, SIN Collective members, the founders of Undocu Studies, BSU members, and the activists who fought so brilliantly and movingly for CRES. Since coming here, I have drawn strength from community near and far—indeed been immeasurably buoyed by the friendship and generosity of Tsering, Sarah, Kara, Veronica, Gautam, Kasturi, Leela Premnath, Sunaina Maira, Layla Maira, Joanna Meadvin, Will Packer, Julie Ha, Beenash Jafri, Juliann Anesi, Tolteka Cuauhtin, Wayne Yang, Maile Arvin, Marisol LeBrón, and Keith Camacho.

In various settings Siraj Ahmed, Don Weber, Jennifer Ho, James Thompson, Jane Thrailkill, Chris Connery, Susan Gillman, Josephine Lee, John Wright, and Tim Brennan posed questions that fortified this project. In a UC Humanities Research Institute (UCHRI) residential research group and beyond, Andy Smith and Curtis Marez went out of their way to offer painstaking feedback and encouragement. In a campus workshop organized by Flora Lu, Sylvanna Falcone offered astute professional advice. Early drafts of parts of this book were first published in *Comparative Literature Studies* (*CLS*) and *American Quarterly* (*AQ*). Sophia McClennan was a deft *CLS* guest editor, and the *AQ* editorial board and reviewer pushed my research in needed directions. Emily-Jane Cohen at Stanford University Press offered razor-sharp advice, strengthening this book. Ever-kind and witty, Faith Wilson Stein steered this book forward, and Jessica Ling, with great patience and warmth, ensured its completion. Robin D. G. Kelley and Chandan Reddy read this book with both care and palpable solidarity, offering incredibly generous, thoughtful feedback. I am truly in their debt.

I wish to thank the archivists and research librarians who facilitated my access to various collections: Alice Birney at the Library of Congress, Paul Moores and Hillary Jenks at Riverside City College, Dean Rowan at the UC Berkeley Law Library, and Eric Van Slander at the National Archives in College Park, Maryland. I am grateful to Seiko Buckingham for permission to reproduce images from the Miné Okubo estate. Fellowships from UC Berkeley's Chancellor's Postdoctoral Program, the American Council of Learned Societies, the Hellman Fund, UCHRI, the Bancroft Library, UC Santa Cruz Institute for Humanities Research, as well as grants from the UC Center for New Racial Studies and UC Santa Cruz's Committee on Research supported this book.

Over the past decade and a half, I have been privileged to work alongside and to learn from scholars, activists, and cultural workers committed to exposing hard truths about U.S. military empire in Asia and the Pacific and to pursuing just solutions to its violence and harm. Their tirelessness is humbling. More than simply critiquing the world in which we live, they courageously seek to transform it. Juyeon Rhee has been the dearest of friends, whose unerring political analysis I value immensely. I have been fortified by her love and support. The same is true of Monica, Ramsay Liem, Paul and Deann Borshay Liem, JT Takagi, Marty Hart-Landsberg, and Hyun Lee. I am fortunate to have Namhee Lee, Bruce Cumings, Kang Jeong-gu, Kim Dong-choon, Lee Daehoon, and Kim Jongmin as models of scholarly courage and to count Sarah Sloan, Gregory Elich, Ji-Yeon Yuh, Haeyoung Kim, An Hyekyoung, Crystal Baik, Joo Ok Kim, Patrick Chung, Alfred Flores, Minju Bae, Jeff Santa Ana, Leo Chang, Koohan Paik, and Arnie Saiki as comrades in a broader anti-imperialist activist-scholarly community.

Finally, I close with the deepest of thanks to family and family friends who waited for far too long while I brought this book to conclusion: my parents Myung Ki and Lorrie Hong, my sister Michelle Hong, my aunt Young-oak Kwon, my dear friends Yukyung Lee and Joan Wada, and last but not least, Joe and radiant Hanŭl. I am grateful beyond measure to all of you for your love. It has sustained me. This book also draws spirit from those who are no longer here. Joe, you have been rock-steady. I could not have written this without you.

A Violent Peace

INTRODUCTION

The Profile and the Target

In the wake of America's decisive victory in World War II something murky entered into U.S. affairs, both domestically and abroad. The principle of indistinction—or the theoretical nonperception of difference—would in short order be enshrined as a postracial ideal at the very heart of American conceptions of liberal democracy. It would simultaneously, however, take institutional form in the militarized practices of racial profiling and area targeting critical to the undemocratic exercise of U.S. police and war power—practices predicated on the lethal conflation of racialized humanity with suspect terrain that refused differentiation on the level of the individual while generating "group-differentiated vulnerability to premature death."[1] As a world-destroying and -remaking force, post-1945 U.S. militarism demands complex, historically layered, and geographically far-reaching analysis. It requires consideration of the racism of the U.S. war machine and the latter's equivocal function as an engine of both life-affirming and lethal multiculturalism. Yet our language for U.S. militarism's at once formative and enduring role in global and domestic affairs, even though this history extends back several decades, is strikingly impoverished and insufficiently attentive to its penetrating reach. Understanding the role of U.S. police and war power within the political economy of postwar U.S. "democracy" entails critically revisiting World War II's structural legacies. How we explain postwar U.S. militarism—its reliance on superior force to achieve political ends in foreign and domestic arenas—depends on our grappling with the transformation of the United States during World War II, a time of Jim Crow, into a boundary-blurring, total-war state, permanently mobilized not only for war abroad but also for war at its very core.

Examining how World War II, a war supposedly fought against the twin threats of militarism and fascism, gave rise to a far-reaching system of militarized unfreedom and imperial subjection requires challenging orthodoxy around the so-called good fight. Here, the pervasive cultural mythos that the 1950s was a time of war-fostered plenty has had the effect of recuperating, in terms of perceived domestic benefits, not only the Korean War, a U.S. war of intervention that left an estimated four million Koreans dead, but also World War II's total-war economy. It has sanctified the guns-and-butter thesis of the welfare-warfare state—namely, that "our economic well-being depends upon the military budget."[2] That World War II saw unprecedented job opportunities for blacks, women, and migrants—segments of the labor force previously excluded or marginalized by reason of race, gender, or nationality—has granted U.S. militarism a potent democratic aura that persists to this day. What President Franklin Roosevelt, in World War II's early years, described in velvet-glove terms as America's "arsenal of democracy" signaled, however, far more than the shifting of domestic industry into war gear and the consequent heralded opening of the labor market. The arsenal of democracy relied on total war's iron-fist infrastructure, which would shape the postwar U.S. welfare-warfare state, mostly in shadowy or unseen ways.[3]

Where it surfaced, warfare's criticality to U.S. democratization efforts would call into question the postwar U.S. global project. Few could deny that Cold War America, with its serial catastrophic wars in Asia, had presented a damning "image of violence" in the form of mass civilian death to the world rather than a galvanizing vision of "revolution, freedom and democracy."[4] As Ho Chi Minh repeatedly pointed out, "U.S. imperialists . . . are clamouring about 'peace,' [while] hurriedly building up many more military bases, dispatching many additional troops to South Vietnam and intensifying the bombing of North Vietnam"; such professions of peace "can by no means fool ours and the world peoples."[5] As he noted, the United States had actively armed repressive client-states in the greater region while turning a blind eye to their counterrevolutionary violence. In Asia and the Pacific, where the Cold War immediately turned hot, the task of keeping the peace would thus prove hard to differentiate from the waging of war. Insofar as democracy could be said to be the legacy of U.S. triumph in the former Pacific theater of World War II, it presumed militarism, if not outright war, as a precondition. Significantly, in that same window, race, long the overt contradiction to U.S. claims to democracy on the world stage, would be strategically enfolded into the Cold War U.S. war machine. Indeed, the desegregation of the U.S. armed forces preceded *Brown v. Board of Education* by several years. Of the dubiousness of military integration as a civil-rights gain during a time of counterinsurgent U.S. war in Asia, Martin Luther King Jr. perceived that the Vietnam War succeeded in aligning "Negro and white boy... in brutal *solidarity* burning the huts of a poor village."[6]

For the inhabitants of Asia and the Pacific, the postwar Pax Americana, the American military "peace" that settled the region in the wake of Japan's defeat, would introduce an anticommunist necropolitical order in which unfreedom would be presented as freedom, democratization as democracy, and militarism as the basis for life itself. In real terms the Pax Americana meant the suspension of decolonizing justice, the deaths of several million civilians, the displacement of many millions more, nuclear ruin that eclipsed the magnitude of the atomic bombings of Hiroshima and Nagasaki, and the creation of a forward-deployed permanent garrison state anchored in hosting sites throughout the region. During an era that some American Cold War historians have breezily described as a long peace, this militarized regime institutionalized the sweep and grip of U.S. power within the former Pacific theater of World War II in the form of the Pacific Command (now Indo-Pacific Command), the oldest and largest of U.S. military commands around the world.[7] Encompassing more than half the earth and 70 percent of the world's oceans, this sprawling military empire extends latitudinally from the Arctic to Antarctica and longitudinally from the western United States to India's west coast.[8] Meant to keep the regional peace, it stands as a testament to a legacy of ongoing, underrecognized war. How do we begin to square this history of catastrophic violence and world-altering terror with a redemptive national narrative of postwar U.S. democracy? How do we account for the formidable structure of counterrevolutionary violence that materialized out of the heated U.S. engagements in Asia and the Pacific during the Cold War—namely, the U.S. national security state, its empire of bases, its permanent war economy, and the military-industrial complex?[9] How and why did most Americans perceive a time of unrestrained war violence to be a period of uneasy peace?

Examination of the Cold War U.S. military behemoth that emerged from U.S. entanglements in Asia and the Pacific requires analysis of the aftermath of U.S. triumph consequent to its total-war strategies in World War II's Pacific theater. Scholars have periodized World War II as a rupture, in a world-historical sense—a global racial break, according to Howard Winant, and the inception of the age of the world target, in Rey Chow's influential theorization. Yet even as Winant locates what he contends was a worldwide shattering of the formal trappings of white supremacy against domestic civil rights struggles and the sweep of postwar global decolonization movements, he does not dwell on how U.S. war strategy flexibly adjusted to these shifting geopolitical conditions or how the U.S. military, embroiled in a counterrevolutionary war in Korea just half a decade after World War II, led the way in institutionalizing colorblindness as postwar U.S. policy.[10] Indeed, at the Cold War's onset Harry Truman's Committee on Equality of Treatment and Opportunity in the Armed Services (the Fahy Committee), in assessing the costs of black demoralization on the Jim Crow military, stressed "the interdependence of the objectives of equal opportunity and military efficiency" in the armed services.[11] We thus must inquire into the centrality of the self-legitimating strategies of U.S. military empire to the racial break itself. In contrast to Winant's thesis, Chow's account of the militarized global dispensation inaugurated by the U.S. atomic bombings of Japan brings into sharp relief how the U.S. war machine positioned the world as a target, always already subjugated at the end of a nuclear kill-chain. Yet Chow does not theorize the target beyond identifying it as "an object to be destroyed."[12] While critiquing the nexus of war, national security, and race specific to Cold War Asian area studies, she assumes rather than explicitly argues the racism of war and militarism. How race inheres in the logic of the target thus goes unaddressed.

Whereas the obsolescence of racism as a ruling idea is at the heart of Winant's account, the emergence of unrivaled annihilatory U.S. war power is at the center of Chow's analysis. If Winant's account illuminates the postfascist liberalization of postwar racial orders worldwide, Chow's thesis sheds needed light on the post-Hiroshima illiberalism of a world order conditioned by the threat of apocalyptic U.S. force. In this regard both accounts look back to World War II as catalyzing U.S. global ascendancy, yet Winant's emphasis is biopolitical whereas Chow's is geopolitical. Winant's racial-break thesis and Chow's theorization of the age of the world target have much to say to each other. Both hint at what I contend is the strategic logic of indistinction that informs the liberalism *and* illiberalism of postwar U.S. military empire in Asia and the Pacific. If World War II expanded the concept of the military target and, with it, permissible indiscriminate death, it also highlighted, for all the world to see, the black soldier's quandary in America's Jim Crow army, fighting for democracy and against fascism on two fronts. As Winant briefly acknowledges, the "embittering return to a segregated or colonized homeland" (133) of soldiers of color propelled postwar movements against formal racism. Not, however, merely a factor in the abandonment of racism as state policy, U.S. war strategy in the first instance drove federal desegregation.

We might remember the call for wartime national unity issued by Robert Patterson, Roosevelt's undersecretary of war. Urging whites to regard World War II as "every American's emergency" and to refrain from racist violence against black veterans in uniform, he reasoned that the danger posed by the enemy was common to all—indeed, that "the aerial bomb draws no color line."[13]

A mere half decade after World War II, the biopolitics of the racial break and the geopolitics of the age of the world target would converge in interoperable ways in the Korean theater. U.S. war planners seized on the Korean War as an opportunity to implement Truman's 1948 Executive Order 9981, which called for the desegregation of the armed forces. In *The Strange Career of Jim Crow*, published shortly after the Korean War's combat phase, C. Vann Woodward observed: "In two historic instances, Negro Americans have been beneficiaries—as well as victims—of the national compulsion to level or to blur distinctions. The first leveling ended the legal status of slavery, the second the legal system of segregation. Both abolitions left the beneficiaries still suffering under handicaps inflicted by the system abolished."[14] This point is worth considering because the apparent racial democratization of the U.S. military in Korea would later be retrieved as evidence of an American civil rights "victory."[15] As historian Daniel Widener contends, "The Korean War provided the impetus for a specific reordering of American racial relations, paving the way for the emergence of the belief that the U.S. military ... represents the most meritocratic, socially equal, and ultimately progressive institution in American society."[16] At the same time, however, this asymmetrical war furnished the occasion for the Pentagon to expand its definition of the military target, stretched to "include every human-made structure," predictably leading to what historian Bruce Cumings has called a "bombing holocaust."[17] As Harold Ickes pointed out in a March 3, 1951, article for the *New Republic*, U.S. aerial bombing in Korea did not "distinguish between the sexes or between the aged and infants" (quoted in Conway-Lanz, 154). Even as late as 1957, while visiting North Korea as it was rebuilding its society in the wake of U.S. aerial warfare, the French documentarian Chris Marker commented: "*Extermination passed over this land.* Who could count what burned with the houses?"[18] As the Cold War dawned, the principle of indistinction at play in the racial integration of the U.S. armed forces—and hailed by liberals as a civil rights milestone—thus had another institutional manifestation in the expansion of the target. In both instances, indistinction as U.S. policy was aimed first and foremost at ensuring the war machine's necropolitical efficiency.

As a modality of racial capitalism, Cold War U.S. militarism in Asia and the Pacific enabled a range of incommensurate political outcomes, cognitively mapped as "representative government for some and despotism for others."[19] Yet to no small degree, investment in the democratizing returns of war *over there*—namely, civil rights gains *here*—contributed to the mystifications of the post-1945 U.S. welfare-warfare state. Reflecting on what impelled her to write her Korean War novel *Home*, Toni Morrison described her fascination with the darker recesses of the 1950s: "I have noticed how people think of it as a golden age, you know post-war, lots of money, everybody was employed, the television shows were cheerful. And I think we forgot what was really going on in the '50s."[20] Here, she clarified, "We forgot McCarthy, anti-communist horror. We forgot that there was a war that we didn't call a war, called a Korean police action. And it was a violent time for African-Americans." Morrison's comments point to the necessity of locating the potent imperialist concoction at the heart of military Keynesianism—the notion that U.S. war violence abroad stimulates universal prosperity, expanded social welfare, and democratization at home—within the lethality of Jim Crow. Not simply a site where the "good life" and other benefits of capitalist democracy could be pursued and realized, the U.S. home front was imprinted, in opaque undemocratic ways, by both Jim Crow and the structural legacies of World War II as a total war. The war's perceived democratic benefits, emblematized by icons like Rosie the Riveter, call for comparative analysis against the total-war state's institutionalization of a permanent war posture against internal dissidence. Insofar as democracy was to be had in this militarized configuration, it calls for critical interpretation, to borrow Ralph Ellison's resonant World War II–era phrase, as "democracy within the teeth of fascism."[21]

If the mass mobilization of society during World War II meant the provisional inclusion of historically marginalized and reviled demographics in the war industries and the consequent enlargement of civil rights, total war also meant the securitized mapping of the home front, renamed the "Zone of the Interior," a term originating in World War I but animated on a vaster and far more complex scale during World War II. Indeed, democracy's arsenal would serve as home to overlapping U.S. military and domestic counterintelligence campaigns, in essence, a testing ground for militarized technologies of surveillance, racial repression, and social control aimed at rooting out "fifth-column" activity in stateside armed forces and civilian populations. In ways that anticipated postwar political-policing measures aimed at neutralizing anti-imperialist, race-radical, and Third Worldist movements, total war furnished the rationale for the targeting of domestic populations as potential enemies of the state—spectacularly in the mass incarceration of ethnic Japanese and covertly in a nationwide FBI investigation into "racial conditions in the United States" (RACON) that, in surveilling and infiltrating black, Japanese, and communist organizations, set the stage for COINTELPRO.[22]

Under the Cold War rubric of civil defense, a securitized conception of national territory that derived from the geostrategic notion of the Zone of the Interior, the United States waged war in its cities. In the late 1960s the Pentagon developed a military-operational plan, "Garden Plot," aimed at preempting urban unrest. It elaborated protocols for the pacification of urban arenas, including profiling neighborhoods according to "population by race," "poor economic and sociological conditions," "concentrated unemployment," "existence of wide-spread sense of injustice," and access to weapons. Through the lens of counterinsurgency doctrine, so-called high-crime areas were thus interpreted as "enemy territory" where armed combatants could "blend into the civilian population when under close surveillance or pursuit," making it difficult for "the pursuing army to distinguish between the enemy and the civilian population."[23] According to one late 1960s analysis: "As in the war in Vietnam, where an American soldier finds it difficult to distinguish among Vietnamese ... so the white American policeman finds it difficult to distinguish among Negroes, the predominant population in high-crime areas" (Black and Labes, 667). The framing of racial profiling in the language of counterinsurgency should alert us to the tactical convergence between U.S. military interventions abroad and the covert domestic wars the United States has prosecuted from the 1960s to the present. Akin to the simultaneously indiscriminate and group-differentiating logic of the *target* with its built-in margin of collateral damage, *racial profiling* presumes guilt not just by association but by location, sweepingly conflating racialized humanity with areas where "mere presence in a certain place" is tantamount to a crime.[24] It turns on the simultaneous visibility of race as perceived threat and the invisibility of those targeted "as 'individuals'" (M. Jones, 165). In her memoir, Black Lives Matter cofounder Patrisse Khan-Cullors reflects on how the wars on drugs and gangs ethnically cleansed U.S. cities, catalyzing the "forced migration" of black and brown communities and enabling "young white people [to] build exciting new lives ... on the bones of ours."[25] More than deterritorializing in its combat operations on foreign soil, the United States has prosecuted wars domestically in unseen or underrecognized ways.

As a boundary-blurring total war, World War II renewed the role of U.S. war power in dispossessing native peoples. Three years after Roosevelt's decision to enter the war, the securitized mapping of the United States as the Zone of the Interior corresponded to a staggering enlargement of military property holdings by 800 percent, one of the largest land grabs in twentieth-century U.S. history.[26] Wartime emergency powers were wielded to justify the seizure of "public lands," indigenous lands that were then placed under military control for a range of necropolitical objectives, many contaminating in their effects, including uranium excavation and nuclear weapons testing. The journey of the atom in the nuclear Pacific thus traced an itinerary from indigenous lands in North America to the atomic devastation of Hiroshima and Nagasaki to U.S. nuclear testing in the Marshall Islands.[27] Just a year into the postwar era, the United States detonated the first in a series of world-shattering high-yield nuclear weapons in the Marshall Islands, with low-yield nuclear tests on Western Shoshone lands in Nevada to come. For most of the Cold War the United States strategically enclosed the Marshall Islands as part of its vast oceanic Pacific Proving Grounds, administering the islands as a strategic trust territory under the Department of the Interior—akin to tribal or "domestic dependent nations" in the United States. Analysis of the post-1945 Pax Americana therefore calls for the necropolitical conceptualization of territory not just in theaters of U.S. war and its sprawling empire of bases in Asia and the Pacific but also within the borders of the settler-colonial state. Not always destroying in order to remake native land as settler home, much less eventuating in privatization of property, but often destroying to destroy, the transformation of indigenous lands into *terra nullius* in the name of national security compels us to examine war power as an ongoing motor of the United States as both military-imperial *and* settler-colonial formation.[28]

Race under the Sign of Total War

This book examines the price of biopolitical inclusion and territorial absorption within the securitized contours of U.S. military empire in Asia and the Pacific. By theorizing a range of people's struggles—black freedom, Asian liberation, and Pacific Islander decolonization—as homologous responses to unchecked U.S. war and police power at home and abroad, I analyze how alignment, participation, and complicity with the U.S. military, under the ideological aegis of the transpacific

Pax Americana, blurred the color line, giving a redemptive liberal veneer to U.S. war politics in Asia and the Pacific. If saturated with violence, the racial integration of humanity into the U.S. war machine was central to militarism's democratizing promise. This democratic makeover notwithstanding, post-1945 U.S. war politics recalled what black radicals, pointing to the ongoing home-front battle for black freedom, criticized as U.S. fascism, often referencing U.S. hot wars in Asia as the external corollary to its domestic counterinsurgencies. Wary of the costs of militarized inclusion, transwar black radical writings rendered visible what their authors called "wars within wars," or the black struggle for freedom in the context of U.S. wars, as a way of countering the U.S. warfare state's propagation of black Americans in uniform as a form of racial uplift. By retrieving a black radical critique of the fascism of U.S. war power, this book explores U.S. militarism's centrality to the political and cultural imagination of conscripted, colonized, and occupied peoples within an era of U.S. "police actions" abroad and a rising police state at home.

With a lens on the double-fronted nature of Cold War racial terror, this study sheds light on the transposability of U.S. military tactics and strategies against "unruly" populations at home and "enemies" abroad. I examine intelligence and racial counterintelligence as the modality of America's informal wars throughout the Cold War—its counterinsurgencies, police actions, low-intensity wars, civil defense, riot-control measures, and political-policing operations. As I demonstrate, World War II served as the occasion for the United States to consolidate the tactics of intelligence warfare and political policing it thereafter deployed in double-fronted ways: both to pacify revolutionary populations in U.S. interventionist wars in Asia and to neutralize black radicals through domestic war operations like the FBI's COINTELPRO and the CIA's MHCHAOS. What surfaced as geographically far-flung, seemingly unrelated, campaigns of state violence—operationalizing the logic of the target and giving rise to racial profiling—were thus fundamentally linked, albeit in covert ways that eluded ready interpretation. Writing in 1971 against the backdrop of the U.S. war in Vietnam and just prior to the activist exposure of COINTELPRO, Eqbal Ahmad, a trenchant critic of evolving U.S. counterinsurgency doctrine, noted the boomerang effect of U.S. wars of aggression abroad. The "practice of counter-insurgency," he pointed out, had "erode[d] the democratic processes and institutions of metropolitan countries."[29] By cognitively mapping U.S. informal war in the long wake of World War II, this book examines the structural linkages between militarized state responses to domestic disorder and foreign war.

Black antifascism, both during World War II and throughout the Cold War, served as a revelatory lens with regard to the centrality of warfare to the political economy of the United States. It disclosed the continuity between the U.S. "police action" in Korea and "the policeman's bullet" at home.[30] Far from hailing "Jim-Crow in uniform," in Claudia Jones's phrase, as a sign of democratic progress, black antifascist critique perceived the lurking fascist dimensions of race within militarized form, foreseeing the prospect of militarized transracial complicity in a fascist agenda of unfreedom, including imperialist war.[31] It thus necessarily framed its analysis of Jim Crow in the military and defense industries not in narrowly domestic terms but against the imperialism of U.S. war power. In his wartime novel *If He Hollers Let Him Go*, Chester Himes described the "filled-up feeling of my country" that his black narrator, Bob Jones, experiences while working in California's war industries: "I felt included in it all; I had never felt included before."[32] Yet the gains to be had as a low-level beneficiary of U.S. war violence soon give way to the unnerving racial feeling pervading democracy's arsenal. All too fleeting, Jones's total-war euphoria morphs into an unshakable "crazy, scared feeling" of losing his job or "getting pulled up by the roots" (30) like the Japanese Americans he witnessed being forcibly removed to concentration camps. Specters of militarized unfreedom like these haunt the war-occasioned national fantasy of upward mobility and multicultural unity. In an unpublished 1940 Federal Writers' Project essay, "The Negro and the War," Ellison argued that war's seduction stemmed from its "offer[ing] a non-economic basis upon which Negroes could participate in the national life." Mobilization against a common enemy was used cynically, as he put it, as "a device for unifying the diverse classes of the fascist state."[33]

By contrast, triumphalist American accounts of World War II as a resounding moral victory acclaim the U.S. war machine's flexible tactics with regard to racialized humanity. Identified in some civil rights histories as a catalyst for racial equality, "war, if not credited with destroying US bigotries outright, is remembered as the 'seed' or 'watershed' from which racial justice developed."[34] The postwar portrait of the integrated U.S. war machine as a social equalizer obscured the black radical critique of its function as a fascistic generator of racial unfreedom. Pointing to "the undemocratic character of the army of American imperialism," C. L. R. James declared at World War II's outset that it was not a workers' war. Black men conscripted into an apartheid army possessed no "control of the means of destruction."[35] In this, James alighted on a core truth that would persist past the racial integration of the U.S. armed forces—namely, the U.S. war machine's incapacity to wage a genuinely people's war. Here we can trace a continuum from the total-war incorporation, under segregated conditions, of black Americans into the U.S. war effort during World War II to the vanguardist multiculturalism of the U.S. military during the early postwar period. As Neda Atanasoski has argued, "Because it authorizes ongoing imperial violence, multiculturalism can be characterized not simply as a new racial technology but rather as the *afterlife of previous racial forms*."[36] As this book traces, militarized multiculturalism evolved structurally from fascistic conceptions of war unity.[37]

Throughout the Cold War, multiculturalism would furnish U.S. interventionist war with its liberal veneer. The brute geopolitics of U.S. militarism and antihumanism of its post-1945 war machine would be superficially belied by the U.S. military's biopolitical inclusivity. Vital to the recuperation of U.S. militarism in Asia and the Pacific—its occupations, base expansions, counterinsurgencies, nuclearization, and wars—as liberalizing racial opportunity was the deployment of desegregated forces to the region, the "humanitarian" baby-lifts of Asian and mixed-race war orphans consequent to U.S. interventions in Korea and Vietnam, the citizenship gateway for Asian GI brides, the forging of "mutual defense" alliances with Asians and Pacific Islanders "liberated" from Japanese rule, and the promise of economic aid for coalition allies. Strategically motivated, this securitized enlargement of the terms of humanity did not translate into meaningful avenues of political participation. Insofar as integration into U.S. military empire meant heightened exposure to death even as it held out the prospect of selective induction to the side of life, it fostered risk-based multiculturalism and subimperial dependency. Indeed, with the dawning of the Cold War, the U.S. concentration camp, the bombed-out cityscapes of Hiroshima and Nagasaki, the frontlines of U.S. wars of aggression in Asia, and the U.S. military uniform would be coded as sites of democratic opportunity for racialized subjects. If the Cold War in Asia and the Pacific catalyzed advances in civil rights for some, this perceived progress obscured the violence of a U.S.-sponsored agenda of freedom through militarization. The expansion of civil rights in a newly desegregated U.S. military, and the assertion of those rights over and against the human rights of occupied peoples, further obscured structural linkages and entanglements between differently subjugated populations.

This book offers a twinned genealogical account of U.S. war and police power, on the one hand, and postwar multiculturalism, on the other, that originates in an untold tale of midcentury U.S. fascism. It employs a comparative methodology that at moments dwells on and dilates junctures of political solidarity and alliances during the Cold War among black Americans, Asian Americans, Pacific Islanders, and Asians yet principally seeks to shed necessary light on how the U.S. warfare state fostered interdependency in a covert framework of counterinsurgency. I attend to the convergence, at times indistinguishability, of U.S. *territorial geopolitics* and *racial biopolitics* within post-1945 U.S. military-empire in Asia and the Pacific. These are this book's structuring terms of comparison. Read as indices of semisovereignty, these dynamics of absorption and inclusion cannot be theorized outside patterns of indigenous dispossession, racial exploitation, and militarized neutralization. They enable an account not only of the strategic blurring of racial lines against the backdrop of U.S. wars and nuclear violence in Asia and the Pacific but also of the overlap between the United States as both military-imperial and settler-colonial formation. Where I highlight racial entanglement, collusion, and critique, I argue for their contextualization as "wars within wars" (Ellison). Thus, rather than take desegregation, assimilation, and racial mobility as untroubling signs of domestic racial progress, this study examines their geostrategic utility. In the early twentieth century W. E. B. Du Bois famously predicted that the color line would be the defining problem of the century. As this book demonstrates, the blurring of the color line would prove central to the hegemonic operations of U.S. militarism in Cold War Asia and the Pacific.

Asia for Americans

In Asia and the Pacific, where, as Lenin forecasted, the rival imperialisms of Japan and the United States would not peacefully coexist in some "ultra-imperialist" alliance but would eventuate in brutal war, American white supremacist ideologies and Jim Crow practices would be challenged by Japan's canny articulation of its own imperialist aspirations in color-line slogans that highlighted the contradictions of U.S. claims to democracy.[38] Beyond the pan-Asianism of its oft-cited catchphrases, "The Great East Asia Co-Prosperity Sphere," "Two Nations as One," or "Asia for the Asiatics," Japan pitched the global legitimacy of its military-imperial enterprise in racially egalitarian mottos—like "Black, Yellow, Red, and Brown"—that appealed to the nonwhite world for solidarity.[39] In this regard World War II in the Pacific theater was less a race war between an Asian people and (white) Americans who perceived each other through the distortions of stereotypes, as John Dower has notably argued, than a pitched battle in which the *flexibility* of warring ideologies around race was put to the test. Although vanquished, Japan emerged arguably unrivaled in this arena.

What Japan powerfully modeled—and where it left the United States in the dust—was its capacity, as a fascistic military-imperial power, to embrace the ideology of multiculturalism as central to its Pax Japonica vision of regional rule. As historian Takashi Fujitani has argued, the transformation of the United States and Japan into total-war states during World War II meant that neither could "afford to ignore even [their] most abjected populations."[40] Although Fujitani's focus does not extend into the postwar period, his insight into the opportunism of the "inclusionary racism" (384) of both U.S. and Japanese war machines sheds crucial light on the total-war origins of the racially incorporative logic of postwar U.S. militarism. In particular, how the United States legitimized its presence as the reigning power in the Pacific in the wake of Japan's defeat—hurriedly abandoning its commitment to Jim Crow in its military ranks—entails inquiring into its former foe's self-fashioning as the "champion of the darker races."[41] To understand the U.S. war machine's shifting racial politics, in other words, we must examine its deterritorializing absorption of the governing logic of the vanquished. In the heat of World War II, Pearl S. Buck reported to the U.S. public that "Japan . . . is declaring in the Philippines, in China, in India, Malaya, and even Russia that there is no basis for hope that colored peoples can expect any justice" from the United States: "Every lynching, every race riot gives joy to Japan. The discriminations of the American army and navy and the air forces against colored soldiers and sailors, the exclusion of colored labor in our defense industries and trade unions, all our social discriminations, are of greatest aid today to our enemy in Asia, Japan. 'Look at America,' Japan is saying to millions of ears. 'Will white Americans give you equality?'"[42] According to historian Ernest Allen, Japanese propaganda went even further: it offered assurances to black Americans in the South that they would be "beneficiaries of a more democratic social order within the United States via the intervention of the Japanese imperial army."[43] The first order of business, following a Japanese invasion, would be the "redistribution of southern farmland" (43). The draw of the Pax Japonica to black Americans in the South therefore resided, at least in part, in its supposed commitment to making good on the unfinished business of radical Reconstruction.[44]

Although Japan's appeal to black Americans necessarily disavowed the racism of its brutal colonial policies toward its Asian and Pacific Islander neighbors, its capacity to exploit discourses of racial unity in ways unavailable to both the United States and Nazi Germany might alert us to how fascist and imperialist ideologies around race, specifically in the Pacific theater, were elastic in their articulation. By calling attention to the overt racism of the United States toward its Asian enemy as well as its formal Jim Crow policies, Japanese military empire, though racist and lethal in practice, vivified an ideological mode of regional rule—fascist, imperialist, *and* multicultural—that held instructive value for its successor. Still sinister in fascist threat but more ideologically supple in its adoption of a color-line stance against white imperialism, Japanese war propaganda rhetorically heralded an era of racial egalitarianism. For black Americans in the 1940s, as George Lipsitz notes, "the Japanese were not just any outsiders.... They were people of color with their own independent nation, a force capable of challenging Euro-American imperialism on its own terms, and possible allies against the oppressive power of white supremacy."[45] American jingoism demonizing the Japanese enemy in a time of Jim Crow, including by translating the Japanese into a well-worn antiblack idiom, was thus unsettled by the seductive power of Japan's multicultural ideology. Nazi race hatred might have resonated as chillingly familiar to black Americans, but Japanese propaganda deploying multiracial banners invited symbolic identification without eliciting structural critique. This was thus a potent fascistic appeal, coded as transnational racial solidarity. Seeking to alert black Americans to the dangers of Japanese color-line propaganda, the Harlem section of the American Communist Party warned: "Imperialism knows no color."[46] In an unpublished editorial for the *Negro Quarterly*, a wartime journal he coedited with black communist Angelo Herndon, Ellison noted that "one of the greatest ironies of the war . . . has been [Japan's] seizing even the psychologucal [sic] instrument of [the] power of imperialism and using it against the Western nations, thus bring[ing] color psychology through a complete circle."[47]

Subimperial Modernity

Engineered out of the spoils of World War II in the Pacific theater, U.S. military empire in Asia and the Pacific, as a system of "domination without annexation," would again—as journalist George Marion noted in 1948—"wait on war" to rationalize its expansion and consolidation.[48] U.S. victory in the region, which the United States treated as "an exclusively American theatre of operations," established the foundations of its system of bases in the Pacific, a vast militarized archipelago stretching westward from California and Alaska to Hawai'i, Okinawa, and South Korea, and southward from East Asia to Singapore, Guam, the Marshall Islands, and Australia.[49] A mere five years after World War II, the United States seized the occasion of the Korean War to fortify its military posture into a permanent regional infrastructure. By the time the Korean War came to a draw, the United States had massively expanded its military-imperial footprint by acquiring basing rights in Taiwan and adding or developing bases in South Korea and Japan—all told, a 40 percent increase of its total overseas military bases.[50] During the Cold War, U.S. wars against China, North Korea, and North Vietnam would demonstrate the U.S. garrison state's counterrevolutionary function, with regional U.S. bases serving as "a dagger . . . aimed at the underbelly of its socialist neighbors."[51]

The political economy of Cold War U.S. military imperialism in Asia and the Pacific has demanded critical analysis—and an explanatory language—beyond that of existing paradigms. As Walden Bello has stated of the postwar Pax Americana regime, it was "in the Asia-Pacific . . . that Washington launched its first experiments in neocolonial control—the sponsorship of formally independent but subservient regimes that could be counted on to promote US strategic and economic interests."[52] (7). Other theorists of U.S. neocolonialism—or what has variously been dubbed "imperialism without colonies," "invisible empire," "leasehold empire," and "informal empire"—have observed the critical role of U.S. militarism within an imperial system capable of domination, even absent formal claims on the sovereignty of postcolonial states.[53] Complicating classic center-periphery models, Cold War U.S. military empire, as a "multi-ringed defense system" structured to encircle socialist nations, must moreover be understood against what Matthias Luce, in his account of "sub-imperialism," has described as the "integrationist tendency of world capitalism" following World War II.[54] By cultivating Third World oligarchies, and in so doing recuperating regional wartime collaborators with Imperial Japan, U.S. military empire fostered a system of dependent capitalism, or "sub-imperialism," in which a spectrum of subordinate "nations [were] shaped into the sphere of influence that serve[d] the sub-imperialist country's capital reproduction" (Luce, "Sub-imperialism," 31–32). Aimed at actively rolling back socialism, the U.S. alignment with manipulable dictatorships gave rise to what critics have called "client fascism" or "subfascism."[55]

Insofar as the unequal, coercive geopolitical dynamics of military occupation, subimperial incorporation, and mutual defense alignment were framed as regional pathways to development, they must be theorized in conjunction with the biopolitical dynamics of desegregation, assimilation, and racial mobility that have typically been construed as equalizing social measures vital to democratic progress in the United States. Both modes of integration were central to securing U.S. dominion in Cold War Asia and the Pacific. In an era when civil rights reforms blurred the domestic color line, the promise of progress specific to the transpacific Pax Americana, its very democratic veneer, resided in the multiethnic, multinational participation of U.S. regional allies in a series of U.S. interventions in the region. Promoting a distinctively militarized form of Cold War internationalism, the United States, under the UN banner, prosecuted an asymmetrical war of aggression in Korea with the support of twenty other nations—in essence, a "subcontracting of counterinsurgency."[56] In the ensuing decade, under the rubric of Lyndon B. Johnson's "More Flags" program, troops from South Korea, Thailand, the Philippines, and South Vietnam, now refashioned as "Free World countries," trained with U.S. forces in Okinawa and served in both aid and combat capacities in Vietnam.[57] As critics noted, this reliance on Third Country Military Forces, or "rented troops," was a "benighted American attempt to internationalize the war as a cover for U.S. intervention."[58]

Yet the U.S. military, too, conceded that the campaign to seek "Free World" or "third-country" support was aimed at "eras[ing] the conception that the Vietnam War was purely an American undertaking supported only by non-Asians."[59] "Asians," the 1975 U.S. Army study *Allied Participation in Vietnam* reasoned, "were well qualified to understand and communicate with the Vietnamese people" without being "the target of anti-European feelings that were a legacy of the colonial period" (81–82). Moreover, "every Korean soldier sent to South Vietnam"—with more than three hundred thousand South Koreans mobilized— saved the United States from "sending an American or other allied soldier" (145) into battle, plus commanded far lower pay.[60] Although the United States maintained operational control over these forces, this study argued that the display of South Korean volunteerism was vital to the "More Flags" initiative's success. To parry charges of flunkeyism, South Koreans were compelled to demonstrate that "they were freely assisting the United States" (135). As *Allied Participation in Vietnam* delicately underscored, however, it was "understood that although [U.S.] directives to Korean units would be in the form of *requests* they would be honored as *orders*" (134, emphasis added).⁶¹ Unsurprisingly, in the verdict of the 1967 International War Crimes Tribunal on Vietnam, a quasi-legal people's forum that examined the U.S. war through the lens of international humanitarian law, South Korea, Japan, the Philippines, and Thailand, far from lauded for sending Asian soldiers as brothers in arms, were named as accomplices to U.S. aggression. At a tribunal hearing, Donald Duncan, a former Army Special Forces soldier, testified that U.S. recourse to Asian mercenaries was aimed at deflecting culpability: "We were continuously told 'You don't have to kill them yourself—let your indigenous counterpart do that.'"⁶² As Justice Lelio Basso summarized: "In its aggression the US has been able to procure a vast and numerous array of accomplices, helpers and followers who have given a ready hand. Practically every country in the Orient has been somewhat induced into this accomplice role."⁶³

Democratization's inextricability from U.S. militarism is the uneasy legacy of native-proxy reliance so central to multilateral regional military collaboration in the U.S. war in Vietnam—or Nixon's doctrine of "using Asian boys to fight Asian boys" (Kuzmarov, *Modernizing Repression*, 21). The lesson for those in the ambit of U.S. military empire was plain: access to postwar modernity could be had at a price—complicity with the U.S. war machine. In uneven ways across the region, U.S. military imperialism thereby fostered economic recuperation via interventionist wars that served as militarized substitutes for the Marshall Plan.⁶⁴ Perversely framed as modernizing opportunities, the Korean War was essential to postwar Japan's economic recovery and the Vietnam War likewise critical to South Korea's compressed development under military dictator Park Chung-hee. Unsurprisingly marginalized in these "democracy-building" efforts was reckoning with histories of colonial violence—whether Japanese, European, or American. The goal was the restructuring of the region as a free-market zone. Economic reconstruction through military force thus displaced the pursuit of decolonizing justice while circumventing local processes of democratic self-determination. In an era of global anticolonial struggles, the Pax Americana offered a transpacific, multinational, ethnically inclusive conception of securitized humanity, a defensive construction of "bonds forged in blood" that posited militarized development as a foil to notions of sovereignty or self-determination based on the people.

In the region where the United States unleashed atomic bombs against civilian populations and waged catastrophic anticommunist wars of intervention, U.S. militarism would be ideologically pitched as the basis for national recovery along purportedly democratic lines. Thus, relative to Japan, the bomb meant not only peace but also capitalist futurity. Examples outside this progressive teleology—*hibakusha* ("bomb-impacted person," or survivors of the Nagasaki and Hiroshima atomic bombs), irradiated Marshallese refugees, disabled civilians, separated family members, war orphans, militarized prostitutes and their mixed-race offspring, Agent Orange–exposed Vietnamese peasants and their descendants, long-term unconverted political prisoners in South Korea—fell within a permissible margin of human ruin or what Hosu Kim and Grace Cho refer to as the "biopolitical excess" of collateral damage.[65] Dependent on its production of war materiel for the United States in the Korean and Vietnam theaters, Japan's economic rehabilitation broadcast a clear message to the region: modernity, democracy, and peace were all possible but only through complicity with U.S. war and police power. Unadjudicated and unredressed, the atomic bombings thus established a paradigm of U.S. impunity that cleared the way for its devastating wars in Korea and Vietnam, as well as the sixty-seven nuclear tests it carried out from 1946 to 1958 in the Marshall Islands that, in magnitude, equaled 1.7 Hiroshimas and Nagasakis per day.

In post-1945 Asia and the Pacific, U.S. militarism would accordingly be framed as a means to a future, despite the fact that its chief products were mass death and ecocide. It would be promoted as a stabilizer of democracy and the basis of capitalist prosperity rather than a crisis-generating architecture responsible for regional repression and instability. In the 1980s Roland Simbulan dared state the obvious by describing U.S. military outposts in the Philippines as "the bases of our insecurity."[66] To no small degree, the counterrevolutionary function of U.S. bases was by design, their purpose to bolster counterrevolutionary conditions in host countries. Unthinkable outside U.S. military backing, governments like the Marcos regime were thereby empowered to wage internal war against revolutionary democracy movements. We might recall that by late 1943, the Joint Chiefs of Staff, forecasting Japan's defeat, developed a blueprint at Roosevelt's request in which postwar U.S. bases figured as essential infrastructure for a U.S.-dominated multilateral repressive apparatus in the Pacific—an "International Police Force." U.S. unilateralism conditioned this Pax Americana vision for the region. As historian Kimie Hara points out, although initially the major Allied powers, "the US, UK, Russia and China[,] were expected to assume world-wide responsibilities for security, the military did not have confidence in future international cooperation."[67] Unsurprisingly, this police force would undertake devastating anticommunist "police actions" in the region.

Encircling China and putting the Soviet Union on notice throughout the Cold War, the U.S. garrison state enabled the projection of U.S. war and police power within Asia and the Pacific; indeed, it continues to do so to this day. By militarizing the constabularies of allied nations and client regimes and modernizing their technologies of repression, the United States trained them to wage war against their own people and to take part in regional U.S. interventionist wars.[68] If "liberated" from Japanese colonial rule via U.S. intervention at the end of World War II, Okinawa, the Philippines, South Korea, and Guam were conscripted as launching pads for the U.S. war in Southeast Asia. In real terms the project of regional democratization thus meant the active suppression and repression of democracy. As antibase and people's democracy activists have for decades sought to bring into view, democracy, far from gifted by the United States, has in fact risen from below in Asian and Pacific Islander nations. Theirs has been a ceaseless battle within the formidable grid of U.S. military imperialism.

Rule without Law

As an extraterritorial expansion of the United States through overseas military bases and an imperial extension of its sovereignty through the boundary-blurring logic of national security, the Pax Americana reconfigured Asia and the Pacific as a geostrategic arena neither wholly external nor recognizably internal to the United States. Crucial to the ideology of American freedom yet outside U.S. territorial bounds, this region was a crucible for democratization as an imposed political project of the United States, realized at the barrel of a gun. Here, we might retrieve Karl Liebknecht's classic critique of militarism's antidemocratic nature—namely, that the "deciding factor in every social relation of power is, in the last resort, the superiority of physical force."[69]

Predicated not on law but on the tyranny of force, U.S. military empire in the region gave rise to securitized conceptions of humanity whose racial logic this book—with its inquiry into racial soldiering, wartime mass detention, racial counterintelligence, collaboration, subimperialism, human radiation experiments, and military mascotry—scrutinizes. It assembles a composite transpacific archive of U.S. war and militarism, placing into conversation a range of principally Cold War texts and objects that bear the deformative imprint of U.S. counterrevolutionary violence in Asia and the Pacific but that for reasons of national location, ethnic literary tradition, genre or medium, or narrowly conceived historic era have typically been interpreted apart. This archive includes minor war writings by major black writers, hibakusha accounts of the U.S. atomic bombing of Hiroshima, Nisei visual renderings of the American concentration camp, fictional reworkings of the occupation of Japan, black radical human rights petitions, GI photographs from the Korean theater, novels about Filipino guerrilla resistance to U.S. military rule, proceedings from anti-imperialist people's tribunals, Okinawan antibase discourse, and Marshallese critiques of U.S. human radiation experiments. Yet insofar as they were shadowed by U.S. military force, I read these cultural and political materials alongside a spectrum of U.S. government documents—congressional transcripts, national security directives, occupation edicts, military counterintelligence logs, army desegregation orders, policy blueprints, racial counterintelligence reports, and FBI case files.

Extending across national borders and unfettered by genre, the cultural archive of the Pax Americana in Asia and the Pacific demands, I contend, a flexible geopolitical reading practice that critically mirrors the supranational penetration of U.S. war and police power beyond and within U.S. territorial bounds as well as in sites not typically understood as arenas of war. It has a place within an undertheorized body of post-1945 cultural production—a politically equivocal body of cultural expression that we might call *art* or *literature of democratization*. The compositional elements of this corpus of writing, visual art, film, and performance—namely, race within militarized form—uneasily recall the mass ornaments of fascist aesthetics yet with a difference in emphasis and perspective. In contrast to the subordination of the human to militarized form in fascist aesthetics, the zooming in on racialized humanity in settings thoroughly conditioned by asymmetrical U.S. force enables disavowal of war's deterritorializing violence in the art of democratization. By backgrounding the conditions of invasive force that grant visibility to a spectrum of racially abject figures—Jim Crow soldier, camp inmate, cannon fodder, war trash, radiation test subject—the art of democratization lends itself to interpretive practices that minimize the structures in which precarious humanity was captured in the first place. It thereby permits liberalizing even humanitarian readings and progressive conclusions that mystify the nature of U.S. militarism as, above all, a modality of mass destruction. In this geopolitical corpus war figures as the enabling condition of democracy and the basis of capitalist futurity. In its suggestion of democratic possibility within the confines of militarized unfreedom, of life possibility in the shattering bounds of the target or the war machine, this cultural archive of U.S. military empire recalls Ellison's phrase "democracy within the teeth of fascism."

Indeed, art of democratization demands interpretation within a genealogy of American "democracy" that black leftists, as earlier argued, critiqued as U.S. fascism. Far from securing for race its rights, U.S. wars abroad—as figures such as William Patterson, Ralph Ellison, James Baldwin, and others maintained—were corollaries for invisible wars against the "enemy" at home. In its engagement with Cold War U.S. militarism, this book thus retrieves the explanatory power of the suppressed legacy of U.S. fascism. In contrast to postatrocity aesthetics that assume a decisive historical break from the genocidal histories that spawned them, the art of democratization—although marked as postwar—never arrives at the time of liberation, much less democracy. In this regard it must be contrasted to the body of Holocaust art and letters that Theodor Adorno called "lyric poetry after Auschwitz" and Elie Wiesel described as "literature of testimony."[70] If the staggering human ruin consequent to Nazism gave rise to a cultural archive positing a clear postwar rupture, both aesthetically and politically, from fascism, the Pax Americana cultural archive in Asia and the Pacific entails grappling with shadowy geopolitical transition and troubling continuity. This corpus of double-fronted counterinsurgent war calls for contextualization within a geopolitical context informed by the stark absence or failure of official mechanisms of justice and the suspension of decolonization. Although somewhat formalized in unequal bilateral instruments—for example, status of forces agreements, visiting forces agreements, mutual defense treaties—that have given legal veneer to U.S. extraterritoriality, Cold War U.S. militarism is characterized less by rule of law than by rule without law.

Crises in sovereignty thus define the art and literature of U.S. military empire in Asia and the Pacific, giving rise to an emergent anti-imperialist human rights idiom. The Pax Americana would, in this regard, prove vital to the creation of a Janus-faced—human/international and civil/domestic—rights regime. If this bifurcation rendered rights meaningful only in their national articulation as civil rights and enabled the United States to place human rights outside its jurisdiction, beyond what Malcolm X dubbed "Uncle Sam's backyard," this book demonstrates how the operative logic of human rights in Cold War Asia and the Pacific was far from settled. It dwells on a shadow human rights history specific to regional peoples' struggles and antimilitarist democracy movements. In such contexts "human rights" and "democracy" were wielded not as military-imperialist jargon but as modes of anticolonial, decolonizing, Marxist, indigenous, and solidaristic expression. I thus read discrepant articulations of sovereignty—expressed in the U.S. setting as black freedom, in insular territorial contexts as indigenous decolonization, and in occupation zones as resistance—as homologous responses to U.S. militarism whose points of affinity and departure call for comparative analysis.

As the Cold War dawned, the United States blurred the color line in liberalizing and deathly ways. It operationalized what I have called the principle of indistinction in its newly desegregated military, technologies of mass destruction, multilateral wars of intervention, and counterintelligence practices. Yet in yoking disparate peoples and communities across the Pacific in lethal subterranean ways, the U.S. war machine also created the inadvertent grounds for solidarity—for the imagining of collective futures beyond the implacable stranglehold of the postwar Pax Americana. Whereas the term *Third World* enabled a transnational imagination of solidarity between decolonizing struggles abroad and within the United States during the era of the U.S. war in Vietnam, the black radical charge of fascism against the U.S. warfare state went further. It rendered visible the illegitimate violence of the U.S. war machine in waging informal wars abroad and at home. More than a legacy of the Cold War, U.S. militarism persists unabated today yet absent a ready idiom of international solidarity that accounts for the multidirectionality of its violence—absent, this is to say, the trenchant critique antifascism enabled. Through recourse to the archives of black antifascism, this book proposes a critical reframing of U.S. militarism: democracy within the teeth of fascism.

"Democracy within the Teeth of Fascism"

The Black POW and the Invisible War at Home in Ralph Ellison's War Writings

Invisible Man, Forgotten War

As the Korean War was coming to a draw, Ralph Ellison pointed to the black American's function as the "key figure in a magic rite by which the white American seeks to resolve the dilemma arising between his democratic beliefs and certain antidemocratic practices."[1] Only "when white men drew up a plan for a democratic way of life," he stated in "Twentieth-Century Fiction and the Black Mask of Humanity," did "the Negro . . . exert an influence upon America's moral consciousness," an influence repressed in the wake of Reconstruction's betrayal "until the Korean War" (28–29). In critiquing the opportunistic racial trappings of American claims to democracy in a historic juncture in which newly desegregated troops had been deployed to the front lines of the U.S. war in Korea, he pointedly upheld that a "people must define itself," clarifying that black humanity could no more be defined by others than freedom be "conferred upon another" (44). Reaching into the American literary past to retrieve a figuration of democratizing possibility, Ellison held out Jim's eventual fate in Mark Twain's *Adventures of Huckleberry Finn* as a humanizing expansion of freedom beyond "market-dominated relationships" (31). Yet in discerning democratic potential in Twain's portrait of humanity that, in his provocative phrase, "masked its face with blackness" (44), he left curiously unremarked the black American soldier's global propaganda value in the heated Cold War moment in which he was writing.

At a moment, that is, when U.S. officials were all too aware that the domestic management of race was pivotal to "the psychological battle against Communism" in the world arena, Ellison had little to say about the U.S. war machine that, in its Cold War renovation, strategically masked its face with blackness.[2] If impossible to recuperate as a "good fight," much less a victory, the Korean War was heralded in progressive terms by the U.S. government as a "breakthrough on the color front," a "successful racial revolution," and "a door of opportunity to

Negroes" (Nichols, 126, 144, 169). U.S. military desegregation in Korea, referred to as the Korean "experiment" in government-supported reports, was trumpeted as "a living example of democracy in action" that *"change[d] the complexion"* of the armed forces, placing the U.S. military at the vanguard of civil rights reform.[3] As Daniel Widener argues, the Korean War impelled the "reordering of American racial relations, paving the way for the emergence of the belief that the U.S. military—the primary purveyors of organized violence on the planet today—somehow represents the most meritocratic, socially equal, and ultimately progressive institution in American society."[4] In this regard, militarized blackface in the Korean theater was vital to camouflaging the illiberalism of a counterrevolutionary war in a distant land against an unknown people—a war that, for all its seeming insignificance, furnished the rationale for the consolidation of a formidable infrastructure of violence central to U.S. postwar dominance: the national security state, the military-industrial complex, the empire of bases, and the permanent war economy.

Yet this contradiction between America's democratic beliefs and its antidemocratic practices on display in Korea occasioned no direct response from Ellison. Insofar as the U.S. interventionist war in Korea was hailed as catalyzing Jim Crow's federal dismantlement by institutionalizing black-white fraternity in the military, Ellison's silence is all the more striking because these concerns and fears coursed as a leitmotif through his World War II–era commentary and fiction. In his early 1940s editorials for *Negro Quarterly*, the short-lived journal he edited with black communist organizer Angelo Herndon, and his late-war short stories, the black soldier's ironic conundrum " 'twixt two things," fascism and democratic possibility, loomed large. War politics also furnished the key theme of unpublished writings from that era, including "The Negro and the War" (1940), an antiwar essay he drafted while with the Federal Writers' Project (FWP), and drafts of an antifascist war novel he later credited as a blueprint for *Invisible Man* (1952).[5]

Some three decades on, however, Ellison would claim he had not abandoned these concerns, even as they were no longer foremost in his treatment. In *Invisible Man*, a novel drafted as Truman called for military desegregation and published as the Korean War was raging, military racial integration is wryly transformed into a chemical mixture—ten drops of "dead black" liquid dissolved into a white graduate base—used to make Liberty Paints' best-selling "Optic White," the "purest white paint that can be found" (200, 202). The addition of these black drops has the counterintuitive effect of enhancing the paint's dazzling whiteness. If starkly visible at first, the black when blended becomes imperceptible, for all intents and purposes neutralized. The compound is not just as white as it ever was but even whiter. Difficult to read as a celebration of democratic pluralism that many critics associate with Ellison, Optic White perversely allegorizes the structural effects of colorblindness within a lethal militarized context. Ellison claimed inspiration struck when he chanced on a replica of "Saint-Gaudens's monument to Colonel Robert Gould Shaw and his 54th Massachusetts Negro Regiment" (xvii) incongruously folded into a vat of Plasticine, a composition that recalled its Civil War referent of a white commander buried in a mass grave alongside his black troops. Yet in *Invisible Man* this emblem of "black and white fraternity" (xvii) is transformed, to the point of dissociation, into a lurid nightmarish sequence. After an explosion at Liberty Paints hurls the narrator headlong into first a "wet blast of black emptiness" and then an obliterating "bath of whiteness" (230), in effect replicating Optic White's formula, he awakens to find himself harnessed to a factory hospital's lobotomizing machine. His mind stripped blank, he floats "in vast whiteness," unsure "where [his] body end[s] and the . . . white world begin[s]," even as psychiatrists hold up signs reading "BOY, WHO WAS BRER RABBIT?" (233, 238, 242). Desperate to be free, the narrator falls to "plotting ways of short-circuiting the machine," a strategy that would surely take him down as well, yet comes to the realization that his ultimate desire is for "freedom, not destruction" (243).

In the narrator's tragicomic predicament we can discern echoes of the supposedly mentally ill, black World War I veterans at the Golden Day, men who fought on behalf of democracy only to be repatriated into unfreedom in the Jim Crow South, as well as Todd, the Tuskegee airman–like flyer strapped into a straitjacket at the end of Ellison's short story "Flying Home" (1944). Reviewing *Invisible Man* in Paul Robeson's *Freedom* newspaper, John Killens condemned the Golden Day episode as a mockery of the black antifascist struggle: "A million Negro veterans who fought against fascism in World War II are rewarded with a maddening chapter of crazy vets running hog-wild in a down home tavern."[6] Yet, in this influential critique, Killens overlooked the ways in which Ellison's Cold War novel, albeit set in the interwar years, anachronistically returned World War II home to American terrain. While conceding *Invisible Man* was "not properly a 'war' novel," Ellison, in casting a backward glance on its genesis, took pains to emphasize it had been "conceived during World War II, and . . . was intimately related to the tensions and dislocations visited upon individual and society alike by warfare."[7] Crucial was his imagination of World War II as a deranged scenario for the black quest for freedom, a view not unlike that of Killens, a veteran who had fought in the Pacific theater. For Ellison the war against fascism heightened the contradictions of the black freedom struggle and in startling ways exposed the U.S. home front to have *already* been an arena of total war. As he stated in his FWP essay, not only would "the South . . . rather see a Negro dead than wearing an army uniform," but also, "in the fluid folklore of Negro rebellion, . . . there are stories of unpopular white officers who did *not* die in bed." Although these below-the-radar "wars-within-wars" (*Invisible Man*, xii) had been thrown into momentary relief during World War II, they had preceded the war and would not end with the formal declaration of peace. In a profound sense, then, Ellison recognized that war for black Americans persisted in ways exceeding the obvious in the postwar domestic scene. Retrospectively claiming he had conceived *Invisible Man* as a war novel, he urged that it, "despite its peacetime scenery" (*Invisible Man*, vii), be read along those lines. No critic to date, however, has done so.

Indeed, more than three decades after its initial publication, Ellison would hint at an encrypted thematic continuity between his war-era writings and his Cold War magnum opus. Noting that he began writing *Invisible Man* in July of 1945, Ellison, in a draft of the 1980 Franklin Library preface, maintained that "the novel draws its tensions from a then contemporary war time scene." Of war's salience to *Invisible Man*, he further insisted that "war could, with art, be transformed into something deeper and more meaningful than its surface violence."[8] In no way implying that war violence be aestheticized, Ellison alluded rather to art's critical capacity to estrange war from its typical contexts, to render its violence visible outside battlefield spectacles and customary legal definitions. In this sense war, too, poses a problem of visibility, at once highly visible and "*un*-visible" (*Invisible Man*, xv). In *Invisible Man* war appears in elliptical narrative traces: the grandfather's final words, the battle royal, the Golden Day vets, Liberty Paints' screaming eagle trademark, the man harnessed to machine, Ras the Destroyer's race-war theories, the zoot suiters, the police murder of Tod Clifton, and the Harlem race riot. Neither bound to conventional expression nor reducible to metaphor, war saturates the novel's domestic milieu, hovering, as it were, on the lower frequencies. Insofar as it does, readers must grapple with the degree to which violence, enmity, unfreedom, *and* war power structure and permeate America's "peacetime" unequal social order.

"I never told you," the narrator's dying grandfather reveals to the alarm of gathered kin in *Invisible Man*'s opening pages, "but our life is a war and I have been a traitor all my born days, a spy in the enemy's country ever since I give up my gun back in the Reconstruction" (16).[9] These militant words from the "meekest of men"—a man born into slavery, declared "free" with slavery's abolition but for all appearances content to keep to his "place" (16)—grip the narrator, haunting him in his repeated failed quests for freedom. Seeking to illuminate their meaning, Ellison, in drafts of *Invisible Man*'s Franklin Library preface, contended that the "state of *civil* war, usually but not always carried out by means short of arms," persisted past "the tragic fraternal strife which errupted [*sic*] in 1860" (emphasis in original). In "The Negro and the War" he elaborated that post-Reconstruction reaction was a "betrayal of the Negro's part in what was actually a revolutionary struggle," adding that the "major issues fought for by the Negro people during this period are still unwon today." That this struggle was unfinished was no prosaic point for him. At stake in recognizing the present as a state of unabating counterrevolutionary war was no less than "the nature of reality" ("Twentieth-Century Fiction," 26) itself. Indeed, radical Reconstruction's betrayal, he argued, rendered "illusion and reality, slavery and freedom, democracy and tyranny" indistinguishable ("Draft—Franklin Library Preface"). The grandfather's curtain-parting words thus represented, in Ellison's view, the "complex wisdom of those who endured and survived enslavement in the world's preeminent democracy" ("Draft—Franklin Library Preface"). Serving as a heuristic for the following narrative, the statement that "Our life is a war" uneasily suggests domestic settings might be recognized as arenas of war, peacetime as wartime, and civilians as potential insurgents. Priming his family for conscious engagement in the battles ahead, the grandfather cautions them to "live with your head in the lion's mouth" (*Invisible Man*, 16).

This disquieting counsel, which sets the tone for the narrator's ensuing trials and tribulations, also links the subterranean war politics of Ellison's Cold War novel to the antifascist politics of his World War II writings, specifically recalling his vivid war-era phrase "democracy within the teeth of fascism."[10] Both expressions, the grandfather's warning and Ellison's antifascist phrase, derive their potency from the unsettling insight that the U.S. home front, or domestic scene, might be recognized as a theater of war. Here we might draw a parallel: if the grandfather's words imply that a de facto war persisted past the Civil War's end and that with radical Reconstruction's betrayal the black revolutionary struggle went underground, so, too, do his words, by recasting Ellison's war-era phrase, suggest that the antifascist struggle in the United States would not end with the Axis defeat. This point is worth emphasizing because the midcentury break—or, some argue, apostasy—that Ellison scholars contend distinguishes the leftist proletarian politics of his war-era writings from *Invisible Man*'s Cold War liberalism, coincided with the disappearance, almost overnight, of antifascism as a politics around which an international left might organize. On the cusp of an era in which U.S. war power would take permanent institutional form while proceeding with brutal unilateralism—all under the liberal cover of integration, coalition, multiculturalism, and democratization—Ellison's visceral phrase potently captured the U.S. welfare-warfare state's structural contradictions. Liberal sovereignty, Mark Neocleous argues, relies on the "*secrecy* of war," typically refraining from calling its "permanent exercise of war power" by war's name, much less nominating its internal "unsocial and lawless" targets "enemies."[11] If Ellison's provocative phrase suggests that, under critical scrutiny, the formal enmity between Allied and Axis powers belies a shadowy identity, it was this political *visibility*, which two-front antifascist critique lent to the *war at home*, that for Ellison made World War II as a total war exceptional.

Insofar as Ellison's analysis of World War II's undemocratic threat was inextricable from his critique of fascism, it lost its moral charge, political legibility, and narrative power as the prevailing Cold War account of fascism insisted on the latter's ideological contiguity with communism—at the very moment in which U.S. war power would be directed against communism as its principal target at home and abroad. As a self-exculpatory discourse wielded by the capitalist bloc, the Cold War catchphrase "totalitarianism" served ideologically to estrange fascism from its genesis and location in industrial capitalism and to yoke it instead with communism, thus evacuating fascism's meaning and warping the clarity of the antifascist critique of militarism, precisely as U.S. war power assumed unprecedented infrastructural form following World War II. Fascism, that is, inheres in the "mass mobilization for nationalist and counterrevolutionary aims, militarized activism, and ... drive for an elitist, authoritarian and repressive state apparatus" (Neocleous, xi) specific to the capitalist system. Historically inextricable from capitalist militarism and its propulsion to imperialist war, it arguably poses a problem as much for the present as the past. Yet it is a sure sign of the durability of Cold War obscurantism around fascism as an explanatory and galvanizing concept that it registers as apparent hyperbole when applied to the post–World War II U.S. national security apparatus, military industrial complex, empire of bases, and permanent war economy. Indeed, in the wake of World War II, as U.S. military empire expanded around the globe, deforming millions of peoples' lives, it became proportionally "*un*-visible" within the domestic arena, even as U.S. war and police power continued to condition everyday life. In this regard black antifascist critique, more than marking a past politics, must be understood as potent in its prognostication, particularly with regard to the war at home.

Inquiring into how the Double-V politics of Ellison's war-era writings—namely, wartime black American support for victory against racism and fascism abroad and at home—persist in *Invisible Man* thus requires asking how U.S. fascism, without the benefit of German and Japanese mirrors, might be recognized in the postwar domestic scene. Few scholars discern continuity across what are viewed as two distinct periods in Ellison's career: the war era, in which he, as proletarian journalist, essayist, and short fiction writer, moved in a rich leftist milieu as an engaged intellectual; and the long Cold War period, when he, after securing his literary reputation on the basis of *Invisible Man*, tilted toward quietist politics and reactionary isolation. That he, in roughly half a decade, produced the makings of an antifascist war novel and what many critics contend is a categorically anticommunist novel may be proof for some of his political apostasy. Yet it also surely serves as commentary on the eclipse and co-optation of antifascism as an oppositional politics in the postwar era.[12] In the context of the Korean War, a "forgotten war" that catapulted the black soldier on desegregated front lines to global visibility and furnished the rationale for the permanent fusion of corporate capitalism to militarism, the literary emergence of Ellison's invisible man may have signaled the sublimation of his World War II–era concerns about the black soldier's democratic quandary in the face of a two-front fascist threat. I argue they moved underground.

Double-V Blueprint, Cold War Novel

From 1942 to 1945, during World War II's late years, Ellison, writing on a Julius Rosenwald Fund grant, began a novel he would move away from but not entirely abandon—a wartime story of a black airman who bails out of an overfreighted plane only to be captured and interned in a Nazi POW camp. The narrative's dramatic tension arises from the protagonist's Double-V struggle to harness revolutionary possibilities for humanizing freedom within camp confines.[13] The forcible grounding of the airman in a fascist site that, however eccentric to the United States proper, serves as a distorted yet telling mirror for the latter, speaks to U.S. democracy's paradoxes. Positioned at the U.S. war machine's helm, the black POW, an overdetermined figure of historical dispossession, emerges as the ironic face and singular redemptive possibility of American democracy in this fledgling novel-of-ideas. The downed flyer not only serves as "*the* image of the American" ("Twentieth-Century Fiction," 26) but also, from his grounded position, signals the tenuous political possibility of transracial fraternity and revolutionary humanity. In retrospect Ellison would describe this story as a war within a war, drawn from a long history of black quests for freedom in the context of U.S. wars. Significantly, he would also credit it as a conceptual influence on his 1952 major work, *Invisible Man*. On the whole, however, this POW narrative of a Tuskegee airman–like figure has received scant critical attention, a reflection in part of Ellison's reluctance to claim it in the early Cold War era.[14]

As *Invisible Man* garnered laurels, Ellison remained mostly silent about this curious effort toward his first novel. According to Arnold Rampersad, it was one of three simultaneous novelistic forays made by Ellison near World War II's end: "One was his Nazi prison camp project (of which fewer than a dozen pages survive). The second, set in a Southern college, has as its principal character a black man named Bard. Then there was a third novel about an invisible man."[15] Whereas the latter two efforts are thematically consistent with the novel that secured Ellison his literary fame, the "Nazi prison camp project" does not obviously coincide with *Invisible Man*'s interwar narrative. Ellison, in fact, dismissed this war project as a false start, referring vaguely to "a short novel which was unsatisfactory, ill-conceived and never submitted for publication."[16] Only later, in a 1981 introduction to *Invisible Man*, would he ascribe precursory significance to it, stating *Invisible Man* "erupted out of what had been conceived as a war novel": "The narrative . . . focused upon the experiences of a captured American pilot who found himself in a Nazi prisoner-of-war camp in which he was the officer of highest rank and thus by a convention of war the designated spokesman for his fellow prisoners. Predictably, the dramatic conflict arose from the fact that he was the only Negro among the Americans, and the resulting racial tension was exploited by the German camp commander."[17]

Filed in Ellison's Library of Congress papers under the misleadingly finished rubric "Airman Novel," this early novelistic effort encompassed, at minimum, a three-page Rosenwald prospectus, several pages of manuscript notations, several pages of hand-annotated typed outlines, and several pages of typed draft fragments, in addition to compiled reference materials including mimeographed letters from repatriated American POWs and newspaper clippings.[18]

Presented in his 1945 Rosenwald application as "a novel of ideas" whose setting "does not depend upon . . . naturalistic depiction" but rather on "highly imaginative" rendering, this proposed novel drew on André Malraux's *Days of Wrath* for its Nazi-camp framework. If total war had thrown the racial contradictions of American democracy on both the home and war fronts into high relief, in "Airman Novel" Sheppard, the protagonist, is confronted with the task of dialectically expanding humanity's terms within the confines of fascism in order to realize a broader, "more human" idea of freedom. Under the direction of Edwin Embree, Rosenwald's outspoken antifascist president, the philanthropic organization, known for funding black education and arts, supported Ellison's Nazi POW-camp project as the war was coming to a close.[19] In *American Negroes, a Handbook* Embree, adapting Lincoln's "divided house" speech, linked U.S. internal colonialism to fascism; his critique of black subordination suggests why "Airman Novel" garnered Rosenwald support: "American Negroes are our colonials. And there is no room in the world for which we are fighting for colonial status. We cannot save a world half nazi, half democrat."[20] We might surmise that Ellison's précis, with its searching exploration of wartime democratic possibilities, resonated with reviewers. The time was ripe for a story that strove to imagine democracy's realization in the face of a two-front fascist threat—Nazi *and* American.

"The essential purpose" of "Airman Novel," Ellison conveyed in his Rosenwald prospectus, "is to determine what type of democratic relationships are necessary for a highly conscious Negro to function with white men and at the same time exercise the fullest potentialities of his humanity" ("Airman Novel"). In both his Rosenwald application and 1981 account of "Airman Novel," the Double-V resonance of his protagonist's dilemma, caught between "native and foreign racisms," is unmistakable. If first and foremost "a novel of ideas," Ellison's war narrative referenced its historical moment. Even if doomed as a realistic tableau—"invit[ing] trouble," according to Rampersad, for "Ralph knew next to nothing about the military, or about prison camps" (180)—the agon between black flyer and his white compatriots in the POW-camp context was not far-fetched from a historical perspective.[21] Among Ellison's papers are news clippings that ironically suggest democratic possibility for black POWs in Nazi confinement. From wartime black newspapers Ellison meticulously saved accounts of repatriated black soldiers who testified to Jim Crow's absence, indeed to the dismantling by Nazi command of any white American POW attempt to establish a color line. A February 23, 1945, article describes the homecoming of the "only Negro among the 463 Yank soldiers returning on the Gripsholm," who indicated the Nazis treated him "just like any other American soldier"; furthermore, "nobody even tried to tell him about the superiority of white Aryans." The caption below his photo dryly reads: "Pfc. Morris Carter of Starksville, Miss., is glad to be back, although in German prison camps he found no Jim Crow rules." In a May 12, 1945, *Pittsburgh Courier* article, "GIs Arrive from Nazi Camps after 3 Months Imprisonment," seven black servicemen avowed that, futile Jim Crow attempts by white American POWs aside, "there was no segregation demanded by the Germans," with the ominous exception of "Jewish soldiers who were removed completely from the camp."[22]

Although Ellison advanced the thesis in his Rosenwald précis that "the need for democracy is implicit in the Negro situation," his proposed war novel's irony resides in its insistence that his protagonist Sheppard's "most satisfying relationship with white Americans" is to be had "in the very teeth of the Nazi."[23] Returning to this provocative theme in notes, outlines, and draft fragments for his antifascist novel, Ellison sounded out the idea that Offlag 369, the Nazi POW camp, "must be [a] functioning democracy," a democracy "achieved under [the] most inhuman conditions of [a] concentration camp." Structured as a political bildungsroman, "Airman Novel," according to his précis, is a "story of the [pilot's] progress from humiliation to humanity," for "here for the first time in his life he is given an opportunity to define and create the type of society he needs." Ellison's draft materials furnish suggestive detail about how Sheppard and his white compatriots—including southerners who, at one point, "beat him"—achieve the political consciousness needed to forge common cause against the Nazi. In notes, we come across Ellison's insistence that these "men develop real comradeship" in the camp. Their solidarity, however, requires a war-specific plot twist: as the highest-ranking American officer, Sheppard is given discretionary authority over the other American POWs. More than an adherence to war protocol, the Nazi commander's inversion of Jim Crow is "a gesture of contempt for democracy." His recognition of Sheppard's rank is calculated to inflame racial tensions among the Americans. Yet rather than use his newfound power to give in to impulses for revenge, even as the sinister Nazi prods him to kill his compatriots, Sheppard, whom the Nazi views clinically as a "test case," "must overcome his hate... and create a fully functioning democracy within the teeth of fascism." Ellison's "Negro hero" thus spares his men's lives and engineers their escape.

It is, moreover, Sheppard's status as Allied enemy, his nationality prioritized over race, that perversely enables the Nazi-camp space to approach the democratic ideals of what Ellison called the "American Creed." We might recall photographer Gordon Parks's ironic observation when assigned as an Office of War Information correspondent to the Tuskegee airmen: "I noticed a sign reading COLORED PASSENGERS and another one reading WHITES ONLY. The four black soldiers moved automatically to the colored side, and so did I. How ironic, I thought; such nonsense would not stop until we were in enemy territory."[24] In a twist on the crisis of self-recognition in Du Bois's concept of double consciousness, Ellison likewise implies the black POW is most fully human when he sees himself through the eyes of someone who regards him *as an enemy*. His notes offer this sketch: "[Sheppard] expects Nazi to regard him with fantasy aspect of white Americans. Nazi doesn't. Instead he is approached as a human being—which startles him. Nazi has no moral interest in him thus sees him as man and enemy." If an allegory for U.S. fascism, Ellison's Nazi POW camp thus does not serve as an easy equivalent for the United States, and the Double-V concept imperfectly obtains. If the analogy between Nazism and U.S. racism was still resonant more than two decades later, with Charles Sims of the black militant Deacons stating in the late 1960s, "See, the Southern white man is almost like Hitler in the South," in Ellison's war novel, the Nazi possesses a seductive edge over "the Southern white man."[25] Ellison posed a thorny question: "How can the american [sic] creed conflict be illustrated in the camp?" Translating unevenly, his staging of the "American dilemma" threatens to slide into a comparative juxtaposition of two versions of fascism, Nazi and American, with U.S. fascism, relative to the black flyer, appearing the worse of the two evils.

The Black Antifascist Dilemma

In "Airman Novel" Sheppard, situated "'twixt" fascism in Nazi and American forms, must figure out a way *not* to go to hell, as it were. Only by rejecting a Faustian bargain with the Nazi commander can Ellison's protagonist "evolv[e] a broader concept of freedom." Resisting the desire to exact revenge against his racist white compatriots, he attempts to tap the humanizing potential in his crisis of conscience: "When flyer is given power he is not satisfied to simply impose it; his need for psychology is ever greater. C. P.'s short coming [sic]." Reluctant, however, to parody the party's shifting positions toward the black freedom struggle, including its "shamefaced support" of "a Jim Crow army," and committed to Marxist analytical tools, Ellison embarked on a maverick attempt to think through the dialectical expansion of the terms of humanity by joining "Marx and Freud."[26] As he explored in his fledgling novel, revolutionary solidarity required a turn in consciousness, a psychology of political fraternity more powerful than the reflex for self-preservation. Borrowing his Nazi-camp framework from *Days of Wrath*, one of two André Malraux works Langston Hughes lent him on his Harlem arrival in the summer of 1936, Ellison probed these novels and other communist writings for what they revealed about the psychological dimensions of antifascist solidarity.[27]

Crucially, *Days of Wrath*—a novel that "alerted the world to the peril of the Nazis"[28]—furnished Ellison with a psychologically inflected, antifascist template, a European model that imperfectly mapped onto the black antifascist struggle. Featuring a partisan named Kassner captured by the Nazis, this tale of political persecution champions international communist brotherhood: "it stirred him even more deeply to feel that they were united not in their persons but in their common devotion, . . . austere and powerful friendship of a sort rare on this earth."[29] Revolutionary solidarity in the novel engenders the possibility of new—in Ellison's phrase, "more human"—forms of social life. In a preface to the novel's English translation, League of American Writers president Waldo Frank stated, "The torment of war, revolution, counter-revolution finally releases the elements of human life from their old forms."[30] Placing Marx and Freud in dialogue, Frank contrasted the communist solidarity's "conscious love" to the mindless submission demanded by fascism: "The conduct of the new type of person is premised, not upon isolation, but upon solidarity. His sacrifice is not for the salvation of his individual soul . . . nor does it follow from the loss of personality in the inebriate herd-egoism of nationalism and devotion to 'Fuehrer' and 'Duce'" (xv).

What Frank identified as new solidaristic forms of humanity, with their intimation of a collectivity-to-come, would be an abiding literary preoccupation for Ellison. At this point, as Lawrence Jackson writes, Ellison believed politically committed writers "had a sacred duty, such as that displayed by the heroic André Malraux, to detail emergent forms of liberating social consciousness" (262).[31] By exploring the psychological dimensions of antifascist fraternity as the basis of global communist revolution, *Days of Wrath* served as both model and foil for Ellison's black antifascist narrative.

If *Invisible Man* closes with the question posed by the narrator from a "hole in the ground"—"Who knows but that, on the lower frequencies, I speak for you?" (6, 581)—in Malraux's *Days of Wrath*, Kassner, "incarcerated in a rather large dark hole" (23) in a Nazi concentration camp, is compelled to speak for other imprisoned partisans: "Deprived of brotherhood as he had been of dreams and hope, Kassner waited in the silence which hung over the desires of hundreds of men in that black termite's nest. He must speak for them, even were they never to hear him!" (92).[32] In his cell Kassner experiences deepening consciousness, with brotherhood transforming into spiritual fellowship. Of his comrades forced by twisted "SA-men . . . to sing the Internationale" at gunpoint, Kassner, with agony and exultation, recalls their "shout[ing] the song with such fierce hope ringing in their voices that the non-commissioned officer had drawn his revolver and fired" (48–49). Joined "in a common bond . . . in which music takes man's head between its hands and slowly lifts it toward human fellowship" (48), these fallen comrades inspirit Kassner, nourishing his will to persist in the struggle. A narrative of revolutionary sacrifice, with an unnamed partisan assuming the place of Kassner, who is sentenced to death, *Days of Wrath* ends with Kassner's return to his wife and child—and, the novel implies, to invigorated antifascist activity.

Traces of Malraux's heroic romance, as a source text for "Airman Novel," can be discerned in Ellison's 1981 introduction to *Invisible Man*, in which he reveals that for his black pilot "there was neither escape nor a loved one waiting" (xii). The fact that home for Sheppard represents neither sanctuary nor domestic bliss but a site of life-or-death struggle warps the narrative horizons of Ellison's antifascist novel, which culminates not in his protagonist's return to family but death. Indeed, in "Airman Novel" hell and home are transposable settings in a single nightmare. Uncanny echoes of home resonate in Sheppard's first meeting with the diabolical Nazi commander. Here, the contrast with *Days of Wrath* is especially revealing. Marking his grim entry into the concentration camp, Kassner's encounter with the "Hitler official" is rendered in straightforward terms: "At the moment when Kassner was pushed into the guard room, a prisoner under cross-examination finished a sentence which was drowned in the shuffle of papers and police boots. Across the table from him sat the Hitler official. He was true to type: heavy jaws, square head, close cropped blond hair, almost shaven over the ears" (Malraux, 11).

In Ellison's Double-V recasting, the meeting between stock Nazi commander and black POW takes on dizzying implications that blur the novel's geographical parameters. "Expect[ing] to find the commander repulsive," Sheppard instead encounters someone resembling "the picture of an American diplomat he had seen in a newspaper." Complicating the Nazi's personification of deathly fascist politics is his morphological likeness to his American double:

> Before him [Sheppard] saw the camp commander seated behind a desk. The face might have been American or English. It was smoothly shaven, the hair slightly greyed and closely clipped. The officer looked at him distantly, then studied a folder for a moment as he motioned for him to come closer. When the man looked up he found himself looking into a pair of the coldest blue eyes he ever [sic] seen. He wanted to remove his gaze, but could not; and suddenly he remembered three lines from *Hamlet*:
>> "Angels and ministers of grace defend us!
>> Be thou a spirit of health or goblin damn'd
>> Bring with thee airs from heaven or blasts from hell . . . "
>
> And as though the commander had read his mind he saw a smile form on the blond face and growing broader become a grin.

The foreign fascist menace's unnerving familiarity prompts reckoning with the fascist menace closer to home. Likened to Old Hamlet, a specter unsettling the distinction between earthly and spiritual realms, the demonic Nazi reveals himself, as the scene unfolds, to be as American as he is German. Ellison theorized these converging fascisms along psychological lines: "Symbolically, the Nazi is a 'Satan' principle, a projection of the accumulated hate and humiliation against the unfairness of [the pilot's] experience at home and in the Army, and also a projection of his own inferiority feelings" ("Airman Novel").

Far more treacherous than Kassner's meeting with the "true to type" Nazi officer, Sheppard's encounter with the camp commander sets the stage for the Nazi's sinister designs and pulls the narrative gravitationally back to the American scene. In their initial exchange the Nazi ventriloquizes slurs drawn from the American idiom:

> "Hello, boy. I'm sorry, *colored* boy. That's what they call you, isn't it?" are the first words out of the Nazi's mouth.
>
> "I've been called many things," he [Sheppard] said, wondering at the kraut's pure English.

"Colonel Nigger! There. How's that?"

"Since you have the advantage—"

"I was born with that, Colonel Black Boy." ("Airman Novel")

This deranged dialogue encapsulates Sheppard's Double-V conundrum in Ellison's novel-of-ideas.[33] For Kenneth Burke, whom Ellison claimed as a "literary 'ancestor'" ("Hidden Name," 162), the three lines from *Hamlet*, which register Hamlet's astonishment at the sight of his father's ghost, mark a shift away from the commonplace; with their utterance, the ordinary is overtaken by "the grandiose, the full-throated and full-vowelled."[34] In "Airman Novel" the Nazi's interpellation of Sheppard similarly unsettles the narrative register by bringing the black antifascist struggle into view. If, as Richard Wright had argued, literature represents a battle over reality, for Ellison it followed that realism, because of its mimetic presumptions, could not adequately capture, much less critically expose, the contradictions of the black American experience of a two-front war.[35] In a 1940 essay he offered insight into his literary method, identifying the irrational, the so-called Negro problem, as "that blind spot in our knowledge of society where Marx cries out for Freud and Freud for Marx" ("An American Dilemma," 311). If fascists in Europe had mastered the psychological dimensions of ideological manipulation, Ellison contended that their nearest domestic counterparts—white southern elites—were not far behind in their cynical exploitation of what he referred to as "political technology" ("An American Dilemma," 311). A jarring homecoming for the black pilot, the Nazi's race-baiting greeting conjures America's blind spot in Offlag 369. Understanding how deeply the slave past encodes the American present, the Nazi makes a mockery of Sheppard's military rank with epithets drawn from the lexicon of slavery and Jim Crow.[36] The home-front image that thus surfaces is not the propagandistic portrait of the dashing Tuskegee airman but its obverse—"lynched Negroes who dared to wear the uniform" of the U.S. Army.[37]

"Airman Novel" intimates that the allegiances of the black American in uniform, as "the human factor placed outside the democratic master plan" yet conscripted into the U.S. war machine, are unsettled. Called to fight for democracy's fragile possibility, Sheppard wrestles with the agon between democracy and fascism in the militarized camp setting, leaving uncertain which one might prevail. The volatility of Nazi-black POW encounter thus resides in its potential for race-blurring alignment—both fascist *and* antifascist, regressive *and* liberatory. Depicted as "a psychologist given to ceaseless intrigue," the Nazi demeans Sheppard in the white supremacist American idiom as a means of dilating the war within the war and thereby unleashing his rage against his white compatriots. Viewing Sheppard as a reactive tool rather than a conscious actor, he exploits the "feeling... experienced by Negroes [that so much] in the U.S. is tinged with fascism" as the ironic basis for black complicity with the fascist enemy.[38] Raising the prospect of black treason, this novel-of-ideas reworks wartime U.S. anxieties that Nazi and Japanese propaganda might capitalize on Jim Crow.[39] As the CPUSA (Communist Party USA) pamphlet *Is Japan the Champion of the Colored Races?* warned: "in every land, in its drive for power, [and] in its efforts to retain power," fascism "fastens upon racial prejudices and animosities, fanning them into a flame to divide the people," drawing in the United States on "ideas rooted deep in chattel slavery."[40]

More than crude antics, the Nazi's goading methods are tactical in nature, aimed at plumbing the depths of Sheppard's demoralization. Discerning the vulnerability of the larger U.S. war effort in the black POW's predicament, he proceeds from a militarized understanding of racial psychology as a vital wartime weapon. Identifying Sheppard as a slave in a Jim Crow army, the Nazi dares him to wield the power of life or death over his white compatriots: "You're slaves, Herr Shappard [sic], not because of your blood (we dont [sic] believe that nonsense, you know) but because you are unwilling to seize upon power." Yet even as he seeks Sheppard's collusion in his twisted machinations, a plot Ellison dubbed "Faust—with definite modifications" ("Airman Novel"), it is the Nazi's performative slide into his American counterpart that confounds the novel's politics of enmity. In a draft note to himself Ellison pondered the ambivalence of affinity plaguing Sheppard, on the one side hounded by the Nazi and on the other tormented by white southerners: "Interview [with Nazi] must set stage: what against what." Implying the terms of opposition *and* allegiance are open-ended, "what against what" describes the crisis of conviction dogging the black antifascist struggle. "Let us agree that Negroes must fight against aggression," C. L. R. James conceded as war broke out in Europe. "But who," he pointedly inquired, "are the aggressors against the Negroes?" (37).[41]

Democracy within the Teeth of Fascism

Race in militarized form furnishes the narrative tension of Ellison's war-era tales of failed flight. Vital to government efforts to ensure black loyalty in World War II, the image of the black flyer was widely propagated to "build up black morale by integrating a more visible 'Negro' into the public sphere of patriotic rhetoric."[42] In this era of "Jim Crow in uniform," to use Claudia Jones's incisive phrase, the state endorsed black visibility in the constraints of hyperpatriotic military form. The message was gradualist: through militarized service and sacrifice to the nation, black Americans moved one step closer to a democratic future. As a potent fantasy of racial overcoming, the black flyer implied military technology's redemptive role in enhancing the humanity of racially reviled subjects. The very war machine vital to U.S. postwar military-imperial ascendancy was thus framed as a vehicle of eventual rights for subjects integrated into its shattering operations. Yet the compositional elements of Jim Crow in uniform as a spectacle of a multicultural democracy-to-come—namely, race bounded by militarized form—uneasily mirrored those of the fascist mass ornament and the inhuman "*ratio* of the capitalist economic system," to draw from Siegfried Kracauer.[43] The relationship to race was extractive and destructive. In no way intended to affirm the integrity of humanity, the harnessing of race to the war machine required that racial labor risk its own obliteration by carrying out, in Fordist fashion, a "form-bursting" (Kracauer 83) lethal agenda geared toward the devastation of distant lifeworlds. Perversely incorporated as a cog into the imperial machinery of mass destruction and therefore simultaneously a target, the black flyer thus represented death superimposed onto a long-standing dream of flight drawn from the imagination of black liberation.[44]

Informed by conflicting visions of freedom, both emancipatory and counterrevolutionary, Ellison's wartime tales of failed flight thus anticipated the narrative tensions of a post-1945 geopolitical body of writing we might call art or literature of democratization. War figures redemptively in this politically equivocal cultural archive as the enabling condition of democracy, which is typically deferred into an indeterminate future. In its portrait of race subjugated by militarized form, however, this literature shares a disquieting morphology with fascist aesthetics—yet with a different emphasis. Whereas the fascist mass ornament exults in how militarized form subsumes the human element, literature of democratization underscores militarism's democratizing possibility by asking, "In what way *more* human" (*Invisible Man*, 354). In this, art of democratization risks mystifying the imperial war machine's antihumanism and profound racial violence by sentimentalizing the human element. Although Ellison's war-era literary explorations of democratic possibility in militarized settings recall the fascist mass ornament's metallization of human flesh, his narratives of black incorporation into the U.S. war machine were an antifascist politicization of art that sought to expose the fascist logic of "Jim Crow in uniform." In this regard, art of democratization encodes both fascist and antifascist potentialities. Insofar as the total war state framed Jim Crow-in-uniform in terms of future democratic prospects for black Americans, it demands retrieval as a militarized origin of multiculturalism as a budding state ideology.

Ellison's tales of failed flight pointedly referenced the Tuskegee airmen, militarized emblems of state-sponsored racial uplift propagated as embodying vanguardist potential relative to the civil rights struggle—a progressive interpretation he disputed. Dismissing the Tuskegee airmen as "subsidized" tokens in the Jim Crow armed forces, he took aim at the "window-dressing air school at Tuskegee," a segregated aviation training site in the South that was "palmed off on the American people as the real thing" ("Editorial Comment [1943]," 301, 299).[45] In a 1942 editorial in *Negro Quarterly*, he identified Franklin Roosevelt's "hand-pick[ing of] a few Negro leaders" as "a game which does not aid the cause of victory over the enemy" (ii). In a subsequent 1943 editorial Ellison lauded "William H. Hastie's resignation from the War Department, where it was expected of him to remain silent" (299). Published by the NAACP in August of 1943 after his War Department resignation, Hastie's *On Clipped Wings: The Story of Jim Crow in the Army Air Corps* denounced Tuskegee's "unholy alliance" with the Jim Crow army, a rare critique in the total-war years of the collusion between civilian institutions and the U.S. warfare state:

> When we find Tuskegee Institute working hand in glove with the Army Air Command to establish . . . a Jim Crow air training program at Tuskegee, such conduct should be exposed and condemned. . . . With callous indifference to the best interests of the Negro and to the larger values of democratic practices in the war effort, Tuskegee is looking out for Tuskegee. The school gets its mess of pottage in profitable Army contracts and the promotion of its own private aviation training program, while the Air Forces have a willing and useful accomplice in their design of keeping the Negro strictly segregated. (10)

In contrast to the enfolding of the Tuskegee airmen into the state's war agenda, Hastie's bailing out from the War Department was a courageous act, Ellison argued, that "lost him prestige among Fascist-minded whites" yet "made [his] name meaningful among thousands of Negroes, bringing eligibility for that support which is the basis of true leadership" ("Editorial Comment [1943]," 299). By stepping down and "integrat[ing] with the Negro masses" ("Editorial Comment [1943]," 300), he augured a "Negro leader" capable of positive action.

In his wartime fiction Ellison thus returned fascism to U.S. terrain through the downward arc of his black airmen protagonists. Cautious yet hopeful about World War II's prospects as *"a peoples' war . . . fought and won by the people,"* he imagined fascism and democracy at opposite ends of a vertical axis.[46] In a war in which air power was critical to U.S. victory, fascistic "dreams of world domination and mass destruction" featured "the airplane as agent."[47] These fantasies of racial annihilation envisioned aviation as "a tool shaped specifically for Western hands," thus granting "the White race" dominance over a "sea of Yellow, Black, and Brown."[48] Uninterested in vying for mastery of the skies, Ellison by contrast refused his protagonists militarized eye-in-the-sky supremacy, repeatedly crashing them to earth. As his short story "Flying Home" (1944) illustrates, the northern black pilot training in a Tuskegee-like setting for wartime duty is likened to a racialized Icarus who believes flight enables a transcendence of American racism. In this tale the pilot's ascendant ideals find realization not in soaring heights but a bathetic plummet onto a white farmer's land.[49] That Todd, Ellison's protagonist, would as likely be brought down over the South as the European theater furnishes the critique of this story of failed flight.[50] If evocative of the flying African freedom tales collected by the Works Progress Administration in 1940 from former slaves living along the Georgia coast—"duh story bout people dat flied off tuh Africa"—"Flying Home" draws its irony from the overlay of the U.S. South and the Third Reich.[51] Discovered by Jefferson, an elderly black sharecropper who stays with him to guard against lynching, Todd, badly injured, must endure trenchant queries: "What was you doin' flyin' over this section, son? Wasn't you scared they might shoot you for a crow?" (162). As this story suggests, for the black flyer, heroically nicknamed "Black Eagle" or "Brown Condor" by the black press, the metonymic slide to "lousy buzzard" or "jimcrow" (155) is but a step away. Confronted with what he takes to be the encrypted censure of Jefferson's supple vernacular, Todd screams: "Can I help it because they won't let us actually fly? Maybe we are a bunch of buzzards feeding on a dead horse, but we can hope to be eagles, can't we?" (161).

By contrast, in "Airman Novel" Sheppard, burdened with a brooding disposition—indeed, "too wise to accept the status quo"—*elects* to bail out when his flak-damaged bomber can no longer bear the crew's weight. Yet this sacrifice is complicated by his view that "participation in the Air Force" does not advance the antifascist cause. Unlike his crew who accept a tokenized role in the Allied war effort, Sheppard finds no satisfaction in state-subsidized uplift. Ellison offers this wry portrait: "He is an intellectual-technician, representative of a new Negro type; and his concern with absolutes, values, meanings, caused him to function as a bad conscience for the rest of the crew. These, for the most part were content with the gains represented in their participation in the Air Force, and his attitude was an uncomfortable one. Thus their relief when he volunteer's [sic] to bail out." In the late-war, "go for broke" moment in which the story is set, Sheppard's decision potentially reads as desertion. Yet even when what awaits him is a Nazi POW camp, structural change, "Airman Novel" implies, must begin from below.

If retrieved in isolation, "Flying Home" might read as an insular critique of Jim Crow. The impact of Ellison's literary explorations of Double-V politics, however, depended on the resonance between the South and the Nazi POW camp to convey fascism's insidious reach. Essential to his democratic literary method was thus an outside figuration of the fascist threat to illustrate the internal menace. As a provocative wartime analogy for the United States, the Nazi camp in "Airman Novel" thus possessed a uniquely estranging capacity to dramatize what white Americans neglected to see in their midst: "the essentially undemocratic treatment of their fellow citizens" ("Twentieth-Century Fiction," 27). If Axis defeat cleared the way for U.S. global ascendancy by signaling that fascism, tidily packaged as Nazism and Japanese militarism, had been vanquished, it left unanswered how home-front fascism had been addressed. In a 1951 Civil Rights Congress petition to the United Nations charging the United States with genocide against black Americans, William Patterson described white supremacist terror as "a crime so embedded in law, so explained away by specious rationale, so hidden by talk of liberty, that even the conscience of the tender minded is sometimes dulled"; indeed, "its very familiarity disguises its horror."[52] In that same juncture Ellison lambasted complacency toward "that ritual of violence closer to home, that ritual in which the sacrifice is that of a human scapegoat, the lynching bee" ("Twentieth-Century Fiction," 37). If thrust into public view during the war, the unresolved matter of fascism at home became "*un*-visible" as the Cold War dawned.

In the early Cold War era, war likewise moved underground in Ellison's fiction. Distinctive as a narrative pattern in his oeuvre, the downed black pilot's descent resurfaces in the downward propulsion of *Invisible Man*'s narrator. If *Invisible Man*'s leitmotif of vertigo invites being read as a critique of racial uplift measures, it also recalls the gravitational arc of "Airman Novel," suggesting a postwar sublimation of Ellison's antifascist exploration of the invisible war at home. In *Invisible Man* the unnamed narrator identifies "men outside of historical time" in aerial terms as "birds of passage ... distant from the centers of historical decision" and obscured by "those lies [their] keepers keep their power by" (439). Yet the novel also implies the power potential of that obscurity. It opens and closes in a blazing squatter's den beneath interwar New York City, a "hole in the ground" plugged furtively into the city's "monopolated" (5) energy source. Wired with 1,369 lights, this incandescent lair "allows [him] to feel . . . vital aliveness" as the narrator eludes detection from the city's fascistically dubbed "master meter" (7, 5).[53] Giving metaphoric expression to postwar democratic contradictions, the vertical tension between images of flight and underground hibernation culminates in the narrator's subterranean solitude.

Just as the black military pilots of Ellison's concept-driven war stories are hurtled to scenes of unfreedom below, the narrator's subterranean position in *Invisible Man* suggests a shift to a politics of immanence.[54] Of a piece with his insistence on groundedness as the vantage of the masses in his tales of failed flight, "low-down" ("The Art of Fiction," 170) or "lowest down" ("Brave Words," 104) signaled for Ellison a revolutionary humanizing possibility.[55] As he put it, "going-under-ground" implied "covert preparation for a more overt action" (*Invisible Man*, 13) and "a will to confront the world"—a posture suggestive of shadowy war.[56] Hovering in "a state of hibernation" (6), *Invisible Man*'s narrator inhabits an emergent space that bears the potential, following Raymond Williams, to generate "new meanings and values, new practices, new relationships . . . which are substantially alternative or oppositional."[57] Thus, rather than read the narrator's descent as a Cold War turn away from a politics of collectivity to individuality—keeping in mind that the emergent, as a site where exclusions are expressed, can appear as "the personal or the private" (Williams, 125)—we might ask how his location implies an as-yet-unrealized oppositional politics.[58] Reading across Ellison's oeuvre, we might consider how the black POW's battle in "Airman Novel" anticipates the invisible war waged by the "spy in the enemy's country" (16) in *Invisible Man*.

Retrieving Ellison's preoccupation with figures that self-ejected from the U.S. war machine enables a critique of American multiculturalism as an incipient state ideology during World War II. Insofar as the downed flyer's quandary allegorized the two-front fascist threat, it pointed to a crisis requiring a solution more far-reaching than military desegregation, which would in short order be realized in the postwar years.[59] Defined by "racism, materialism, and militarism," Cold War

America, as Martin Luther King Jr. observed two decades after the racial integration of the U.S. military, offered a damning "image of violence" to the world, not a galvanizing vision of "revolution, freedom and democracy."[60] If superficially evocative of the unified black-white front so central to the midcentury antifascist struggle—and Ellison's notion of democratizing art—the alignment of "Negro and white boy . . . in brutal *solidarity* burning the huts of a poor village" (King, 33) in Vietnam signaled its perversion. These "strange liberators" had been sent "eight thousand miles away" to "kill and die together for a nation that has been unable to seat them together in the same schools" (King, 34, 33). In the U.S. war in Vietnam King discerned fascism's specter: "What do the [Vietnamese] peasants think as we ally ourselves with the landlords and as we refuse to put any action into our many words concerning land reform? What do they think as we test out our latest weapons on them, just as the Germans tested out new medicine and new tortures in the concentration camps of Europe?" (35).

Here we might recall Marxist anthropologist Bernhard Stern's early World War II prediction: "Discredited because of the role of Italy and Germany," fascism would "'arrive on an antifascist platform'" in the United States.[61] In this, he anticipated the U.S. military's Cold War renovation, propagated as a civil rights advance and an image of U.S. multicultural democracy around the world. We might return to Ellison's unpublished 1940 FWP essay "The Negro and the War" and note its concern that militarized black-white fraternity might be complicit in fascist agendas of unfreedom, including imperialist war violence. Powerfully critiquing the fascism of U.S. militarism, Ellison argued war's seduction stemmed from its "offer[ing] a non-economic basis upon which Negroes could participate in the national life."[62] Mobilization was cynically used as "a device for unifying the diverse classes of the fascist state," or what scholars of fascism have described as the "noneconomic harmony of the nation in arms."[63] The perils of a prior Du Boisian "close the ranks" stance urging blacks to enlist, Ellison cautioned, would be unduly born by the black proletariat in a war promoted by "reactionary forces, including their own middle class leaders."[64] In denouncing the black leadership's complicity, Ellison was not far removed from C. L. R. James's critique of the top-down galvanization of the black masses for war: "Some people, . . . Negro leaders included, state that there is a possibility of Negroes gaining their rights and participating freely in American life, if they show that they are willing to die for 'democracy'" (41). Ultimately, the Communist Party's shift from "This is not the Negro's war" to its embrace of "All Out for the War of National Liberation" was a move from an antiwar stance to a Popular Front politics that Ellison struggled to reconcile.[65] Reflective of the former, his FWP analysis of imperialist war and the black freedom struggle's global dimensions—its solidarity with labor even in "enemy" countries—represented a profound grappling with race, capitalism, and U.S. militarism. Even as he later deemed World War II to be "potentially [a] peoples' war," his early emphasis on the war's imperialist nature and portrait of the black freedom struggle as "wars-within-wars" can be discerned in his subsequent writings. Although Eric Sundquist deems Ellison's 1943 *Negro Quarterly* editorial, which advocated for "critical participation" in the war, to be his "fullest essay on the war," it cannot fully counter his early skepticism toward imperialist war, so searchingly explored in his unpublished FWP essay.

The War at Home

Committed to the idea that democratizing art had an obligation to call forth America's "blind spot ... where Marx cries out for Freud and Freud for Marx," Ellison cast light on a hazy zone between racial feeling and structural racism that was materializing as a matter of official U.S. concern during the war.[66] His portrait in "Airman Novel" of the Nazi as "a psychologist given to ceaseless intrigue" where the black POW was concerned uneasily mirrored the U.S. government's obsession with what it deemed to be the problem of "Negro morale." War planners approached black American social psychology as a national security issue requiring state intervention. Signed by Roosevelt into law on June 25, 1941, Executive Order 8802, which recommended the eradication of discriminatory practices in the war industries, conceded racism's harmful impact on "Workers' morale and ... National unity."[67] In 1942 a consortium of psychologists affirmed to state agencies: "Our whole national effort—in factories, in Washington, on ships at sea and in air, and in the army lines—depends on morale."[68] Cited by the postwar President's Committee on Equality of Treatment and Opportunity in the Armed Services ("Fahy Committee"), the report "Historical Background of the American Negro in Aviation" (1945) likewise cautioned that prejudice "can do plenty of damage to our American or world security."[69]

Yet government consensus around the "Negro problem" was conditioned by disavowal. The "Negro American," Stern remarked, "may ask whether fascism is really an alternative for him or merely another word for the prevailing system" (378). Nowhere, however, did the state grapple with the systemic challenge posed by black antifascist critique. As with other "pseudoscientific sociological concept[s]" masking the structural nature of racial inequality, "Negro morale" enabled whites to "refuse to recognize the vast extent to which they too benefited from [black] second-class status" (Ellison, *Invisible Man*, xv). More insidiously, by transforming an effect of racial alienation into a national security concern, the wartime state sanctioned an array of securitizing responses, including the development of domestic psychological warfare, that targeted the very population—black Americans—it feared was demoralized in the first place.

All too aware that U.S. victory required black identification with the war effort, Roosevelt commissioned surveys on black morale from wartime propaganda agencies—the Office of Facts and Figures (OFF) and the Office of War Information (OWI)—that amounted to domestic intelligence-gathering operations. Treated as an urgent national security matter, government findings were kept under wraps. In 1943 black social scientist Roscoe Lewis noted that even as the government had yet to release its studies on black wartime morale, the causes of "brooding bitterness" were plain: "lynching, the court-martialing of Negro soldiers for 'rioting' in a Southern town, [and] . . . prevention of friendly contacts between white and Negro soldiers."[70] Indeed, the surveys found that "Negro bitterness toward Army segregation and Navy exclusion was deep seated, sprang from feelings accumulated through the years and was merely brought into sharp relief by the draft and the war."[71]

By a curious coincidence, while the OWI was conducting a survey in Harlem on "the black man's attitude toward the war," Ellison was interviewing Harlem residents for an FWP history initiative on "Negroes of New York."[72] Whereas the OWI survey was tied to government efforts to neutralize black discontent, the FWP, especially the New York office, was viewed as a hotbed of leftists seeking to foment unrest through "subversive propaganda."[73] That both agencies were simultaneously questioning Harlemites aroused local suspicion. In a 1942 *New Masses* article, "The Way It Is," Ellison described an interviewee identified by the pseudonym "Mrs. Jackson" probing his purpose: "So you want to know about how we're doing? Don't you live in Harlem?" and "You're sure you're not one of these investigators?"[74] Despite her reservations, she resolved to take part, stating, "I *want* them to know how I feel" (9). Serving as Ellison's "profile of Harlem," Mrs. Jackson, whose son was in the army, offered this take on the two-front fascist threat: "we got to fight the big Hitler over yonder even with all the little Hitlers over here" (9, 11). In a similar vein, *The Militant* noted that convincing black Americans that "Hitler is their main enemy when they can still feel on their backs the oppression of the American ruling class" would be a hard sell.[75] Indeed, blacks who minimally benefited from the New Deal had to accede to what Claudia Jones called the "war-deal" (*Jim-Crow in Uniform*, 9), their lives mattering insofar as the state's necropolitical demands were concerned. Ellison ended his piece by editorializing about the war at home: "The Mrs. Jacksons cannot make the sacrifices necessary to participate in a total war if the conditions under which they live, the very ground on which they must fight, continues its offensive against them." He then added a parting shot against the OWI: "Nor is this something to be solved by propaganda. Morale grows out of realities, not out of words alone" (11).

Far from prompting structural reflection on the state's role in fostering racial inequality, however, the specter of black demoralization spurred government propaganda efforts as well as racial intelligence and counterintelligence programs targeting black Americans as the state's likely enemies.[76] Demoralization led to disaffection, which led to sedition, or so the argument went. Construed as borderline seditious, black sentiment that American society was "tinged with fascism" (Ellison, "Editorial Comment [1943]," 296) justified the expansion of the state's political policing apparatus, which in its repressive effects only substantiated black antifascist critique. As the United States declared war against fascism abroad, the wartime logic of emergency engendered the conditions whereby fascism could take hold domestically.[77] Expressions of disaffection and demoralization in the Jim Crow armed forces and a home front deformed by police brutality, lynchings, race riots, discrimination in the war industries, and grinding black poverty were interpreted as harbingers of sedition, sabotage, and espionage. Adopting a decontextualized view of disaffection as "a state of mind indicating a lack of affection for the United States government," intelligence agencies cast a wide dragnet, surveilling not only so-called enemy aliens but also black Americans for signs of unpatriotic affect.[78] Noting "the 'Slap the Jap' hysteria following Pearl Harbor has carried over to increasing hatred of the 'enemy' closest at hand, the Negro," Lewis emphasized that black morale required faith in democracy's attainability.[79] Yet signs of a rising police state, intensified by what novelist Chester Himes referred to as the "tight, crazy feeling of race as thick in the street as gas fumes" (30), were hard to ignore. Unleashing its police power in the name of wartime necessity, the government not only spectacularly mass-incarcerated Japanese Americans but also deployed armed force against striking war-industry workers, threw draft resisters and antiwar union organizers into jail, and clamped down on journalistic freedoms.[80] "*Is it now? Is now the time?*" wonders Bob Jones in Himes's *If He Hollers Let Him Go*. "I was the same colour as the Japanese and I couldn't tell the difference. 'A yeller-bellied Jap' coulda meant me too" (4, emphasis in original).

Yet even as the combustible "feel[ing of] race trouble" was "never more than two feet off" (Himes, 4) during the war, color-line politics were being recoded in opaque, undemocratic ways that would inform the postwar emergence of antiracism and anticommunism as linked state policies. The rise of Cold War multiculturalism must be historicized against government anxiety about the threat black demoralization posed to U.S. war power during World War II. In the first instance the calculation behind desegregation as federal policy was the war machine's efficiency. On the Korean War's cusp the Fahy Committee, casting a backward gaze on World War II, argued that "the nation's manpower cannot be used with *maximum efficiency* unless the armed services offer to all men in uniform equal opportunity to discover and exploit their capabilities."[81] If construed as civil rights progress, postwar military desegregation signaled something more sinister afoot: the institutionalization of a permanent war posture against enemies abroad *and* at home. Globally, U.S.-backed political policing, so central to anticommunist nation-building, ensured the security conditions for capitalist profitability. Domestically, in the name of civil defense—a Cold War euphemism for the war at home—covert warfare methods were applied to subjects viewed as the internal enemy. In this regard World War II inaugurated the operationalization of political intelligence on an unprecedented scale in "the Zone of the Interior" (ZI), a geostrategic term roughly denoting the continental United States.[82] If usually understood as "national territory not included in the theater of operations" ("Order of Battle," 1), the ZI nonetheless served as the staging ground for the U.S. prosecution of wars within wars.

For U.S. war planners World War II, viewed as a multidirectional national security threat, required novel tactics for mobilizing domestic populations *across the color line*. It did so in overt and covert ways, including in a clandestine political arena that the Office of Strategic Services (OSS), the CIA's precursor, dubbed "morale operations" (MO), or psychological warfare. This nascent "science" was aimed at neutralizing the threat from two conflated demographics: foreign and domestic enemy populations, including U.S. nationals viewed as racially or politically disaffected, or both.[83] Central to the defeat of such foes—"by truth and by lies, by means fair or foul," in the OSS's telling phrase—was the collaboration of racialized figures mobilized by the burgeoning national security state as native informants, undercover experts who could move unnoticed and with ease in target populations. The racial profiling of subjects likely to be disaffected and their framing as potential enemies blurred the color line during a time of Jim Crow. The state operationalized networks of spies, informants, infiltrators, agents provocateurs, and rumormongers as part of its domestic war machine. Not coincidentally, the racial and securitized double-connotation of "spook" originated in World War II, a perilous era for the "'enemy' closest at hand." As Malcolm X recalled of those years, "Military intelligence units stationed 'black spies in civilian clothes' in African American neighborhoods to watch for subversive activity."[84]

In this total-war context "any Negro demand for justice," Ellison remarked, was viewed "as treasonable, [and] any Negro act of self-defense as an assault against the state."[85] At risk of prosecution for riots, protests, strikes, mutiny, sedition, disaffection, and other forms of insubordination, the black soldier was often singled out for severe punishment "when he was only one offender among many, and sometimes even when he was the victim."[86] More than 80 percent of U.S. soldiers executed for capital crimes in the European theater were black, even though they represented just 10 percent of the U.S. armed forces. Stateside, the fact that black soldiers hazarded the death penalty by "taking up arms against lawful authority in a time of war," as military historian Stanley Sandler writes, testified to the unbearable conditions they faced. "Blunt" reports by army observers revealed that a significant number of enlisted black men harbored "'implacable hatred for the Army.'"[87] Truman Gibson, the War Department's special civilian aide on racial affairs, went so far as to caution Secretary of State Henry Stimson that black soldiers "would much rather fight their domestic enemies than their foreign foe."[88] That some were willing to die by taking up arms against the enemy at home deeply alarmed U.S. war planners.[89]

Although underreported by the government, fiery outbreaks of racial violence on and near stateside U.S. military bases, as well as civilian race riots deemed "the worst . . . since the 'Red Summer' of 1919" (Sandler, 106), gave new meaning to World War II as a total war. For the war's duration the ZI served as the setting for twenty documented instances of militant resistance by black troops in the army.[90] According to Fisk University's Social Science Institute, in 1943 alone there were 242 race riots or disturbances in roughly fifty American urban centers, including Los Angeles, Detroit, New York, and southern cities, many of which involved black soldiers.[91] If described in burnished terms as the "arsenal of democracy" because of the significance of U.S. industrial production to the Allied war effort, the home front was riven by widespread racial conflict.[92] Tellingly, Mrs. Jackson, whom Ellison interviewed for the FWP history project, confessed she longed for her army sergeant son's deployment, "cause then my mind would know some ease" ("The Way It Is," 11)—the implication being that she would rather see her son on the front lines of declared war than on the guerrilla terrain of the war at home.

Ellison reworked the hidden history of the war at home into *Invisible Man*, noting the absence of an official archive for matters contradicting "those lies . . . keepers keep their power by" (439). The August 3, 1943, Harlem riot, which left five dead, several hundred injured, and more than five hundred arrested, was catalyzed, according to the NAACP journal *The Crisis*, by a "wildfire story . . . of the shooting of a Negro soldier in uniform by a civilian policeman." Although the white police officer, James Collins, in fact wounded the black soldier, Robert Bandy, the rumor of Bandy's death drew its logic from a geography of underground war in which, according to *The Crisis*, "the gun in the hands of a good New York policeman doing his duty was the gun in the hands of Dixie cops shooting down men in the uniform, if you please, of the Army of Democracy":

> Negro soldiers have been shot down by civilian police in Alexandria, La., in Little Rock, Ark., in Baltimore, Md., in Beaumont, Tex., and in a half dozen other places. They have been humiliated, manhandled, and beaten in countless instances.
>
> The Harlem mob knew all this. It hated all this. It could not reach the Arkansas cop who fired a full magazine of his revolver into the prone body of a Negro sergeant, or any of the others, so it tore up Harlem.[93]

In *Invisible Man* this war-within-a-war is transformed into an interwar race riot, ignited not by the police shooting of a black man in uniform but by the police murder of Tod Clifton, whose cause of death is "resisting reality in the form of a .38 caliber revolver in the hands of the arresting officer" (458). "He thought he was a man," states the narrator in an improvised street eulogy, "when he was only Tod Clifton," a black man confronted by a "cop [who] had an itching finger and an eager ear for a word that rhymed with 'trigger'" (457). The narrator describes Clifton as a casualty of an ongoing invisible domestic war—"he was black and they shot him. . . . It's an old story"—and the funeral procession as "a prayer for the unknown dead soldier" (456, 452). Anticipating the 1960s race riots, nearly all sparked by antiblack police brutality, *Invisible Man*'s race riot reveals the domestic arena's militarized contours during a time of supposed peace—a subterranean "crash of men against men with most of the guns and numbers on the other side" (553). Submitted to the UN a year prior to *Invisible Man*'s publication, the Civil Rights Congress petition *We Charge Genocide*, which charged the United States with genocide "against the Negro people," observed that the form of counterrevolutionary violence had shifted: "Once the classic method of lynching was the rope. Now it is the policeman's bullet. . . . We submit that the evidence suggests that the killing of Negroes has become police policy in the United States."[94] On the postwar home front the practice of "keeping the peace," as these critics remarked, was indistinguishable from the waging of war.

The Enemy Within

During World War II the FBI embarked on an investigation, "Foreign-Inspired Agitation among the American Negroes," which linked "African Americans with the triple specter of spies, sabotage, and subversives."[95] This nationwide investigation was carried out by undercover operatives planted in a wide spectrum of organizations and institutions and a fleet of researchers who scoured open sources of information to map the political terrain of "racial conditions" during a time of heated racial protest and agitation. Not declassified until 1980, when historian Robert Hill obtained it through FOIA request, *Survey of Racial Conditions in the United States*, an FBI internal security division report, covered the range of wartime black protest: "black workers in defense industries; racial conflicts in the military; the influence of the outspoken wartime black press; Japanese influences on the antiwar sentiment among blacks; Communist Party organizing and membership in the black community; African-American Islamic Movements; and the upsurge of independent black organizations, including . . . the March on Washington Movement and the . . . NAACP. . . . The overriding goal of the survey was to monitor and find a way to stem the rising tide of wartime racial protest and racial disorder that swept the country from 1940 on" (Hill, *The FBI's RACON*, 5).

Central to this project was the ideological construction of subjects racially excluded from the benefits of American democracy *as enemies*. If black debate centered on whether black Americans should participate in the U.S. war effort to defeat the fascist enemy abroad and at home, the U.S. government was waging a largely invisible war against what it construed as an internal threat. Often associated with the Cold War, the institutionalization of counterintelligence, surveillance, and infiltration, all practices that frame civilians as potential enemies, is a dubious legacy of World War II as a total war. Not only could civilians be mobilized for the U.S. war effort, but also, they might be working against it.

At the same time this FBI investigation was under way, the U.S. Army Counter Intelligence Corps (CIC) placed "colored agents ... undercover" among black troops in the Jim Crow military:

> One agent was placed under cover [sic] as a prisoner in the stockade and others were assigned to interview guard personnel and other prisoners. The soldiers had said in their letters [home] that "torture houses" were being constructed to kill Negro soldiers, when actually small solitary confinement houses were being built within the stockade for normal punishment purposes. They said that whites wanted to make slaves of the colored people in the Army; that white soldiers never got guard house sentences while Negroes were always given six months; that the Army was more interested in killing the Negro than the Nazi.
>
> The undercover agent gathered several incriminating statements. One suspect stated that if he were at liberty to kill his enemies "there would not be a white man on the base within one week." Both affirmed that if sent overseas they would kill everyone not black. The other suspect told his fellow prisoners that he hoped America would lose the war and that the Germans would soon invade the country. He alleged that he would sabotage the installation when released from the stockade.[96]

Living with their heads in the lion's mouth, these soldiers were at war, only not against a foreign enemy. For Ellison this type of story was an all-too-familiar, baleful American tale, crystallizing the dilemma of the black freedom quest in the menacing confines of unfreedom. In an era in which the postwar Pax Americana's militarized politics were already under way, with war planners anticipating U.S. victory in both theaters, Ellison explored the undemocratic flip side of the Double-V slogan. If World War II, according to the wartime black papers, was a two-fronted fight for victory, it was also the case, he argued, that "when this country declared war, it was as much against the black man as against the foreign enemy" ("The Negro and the War").

In her essay "Racism and Fascism" Toni Morrison states, "Let us be reminded that before there is a final solution, there must be a first solution, a second one, even a third. The move toward a final solution is not a jump. It takes one step, then another, then another."[97] The first step, she speculates, might look like this: "Construct an internal enemy, as both focus and diversion" (384). A subsequent step might be "Criminalize the enemy. Then prepare, budget for and rationalize the building of holding areas for the enemy—especially its males and absolutely its children" (384). What has been held out as Cold War liberalism enshrined the war power deployed by the United States during World War II against the internal menace, thus legitimating, as Neocleous argues, the "permanent exercise of war power against . . . unsocial and lawless elements" as police power: "Seen through the lens of sovereignty, these elements are the enemies of security; through the lens of property, they are the enemies of improvement; through the lens of police, they are disorderly. The outcome can only be war and war again" (82). It is precisely with regard to this secret war, this invisible war, that Ellison's war writings offer an illuminating critique of the lurking fascist dimensions of U.S. democracy—"democracy within the teeth of fascism."

Revolution from Above
Ōe Kenzaburō, the Black Airman, and Occupied Japan

The Black Pacific

If we can imagine something called "the black Pacific," it demands contextualization against U.S. military-imperial exploits in Asia and the Pacific, a legacy founded on force in which race has borne an uneasy relationship to the U.S. war machine. From the turn-of-the-century U.S. seizure of the Philippines onward, the asymmetry of U.S. war power has found expression in racially coded images of merciless violence unleashed from above. In its belligerent trajectory "screaming into the Pacific," the eagle, invoked in soaring flight as a symbol of American liberty, was reimagined in predatory motion, descending with fearsome speed.[1] Associated with catastrophic force, the swooping eagle has served as one emblem of the post-1945 American "peace" regime in Asia and the Pacific, an arena of imperial dominion in which unfreedom would be presented as freedom, democratization as democracy, and militarism as the basis for life itself. By World War II, the eagle Mark Twain had earlier described as turning swaths of the Philippines into a "howling wilderness" morphed into a metallic B-29 Superfortress, and the talons that laid waste to Japanese cities took various destructive forms: incendiary wind, jellied gasoline, and atomic bombs.[2]

Central to modern warfare, the technological capacity to administer mass death from on high has presumed and enacted a spectrum of comparative humanity—superhumanity, subhumanity, nonhumanity—giving rise to an expanded policing order featuring the "pilot as policeman, bomb as baton."[3] In a 1939 essay, "Aviation, Geography, and Race," the pro-Nazi American pilot Charles Lindbergh described mastery of the skies in possessive racial terms. He envisioned aerial superiority as playing a civilizational function in erecting a "barrier between the teeming millions of Asia and the Grecian inheritance of Europe—one of those priceless possessions which permit the White race to live at all in a pressing sea of Yellow, Black, and Brown."[4] Lindbergh's overtly white supremacist theories would give way to racially blurred practices of asymmetrical warfare as the twentieth century wore on. Structural reckoning with the U.S. war machine's shattering necropolitical effects therefore entails that we be vigilant in confronting the racial logic of its outsized "production and exploitation of group-differentiated vulnerability to premature death."[5] Less an interplay between identifiable or isolable combatants than a dynamic between "a vast, mechanized, highly technological force" and an abstract target, modern U.S. warfare requires analysis of racism that centers on the war machine's industrial function: extermination.[6] Inheriting from historical imaginaries of conquest that collapsed native humanity and terrain as a *terra nullius* for imperial designs, conceptions of the target as a site of mass anonymous death recode race along spatial lines.

The Pax Americana's precipitating conditions in Asia and the Pacific were thus twofold: dominion above and indiscriminate wasteland below. The U.S. atomic bombings of Japan that brought war in the Pacific theater to a spectacular close mapped the racialized divide between life and death onto the separation of air from ground, even as the ruling ideas about race were shifting. Indeed, the planes that transported the atomic bombs would also be ideologically cast as carriers of democracy, and ground zero would be construed as the basis for reconstruction. Having defeated the foe, the U.S. war machine shifted gears to reengineer its civil society. Both death and revolution thus came from above, signaling an era's onset in which Japan's "democratization" would take place in U.S. militarism's ambit. Theodore Cohen, General Douglas MacArthur's labor-relations chief, recalled the euphoria of "democratizing [Japan] by means of that least democratic of institutions, the Army": "the exhilarated American staff felt able to do anything it was asked to do: disarm a world power, demobilize its armies, govern it, and transform its basic institutions. Their horizons were unlimited. After all, they had won the war."[7] Yet the war machine that wreaked indiscriminate ruin in Tokyo, Hiroshima, Nagasaki, and other Japanese cities did not deactivate with the Occupation.[8] Here we might recall Karl Liebknecht's early twentieth-century insight into militarism: "The deciding factor in every social relation of power is, in the last resort, the superiority of physical force."[9] In this, he anticipated the criticality of U.S. war power to Japan's reconstruction and its long postwar history as a U.S. client-state.

Propagated as democracy's world-historical expansion where none had broadly existed, the U.S. "revolution from above" in Japan, which in retrospect would appear "the most successful of the American postwar interventions" (Cohen, 6), was ambivalent in its democratizing effects. As a regime change that bore the revolutionary promise of democracy and freedom, it obliquely recalled Reconstruction.[10] Resonant here is W. E. B. Du Bois's account of Reconstruction as "a dictatorship backed by the military arm of the United States by which the governments of the Southern states were to be coerced into accepting a new form of administration."[11] Japan's defeat, too, served as the basis for sweeping social transformation. Yet U.S. militarism's structural durability and political function in postwar Japan contradicted its purported democratic telos. As the occupation drew on, MacArthur came to view centralized state and police power as a "bulwark against revolution."[12] His goal of restoring Japan along anticommunist lines turned on the emperor's retention. Thus, even as the Occupation's bywords were "democratization" and "demilitarization," deimperialization was off the table. Moreover, as the key Asian U.S. client state, Japan anchored an expanding "empire of bases" that extended U.S. war power throughout the region.[13] The ultimate nature of Japan's democratization was thus unsettled: did U.S.-engineered regime change signal freedom or repression, demilitarization or remilitarization, revolution or counterrevolution?[14]

In Occupied Japan, Reconstruction's echoes reverberated on multiple registers, including skepticism about an imposed revolution's democratic potential.[15] Yet unlike the protracted reaction that followed federal troop withdrawal from the American South and signaled the eclipse of radical Reconstruction, the paradox of democratization in Japan resided, in part, in the fact that U.S. soldiers never left Japan. Characterized by class preservationism, Reconstruction's betrayal was marked by the Republican Party's reconciliation, as Marxist historians have noted, with "the former enemy."[16] Unfreedom thus arrived in freedom's garb, a contradiction that has preoccupied leftist historiography of Reconstruction following the 1935 publication of Du Bois's landmark *Black Reconstruction in America*. As Du Bois argued, Reconstruction did not end "exploitation of the dark proletariat," much less ensure labor's emancipation, but instead gave rise to a "dictatorship of capital" (16, 239), thereby inaugurating a long era of counterrevolution. Not singular to the United States, this "epic struggle between the dictatorship of capital (plutocracy) and the dictatorship of labor (democracy)" would be globally restaged in colonial contexts.[17] If in theory an occasion for radical transformation, war ruin could be and indeed was seized as an occasion for rehabilitating capitalism.

Early postwar Japan, albeit wretched as far as the daily lives of the Japanese were concerned, was likewise a landscape of opportunity for the investor—as one American visitor tellingly put it, "a carpetbagger's dream."[18] U.S. Army Counter Intelligence Corps (CIC) documents reveal that by mid-1946, rightists, ultranationalists, and militarists no longer constituted the principal target of political policing and were, in some cases, depurged.[19] Instead, a new enemy entered the crosshairs of the U.S. war machine. In a red-baiting shift, CIC trained its sights on the Japanese Communist Party, whose members, on release from prison, rapidly organized around workers, protesting American capital's "colonization of Japan."[20] The CIC, which deemed itself "the eyes and ears of the Occupation" and, in remote areas, its "sole representative" (*CIC in the Occupation*, 38, 29), enlisted the Japanese police in routing out labor organizers with alleged Communist Party ties. Conceding that rampant food shortages, skyrocketing inflation, and the Occupation-imposed wage scale made it impossible for "the Japanese worker . . . to provide for himself and his family" (*CIC in the Occupation*, 84)—all when more than thirteen million were unemployed and large swaths of the country lay in ruins—the CIC nevertheless aimed for total compliance with MacArthur's no-strike order. Although Japan's new constitution granted unions the right to organize and bargain collectively, leading to a massive surge in union membership, command control over labor and austerity defined the U.S. postwar program. In the purge of Japanese affiliated with the Japanese Communist Party—a party MacArthur blasted as a "satellite of an international predatory force and a Japanese pawn of alien power policy"[21]—we can discern the ideological seeds of anticommunist U.S. police actions to come, wars in Korea and Vietnam that, in turn, would stimulate Japan's rebuilt economy. In the dawning Cold War order, wartime allies thereby morphed into peacetime targets whereas former rightist foes in Japan and the region were rehabilitated as linchpins of anticommunism. In this new dispensation, undemocratic Asian regimes, often helmed by pro-Japanese collaborators, were actively cultivated, installed, and backed by the United States in order to "contain" communism's perceived threat.[22]

As an equivocal vehicle for democratic change, the U.S. war machine thus incorporated proxy governments and their militaries into its strategic posture as it launched serial hot wars in the region. With an eye to postwar U.S. regional dominance, it strategically recoded both lines of enmity and the color line virtually overnight. The transformation of the U.S. war machine complicated the racial logic of asymmetrical warfare, especially as multinational anticommunist unity became the driving U.S. foreign policy imperative for the Cold War's duration. Just three years into Japan's occupation, President Truman issued Executive Order 9981, recommending the U.S. military's desegregation. In so doing, he set the stage for the reconfiguration of American race relations in far-flung settings conditioned by U.S. military force against local nonwhite populations.[23] While the struggle against Jim Crow was being waged at home, U.S. policies in Occupied Japan fostered "a subtle but distinct colour bar," reserving facilities for exclusive U.S. military use with signs that read "Japanese Keep Out" or "For Allied Personnel Only," in addition to marking separate entrances for Americans and Japanese in downtown Tokyo public buildings.[24] The racial liberalization of the U.S. military thus occurred in the illiberal context of unprecedented U.S. expansionism in the Pacific. In theory colorblind within its own ranks by the early Cold War era, the U.S. military shed the Jim Crow legacy that bedeviled U.S. claims to democracy during World War II, thereby enabling the United States to parry charges of imperialism in the global arena.[25]

To the extent U.S. military outposts in Occupied Japan served as extraterritorial settings for the enlargement of black civil rights, Reconstruction's unfinished business would ironically and superficially be realized in the Pacific. Yet insofar as the "freedom dreams" of the black Atlantic found fugitive passage into the Pacific via the U.S. war machine, they were complicated by their association with asymmetrical U.S. military-imperial power.[26] Moreover, democratization, as a Cold War project, did not inflame the revolutionary imagination; rather, it took the counterrevolutionary form of U.S. interventionist wars in the region. Ambivalently positioned on the front lines of such wars, black soldiers have historically been aligned both with and against the imperial war machine. Testament to the U.S. practice of racial soldiering, they have surfaced in ways that have pointed to the unfreedom of the U.S. home front. Within the longer transpacific history of U.S. military empire, we might think of legendary buffalo soldier David Fagen, who crossed the line to lead *insurrecto* troops in the Philippine-American War; Dorie Miller, cook third-class in the Jim Crow armed forces, who emerged from below deck to gun down Japanese planes at Pearl Harbor; and black GIs aligned in "brutal solidarity" with America's multiethnic, multinational military in its war in Vietnam.[27]

The tale of the screaming American eagle thus links the black Atlantic to the black Pacific as a catastrophic geography of death in its own right. In the post-1945 era it has called for analysis of the war machine's equivocal function as an engine of lethal multiculturalism. In Paul Gilroy's famed account of the black Atlantic, the slave ship figures as "the *living means* by which the points within that Atlantic world were joined."²⁸ By contrast, in the geo-imaginary of the Pacific, the plane appears as a technology of U.S. military might that serves less to articulate "discontinuous histories" (Gilroy, 17) than to produce discontinuity as an intended effect. The aim is to shatter the world below. Yet race in the form of premature death also enters the U.S. war machine, as Jin-kyung Lee has argued, as necropolitical labor freighted with the work of obliterating the enemy while being itself vulnerable to annihilation.²⁹ In this regard, scenes of asymmetrical U.S. warfare might be understood as dramas in comparative subhumanity in which the operators of machineries of death and the inhabitants of the target have been unevenly placed into inexorable kill-or-be-killed motion against each other.

Naming the grim relation between pilots and the masses below, the *kill-chain* assumes hierarchy and discontinuity as structural givens. Subordinated to the war machine's necropolitical function, the pilot, for all intents and purposes, has been mechanistically integrated into a "human-plane system," a hybrid human-nonhuman militarized technology aimed at the distant destruction of the lifeworlds of others.³⁰ The pilot, in other words, is aligned with lethal machinery rather than the humanity of the target. Such a system historically assimilated black men not into humanity's ranks per se but as "well-oiled working parts of a grand mechanical system."³¹ Yet in the war machine's incorporation of racialized flesh we might detect a "counterculture of modernity" (Gilroy, 1) specific to the black Pacific, an emergent possibility linking black pilot and Asian target and suggestive of solidarity—namely, a relationality born of differing positions of dehumanization relative to the U.S. war machine.

The Crane and the Eagle

Published five years after the formal end of U.S. Occupation, *Shiiku* ("Prize Stock," 1958) plays on vertical metaphors of the American revolution from above. An ironic meditation on the U.S. occupation and postwar democratization of Japan, this novella garnered 1994 Nobel laureate Ōe Kenzaburō Japan's Akutagawa Prize, catapulting him to postwar prominence.³² It takes place during a late-war summer when "'enemy' planes" resembling birds to Ōe's rustic child narrator "had begun recently to traverse the sky" (Nathan trans., 118). When one hurtles down to the earth and villagers capture the American pilot, the action of Ōe's strange tale begins.

In the crashing bird we might detect an overdetermined resonance. As the Pacific War drew to a close, the sacred crane (the Japanese emperor) and the American eagle (MacArthur) descended onto Japanese terrain. These converging trajectories signaled the onset of Japan's democratization.[33] Fixed in the wartime generation's sensual memory, the emperor's symbolic downfall occurred on August 15, 1945, when the Voice of the Crane broadcast his nation's surrender over the radio. Ōe recalls his fellow Ōse villagers' incredulity at hearing the emperor's reedy, all-too-human voice: "How could we believe that an august presence of such awful power had become an ordinary human being on a designated summer day?" (Nathan trans., n.p.). According to John Nathan, Ōe experienced this desacralization as a recurring fever-dream: "Sick with a fever, he . . . beheld the Emperor in a terrifying nightly dream, soaring across the sky like a giant bird with white feathers. Then Hirohito went on the air and spoke in the voice of a mortal man."[34] Hirohito's iconoclastic "humanization" marked Japan's entry into the postwar era. The transition's success required his explicit demilitarization. Identified with a nationalist ideology of sacrifice, the emperor, as "a god, the authority of the nation, the organizing principle of reality," had, after all, galvanized the total-war mobilization of Japanese society.[35] Not even Ōe's home "in a valley surrounded by a dense forest on [a] remote island" could escape his authority: "We had even prayed at our shrines for victory at war to the Emperor who was a god. And the 'August True Reflection' of the Emperor, His photograph, reproduced in large numbers, was installed in the alcove of honor at all our national schools. In case of fire, the principal was obliged to risk his life if necessary to carry the Imperial Portrait to safety first of all" ("Day the Emperor Spoke"). A child during the war years, Ōe recalls his indecision when asked by his elementary school teacher, "What would you do if His Majesty commanded you to die?" ("Day the Emperor Spoke"). Knowing the required answer was that he would kill himself, Ōe, who seditiously wished to live, paused. In Ōe's account this hesitation earned him a flogging.

If indelibly associated in Ōe's mind with militarized authoritarianism, the hawk that presided over Japan's wars of aggression was reimaged after its defeat as a benign marine biologist, amateur botanist, and model family man, in short, rehabilitated as a peaceful crane. With his flexible symbolic properties, Hirohito proved of inestimable value to the Occupation.[36] On the orders of the Supreme Commander for the Allied Powers (SCAP), namely, MacArthur, Hirohito released a "Declaration of Humanity" (*ningen sengen*) on January 1, 1946, as the basis for the "Construction of a New Japan": "The ties between us and our people . . . are not predicated on the false conception that the Emperor is divine and that the Japanese people are superior to other races and fated to rule the world."[37] MacArthur promptly issued an approving statement: "The Emperor's New Year's statement pleases me very much. By it he undertakes a leading part in the democratization of his people."[38] In the interregnum Hirohito, in his appointed role as "America's man in Tokyo," modeled like no one else could a pro-American stance.[39] He was deployed as a vehicle for SCAP-mandated reforms, yielding to U.S. hegemony in Japan.[40] Of the China hands pushing for Hirohito's prosecution, MacArthur groused, "They don't understand. . . . I can't possibly accomplish the transition without him."[41]

The symbiosis between emperor and occupier thus facilitated the near-instantaneity with which the drama of transitional authority played out: atomic ruin, emperor's surrender, MacArthur's assumption of unbridled power, and GIs bearing gifts of Hershey bars and Lucky Strikes throughout the archipelago. As Hirohito descended to earth, MacArthur ascended to heaven. Both Japanese and U.S. Occupation histories leave undisputed the general's prime-mover status: "MacArthur bestrode the land like a Colossus, and the Japanese called him 'father'" (Cohen, 53). Toshio Nishi notes: "MacArthur demonstrated his supreme authority when he told the US Senate in May 1951 that his orders to the Japanese people 'were not subject to the controls of any higher authority'" (286). Emblematizing the revolution from above, the eagle in occupied Japan was MacArthur. In *Beneath the Eagle's Wings* John Curtis Perry writes that "MacArthur epitomized the American presence in Japan": "His godlike power, his ignorance of Japanese culture, his pronounced ethnocentricity, and his enormous self-confidence as well as the success he enjoyed there were common to the whole enterprise" (78).

Reinforcing MacArthur's stamp on the Occupation were the optics of the transition. His commanding carriage, unadorned self-presentation, and staged arrival amounted to a performance of U.S. postwar hegemony. The widely circulated photograph of his meeting with Hirohito drove home the message about the changing of the gods: "On 27 September 1945, Hirohito, the living god for ordinary Japanese, paid a courtesy visit to MacArthur. The *Asahi* published a picture of the short, stern-faced Emperor, with a formal tie standing still beside the tall, relaxed MacArthur" (Sugita, 16). Not just a study in contrasts, but a portrait of the complementary workings of postwar power, this image of

MacArthur hosting Hirohito in the emperor's own former dominion bespoke a near-total supersession of authority. This image of conquest complemented a mass-mediated photograph of MacArthur's arrival on Japanese soil a month prior. As the foreign face of Japan's future within a U.S.-dominated world system, MacArthur landed on August 30, 1945, at Atsugi Airfield, where kamikaze pilots, in service to the emperor, had been trained. In a canny performance of militarized peace he stepped out onto the tarmac noticeably weaponless: "The victor displayed his superior force by conspicuously concealing it; MacArthur carried no gun, not even a sword. The Japanese people, long expert in the art of self-presentation, appreciated the man's style" (Nishi, 285).

A Rare Species of Bird

Written in the wake of the Occupation, and on the threshold of mass protests against the 1960 renewal of the U.S.-Japan Security Treaty, *Shiiku* recasts MacArthur's dramatic landing and the emperor's humanizing descent, situating these twinned events in the prior wartime era and revising them along provocative racial lines. Conflating U.S. occupier and Japanese emperor in the image of the plummeting plane, an exposed negative suggesting American eagle and Japanese crane, Ōe alters the Occupation script toward ambiguous ends. Restaging Hirohito's descent and MacArthur's arrival as the crashing to earth of a black American airman—an unnamed captive figure rather than an occupying army—*Shiiku*, as an "ironic picture of Japan's relationship with America," shifts focus from the historic revolution from above to the emergent possibility of democracy from below.[42]

As an ahistorical plot twist, the pilot's racialization is essential to the imaginative value of Ōe's tale. It counters the historical absence of black airmen in U.S. bombing campaigns against Japan and effaces the white pilots who flew the B-29 bombers that firebombed Tokyo and dropped atomic bombs on Hiroshima and Nagasaki. Of *Shiiku*'s flawed facticity, Ōe has stated:

> The time of the story is near the end of the Pacific War, and the account begins with the shooting down of a U.S. bomber on an air-raid mission. A black airman falls by parachute into the deep woods that surround the mountain Village and is taken prisoner by the villagers, most of whom are farmers. I have been told that during the Pacific War, at least, there were no black American airmen. During my boyhood years, however, there was a tale—although highly doubtful as fact—narrated in the village as a piece of "new folklore," telling of farmers

in the mountains of Kyushu . . . murdering a black American soldier who had parachuted from his bomber. Thus my story is based solely on a rumor that bears reality in terms of narrative folklore.[43]

In its premise Ōe's novella uncannily mirrors Ralph Ellison's unpublished wartime novel of a black flyer interned in a Nazi POW camp. Yet *Shiiku* reflects the complex racial and colonial dimensions of the Pacific theater, where the United States deployed a Jim Crow military to fight against an Asian fascist foe. It imagines democratization to be a searching horizontal process that occurs between subaltern subjects located in Japan's margins, far from "the insular, unaccommodating, and emperor-focused culture of the rest of Japan" (Ōe, "Speaking on Japanese Culture," 32).

Shiiku describes the fragile unfolding of friendship between the narrator, a Japanese boy called "Frog" (a derisive nickname the town clerk applies to all the village children), and the downed pilot, referred to by the epithet "the catch."[44] Metonymically associated in the first instance with his plane, the bomber pilot is first naturalized, in the child narrator's description, as "a rare species of bird" (118). He enters the village as a cipher. Captured after parachuting into a nearby forest, "the *catch*, instead of a flying suit of burnt-ocher silk and black leather flying shoes, wore a khaki jacket and pants and, on his feet, ugly, heavy-looking boots" (114, 123). With an "iron chain of a boar trap . . . locked around his ankles" (123), he makes for an abject spectacle. With his descent to earth, he is thereafter cast in gravity-bound, sensory, bestial terms.

Ōe's animalization of the pilot invites contextualization against the rigid hierarchy that casts Frog's village as closest to the earth, a human substratum that verges on the animal. Drawing on tropes of degradation, Ōe crafts a portrait of the airman, one face of U.S. victory in the postwar juncture in which he was writing, as uncertain humanity, as the human in limbo. Not unique to the black soldier, this portrait of suspended humanity is contagiously refracted throughout the novella, first finding expression in the odor of a corpse at the crematorium, "like the sticky fluid certain kinds of beetles leaked" (114), and thereafter extending to the members of Frog's ostracized village. Enlivening the village idiom, including Frog's narration, creaturely metaphors mark the people of his "old but underdeveloped homesteaders' village" (114) as close to the earth. Occupying the bottom of a militarized administrative order governing Tokyo center, prefecture, town, and village in *Shiiku*'s total-war setting, Frog's hamlet, although isolated because of flood and landslide, wields no independent authority but must defer to dictates from on high. Obliquely depicted, this centralized bureaucracy conditions the villagers' social status, ensuring their subhumanity. Yet animality also inheres in the target's kill-chain logic. When the "enemy plane" passes overhead, its roar "drown[s]" Frog and his playmates "like insects trapped in oil" (116), immobilizing them through sheer force of sound. Far from crystallizing in a single subjective center, near-animality and its correlate, near-humanity, slide from bestialized black soldier to Frog, "a miserable and meager creature" (133), and back again.

Brought to bear in *Shiiku* on a POW whose fate is unsettled and villagers "treated like dirty animals in the *town*" (114), tropes of degradation are a signature of Ōe's idiom. As an expression of "the peculiar logic of the 'inside out' (*á l'envers*), of the 'turnabout,' of a continual shifting from top to bottom," carnival and its kindred literary concept, grotesque realism, have been vital to his account of Japan's overnight metamorphosis from fascist military empire to U.S. client state.[45] In analysis of Rabelais, Mikhail Bakhtin contends that degradation, "the lowering of all that is high, spiritual, ideal, abstract . . . to the material level, to the sphere of earth and body" (19), is grotesque realism's essential principle. For Ōe, a voice of postwar conscience, degradation has furnished the grounds for Japan's genuine democratic transformation. With Hirohito's humanization the Japanese national polity was unseated from its apex as humanity's standard in Japan's racialized empire to its nadir as prostrate subhumanity in a U.S.-dominated regional order. By the war's end, Japan was in ruins. Three million Japanese were dead.[46] U.S. bombing campaigns decimated a majority of urban housing, leaving fifteen million homeless.[47] If critical of U.S. militarism, Ōe has also located democratizing possibility in this abjection. Only through defeat could Japan, in his view, recognize the humanity of those it subjugated—Chinese, Koreans, Okinawans—as well as stigmatized war remnants such as *hibakusha* (atomic-bomb survivors) and *zainichi* (ethnic Korean residents) in Japan's postwar landscape.

"I dream about the Japanese people's true life," Ōe stated in a 1995 conversation with Kim Chi-ha, South Korean poet and former political prisoner, "and the future of the *saengmyông gondongch'e* (life-sharing community) of the Asians."[48] If at first glance reminiscent of the "Greater East Asia Co-Prosperity Sphere" slogan under which Japan waged aggressive regional war, Kim's concept of "life-sharing community" turns on Japan's deimperializing transformation. As Taiwanese scholar Kuan-Hsing Chen contends, deimperialization requires that "critical intellectuals in countries that were or are imperialist ... reexamin[e] their own imperialist histories and the harmful impacts those histories have had on the world."[49] The dialectical interplay of decolonization and deimperialization, he argues, "is a precondition for reconciliation between the colonizer and the colonized" (vii) and their mutual movement toward democracy. Against his nation's role as a cornerstone of U.S. military empire in Asia and the Pacific, Ōe has insisted that Japan, despite its postwar economic rise, must rightfully be understood as a margin, not the center, of the region.[50] Claiming anti-imperialist status as a peripheral writer, Ōe has maintained that "Japan is on the periphery of Asia" and only "from the periphery" can "the story of the human being" be told.[51]

For Ōe, Japan's peripheralization has meant the abandonment of its wartime conception of the human, understood along ultranationalist lines. Aimed at illuminating Japan's obscured margins, Ōe's turn to grotesque realism as a "literary weapon" ("Japan's Dual Identity," 98) in *Shiiku* permits a double deimperializing move: the revelation of subhumanity in Imperial Japan under the sign of black American subhumanity and vice versa. However superficially evocative of color-line slogans propagated by Japan's fascist war machine, "Black, Yellow, Red, and Brown," Ōe's linking of histories of dehumanization enables a critique of Japan's framing of the Pacific War as a race war, with black Americans and Japanese supposedly natural allies with a shared foe in white supremacy.[52] As evidence of a mindless subscription to Japanese propaganda, the character Harelip's exclamation, "He's a black man, he's no enemy!" therefore serves as a reactionary foil to Frog's more uncharted alliance with the black POW.[53] Questioning whether Pax Japonica demagogic slogans calling for a united front against white imperialism possess democratic value, *Shiiku* instead posits mutual subhumanity and near-animality, not black identification with Japanese imperialism, as grounds for insurgent political possibility. The novella insists on mutual degradation, refusing to stage Frog's cross-racial encounter with "the catch" on assuredly human ground. Instead, democratization's fragile prospect emerges from the growing bond between Frog and a POW likened to "a domestic animal" (146). On the night the pilot is caught and confined to the cellar of the storehouse where Frog's family makes its home, Frog inquires of his father:

"What are you going to do with [the soldier]?"
"Until we know what the town thinks, rear him."

"Rear him? Like an animal?"

"He's the same as an animal," my father said gravely. "He stinks like an ox."

(126–27)

Frog describes his elation at this news: "I hugged myself with both arms, I wanted to throw off my clothes and shout—we were going to rear the black soldier, like an animal!" (127). With the POW's fate yet to be determined by the Imperial Army, the town clerk, assuming the "arrogant tone of a minor bureaucrat" (140), shifts responsibility for the soldier's confinement onto the villagers. In the ensuing reprieve Frog and the other children turn the force of their imagination to their "rare and domestic animal, their animal of genius" (153) whom they, beyond adult supervision, "rear" as a special playmate. In this interlude the children are "joined to [the soldier] by a sudden, deep, passionate bond that was almost 'human'" (147).

In Ōe's tale of strange and deliberate reversals, the children's world appears to invert the order of things, allowing for a sense of removal from the militarized status quo. In a setting permeated by top-down authority, with Frog's village at the bottom of a system elevating the military above prefecture, prefecture above town, town above village, and emperor above all, the defamiliarizing presence of the POW momentarily enlarges insurgent possibility. Against prescriptive social authority, Frog forges a bond with the American soldier. He recounts, "My brother and Harelip and I fell into the habit of spending the daylight hours in the cellar where the black soldier sat, our chests hammering with the excitement of breaking a rule at first" (144). This capacity to imagine and enact the breaking of rules demonstrates the emancipatory impact of the POW's presence in the children's world. If, during the war, "the Japanese had no other way of realizing themselves than by nullifying themselves in a fusion with the Emperor" (Ōe and Kim, 293–94), by contrast, Frog's intensifying attachment to the black soldier gives way to alienated national self-consciousness. Through a shift in allegiances from fascistic fantasies of imperial totality to a more abject subjectivity as "a totally insignificant Japanese boy" (137), it is possible to discern a groping toward an as-yet-unnamed social relation—an orientation toward the POW that hints of something anarchic and liberatory.

Free yet fundamentally unfree, the POW, as the occasion for the children's crude games, becomes the inadvertent basis of their discovery of their own freedom. Without adult permission Frog, in the first of a series of antiauthoritarian gestures, unlocks the boar-trap around the POW's wounded ankles with his father's key. As he gratefully notes, the soldier who entered their territory in a plane resembling a bird does not "drop ... upon us like an eagle" (145). Thereafter, the children begin "taking the black soldier out of the cellar frequently, for walks along the cobblestone road": "The adults said nothing. When they encountered the black soldier surrounded by us children they merely looked away and circled around him, just as they stepped into the grass to avoid the bull from the headman's house when it came along the road" (149). By "liberating" the soldier, the children loosen the hold of adult authority over themselves. On their own cognizance they entrust the soldier with tools "that could have been used as weapons" (146), bathe with him in a nearby spring, and urge him to copulate with a goat.

That the children's world remains unmilitarized—an exception to the total-war context and thus permissive of alliances across enemy lines—is *Shiiku*'s central fiction. Set in the rural margins, Ōe's oneiric tale foregrounds Japan's periphery against its militarized center, the village against the town, and the children's world against that of the adults. Although situated in a totalizing emperor system, the village, as a subaltern site in an imagined Japan, hints at an internal remove—what Ōe describes as a "village culture" that resists Tokyo's "homogenizing, centristic culture" ("Speaking on Japanese Culture," 35). If premised on the Imperial Army's overstretch in the late-war period, the POW's "freedom" turns on the conceit he has been released to the children's world, unshackled not only from the crude boar-trap around his ankles but also from the U.S. war machine. Of his place among them, Frog muses: "We could not believe that this black man like a domestic animal once had been a soldier fighting in the war" (146). Frog rejects enemy consciousness, turning away from militarized authority that extends from the adults to the emperor. Ōe details his wordless attempts to find common ground with the POW outside the hierarchies shaping the novella's social world. In this way *Shiiku* envisions democracy emerging from a setting thoroughly conditioned by militarism.

Coming from the Territory

In a 1966 essay, "Huckleberry Finn and the American Dream in the Shadow of the Vietnam War," Ōe reflects on how the past and present collided for him while he was in the United States the prior summer, stoking racial fear akin to that experienced by "Nisei ... sent to a concentration camp" and "black youth" inducted into the Jim Crow U.S. Army.[54] Chatting with a French woman writer at a Harvard crosswalk, Ōe noted that General Curtis LeMay's prescription for Vietnam—"Bomb them back into the Stone Age"—had originated in his blueprint for dropping atomic bombs on Japan in World War II and plan for incinerating North Korean cities during the Korean War. That the Japanese government decorated the strategist behind the bombings of Japan, Korea, and Vietnam was, Ōe stated, "a betrayal of human beings in Hiroshima." Immersed in this discussion about Asia as historic target of the U.S. war machine, Ōe suddenly found himself the object of racial profiling when Americans in a passing car yelled out, "Hey, did you learn your lesson?" and hurled the dated epithet "yellow peril" at him. Jolted into enemy consciousness, indeed perceiving himself as "a bespectacled buck-toothed ugly midget figure that was an exact caricature of the 'Jap,'" Ōe recalled the date, August 15, the twentieth anniversary of Japan's surrender. With a copy of Mark Twain's 1885 *Adventures of Huckleberry Finn* in his pocket, he was besieged by "mutually contradictory remembrances and emotions concerning America" regarding the "lesson" of Japan's defeat.

In this essay Ōe lays claim to an inheritance of democracy imposed from without, a legacy of militarized liberation with freedom as its face, unfreedom as its obverse. He hails Huck as "a free hero" whose "antisocial flight" modeled an imagination beyond "fear or hatred of America, or total dependence on America" for postwar Japanese children. Yet he simultaneously laments his inability to free himself "from the oppressing, demonic power of the word America." Preoccupied with the contradiction of Japan's democratization, Ōe has repeatedly cast freedom in imperiling conditions in his writing. In his oeuvre freedom tempered by racial abjection is an effect of democratization. In an autobiographical description that recalls Frog, Ōe describes the "paradox of Japan's surrender and postwar period" that he experienced: "one patriotic boy in a village found that he had to cope with a gigantic seed of submission. At the same time he also began his apprenticeship, living through the postwar period with a gigantic seed of liberation and renewal."[55] Ōe's postwar apprenticeship in democratic practice bears noting: as an opponent of the 1960 U.S.-Japan Security Treaty renewal, a critic of South Korea's U.S.-backed military dictatorships, a detractor of Japan's ruling Liberal Democratic Party (LDP)'s resurgent militarism and historical revisionism, an antinukes peace activist, a disability rights advocate, and a self-identified "democrat with a small d" writer.[56] Notwithstanding these commitments, Ōe identifies his membership in "the 'children's generation' of the intellectuals who, after defeat in the Pacific War, hoped and struggled to create a new culture of Japanese people and thereby resuscitate Japan" as his shaping political experience.[57]

Central to Ōe's political awakening was his reading of *Adventures of Huckleberry Finn*, which he credits as the "most important book of my boyhood."[58] Ironically, the very U.S.-sponsored project of political reconstruction that Twain lambasted in turn-of-the-century anti-imperialist broadsides—"We can make them as free as ourselves, give them a government and a country of their own, put a miniature of the American constitution afloat in the Pacific, start a brand new republic to take place among the free nations of the world" (quoted in Zwick, *Mark Twain's Weapons*, 5)—furnished the very context in which Twain's novel would be widely read in postwar Japan. As Tsuyoshi Ishihara notes, Occupation-mandated curricular reform resulted in *Adventures of Huckleberry Finn*'s broad circulation. Viewed as "work[ing] for the freedom and equality that are the foundation of democracy," Huck was idealized by Japanese translators as a model for postwar children.[59] In his introduction to *Huckleberry no Boken* (*Adventures of Huckleberry*, 1948), Keisuke Tsutsui identifies "children, who will contribute to the democratization of Japan in the future" (quoted in Ishihara, 72) as his intended readers. Huck, who chose "to light out for the territory" rather than return to education's manacles, thus would be put back in school once again, so to speak, in the "territory" of Occupied Japan.[60]

By contrast, Ōe maintains that his furtive first encounter with the novel occurred when it was categorized as wartime "enemy literature"—not as a laudable primer in democracy.[61] In his telling, his seditious embrace of the novel was akin to Huck's illicit association with Jim, prompting him to spurn the emperor system and expand his sense of humanity beyond narrowly national affinities: "Presently I found myself clinging to a symbol of hope—a book my mother had dared to obtain for me secretly, even though it was enemy literature: 'The Adventures of Huckleberry Finn.' Huck had turned his back on the teachings of his church and resigned himself to going straight to hell rather than betray the black slave who was his friend. I couldn't help feeling trust for him and for the soldiers who were his countrymen. This reliance seemed to open on the joy of life" ("Day the Emperor Spoke").

From the dilemma "'twixt two things" Huck faces regarding Jim, either to "steal Jim out of slavery" (Twain, 270) or to betray his whereabouts to Miss Watson, Ōe retrieves no less than the challenge of democracy itself.[62] Having accepted his own damnation, Huck, an "embattled cultural hero" (Wilson, 34), turns against a dehumanizing system that narrowly privileges him. His democratizing "resolution to turn his back on his times, his society, and even his god" (Nathan, n.p.) made him a revolutionary archetype for Ōe, who witnessed Japan's radical shift in political systems firsthand.

As a post-Reconstruction novel set prior to abolition, *Adventures of Huckleberry Finn* serves as a curious source text for *Shiiku*, a post-Occupation novella set in the Pacific War's late years. In his reworking of Twain, Ōe suggests a correspondence between the paradox of democratization in Japan and radical Reconstruction's betrayal in the U.S. South. Unfolding along the lines of *Adventures of Huckleberry Finn*'s infamous evasion sequence, *Shiiku*'s middle pages, in which the narrative opens to the children's world, recall the controversial "second slavery" episode—the "charade of Jim's mock liberation"—in Twain's novel.[63] At issue is Tom's failure to disclose that Jim has already been freed. As scholars have argued, Twain's restaging of the tragedy of slavery as child's play, or farce, allegorizes the violation of black freedom in Reconstruction's wake: "Twain had rendered Jim's liberation in *Huckleberry Finn* at that precise moment in American history when barely realized liberties were being wrenched one by one from the grasp of the emancipated black man in the South. Between 1876 and 1883, the period during which he worked on the novel, the Reconstruction was nullified, the ambitious programs of the Radical Republicans abandoned and the fate of the Negro restored to the keep of his former master, a fate manifest in the annual toll of lynchings."[64]

We might also consider Du Bois's reflection that the "slave went free; stood a brief moment in the sun; then moved back again toward slavery" (30). Black Reconstruction's foreclosure, as the forfeiture of "the right to rule extended to all men, regardless of race and color" (Du Bois, 184), was a death blow to democracy with global repercussions.[65] As a "founding stone ... of modern industry," the repression of black American workers, as part of a "dark and vast sea of human labor" that was "enslaved in all but name," animated "new dreams of power and visions of empire" (Du Bois, 15, 5). "Out of the exploitation of the dark proletariat," he contended, "comes the Surplus Value filched from human beasts" (16). As Ōe explores in his fiction, the dialectic of democracy in postwar Japan, if packaged as a revolution from above, required horizontal association among "human beasts."

Interweaving Japanese and American legacies of imperialism and dispossession, *Shiiku* thus revisits Twain's pairing of rustic white child and enslaved black adult, yet it does so with a twist.[66] Ōe racializes Frog, his Huck-like figure, as native to the periphery. Frog, this is to say, is no settler who lights out for the territory, a concept inextricable in the Pacific from the extraterritorial U.S. military presence.[67] Rather, Ōe's debasement of Huck is vital to his imagining "anew what kind of image of human being *Adventures of Huckleberry Finn*" ("Huckleberry Finn and the American Dream") might incite. Albeit a "low-down" (268) figure in Twain's original portrait, Huck is assured of his humanity in a white supremacist system that accords him propertied personhood while brutalizing Jim. Even as this guarantee positions Huck to be able to "redistribute the social and political rewards of whiteness to the black ... body" (James, *Freedom Bought with Blood*, 11), it leaves intact dominant American ideologies of freedom, including those romanticizing the frontier as a site of free soil and unfettered self-realization. By contrast, Frog comes from *dojinburaku*, or "indigenous village," as Ōe renders Twain's "Injun Territory" (347) in his essay "Huckleberry Finn and the Problem of the Hero." All signs suggest Frog and the villagers' caste-like ostracization as "peripheral human being[s]" (Ōe, "Being a Writer") in Japanese society.[68] In this regard Frog cannot raise the POW, to adapt Du Bois, "from the plane of chattels to the rank of human beings" (Du Bois, 60). Rather, in *Shiiku* despised subjects converge on the level of near-animality.

Remarkably, few critics have commented on *Shiiku*'s subhuman continuum.[69] Speculating that Western critics have found the "racial elements" of Ōe's bestialized portrait of the black POW discomfiting, Reiko Tachibana notes that the novella, although ripe for comparative analysis, has generated little discussion in Japan or the United States.[70] The most influential theorization of "Japan's image of the Black Other" remains John Russell's culturalist thesis that "the position blacks have come to occupy in the Japanese hierarchy of races not only echoes Western racist paradigms but borrows from them" (18, 5). According to accounts like these, the presence of antiblack racism in Japan is testament to the global reach of white supremacist ideology and the "indigenization" of imported prejudices, a dynamic intensified by the "distributive currency of American mass media and popular culture" (Russell, 5) within the postwar era. Following Japan's defeat, American racism has been uncritically *translated*, to extend the argument, into the Japanese cultural idiom and social practices. Of the proof of this during the Occupation, the *Pittsburgh Courier* bitterly remarked: "The Japanese [are] looking down on the colored soldiers as inferior because they see them discriminated against by their fellow Americans.... Here is the first lesson in 'democracy' and we may be sure that the Japanese, apt as usual, are learning it" (quoted in Perry, *Beneath the Eagle's Wings*, 171). Yet arguments like this rehearse their own presumptions and omissions. Not only do they assume Japanese identification with whiteness and assent to the supposed Japanese penchant for mimicry, but also, even when acknowledging the militarized circumstances behind the U.S. presence in Japan in the first place, they neglect the structural racism of U.S. militarism. Race and racism are therefore cast, in the first instance, in exogenous terms.

By contrast, race, in Ōe's tale of the black Pacific, necessitates extraliterary contextualization within a Japan peripheralized by its defeat. These local conditions complicate any unidirectional translation of American racism into Japanese terms. Indeed, in its conflation of successive systems of militarized unfreedom, Japanese and American, *Shiiku* prompts the question of whether Frog serves as an uneasy translation of Huck or Jim. This ambiguity is central to its exploration of not only emancipation as an asymmetrical, racialized process but also unfreedom as an overdetermined historical dynamic. If the black Atlantic surfaces in Ōe's invocation of slavery, Jim Crow, and black disposability, the necropolitics of the militarized Pacific also permeate his imaginative reworking of Twain's novel. The mise-en-scène of top-down dramas of democratization—race within militarized form—thus unfurls on intersecting historical registers: black captivity and U.S. occupation. In this regard, *Shiiku* invites being read less as a tale of an encounter between American Jim and Japanese Huck than an account of an evolving relationality between American and Japanese versions of Jim.

As markedly subaltern figures, *Shiiku*'s main characters—a dirty, barefoot boy from Japan's margins and a black POW from the Jim Crow U.S. military—moreover, make for ambivalent national representatives and thus unstable portraits of enmity. Although Ōe himself notes that his fiction often features "unconventional pairings" ("The Art of Fiction," 47), *Shiiku* specifically recalls historic antifascist arguments for class-based solidarity across color lines and national divisions. Seeking to debunk Imperial Japan's "demagogic pose of protecting the colored races," the 1938 black communist pamphlet *Is Japan the Champion of the Colored Races? The Negro's Stake in Democracy* observed that "at the bottom of Japan's social pyramid" were rural farmers whose "starvation rent-in-kind" of "two-thirds of their crops" was "a sort of sharecropping system similar to . . . our own."[71] Published on the cusp of war, this tract argued that black labor in the United States had a unity of interests with Japan's rural poor belied by their countries' intensifying hostility toward each other.

Yet *Shiiku*'s setting is ultimately conditioned by the uncertain nature of the war—neither clearly antifascist nor anti-imperialist—in the Pacific theater, and it is war that ultimately deforms social possibility, shaping Ōe's exploration of democracy from below. If Ōe complicates Twain's Huck-and-Jim pairing by revising "Huck" along racial and subaltern lines, he militarizes "Jim" as a bomber pilot in the "territory." By placing the black POW in a remote Japanese village, Ōe provocatively relocates the historic violence of black captivity to the Pacific. Yet *Shiiku* also implies black collusion with catastrophic U.S. military-imperial power in the context of a war in which civilians in Japan were deemed permissible targets of aerial warfare. We might recall Du Bois's famous argument that the participation of freedmen transformed Union forces into "armies of emancipation" (Du Bois, 55) and the Civil War into a general strike against slavery. By contrast, the airman in *Shiiku* is positioned in a Jim Crow military in a region long imperialized by the United States. If identified with captivity down below, he also descends, in a trajectory suggestive of bombardment, from above. Moreover, when *Shiiku* was first published, the POW's racialization would have referenced not just black servicemen in the segregated U.S. military but more immediately the desegregated Occupation forces. Following Japan's defeat, democratization would have meant black integration into the U.S. war machine as the United States consolidated its permanent war footing in Asia and the Pacific.

In *Shiiku*, military-imperial power, both Japanese and American, thus shapes Ōe's rural utopia, conditioning its narrative possibilities. It is in a pastoral setting, supposedly beyond the reach of total war, that Ōe animates the sign of race, leading to a fatal encounter between a Japanese boy and a black U.S. serviceman. In the penultimate scene Frog, having learned the "authorities had decided the black soldier was to be turned over to the prefecture," naively hastens to warn him: "Slipping past the adults I ran back to where he was sitting in the square in front of the storehouse. Slowly lifting his dull eyeballs he looked up at me halted in front of him and gasping for breath. I was able to convey nothing to him. . . . I shook the black soldier's shoulder as he sat there, and shouted at him in dialect" (155).

Echoes of Huck coming to free Jim resound in this scene, yet Frog cannot steal the POW free, and optimism devolves into tragedy. Misconstruing Frog's wild gesticulations as a lethal warning, the soldier, "like an agile beast . . . leaped at me and hugged me tightly to himself, using me as a shield"; as Frog "writhed in his arms I comprehended the cruel truth. I was a prisoner, and a hostage.

The black soldier had transformed me into the *enemy*" (157). If the narrative has hitherto hinged on "the warm, everyday familiarity that had flowed" (157) between these characters, this scene dramatizes the fatal consequences of a literal failure in translation. In an instant Frog, "like a weasel caught in a trap" (158), occupies the captive position previously associated with the POW. If *Shiiku* opens with an implied superimposition between the black pilot and Hirohito, it closes with another imagistic overlay. With Frog taking the prior position of the black airman, the host becomes a hostage in his own home. As "the *enemy*," Frog is thrust into war's oppositional idiom. He becomes Japanese and the soldier American. This binarizing politics finally makes impossible the moral expansion of humanity for which Twain's novel has been celebrated.

For Ōe, the democratizing power of *Adventures of Huckleberry Finn* turns on Huck's hell-bound decision, yet in *Shiiku* the impossibility of this decision suggests the limits to democracy in militarized settings. Published in the wake of Japan's surrender when U.S. military leaders, aiming to ease the fears of the U.S. public about Japanese savagery, issued assurances about the childlike docility of their former foe, *Shiiku* reworks these anxieties into its tale of rearing and domestication.[72] In the tragic conclusion, after the adults break through the cellar door, Frog, able to make only "a shrill, feeble sound . . . like the scream of a small animal" (160), witnesses his father wielding a hatchet, crushing the soldier's skull and his son's hand—as well as the fragile possibility of democracy from below. The POW's death ensures that the village, cut off from both the nearest town by landslide and the Pacific theater's distant battles, cannot assume its previous social contours. It is "enveloped in the war" (166). Published a half-decade after the Occupation, *Shiiku* closes with a final ironic reversal. In this closing sequence the boy who started out as Huck, Ōe's barefoot liberator, evokes Jim, and the captive bomber pilot who at first raised the specter of Jim Crow fatally conjures the screaming eagle.

Ospreys in Okinawa

At a late September 2012 rally organized by the Article 9 Association, a group Ōe cofounded in 2004 to protest Japan's remilitarization, Ōe underscored the aerial threat U.S. national security posed to Japanese democracy: "The accident-prone Osprey aircraft will soon be deployed at the U.S. Marine Corps' Futenma Air Station in Okinawa, although tens of thousands of local people gathered to show their opposition. And Japan cannot say anything to the United States about this issue."⁷³ The axes of power in Ōe's statement are worth noting. Against the image of Okinawans protesting en masse in the streets, the Osprey loomed as a vertical symbol of militarized tyranny. Describing its deployment as a sign of Japan's subordination to the United States, Ōe asked his fellow protestors, "Under these circumstances, can we say Japan is an independent democratic country?"

Yet even as Ōe pointed to U.S. militarism's undemocratic reach into Japan, his remarks implied the outsized nature of Okinawa's involuntary role in bearing the brunt of the U.S. military presence in his country. Albeit a mere 0.6 percent of Japan's territory, Okinawa has been sacrificed as the nation's principal basing site. As Arasaki Moriteru, cochair of the Okinawa Citizens' Alliance for Peace, has stated: "the Japan-US Security Treaty system rests on structural discrimination against Okinawa."⁷⁴ With its 1972 reversion to Japan after nearly three decades of unbroken U.S. military rule, Okinawa, far from liberated from the yoke of U.S. militarism, saw its basing burden increase. It hosts not only 74 percent of all U.S. bases in Japan but also the highest density of U.S. bases worldwide.⁷⁵ A staggering 20 percent of its land and 40 percent of its airspace fall under U.S. military occupation.⁷⁶ Noise pollution from military aircraft is so intense that 37 percent of the population indicates being routinely disturbed.⁷⁷

The militarized marginalization of Okinawans maps onto their historic treatment as despised national minorities on a continuum with Ainu, *burakumin*, and Koreans in Japan.⁷⁸ In June of 2012 the International Movement against All Forms of Discrimination and Racism submitted a statement to the United Nations Human Rights Council accusing both Japan and the United States of violating the human rights of Okinawans as the indigenous peoples of the Ryukyus: "Given the fact that the US military can have their bases anywhere in Japan . . . , [the] disproportionate concentration of US military bases in Okinawa must be regarded as clear discrimination against Ryukyuans."⁷⁹ This critique begins to disclose the world-shattering racism of militarism even or precisely when overtly racist language is absent. Indeed, Okinawa's postwar dilemma calls for nuanced analysis of the U.S. war machine's structural violence, which collateralizes the lives of both foes and declared allies.

Vigorous Okinawan opposition to U.S. militarism throughout the postwar period, even by those whose livelihoods depend on the bases, has called Japan's democracy into question. Ōe referenced "the Okinawa problem" when he spoke with the *New Yorker* in 1968, near the end of a decade that began with his protest against the renewal of a security treaty granting the United States the right to maintain military bases in Japan and that culminated with the publication of his *Okinawa Notes* (*Okinawa nōto*, 1970).[80] Okinawans, he explained, were taking their resistance to U.S. war and militarism to the streets. Okinawa was "the pivot today," a military colony implicated in America's "very dirty war" ("Talk of the Town," 25) in Vietnam. In identifying Okinawa's subimperial role, Ōe alighted on a truth that Admiral U. S. Grant Sharp bluntly conceded in late 1965: "without Okinawa we couldn't continue fighting the Vietnam War."[81] As an "unsinkable aircraft carrier," Okinawa, in the indictment of the 1967 Russell Tribunal on U.S. war crimes in Vietnam, served as an invaluable "supply, sortie and nuclear base for the US aggression against Vietnam, and a place from which to dominate the Asian countries of the Far East."[82]

Even as he maintained that at first, "the American Army meant democracy to Japan," Ōe, in his *New Yorker* interview, implied a critical distinction between mainland Japan and Okinawa with regard to the Occupation.[83] For mainland Japanese, MacArthur's persecution of communist leaders who "stood outside American Headquarters in 1945 shouting '*Vive MacArthur!*'" was, according to Ōe, "the beginning of the contradiction for us" ("Talk of the Town," 26). Yet if red-baiting typified the "reverse course" stage when Occupation officials abandoned radical democratic reform on the mainland, outright U.S. military tyranny was the postwar norm in Okinawa from the start.[84] U.S. military rule came on the heels of a brutal ground battle resulting in the deaths of a quarter of the Okinawan population.[85] The Japanese Imperial Army ordered civilians to commit mass suicide and deployed them as human shields against invading U.S. forces.[86] Both armies massacred civilians.[87] Herded by the Americans into concentration camps, survivors, on release, were strangers in their ancestral homeland. Cordoned off by barbed wire, U.S. bases occupied the land where their houses and farms once stood. In the early Cold War decades the United States stockpiled weapons of mass destruction and erected more than eighty military installations in Okinawa, putting these resources into lethal play first in the Korean War and then during the Vietnam War.[88] For Okinawans and those regional peoples on the receiving end of U.S. violence, the postwar period thus had an aspect, according to Ginowan village chief Toubaru Kamerou, of "a war not yet ended" (quoted in Toriyama, 404). To no small degree, Okinawa's collateralization by the U.S. war machine has been the price for mainland "recover[y], develop[ment] and prosper[ity]," as Ōe has argued.[89]

As a space of heightened contradiction and thus democratic possibility, Okinawa, for Ōe, has emblematized "peripheral Japanese culture" ("Speaking on Japanese Culture," 33), a framing of Okinawa that envisions its place within Japan despite its colonization by both Japan and the United States. If arguably representative of peripheral Japanese culture, Okinawa's marginalization within Japan has unquestionably translated into its geostrategic centrality to the imperial U.S. war machine. On the "Okinawa problem" as the contradiction that U.S. militarism poses to democracy-from-below in Japan, time, in key respects, has stood still. As Ōe remarked in 2005: "I have always continued to write about the problem of the U.S. base on Okinawa, the fact that even today there is a big U.S. Army base there, with nuclear weapons, and every month a big warship carrying nuclear arms comes to Japan there" ("Starting from Zero"). Discerning Japan's movement "toward actively participating in United States wars," Ōe has criticized the nation's remilitarization under the LDP's postwar hegemony.[90] Okinawa's value as a key outpost for U.S. and Japanese military power projection in the region is a critical context for the Osprey deployment. As Oguma Eiji points out, "Establishing a military base here means being able to place Tokyo, Seoul, Beijing and Hanoi within the range of strategic bombers" (*The Boundaries*, 4).

Here it is crucial to understand that the Osprey was designed, first and foremost, to facilitate expeditionary warfare.[91] With an aerial refueling capability that enables it to reach the Philippines or South Korea, the Osprey, as a replacement of Vietnam War–era helicopters across the U.S. armed forces, has been pitched as essential to the forward deployment of the Marines in the Pacific even though its irrelevance to the defense of Okinawa or Japan is incontestable. Indeed, what Ōe has dubbed the "accident-prone Osprey" jeopardizes Okinawan security on multiple levels, including by making the Ryukyus a target for U.S. foes. As Sakima Kiyoko, director of an antiwar art museum next to the Futenma airbase, has stated: "They see us as the 'Evil Island'; all over Asia, because everything that is dangerous and flies takes off from here."[92] Given the Osprey's notoriety as "one of the killingest experimental planes ever," with thirty fatalities plaguing the evaluation stage alone, its deployment to Okinawa—as critics have charged—bespeaks the hubris of the American military-industrial complex in offloading flawed products to U.S. client-states, crushing local democratic dissent in the process.[93] Manufactured by Bell and Boeing, the hybrid aircraft can travel at fixed-wing speeds for greater distances than helicopters yet with Icarus-like folly, its rotors can lose "their grip on the air" during landing and "the bird drops out of the sky" (Berler).[94]

That U.S. base installations sit in patchwork proximity to populated civilian areas makes its use in Okinawa all the more egregious. As predicted by Ōe, the Osprey was bound to malfunction, and in late 2016 one crashed off Okinawa's coast.[95] From the ground-level perspective of those that inhabit the militarized Pacific, the Osprey's hurtling toward the earth was a vector of racism.

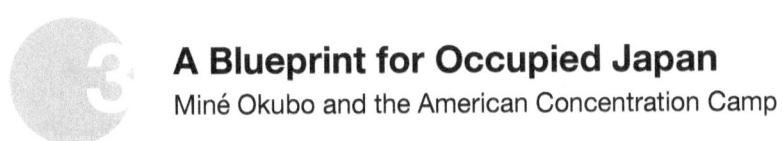
A Blueprint for Occupied Japan
Miné Okubo and the American Concentration Camp

Democracy in Confinement

On October 5, 1943, Miné Okubo, incarcerated at the Topaz concentration camp in Utah, received a telegram from Deborah Calkins, associate art director for *Fortune* magazine, inquiring if Okubo could create two drawings for its end-of-the-year issue.[1] One, Calkins specified, should be a portrait "of [a] large group of Japanese b[ow]ing before [a] state Shinto shrine" and the other a scene of combat death featuring "two or three Japanese soldiers in dr[i]fting sand" on an "island beach" in the Pacific.[2] Slated to accompany a "leading section" on "the subject of Japan," these half-page images should convey "futility and ultimate defeat." To stoke Okubo's imagination, *Fortune* was willing to mail "documentary photographs for detail if desired." Yet the publication was hoping for more than drawn versions of original photos. It urged the Nisei artist to exercise "special forsight [sic]" relative to Japan. Apparently citing her compressed work schedule as art editor of the famed Topaz literary quarterly *Trek*, Okubo initially declined, yet Calkins prevailed on her to reconsider, even offering a deadline extension.[3] This exchange proved fateful. Okubo's illustrations would enliven the pages of the December 1943 issue of *Fortune*, a signature Henry Luce publication known for its documentary style and lavishly formatted during the lean war years, "like an oversized art magazine."[4] Identifying the Pacific theater as the pivotal site where "the war finally has to be won" even as it predicted American victory as "inevitable," the magazine soon recommissioned the artist for its special April 1944 issue titled "Japan and the Japanese: A Military Power We Must Defeat, a Pacific Problem We Must Solve."[5] With this evidence of outside employment Okubo gained leave clearance from the War Relocation Authority (WRA), the government agency in charge of the camps, and the California-born artist relocated permanently to New York in January of 1944.[6]

Rightfully recognized for her detailed portraits of the removal and mass incarceration of approximately 120,000 West Coast ethnic Japanese, two-thirds of whom were U.S. citizens, Okubo viewed her wartime role to be "an observer and reporter" (Gesensway and Roseman, 73) of camp life. By the time she left Topaz in early 1944, she had generated a vast corpus of images, born of direct observation, conveying "what happens to people when reduced to one status and condition."[7] All told, she produced roughly two thousand portraits of camp life in a two-year interval, images rendered in a range of styles and materials—ink, charcoal, tempera, gouache.[8] A fraction of this oeuvre appears in *Citizen 13660*, her account of life behind barbed wire, yet it is this illustrated memoir, published in 1946 as the last camps were being closed, that almost singularly defines her legacy today.[9] Indeed, in the decades after the war, the overwhelmingly affirmative reception accorded to *Citizen 13660*, a work distinguished as the first published book-length Nisei account of the camps, has confirmed Okubo's standing as a major visual chronicler of and historic witness to that experience. To no small degree this reputation, which Okubo herself assiduously cultivated, was buttressed by the memoir's mobilization as documentary proof of government injustice and a self-evident argument for reparations in the 1970s and 1980s Japanese American redress struggle.

As a retroactive interpretive lens, however, *Citizen 13660*'s recuperation in the politics of the redress movement arguably obscures more than it illuminates Okubo's wartime artistic legacy. Much has been written of how her sketches breathed necessary humanity into "Citizen 13660"—the latter a synecdoche for Japanese Americans stripped of their rights. Yet, in lauding its subtle exposé of the camps as an unwarranted, dehumanizing carceral system, such accounts read the memoir as a reproof of government policy, aligned against rather than with state objectives, an interpretation that neglects her memoir's political value in its earliest circulation. Seldom, moreover, are Okubo's images of camp life situated in a continuum with her early war repertoire, a range of public art that included Works Progress Administration (WPA) frescoes and army-commissioned murals. What therefore goes unremarked is the significance of her cultural work to the U.S. war effort and the postwar peace, the Pax Americana that reconfigured the Asia-Pacific region as a U.S. security zone after Japan's military defeat. Writing for the December 1945 issue of *NOW*, journalist Larry Tajiri perceptively identified the Nisei as key to the region's securitization, describing them as "an important cog in the machinery of peace in the Pacific and in the future of international security."[10] Construed by U.S. occupation forces as a "bridge between the American military and the people of Japan," they proved their mettle as "a human secret weapon" (107, 105) whose work in intelligence and propaganda was critical to U.S. victory in the Pacific theater.[11] Insofar as Okubo's portraits of the camps were strategically mobilized during the war and its early aftermath as Nisei cultural contributions to U.S. war aims, their geopolitical framing merits retrieval and reevaluation.

As Okubo stated on her leave-clearance form—infamously also known as the "loyalty questionnaire"—her preference for postcamp employment was "defense" propaganda along the lines of "war posters, moral[e] posters, [and] creative painting mural work."[12] That the Nisei had a vital role to play on the wartime cultural front was articulated as early as 1942 in "On the Japanese Question in the United States," a report submitted to the WRA by U.S. naval officer K. D. Ringle.[13] Maintaining "the nisei could be accorded a place in the national war effort without risk or danger," Ringle urged the agency to promote "a history of the entire evacuation and resettlement program from the point of view of those affected," emphasizing the ideological value of an account "with accompanying pictorial illustrations."[14] In his view such representations "would go farther than anything else toward committing [Nisei] loyalty to the United States." However implausible this instrumentalizing interpretation of her work may be to us today, the WRA actively propagated Okubo's images of camp life as evidence of the democratic potential of the American concentration camp from a Nisei perspective. Far from a transparent indictment of government wrongdoing in its initial circulation, *Citizen 13660* was actively promoted by the WRA "as part of a larger program of assimilation and absorption they had designed for the Nisei" (Robinson, *Pacific Citizens*, 160). Okubo, who signed a collective statement from camp inmates to WRA head Dillon Myer declaring that "loyalty to our country is something to be expressed without reference to past grievances or wounds," cooperated with the WRA's agenda "not only in her choice of illustrations for the book [*Citizen 13660*], and in the brief texts she wrote to accompany them, but in her various public statements characterizing herself as a writer" (Robinson, *Pacific Citizens* 160).

Not restricted to *Citizen 13660*, this elasticity around the political significance of Okubo's wartime oeuvre was nowhere more provocatively on display than in artwork she produced for *Fortune*. Asked to visualize what the editors termed, in a curious turn-of-phrase, "the citizen-subject" of Japan for the magazine's late-war readership, Okubo drew, quite literally, a continuum between

Japanese Americans like her, who had been mass-incarcerated in the United States, and Japanese civilians in Japan whom she had no occasion to encounter firsthand.[15] Neither assuredly citizens possessed of rights nor subjects rendered so thoroughly abject before military-imperial authority as to be unsalvageable, the citizen-subject of Japan was a hybrid figure in another respect. Cast along prepolitical lines, it furnished the grounds for competing sovereign claims. Imagined as situated between the United States as a democratizing force and Imperial Japan as a moribund society, the citizen-subject that Okubo visualized for *Fortune* signaled a productive indeterminacy, a state of potentiality ripe for democratization. The global viability of the postwar U.S. democratizing project entailed not just the rehabilitation of Japan and Japanese Americans but also the liberal recuperation of the American concentration camp. At stake was no less than the identity of the United States itself as a democracy, with the specter of racial unfreedom clouding its postwar mandate to decide the terms of the peace. By deploying police power against a domestic population racially conflated with the enemy, the United States, critics charged, verged on fascism.[16]

Here, *Fortune*'s special issue, "Japan and the Japanese," intimated that any grievances on the part of Japanese Americans about U.S. policies of mass incarceration might be displaced to the arena of free enterprise. This proposed model of recovery would have global applicability in the postwar period. The rehabilitation of the minority demographic construed as the enemy alien and the enemy nation required, or so the logic went, entrepreneurial avenues of self-advancement rather than official redressive measures. Animating the magazine's vision for Asian postwar recovery under U.S. auspices was the region's looming significance and untapped value, limited in scope and scale only by the failure of the U.S. geopolitical imagination. In "The American Century," a 1941 editorial anticipating U.S. victory, Luce, the China-born son of American missionaries behind the *Time*, *Life*, and *Fortune* publishing empire, posited the challenge in opportunistic terms. Asia could be "worth to us exactly zero—or else . . . four, five, ten billions of dollars a year," and the latter were "the terms we must think in."[17] Premised on U.S. global dominion or "the right to go with our ships and our ocean-going airplanes where we wish, when we wish and as we wish," what Luce euphorically dubbed "American internationalism" would, *Fortune* predicted, facilitate Asia's economic recovery.

As historians like Bruce Cumings note, however, "American internationalism" fostered an uneven regional recuperation through interventionist wars that served as militarized alternatives to the Marshall Plan.[18] Perversely framed as reconstructive occasions, the devastating Korean War was foundational to postwar Japan's economic recovery and the brutal Vietnam War likewise critical to South Korea's compressed development. Luce's proposal on how to govern the peace-to-come, what he called "America's Vision of Our World," may have elaborated a "rationale for an expanded American state-form and understanding of national mission after World War II," yet it disavowed the basis of economic recovery in the U.S. sphere of influence in Asia and the Pacific—namely, participation, alignment, and complicity with U.S. militarism.[19] "Democratic" rehabilitation for the enemy abroad and "enemy alien" at home, in other words, was contingent on their compliance within the militarized ambit of U.S. power. Central to this fraught vision of democracy budding in unfree settings was, I contend, the work of Nisei cultural producers whose direct experience of "democracy" in confinement was construed as uniquely situating them to make the case for the U.S. democratization project in occupied Japan.

Somber in tone, Okubo's images for the December 1943 issue of *Fortune*, the first of the two issues she would illustrate, bookended an article, "The Japanese Predicament: Too Few Ships, Men, Machines; Too Much Empire." In keeping with its title, the article described the risks of Japan's territorial ambitions and military overstretch. Featuring, following Calkins's instructions, Japanese subjects bowing in rigid unison before a Shinto shrine (fig. 1), Okubo's opening drawing bore an alarmist caption about the militarized value of conformity: "Submissiveness Is a Japanese Weapon That Our War Engineers Cannot Reproduce." At first glance, the image appears to illustrate Japan's fascistic advantage; as the article maintained, "submissive obedience" was a formidable tool specific to Japan's war arsenal, one the United States lacked.[20] Yet Okubo's closing drawing, captioned "In Death Two Japanese Find Fulfillment," showcased the potential of Japan's antidemocratic weapon to backfire. Its most salient detail a *Hinomaru* clutched in a death grip by one of two corpses at the foreground of a landscape littered with dead bodies, this image encapsulated the perils of blind devotion. "It is one thing to die for the Emperor," *Fortune* editorialized, yet another "to accept rationing, to maintain price levels, and to accept harsh criminal laws aimed at forcefully suppressing all criticism of the non-divine government." Even within what it sought to visualize as "the Japanese predicament," *Fortune* was quick to shed light on theoretical rumblings of democratic discontent.

Figure 1. "Submissiveness Is a Japanese Weapon That Our War Engineers Cannot Reproduce," by Miné Okubo, *Fortune*, Dec. 1943, 124. Image courtesy of Miné Okubo Estate.

As a visual interpreter of Japan for two late-war issues of *Fortune*, Okubo was thus enlisted to exercise "special for[e]sight" into the postwar period by envisioning the place of the citizen-subjects of a defeated Japan within an emerging Pax Americana world order. The recuperative task was multifold. Commissioned to produce images that both anticipated and made the case for America's war victory and Japan's defeat, Okubo strove to visually rehabilitate both the "enemy alien" on the home front and the enemy in the Pacific as democratically inclined subjects capable of thriving in settings conditioned by U.S. militarism. Militarism conditioned each of the entangled policy phases of this U.S. project of "democratic rehabilitation," including the total-war policy of Japanese American mass incarceration; the late-war leave-clearance policy of selective integration, but continued state surveillance, of Japanese Americans; the transwar policy that had Nisei serving in U.S. military intelligence as "a human secret weapon" vis-à-vis first Japan and then Korea; and the postwar policy in which Nisei, including artists like Okubo, performed a range of roles, direct and indirect, relative to the occupation of Japan.[21] As her wartime cultural work for *Fortune* suggests, these projects were entwined on the level of their logic. The rehabilitation of the Japanese "enemy" in the Pacific was perceived as hinging on the Americanization of the alienized Japanese American, all within the militarized contours of a U.S.-sponsored "peace."

Yet shadowing *Fortune*'s forecast for the postwar peace—its dual vision of a defeated Japan incorporated into the U.S. sphere of influence in Asia and the Pacific as well as alienized Japanese Americans assimilated into American society—were lingering concerns about U.S. accountability in the aftermath of what some deemed a brutal race war. As "imaginators" of the U.S.-sponsored democracy-to-come, Nisei cultural producers like Okubo were enlisted to recuperate the American concentration camp by envisioning it as an incubator for democracy.[22] Tasked with mediating the racialized divide between the camp and the outside world, Okubo crafted what might be called a *democratizing aesthetic* that affirmed the legitimacy of postwar U.S. global leadership. By exploring the continuum between her renderings of Citizen 13660 and the citizen-subject of Japan, I thus seek to shed light on the role of Nisei cultural producers in imagining a postwar peace inclusive of a rehabilitated Japan. As historian Takashi Fujitani argues, "in the postwar as in the wartime years, the elite mainstream in academia, government, and the media continued to conflate issues concerning Japanese Americans and Japanese, with the former becoming the domestic 'model minority' and the latter reconstituted into a kind of 'global model minority.'"[23] Along these lines it merits scrutinizing how, as the Cold War dawned, Nisei portraits of camp life were repurposed as commendable lessons of ethnic Japanese subjects not just adapting to militarized structures but "thriving under the American system."[24] Far from discarded in the postwar period, the essentializing logic of "ethnic affiliations" so critical to the securitized wartime construction of Japanese Americans as the enemy within and Japanese imperial subjects as the enemy without was revised as a salutary continuum between two groups of Pacific citizens ripe for democratization.[25]

The embattled role played by Nisei cultural producers in modeling Pacific citizenship within the confines of unfreedom was nowhere illustrated more poignantly than in the wartime quandary of Okubo's fellow artist Isamu Noguchi. Persuaded by Commissioner of Indian Affairs John Collier to voluntarily enter the Poston camp in Arizona, Noguchi soon withered in its claustrophobic confines. In a September 1942 letter to him, Okubo, incarcerated at Tanforan in California, drily remarked: "when the rest of the radicals arrive there, you will have friends."[26] Her reference was to the Nisei Writers and Artists Mobilization for Democracy, a San Francisco–based antifascist organization dedicated, according to Noguchi, to twinned pedagogical goals: "First to present to the public at large a clear and accurate picture of the American citizen of Japanese extraction. . . . Second, to perform an educational service to the Nisei themselves by dispelling whatever confusions may exist among them as to democratic principles, the issues involved in the war, and their duties as American citizens, thereby promoting their morale and consolidating their trust in American institutions."[27]

As Robert Maeda explains, "Noguchi and the members of his group ... were concerned that their fellow Nisei might be swayed by Japan's militarist view that it was waging a race war and that their internment would be corroboration of America's racist treatment of Japanese, thus strengthening Japan's propaganda efforts" (156). Swayed by Collier's "visionary" view of the camps as a vibrant "Colony" of democracy—"Though democracy perish outside, here would be kept its seeds" (Maeda 159, 156)—and conviction that "what the Mojave Indians couldn't do ... the Japanese could do," Noguchi resolved to donate his artistic energies to Poston in the hopes of furthering the cause of democracy.[28] Central to his politicized understanding of art was his conception of the American concentration camp as a laboratory for democratizing art. "We who are artists know that any culture worthy of the name ... dies under fascism," Noguchi stated, albeit with waning confidence from Poston, where he was forcibly made "aware of a color line [he] had never known before."[29]

In "I Become a Nisei," an unpublished essay drafted in May of 1942 and intended for *Reader's Digest*, Noguchi thus emerged as a curious apologist for race-based incarceration: "For many a Nisei, [the camp] is opportunity. . . . It is planned to build here a community, dedicated ... to the proposition that the spirit of freedom may be nurtured and grow even in confinement." In his account of life behind barbed wire he described Collier's disembodied "voice" coming to him "out of the blinding dust": "While not fighting the fight for freedom you will contribute yet to the victory. . . . You are the middle people who will help teach Asia the meaning of democracy." Incarcerated Nisei, identified as incipient democratic subjects, were thus held out as marking a political stage between warring ideologies in the Pacific: Japanese fascism and U.S. democracy. It is no stretch to extrapolate from this interpretation of the camp as a model democratic outpost an uneasy blueprint for occupied Japan.

Americanizing "America"

"Cameras and photographs," Okubo recalled in her 1983 preface to *Citizen 13660*, "were not permitted in the camps, so I recorded everything in sketches, drawings, and paintings" (ix). Not permitted access to conventional means of recording technology endowed with evidentiary weight, Okubo resorted to the drawn medium to document everyday scenes of camp life. A first-person chronicle, Okubo's visual memoir everywhere suggests keen observation and close, if hasty, rendering. It began "as a special group of drawings made to tell the story of camp life for my many friends who faithfully sent letters and packages to let us know we were not forgotten. The illustrations were intended for exhibition purposes" ("Preface," ix). Meant for the gaze of friends who, as she quipped, "told me how lucky I was to be free and safe at home" (*Citizen 13660*, 61), her drawings function as hand-drawn exposures, revealing scenes internal to Tanforan and Topaz.

Yet far from a stealthily realized project—indeed, other inmates would recall her as always with sketchbook in hand—Okubo's recording of camp-life minutiae, as documents in her "evacuee case file" attest, generated official WRA interest and support. Unlike Dorothea Lange's and Ansel Adams's photographs of the camps, which were censored and removed from circulation, Okubo's drawings were deemed "definitely loyal" by administrators who vetted her sketches and writings for *Trek* prior to publication.[30] The agency, moreover, approved of her aim to "write a book on her experiences," going so far as to single her out as part of a cadre of talented young "evacuees" whose "special abilities and talents" might productively align with its agenda.[31] Key WRA administrators served as some of the earliest glowing reviewers of her 1946 memoir, thus begging the question of the exceptionality of Okubo's portraits of camp life. If the camps, given their location in remote interior settings, were "designed not to be seen," then what do we make of Okubo's images, which were intended for show and endorsed by the WRA?[32] In other words, if not as an indictment of profound racial injustice, then how were Okubo's images of life behind barbed wire circulated and read in their historical moment?

Unsettled in terms of their political end point, Okubo's images were emplotted into urgent arguments for assimilation that sought to recuperate the camp along liberal lines. This was most starkly on show in her depictions of the camp as a yet-to-be-Americanized "America," an arena of "democratization" structured by military force. In this typical sketch of Tanforan, the prominent flag, installed outside the post office (fig. 2), distinguishes it from rows of barracks in the distance. In the scene of mass detention it ironizes a war fought for "free[dom] and safe[ty] at home."[33] Depicting the wartime United States from its intensely militarized interior, this scene might be confused with a military outpost or Pacific territory populated solely by Asian subjects. Produced in the name of wartime emergency, the camp has been securitized; whatever risks its inmates theoretically pose are contained within its patrolled bounds. Yet the militarization of lived space has yet to manifest itself in any self-sustaining social order. In *Citizen 13660* images of ever-present crowds, packed living quarters, and endless weary lines function

Figure 2. Post office at the Tanforan WCCA camp, from Miné Okubo, *Citizen 13660* (New York: Columbia University Press, 1946), 61. Image courtesy of Miné Okubo Estate.

as visual tropes of potentially volatile arrangements in camp confines. Whether intimations of democracy in the offing or their dystopian opposite, scenes like this beg the question of what civilian life means in the context of mass captivity. In one drawing after another in Okubo's memoir, the geometry of U.S. military form furnishes an uneasy backdrop for fluid social formations, suggesting less secure design than a deeply uncertain forecast for the future.

Beyond camp courses instructing inmates "How to Make Friends" and "How to Behave in the Outside World" (*Citizen 13660*, 207), assimilation during the transwar years, as the securitized process of making the alien familiar and neutralizing the threat of the foreign, was also a reading practice and an effect of literary reception. Indeed, in their early circulation, Okubo's images derived their social meaning from the transactional function of "Okubo," her comics-style avatar, as witness to and mediator of the scene of camp life before her. If evocative of the camera image, her sketches foreground mediation in a way distinctive to the drawn medium. Far from profilmic equivalents, they convey what Okubo could not have seen, for bordering nearly every image in *Citizen*

13660 is her image of herself.³⁴ In the bottom right corner of the post-office scene, "Okubo," with flyaway bangs and crosshatched shirt, stands out from the queue. A representational quandary specific to visual autobiography, the first-person subject whose point of view structures the reader's must be exteriorized, a first person made third. Yet by formalizing "Okubo," *Citizen 13660* facilitated a visual frame beyond her own: that of the outside viewer. I saw it, her images affirmed, therefore you can see it. By situating the outside viewer within their coextensive space, her sketches performatively blurred boundaries in the early postwar era between inside and outside, "Japanese" and "American," historical witness and secondhand viewer. In this way bridging racial worlds cleaved apart in the name of national security—one a site of unfreedom produced by dominant fear, the other a space of freedom cushioned by distance—"Okubo" functions as both border and vehicle between those worlds, neutralizing the risk of race for the memoir's ethnically non-Japanese readers.

Its defiance of the laws of perception notwithstanding, "Okubo" moreover authenticates *Citizen 13660*'s scenes of camp life. Her stylized self-figuration as a viewer in the frame serves as a testimonial conceit, verifying her presence as historic witness. By granting postwar viewers vicarious access into the camp, however, her images dematerialized the structural racism of the camps and mass incarceration as a wartime experience. Tellingly, in its early reception, Okubo's memoir elicited plaudits from a range of elite white liberal voices. WRA director Dillon Myer, WRA public relations chief M. M. Tozier, Nobel laureate Pearl S. Buck, *Survey Graphic* literary critic Harry Hansen, writer Carey McWilliams, and *Common Ground* editor M. Margaret Anderson converged in their assessment of the authenticity and pedagogical value of Okubo's tableaux for postwar readers. Described as an unvarnished historical record—"a revealing pictorial record which should take its place among the documents of World War II" in *Library Journal*; "documentary evidence" and a "graphic report" in the *St. Louis Post-Dispatch*; "an honest record" in the *Chicago Tribune*—*Citizen 13660*, in McWilliams's estimation, "convey[ed] to those who knew the centers the exact feeling and impression of the scene and the people."³⁵ Praise for the memoir thus made postwar bedfellows of liberal administrator and liberal critic of the camps alike. Tozier, in unison with McWilliams, lauded Okubo's "vivid talent" for capturing the "truth" of the camp experience and conveying it to readers who, for reasons of distance, time, and race, had no occasion to experience the camps.³⁶ Stunningly, Tozier claimed Okubo's images granted him his "first" encounter with the camp experience: "Miné Okubo has succeeded in giving the reader *a strong sense of participation* in the evacuation and relocation center experience.... After reading [*Citizen 13660*], I felt that I knew for the first time what camp life looked like, smelled like, and felt like to the evacuated people" ("Excerpts," emphasis added).

By such accounts anachronistically transporting its readers as surrogate witnesses onto its sensory terrain, *Citizen 13660*, by eliciting identification with "the evacuated people," facilitated the erasure of structural differences. This postwar leveling of difference was central to the democratic rehabilitation of a subject who in wartime was cast as an enemy within. If the postwar race novel, as Jodi Melamed contends, served as an affective vehicle for "white Americans . . . to learn the supposedly inside stories of people of color," *Citizen 13660*'s early reception—premised on readerly identification with the incarcerated, hence a blurring of racial lines—attests to the significance of transracial identification in recuperating the "enemy" along familiar lines.[37] If the fascistic threat of the camps resided in the government's failure to distinguish between Japanese nationals and Japanese Americans, their liberal recuperation turned, to no small degree, on an uncritical collapsing of difference between those on the "inside" and those situated "outside." Central to the arguments for erecting and dismantling the camps, in other words, was the principle of indistinction.

In this regard, Okubo's work aligned with the assimilationist objectives of the WRA, which oversaw not only the removal process and camp administration but also the "resettlement" program as the war drew to an end. If the Ringle report highlighted the instrumental value of Nisei self-representation relative to the war effort, the endorsement of Okubo's work by WRA officials must be understood in the context of the agency's goals of managing Japanese American integration into the larger population, in essence settling camp inmates-cum-pioneers back east. At stake in the dispersal of subjects framed as security threats and their absorption into communities whose racial hostilities could not be determined was less their ability to perform "Americanness" than in "Caucasian" identification with "Citizen 13660" and the latter's real-world equivalents. From Myer, WRA director from 1942 to 1946 and Bureau of Indian Affairs head from 1950 to 1953—and thus, in Richard Drinnon's indictment, "director and commissioner of twin calamities" and personification of the "banality of evil, U.S. style"—we have this remarkable assessment of the value of Okubo's memoir: "The book is a reproof to those who would malign any racial minority, and it should help to forestall any future mass movements of the type she portrays" ("Excerpts").[38] That the empathetic chorus commending *Citizen 13660* included "former jailer[s] of the Japanese Americans" (Drinnon, 225), figures whose bureaucratic function had been premised on disidentification with those they governed, points to the ideological function of work by formerly racially proscribed Nisei artists like Okubo in shifting the contours of postwar racial terrain in the United States.

If forcibly uprooted from the West Coast and divested of rights during the war, the Japanese American was renaturalized as a bona fide citizen in part through a postwar cultural dynamic of readerly identification. Through the conceit of empirical access, *Citizen 13660*'s early readership grappled with the injustice of the camps in troublingly self-referential, vicarious terms. If Okubo's lens offered a corrective to jingoistic views of Japanese Americans as saboteurs loyal to Hirohito, her memoir's early reviewers uncovered evidence of another suppressed link in her images: the national identity of Americans with those incarcerated within barbed-wire enclosures. Indeed, through a syllogistic series of identifications, "Citizen 13660" was rehabilitated as "Carey McWilliams," "M. M. Tozier," and even "Dillon Myer." Yet by dematerializing the conditions that prompted the mass roundup of West Coast ethnic Japanese in the first place, readerly empathy worked in tandem with the WRA's liberal objectives of rehabilitating the "Japanese" along avowedly American lines. In doing so, these readers, including those who had opposed forced removal in the first place, perversely affirmed the "democratic" value of the camps as an assimilationist experiment. Indeed, by blurring the wartime color line, transracial "American" identification with "evacuees" facilitated the government policy of ethnic dispersal, transforming "a harsh wartime measure into an instrumentality for strengthening democracy itself."[39]

Little Tokyos

In World War II's long wake *Citizen 13660* traced an itinerary whose defining end points, in particular its reanimation in the Japanese American redress movement of the 1970s and 1980s, have made its murky starting points difficult to recover. In an appended 1983 preface, based on her 1981 testimony before the Commission on Wartime Relocation and Internment of Civilians (CWRIC), a bipartisan federal committee that recommended reparative measures, Okubo reflected on the camp's salutary scattering effects on her generation: "For the Nisei, evacuation had opened the doors of the world. After the war, they no longer had to return to the little Tokyos of their parents" (x). Here, we might observe the crisscrossing trajectories of Okubo, a.k.a. Citizen 13660, and her book *Citizen 13660*. Whereas wartime government orders propelled Okubo eastward, from California to Topaz to New York, where her *Fortune* assignment awaited her—her memoir moved in the opposite direction in the postwar years, eventually finding a place in Tokyo. Almost four decades after its initial printing by Columbia University Press, *Citizen 13660* traveled with distinction within the world republic of letters.[40] In 1983 the University of Washington Press, a publisher committed to Asian American letters, reissued the memoir. A year later, *Citizen 13660* received the American Book Award, earning it a place in a U.S. multicultural literary canon, and Ochanomizu Shobo, a Tokyo publishing house, translated it into Japanese. If Okubo had been relieved of having to return to the West Coast's "little Tokyos," the "Okubo" of *Citizen 13660* went an ocean farther, landing in Tokyo.

The belated transpacific reception of the earliest published Nisei memoir of the camps is all the more notable because Okubo mistakenly believed her illustrations for *Fortune*'s April 1944 issue had been reproduced in a late-war Japanese edition of the magazine, some two decades before such an edition even existed. To some degree, Okubo's belief that her camp-life images were circulated in Japan decades before they actually were is symptomatic of the securitized internationalism of the *Fortune* issue, "Japan and the Japanese," she had been asked to illustrate. Premised on U.S. victory in the Pacific, this issue reinforced the necessity "not only to defeat Japan in war but to keep her in peace," indeed "at close range."[41] To this end the editors argued the urgency of "understand[ing] the nature of the enemy so that we may destroy, and remake, the nature of his ambition."[42] Conceived after *Fortune* received "a flood of requests" that it republish its September 1936 thematic issue on Japan, the April 1944 issue represented the editors' decision to offer an entirely updated portrait of the country and its people.[43] Not credited to individual authors, the articles instead reflected the collaboration of Asia specialists, including Herrymon Maurer, Claude Buss, and Carl and Shelley Mydans—the latter three repatriates from Japan's internment camps in Asia—and "artists of Japanese extraction" ("Fortune's Wheel," 4), including Okubo. Comprising Americans repatriated from Japanese camps *and* released from an American concentration camp, *Fortune*'s team thus put Asia analysts and "native" informants, both Japanese and Japanese American, in league with each other.

Although written from a policy perspective by white American "experts" on Asia, the issue reflected *Fortune*'s investment in the "myth-making power of the artist [to] provide an image for a new society" and the work of artists as vital "imaginators" (Augspurger, 193, 210) of a democratic future under U.S. capitalist auspices. Unable to send photographers to Japan during wartime, the magazine, famed for its "designed realism" (Augspurger, 76) and visual modernism, instead drew on "the services of experts" ("Fortune's Wheel," 4)—namely, ethnic Japanese artists in the United States. Its reliance on Okubo reinforced what Caroline Chung Simpson has referred to as the "American propensity for seeing Japanese Americans as Japanese aliens" and Nisei "as go-betweens in occupied areas of the Pacific."[44] Of the three commissioned artists—Okubo, Yasuo Kuniyoshi, and Taro Yashima—Okubo's contribution was the greatest in volume. She alone, moreover, was asked to represent both sides of the Pacific—life in Japan *and* the Japanese American experience. *Fortune*'s editors anxiously justified including artwork by artists originally from Japan, describing Kuniyoshi as "a vigorous political worker for the democratic cause," and Yashima as an "antifascist" whose art had led to imprisonment and torture in Japan.[45] Unlike these Japan-born artists, however, Okubo, as the 1972 Oakland Museum catalog of her work pointed out, "was born an American in Riverside, California[, had] never been to Japan and [spoke] little Japanese."[46] Despite this handicap, not only did "Miss Okubo's drawings of camp life," *Fortune*'s editors declared, "exactly suit . . . our purpose" ("Fortune's Wheel," 4) for the opening essay, "Issei, Nisei, Kibei," but also, she created intricate renderings of Japanese "citizen-subjects," Japanese masses, and Japanese industry, dwellings, and urban sites for two additional articles, "The Citizen-Subject" and "What to Do with Japan."[47] The artist whose *Citizen 13660* would give human faces to Japanese Americans incarcerated in wartime thus assumed a weighty representational role as visual interpreter of the citizen-subject of Japan.

Proceeding, then, from a fraught epistemological basis, *Fortune*'s late-war issue sought to address government agencies, military intelligence, and its designated audience, American business—readers empowered not just to shape the peace but also to capitalize on Japan's defeat. Littered with war-industry advertisements forecasting a booming postwar market—"Commanding Position," "The World May Be Shrinking," "When It's Over, Over There," "Realistic Crystal Gazing"—*Fortune* offered a Pacific policy blueprint that reflected Luce's free-enterprise ideology.[48] And it did so while laboring to distinguish itself as a racially liberal alternative to Hearst-brand jingoism.[49] In the article "Issei, Nisei, Kibei," supplemented by seventeen of Okubo's camp-life sketches, most of which reappeared in *Citizen 13660*, *Fortune* condemned Hearst's "campaign of hate and fear," holding the man and his newspapers accountable for the "110,000 people evicted from the West Coast":

> For decades the Hearst press has campaigned against the Yellow Peril within the state (1 per cent of the population) as well as the Yellow Peril across the seas that would one day make war. When that war prophecy came true, the newspapers' campaign of hate and fear broke all bounds. And, when Hearst called for the removal of all people of Japanese ancestry, he had as allies many pressure groups who had for years resented the presence of Japanese in this country. . . . War turned the antagonism into fear, and made possible what California had already wanted for decades—to get rid of its minority. ("Issei, Nisei, Kibei," 8, 22)

Seeking to offer, by contrast, a cool-headed prescription regarding the future of the ethnic Japanese minority in the United States, *Fortune* dismissed fearmongering "innuendoes" that "explosions, train wrecks, fires, and serious accidents" (Hedda Hopper, quoted in "Issei, Nisei, Kibei," 32) ensued on the WRA's release of seventeen thousand Japanese Americans from the camps. Not one, the magazine averred, had been "convicted of anti-American activity" ("Issei, Nisei, Kibei," 32).

Central to *Fortune*'s take on the war-era American concentration camps was what it maintained was their *democratic* difference—and not just when compared to the lethal Nazi variety. Presenting the U.S. mass incarceration of Japanese Americans and Japan's internment of American POWs as an instructive study in contrasts, "Issei, Nisei, Kibei" characterized the treatment of "Japanese held in this country" as reflective of an entrenched—indeed "instinctive"—democratic tradition.[50] The magazine made no mention of the camps' securitized function as sorting houses for subjects whose loyalties were tested beyond that of any other "enemy alien" group. Instead, the essay made recourse to U.S. exceptionalist discourse, advancing the thesis that "when the facts about Japanese brutality to the soldier prisoners from Bataan were made known," Americans "without being told knew that prisoners in the U.S. were fed three meals a day and had not been clubbed or kicked or otherwise brutalized" ("Issei, Nisei, Kibei," 8). Thus, even as it disclosed select administrative abuses, "Issei, Nisei, Kibei" emphasized the necessity of abandoning theories of disloyalty, pushing for assimilation over de facto "Indian reservation[s]" (8, 102), and appealing for public cooperation as Japanese Americans were released eastward.

Yet if the article's aim was clearing the rumor-thicket propagated by Hearst publications, *Fortune* contributed to an obfuscation of the camps at nearly every turn.[51] Careful to use WRA euphemisms—"évacuées," "assembly centers," and "relocation centers"—in its analysis, *Fortune* steered clear of the freighted term *concentration camp*, which Franklin Roosevelt initially used to describe the camps.[52] Emphasizing the camps' strictly custodial, temporary nature, the magazine conjured the specter of race but only to argue the value of assimilation over permanent exclusion. In this regard *Fortune* converged with Noguchi, who insisted "the American answer" to wartime crisis was "a way so different from the Axis." The WRA's objective, in his parsing, was "not just relocation in camps but in the heart stream of America. Their plan is to foster democratic participation and opportunity, to teach the Nisei to stand on his own two feet" ("I Become a Nisei"). Toward this end *Fortune* insisted on the overdetermined expression "little Tokyos." Far from consistent in their usage, the magazine's editors first mobilized the term to describe the prewar urban ethnic enclaves located along the Pacific coast. Like McWilliams, who contended that the "character of the Little Tokyo community itself" was a "principal influence . . . [in] retarding acceptance" of Japanese Americans,[53] *Fortune* argued the necessity of dismantling "little Tokyos": "Back in December, 1941, there was understandable nervousness over the tight little Japanese communities scattered along the West Coast. The long coast line seemed naked and undefended. There were *colonies of Japanese fishermen* in the port areas, farmlands operated by Japanese close to war plants, and *little Tokyos* in the heart of big coastal cities. There were suspected spies among the *Japanese concentrations* and there was fear of sabotage" ("Issei, Nisei, Kibei," 22 [emphasis added]). Rather than read these little Tokyos—in their initial definition "Japanese concentrations" located "in the heart of big coastal cities"—as a foreseeable outcome of restrictive covenants, the editors construed an effect of racial exclusion as a transparent reason for racist fear.

Yet denoting more than the dismantled West Coast ethnic enclaves, "little Tokyos," wielded in the plural throughout "Issei, Nisei, Kibei," emblematized the lurking dystopianism of intensely racialized space—"tight," "concentrat[ed]," and with a dreaded capacity for proliferation. *Fortune*'s editors purposed one of Okubo's drawings to demonstrate how those potentially seditious little Tokyos, which were terminated as a consequence of removal policy, might prove to be the latter's unwitting outcome (fig. 3). Whereas in *Citizen 13660* this crowded scene depicts the Tanforan mess hall after multiple busloads of Bay Area Japanese Americans

Figure 3. Tanforan mess hall, by Miné Okubo, from "Issei, Nisei, Kibei," in "Japan and the Japanese," special issue, *Fortune*, April 1944, 22. Image courtesy of Miné Okubo Estate.

have been dumped at the former racetrack (Okubo and her tall brother among them), this image, as presented in *Fortune*, fails to mention the poor planning behind the packed circumstances. Rather, the magazine's editors marshaled this image as proof of how the very WRA policy intended to dismantle little Tokyos on the West Coast had nightmarishly reproduced their possibility in the camps, indeed "made [them] more ingrown than ever" (32).

Albeit not a part of the camp lexicon, which included "Caucasian" for camp administrator, the epithet "little Tokyos" had broad social currency within the larger cultural landscape during the transwar years.[54] Raised as an alarmist foil against which assimilation as a liberal method of racial rehabilitation could then be vigorously advocated, little Tokyos represented an overdetermined biopolitical concept with regard to a minority demographic framed and segregated as a security threat. Beyond the prewar ethnic enclaves along the Pacific coast, this term, as deployed in *Fortune*, described the "crowded barracks villages of between 7,000 and 18,000 people" ("Issei, Nisei, Kibei," 32). The danger of the camps, according to the magazine, resided in their concentration of "isolated, discarded, and therefore ingrown people" within "a compact racial island of their own frustrated people . . . almost completely detached from American life" ("Issei, Nisei, Kibei," 78). Not just individual little Tokyos but more ominously, a miniature version of the Japanese archipelago, "the nine remote inland sites . . . on federally owned land" ("Issei, Nisei, Kibei," 32) could be integrated into the "American" way of life, but only through the committed execution of policies of "resettlement," educational guidance, and assimilation.

Fortune thus vigorously advocated "resettlement" as the solution to the little Tokyos that had sprung up on federal lands. At stake was the progressive value of an otherwise disastrous mass removal policy.[55] Against accusations that the WRA had "turn[ed] loose, for resettlement, 'dangerous Japs,'" *Fortune* reminded its readers: "from the very beginning WRA's prescribed purpose was to help the *évacuées* to find some place to live outside the prohibited [Western Defense] zone" ("Issei, Nisei, Kibei," 74).[56] Countering interpretations of the camps as a glaring manifestation of the wartime color line, *Fortune* pointed to their interim function in the government's broader assimilationist agenda—a regrettably illiberal means, as it were, to a liberal end. Indeed, in a 1945 *Survey Graphic* article, "Japanese American Relocation: Final Chapter," WRA director Dillon Myer conceded that the camps were "tightly ingrown, racially segregated communities, where it [was] easier and easier to think and talk 'Japanese' and to forget the normal life outside."[57] Describing relocation as "an exciting adventure in the democratic method," he called for public support of the camps' "speedy liquidation" so as to avoid "the only alternative—the permanent maintenance of centers for people of Japanese descent as 'rejects' which our democracy has failed to absorb" (66, 62).

In other words, even as *Fortune* condemned the racist reaction to the little Tokyos on the West Coast, the magazine had no qualms about deploying the same term as an argument for the closure of the camps and the dispersal of Japanese Americans to the eastern United States. In opportunistically seizing on the term, it was not alone. In an April 2, 1942, letter to the WRA, Mike Masaoka, Nisei leader of the Japanese American Citizens League (JACL), raised the specter of little Tokyos in his advocacy for "maximum possible 'intercourse with "white" Americans'": "We do not relish the thought of 'Little Tokyos' springing up in these resettlement projects, for by doing so we are only perpetuating the very things which we hope to eliminate: those mannerisms and thoughts which mark us apart, aside from our physical characteristics. We hope for a one hundred per cent American community."[58]

"Resettlement" as an assimilationist enterprise required not only the dispersal of Japanese Americans within predominantly white American communities but also, as *Fortune* made clear, their capacity to propel themselves forward without state aid. Nowhere did reparations enter into the discussion. Rather, the publication categorized Japanese Americans as subjects with a historic loathing to turn to the state. In "Issei, Nisei, Kibei" *Fortune* reminded its readers that "the record of Japanese-Americans during the depression indicated that they did not take to public relief" and "almost never appeared on WPA or home-relief lists" (74, 78). With this aversion to state aid, "it is now galling [for them] to be distrusted wards of the nation" ("Issei, Nisei, Kibei," 78). Thus unlikely to be a postwar liability, Japanese Americans were extolled as a productive labor force whose integration into American society would benefit the nation as a whole.

To make its case, *Fortune* presented select camp sketches from Okubo's portfolio as evidence of Japanese Americans' hardy resilience and forward orientation. The first strip of line drawings in "Issei, Nisei, Kibei" narrates the initial mass-removal phase along pioneering lines. These sequential images imply the rhythmic procession of a goal-oriented journey. The first frame depicts "Okubo," her brother, and a few others alongside their belongings in a truck headed for Tanforan; the second captures "Okubo" as she arrives at a camp bustling with the activity of inmates who have settled into everyday routines of gardening, laundry, and gossiping; the third offers an interior shot of "Okubo" sweeping dung from her new home's stall floor. It is worth noting that Okubo would include nearly all these sketches in her memoir albeit without the progressive teleology imposed by *Fortune*'s editors.

In an early scene in *Citizen 13660* Okubo ironically notes that Japanese Americans were instructed to "bring work clothes suited to pioneer life" (15), yet her memoir, with its leitmotifs of uncertainty and impermanence, largely refuses a romanticized frontier reading of camp life, even as it highlights the inmates' productivity. In *Fortune*, however, the settler-colonial theme was dilated, with line drawings arranged and captioned to convey a "can-do" spirit in the context of mass captivity. While conceding the camp's makeshift, uninhabitable conditions, the magazine underscored Japanese American hard-scrabble ingenuity. As displayed in *Fortune*, this sequence of Okubo's images narrates inmates as valiant patriots (fig. 4).

Intimating that WRA's little Tokyos, too, might be viewed as a microcosm of home-front spirit, this triptych's emphasis on "making do" and maintaining morale reflected the total-war securitization of U.S. society. Yet more to the point, this trio of images specifically thematized the work of "democratization."

Figure 4. Sequence of line drawings by Miné Okubo, from "Issei, Nisei, Kibei," in "Japan and the Japanese," special issue, *Fortune*, April 1944, 32. Image courtesy of Miné Okubo Estate.

Doing their part in carceral little Tokyos for U.S. victory, Japanese Americans, the captions state, "improvise" and "persist." In "Victory Gardens," the second image, recycled box-sides read less as advertisements for "Wonder Bread" and "Kotex" than as evidence of frugality. Indeed, the reuse of discarded materials performatively designates the figures in this triptych as the *salvage*. In sociological research on the camps the salvage, in contrast to the spoilage, referenced those inmates whose recuperability in postwar American society was foretold by their belief—and demonstrated through their actions—that "a 'good life' could be built up in these isolated, war-duration communities."[59] Even, that is, in militarized confinement, they modeled their faith in the American system.

As Okubo's triptych suggests, the hybrid formula for exemplarity in the face of adversity, American can-do spirit bolstered by Japanese rectitude, determined who in this population would thrive under American authority.[60] The quasi-collectivist concept of the Japanese American victory garden might have recalled for *Fortune*'s liberal readers a 1943 *Survey Graphic* article, "Japanese Colony: Success Story."[61] Describing Japanese American resettlement in Utah in settler-colonial terms, this article focused on the "Food for Victory" campaign of Fred Wada, a "voluntary evacuee" (Fisher, 41) from Oakland, California, as a laudable total-war response to Roosevelt's wartime call for "increased output of both food and munitions": "[Wada] reasoned thus: . . . Japanese Americans are not allowed to make munitions, but they can raise food. He decided to set out, as a patriotic task, to find unused land, form a corps of Americans of Japanese ancestry, and try to break all records at raising crops. The band would not wait to be rounded up by the army, becoming expensive wards of the government. They would go eastward of their own free will and break land like the early pioneers."[62]

Like those Japanese Americans whom *Fortune* described as averse to state aid, Wada was presented as a "Success Story" from whose productive example the larger nation could learn a thing or two. "American" in character, his "Japanese Colony" in Keetley, Utah, stood as proof positive that fields covered with "a mass of sagebrush" could flourish as "acres of vegetables" (Taylor, 334). Against any challenge to his right to U.S. citizenship, *Survey Graphic* held up the Nisei "pioneer," going for broke in Japanese colonies on the home front, as a model of the salvage whose record-breaking "story of patriotism" might prove inspirational "to other loyal Americans" (Taylor, 334).

Art of Democratization

Ideologically framed as the model minority during the racially turbulent 1960s, the Nisei, as William Petersen infamously argued in "Success Story, Japanese-American Style," "established this remarkable record . . . by their almost totally unaided effort."[63] Few historians have traced the origin of this idealization of the Nisei back to the wartime milieu of the American concentration camp. Doing so, however, discloses the securitized premise of the model minority myth. As subjects imagined as loath to turn to the state and able to thrive in the face of state-sponsored adversity, Japanese Americans were construed as signifying democratic possibility in the confines of unfreedom. More than the comparative racial thesis that would emerge during a time of nationwide race riots in the 1960s, this template of resilient racialized subjects flourishing within militarized contexts would have broad applicability to postwar U.S. democratization projects abroad.

As *Fortune*'s special issue "Japan and the Japanese" begins to suggest, cultural representation served as a key ideological arena for the mediation of transracial encounters, facilitating "American" empathy and identification with those on the receiving end of U.S. foreign policy. This fiction of universality papered over the asymmetry of a world order unilaterally structured by what Luce called "American internationalism." Purposed to justify the U.S. democracy-to-come in Asia and the Pacific, Okubo's images of camp life, yoked visually and thematically to her commissioned images of Japan, were aimed at reassuring *Fortune*'s readers by reflecting "America" from within the WRA's little Tokyos. Yet the ambivalence of these images derived from the difficulty of interpreting the camp as a laboratory for democracy. By drawing race in familiar "American" forms, Okubo suggested the salvageability of Japanese Americans *as Americans*. The disquieting irony of her representations of militarized mass captivity, however, arose from the camp's shared morphology with structures of unfreedom associated with fascist biopolitics. Even as Noguchi insisted on the difference of the American concentration camp "from [that of] the Axis," what he and other leftist artists decried as the "fascist line of race bigotry" troubled cultural attempts to recuperate the camp along democratizing lines.

If, in the prewar era, the antifascist American Artists' Congress called for artists to resist all reactionary forces, in particular those seeking to conscript them as "a propaganda instrument" of fascism, by the late-war years, the state-sanctioned work of artists like Okubo, harnessed toward postwar Pax Americana ends, heralded what we might call an *art of democratization*.[64] The compositional elements of this aestheticized war politics—namely, race within militarized form—uneasily recalled fascist war spectacles, including human–war machine hybrids. Yet in contrast to the subsumption of the human by militarized form in fascist aesthetics, the foregrounding of racialized humanity in the art of democratization was aimed at disavowing the impact of state violence. By backgrounding the degree to which brute force served as the enabling condition for the visibility of racially reviled humanity, art of democratization lent itself to interpretive practices that minimized the structures in which race was captured in the first place and, in so doing, colluded in that originary violence.

In Okubo's recollection her artwork for *Trek*, the Topaz literary magazine, so moved *Fortune*'s editors that they invited her to move to New York, thus facilitating her leave clearance from Topaz. We might surmise they were especially drawn to the humanity of *Trek*'s first cover (fig. 5), which poignantly illustrates a Japanese American family's first "Christmas celebration" inside the camp, insofar as they reproduced her less-finished comics version of it (see fig. 3) in the article, "Issei, Nisei, Kibei."[65] What comes to the fore in this holiday scene of an incarcerated family "improvis[ing] a Christmas celebration" ("Issei, Nisei, Kibei," 32) are soothingly familiar rituals and forms: the father's Santa costume, the gift exchange, the hanging stockings, the substitute Christmas tree, the cast-iron stove. Presented in a distinctively "American" visual mode, this image of a family making-do, a version of which appeared in *Fortune*, might have evoked the grinding poverty and distinctively American grit of Lange's Depression-era black-and-white documentary photography for midcentury viewers. Yet unlike Lange, whose WRA-commissioned photographs of camp life were deemed palpably critical and impounded, Okubo's December 1942 *Trek* cover received the green light from WRA censors; in catching *Fortune*'s attention, her cover art served, moreover, as her ticket out of Topaz. As a portrait of democracy in confinement, Okubo's heteronormative rendering of nuclear-family domesticity

Figure 5. Cover by Miné Okubo, *Trek* (Dec. 1942). Image courtesy of Miné Okubo Estate.

behind barbed wire would likely have elicited transracial identification from *Fortune*'s readers. It would have done so, moreover, on the level of content, shared *American* humanity, rather than on the level of implied form or structure, militarized mass incarceration.[66] Only by disavowing state violence—and its socially nonnormative or queering effects—could the assimilation of racialized others, a key ideological operation of the art of democratization, take place.

Although not a makeshift Christmas celebration, another of Okubo's drawings in the same April 1944 issue visualized a family gathering—in this case in Japan (fig. 6). Recalling the finished style and careful layout of her *Trek* covers rather than *Citizen 13660*'s hasty line drawings, this scene signaled Okubo's attempt, at *Fortune*'s request, to "document" intimate details of a late-war Japanese household for its readership. Appearing as a half-page illustration for an article on Japanese wartime civil society titled "The Citizen-Subject... Tightens His Belt and Wipes Off His Smile," this drawing was meant to depict the average "two-room wood and paper house" in Japan, with the main living space doubling as dining room and bedroom, and the brazier serving as "cookstove and furnace" (178). In this tableau a worker and his family, partaking of an austere meal, just "A Bowl of Rice and a Pickled Plum" ("Citizen-Subject," 148) per person, ostensibly represented the average Japanese family. Meant, like the household items, to perform double duty, the scene's spare aesthetic might have communicated for *Fortune* subscribers a distinctive "Japaneseness," yet it also conveyed something all too familiar: the wartime necessity of rationing. In ascribing to the Japanese family a recognizable humanity, this image contrasted with "the most common caricature of the Japanese by Westerners"—namely, "the monkey or ape" (Dower, 84). Enumerating rationing rules imposed on Japanese civilians, the article distilled a principle that would have hit home for *Fortune*'s war-weary readers: in times of war "civilians do without" ("Citizen-Subject," 147).

Beyond Okubo's distinctive style and its careful geometry of forms, intense crosshatching, and fullness of human shape that attested to her brief WPA apprenticeship under Diego Rivera, the embedded social architecture of this interior scene aligned it with the Americana of the *Trek* covers that compelled *Fortune* to contact her. In contrast to the lurking social chaos of the claustrophobic Tanforan mess hall (see fig. 3) and the latter's hint of disaffected little Tokyos, this supposedly typical portrait of a Japanese family attempting to carry on despite the war shared with her depiction of a "Christmas celebration" in the American concentration camp a sense of normalcy in extraordinary circumstances. Poignant in its

Figure 6. Japanese worker and family, by Miné Okubo, from "The Citizen-Subject... Tightens His Belt and Wipes off His Smile," in "Japan and the Japanese," special issue, *Fortune*, April 1944, 149. Image courtesy of Miné Okubo Estate.

depiction of "belt-tightening"—a theme requiring no translation—and soothingly heteronormative, it implied nothing of the militarized fanaticism and perversion associated with Japan in the U.S. media. Rather, the fungibility between this scene and the Japanese American household depicted in "Issei, Nisei, Kibei" would have suggested the recuperability of the Japanese themselves. In "Japan and the Japanese" the continuity between Okubo's images enabled a syllogistic conclusion: just as "Citizen 13660" could be repatriated as an American subject, so, too, could the citizen-subject of Japan be rehabilitated under U.S. postwar occupation.

As an overdetermined reference for the prewar ethnic Japanese urban enclaves along the Pacific coast and the WRA's wartime camps, "Little Tokyo" thus took on a third meaning in *Fortune*'s April 1944 issue. As a metonym for U.S.-occupied Japan, "Little Tokyo" augured the flexibility of the Japanese under militarized U.S. postwar governance. In *War without Mercy*, a study of the Pacific War's racial politics, John Dower notes, "After the war years themselves changed over into an era of peace between Japan and the Allied powers, the shrill racial rhetoric of the early 1940s revealed itself to be surprisingly adaptable" (13). "Idioms"—and here we might include "little Tokyos"—"that formerly had denoted the unbridgeable gap between oneself and the enemy proved capable of serving the goals of accommodation as well" (Dower, 13). Tellingly, a "favorite simile" of General Douglas MacArthur for Occupied Japan was "concentration camp"; indeed, in a May 6, 1946, memo he described the country as "a vast concentration camp under the control of the Allies."[67]

Fortune thus alighted on the transpacific dimensions and implications of the little Tokyos created as a result of U.S. removal policy and discerned in the latter a democratizing opportunity. Its analysis of a national policy regarding a racially proscribed minority, what the editors described as "our treatment of Japanese held in this country" ("Issei, Nisei, Kibei," 8), took on the proleptic tone of postwar foreign policy, and Okubo's images were central to this slippage. Anticipating the casting of Japanese Americans as a model minority and construing "Japan and the Japanese" as a "problem we must solve," *Fortune* positioned Okubo's work as an exemplary model of democratic recovery, implying that Japanese Americans schooled in the undemocratic crucible at the heart of U.S. democracy had a crucial pedagogical role to play relative to U.S. plans for Japan, a Japan that would be destroyed and remade in the context of U.S. victory. If, as McWilliams noted, a "few observers have long recognized the importance of the Nisei in America in terms of the future of Japan" (13), *Fortune* capitalized on this fraught insight, adapting Nisei representations of camp life to illustrate their prescriptions for the U.S. occupation of Japan. Seeing fit to introduce this issue with a portrait of Japanese American mass incarceration and rehabilitation, *Fortune* detected in Okubo's artwork a potent capacity to elicit readerly identification with the Japanese on the terrain of culture. If central to the rehabilitation of Japanese Americans as "American," the domestication of the "foreign" would prove valuable to the U.S. democratization project in Japan.[68] In a 1976 essay for *Pacific Citizen*, the JACL newspaper, "The Trend Is Toward Assimilation," Okubo herself startlingly argued, "The dropping of the atomic bomb in Japan set off unexpected forces *favorable* to Japan." She then clarified: "It alerted the world attention to Japan and they saw Japanese people as people like any other race. There was much sympathy and understanding from everywhere. The United States occupation of Japan to help rebuild Japan into some form of a democracy westernized Japan."[69]

In her 1981 statement before the CWRIC, Okubo testified, mistakenly, to the *Fortune* editors' decision to "write this article ["Issei, Nisei, Kibei"] and put it in the same issue of *Fortune* in Japan" ("Statement," 17).[70] Although *Fortune* had no Japanese version in 1944 and would not until *Fortune Japan* was established in 1963, her mistake is revealing. That Okubo was enlisted to serve as a native "imaginator" for a *Fortune* issue aimed at disseminating knowledge about Japan and the Japanese for U.S. state agencies, army intelligence, and American business discloses the logic of ethnic affiliation that the magazine sought to harness in propagating its vision of a defeated Japan under U.S. military occupation. Whereas it decried the racism of the Hearst press in "campaign[ing] against the Yellow Peril within the state ... [and] across the seas," *Fortune*'s own conflation of Japanese Americans and the Japanese, apparent in its overdetermined construction of "little Tokyos," arguably contributed to the obfuscation of where and why the camps occurred. In her CWRIC testimony Okubo lamented American ignorance: "Many generations do not know that this ever happened in the United States. Whenever I speak about evacuation, they think it happened in Japan. I wish to present a copy of *Citizen 13660* to the Commission for their record" ("Statement," 17). Had Okubo submitted the April 1944 issue of *Fortune* instead, the confusion, we might imagine, would have been compounded.

# Possessive Investment in Ruin
The Target, the Proving Ground, and the
U.S. War Machine in the Nuclear Pacific

Nuclear Mementoes

In the years immediately following the U.S. atomic bombings of Japan, American GIs, as both occupiers and tourists, galvanized the commodification of nuclear apocalypse into consumable miniaturized form. Eager to capitalize on its nuclear heritage even as it sought to shed its reputation as an atomic desert, Hiroshima advertised itself in prefectural pamphlets as a place with much to offer tourists. Stationed in Occupied Japan, the cartoonist Bill Hume remarked the feverish reconstructive energy of the times, with "Japan's business and social world [spinning] crazily beneath an American welcome mat."[1] A site of R and R for U.S. military personnel deployed to the nearby Korean theater and a Cold War object lesson in the shattering consequences of defeat, Hiroshima self-consciously preserved vestiges of atomic devastation, most famously the Genbaku Dome, as part of its postwar topography. Renovated as a "peace city" and an international tourist destination, the municipality encouraged entrepreneurship around the disaster. Of those "mak[ing] their living" out of the bombing, *Life* magazine in 1952 noted the spectrum of thanatourist undertakings by locals: "They trade in heat-fused souvenirs of glass or stone, conduct sightseers through the ruins, sell pamphlets which detail what happened."[2]

For years a fixture next to the Genbaku Dome, Kikkawa Kiyoshi ran the Atomic Bomb Casualty Shop, a souvenir stand frequented by GIs. Its name a play on the Atomic Bomb Casualty Commission (ABCC) created by President Harry Truman in 1946 to conduct long-range biomedical research into the effects of radiation on the survivors of the Hiroshima and Nagasaki bombings, Kikkawa's commercial venture offered simulacra of firsthand memories of his city's decimation. Among his wares were mass-produced yet homely albums tied with colored ribbon that featured photos of atomic devastation as well as grim *cartes de visite* and postcards of incinerated rubble and human ruin, all of which he autographed in bold black marker in English and Japanese, often adding the epithet, "BOMB VICTIM NO. 1," and the no-nukes slogan, "NO MORE HIROSHIMAS." Of the postwar phenomenon of *hibakusha* (explosion-affected people) hawking atomic souvenirs to tourists, *Life* discerned a latent political critique: "Even the Communists do not directly make anti-American capital out of the pictures" (24).

To the extent it made capital out of nuclear atrocity, however, Kikkawa's shop held up an uneasy mirror to the ABCC, an agency criticized by many Japanese as exploitative of hibakusha and indifferent to their suffering. The ABCC had subjected hibakusha to radiogenic study, claiming their blood, tissue, and semen samples as national security data intended, in theory, to bolster Cold War "civil defense" preparedness in the United States. As M. Susan Lindee states in her account of the agency, "American investigators needed to know how and why people died in the wake of an atomic attack"—information vital to triage protocols and weapons development.[3] Of the unabashedly instrumental nature of ABCC's human radiological research program, historian Ienaga Saburō was not alone among Japanese observers in commenting that "residents of those two cities [Hiroshima and Nagasaki] were human guinea pigs in the first use of atomic weapons in warfare."[4] Indeed, even as it extracted biomedical value from these "martyrs of the new atomic age" (Lindee, 122), the ABCC denied hibakusha medical care, reasoning that doing so could be interpreted as "an act of atonement" tantamount to reparations for the bombings.[5] *Life* reproduced the impatient query of "the wife of the much-scarred Kiyoshi Kikkawa": " 'If you Americans atom bombed us, and some of us survived, don't you think . . . you should help us regain our health?' " (24).

First identified by the U.S. press as "Atomic Victim #1" when photographed at Hiroshima's Red Cross Hospital, Kikkawa thereafter readily advertised himself as such. To GIs with cash and compact cameras in hand, Kikkawa transformed himself into a marketable spectacle, baring his keloid-covered back, a corporeal testament to past violence reminiscent of the ex-slave Gordon's "scourged back" in the famed Civil War photo. Although keloids were a visible marker of hibakusha status in Hiroshima, the ABCC again sidestepped the issue of U.S. accountability by deeming them a response to skin injury particular to some racial groups rather than an effect of radiation. For the customers at Kikkawa's shop, however, images of his scarred flesh authenticated their postwar encounter with atomic Hiroshima. In her poem "America Comes Out as the World's Top in Anything," fellow hibakusha Kurihara Sadako memorialized the obscenity of the victor's gaze:

> In Hiroshima
> Mr. Kiyoshi Kikkawa was labelled, "Number One Atomic Bomb Sufferer."
> On the entire surface of his back
> Keloid like lava, have risen;
> The five fingers of his now crooked right hand
> Have ceased to move,
> And are turned inward, sticking to each other,
> The entire hand twitching due to atomic bomb disease.[6]

Neither grief nor guilt, however, appears to have been the prevailing GI response to Kikkawa's disfigured flesh. Indeed, some GIs snapped photos of themselves cheerily flanking his back, their forward-facing countenances a contrast to his backward-facing orientation.

As Hiroshima morphed from a "City of Death into a City of Life," emerging as a bustling postwar metropolis, these privately held photos of the uneven, almost earthen, surfaces of Kikkawa's skin enabled the reenactment of an originary American claim on Hiroshima, a possessive national investment in a site where "the soil . . . was mixed with the bones of the dead."[7] Signaling an intimate shift in scale from macro to micro representations of ruin, these images played to the voyeurism and triumphalism of the victors by invoking a proprietary right to atomic ruin.[8] Thus, if at first spectacularized in god's-eye images of an incinerated cityscape, evidence of Hiroshima's devastation shrank in more ways than one in the postwar years, taking the form of purchasable memorabilia, including photos of Kikkawa's back. These mementoes of World War II's culminating violence and the Cold War's inaugural act could be shared with friends and family back home.[9] In the aftermath of *pikadon*—the bomb's "flash-boom"—images of Kikkawa's now-cooled flesh, with its "lava"-raised terrain, testified to the violent conflation of humanity and earth in the target, standing in for what was rapidly receding from view: Hiroshima's radiation-blasted topography.

Not merely vestiges from the past, however, much less a past that must never be repeated, the nuclear ruin of Hiroshima, Nagasaki, and the Marshall Islands was emplotted into a Cold War U.S. macronarrative of apocalypse to come, a narrative teleologically conditioned by the imperative of U.S. survival at any and all costs in the new atomic era. In an inversion of the directionality of both actual and possible U.S. nuclear aggression, the defensive national fiction of "an American community under total and unending threat" stimulated the hubristic proliferation of the military-industrial complex. It naturalized a nuclearized domestic dispensation, a high-alert posture in which the incursion of "militarism in everyday life" was justified in the name of national security.[10] The nuclearization of reality for Americans extended far beyond domestic duck-and-cover drills, personal fallout shelters, and air-raid sirens.[11] The Cold War U.S. posture of all-out defense against impending nuclear doom entailed imperial consensus around the anticipatory staging of apocalypse writ small.

The sanctity and primacy of life *here*, that is, required the rehearsed obliteration of life, land, ocean, and home *over there*. Throughout the Cold War the U.S. nuclear regime turned on a flawed "model of isolation" premised on the nonintersection, as Elizabeth DeLoughrey has argued, of "'test' and 'control' groups, and the presumed isolation of the Marshall Islands colonies from the continental US and its responsibility to the rule of law."[12] This fiction was contradicted on multiple fronts. Ecologically, global deposition patterns of nuclear fallout obviated the deictic *here*, with its imperial supposition of existing at a safe remove from *there*. Politically, the United States treated the Marshall Islands in sovereignty-breaching ways as an insular territory subject to its dominion. It deflected accountability by exploiting its strategic trusteeship over Marshallese territory, which—akin to tribal or "domestic dependent nations"—was administered by the Department of the Interior. Even as the United States was geographically vulnerable to radioactive fallout from these nuclear tests, it asserted immunity from the atrocities it committed against the Marshallese people, including the devastation of their bodies, lands, waters, and lifeways. Insofar as the U.S. atomic bombings of Japan and high-yield atmospheric nuclear tests in the Marshall Islands surfaced into national discussion, they were not framed as massive human rights violations, let alone apocalyptic in and of themselves. Rather, these acts of nuclear aggression were construed as possessing future import for American lives. In the militarized cartography of the Pax Americana in Asia and the Pacific, deterritorialized zones of death—Hiroshima, Nagasaki, Bikini, Eniwetok, Rongelap, and Utirik—thus took on proleptic value as proxy, sacrificial sites for the United States imagined as the future victim of nuclear terror.[13]

Typically periodized apart, the U.S. atomic bombings of Japan and its Marshallese nuclear tests thus demand theorization along a continuum. Far from marking an end to World War II, the total-war obliteration of Hiroshima and

Nagasaki inaugurated a pattern of permissible nuclear ruin on the external and internal margins of U.S. military-empire that unsettled conventional distinctions between war and peace, enemy and friend, death and life. The U.S. determination to test novel nuclear weaponry in times of war, as well as supposed peace, blurred lines of enmity by consigning all-but-defeated foe and "liberated" territory alike to nuclear devastation. Binding sites designated externally as targets and internally as proving grounds was, in other words, their utility as distant or marginalized lands, atmospheres, and peoples that substituted for those "at home." The post-1945 U.S. garrison state exercised unilateralism in arranging these sites and demographics according to a racialized hierarchy of value. Desirable not for their life-sustaining capacity, much less honored for their lived social meaning, these surrogate zones of nuclear experimentation were instead valued for their disposability. In other words, these lands and peoples were *valued* as dystopian, theoretically parallel universes—sites that could be *devalued* by being laid to waste and thereafter subjected to scientific scrutiny. In reference to uranium mining on Diné (Navajo) lands, Traci Brynne Voyles describes "pollutable" indigenous environments as wastelands either defined by their perceived lack of value or valued "for what can be mined from beneath them."[14] But in the broader imperial geography of nuclear disaster linking indigenous sites of uranium extraction to targeted Asian cities and Pacific Island proving grounds, the concept of wasteland accrued a further meaning. Insofar as the irradiated bodies of these created wastelands redounded to the "benefit of life" in the imperial center, they were, to read Locke's labor theory of value against the grain, perversely propertized as *improvement*.[15] As Lindee writes in her ABCC study, "Bodies scarred by radiation were a critical military commodity" (258). Yet by violently joining geographies and peoples, obviating time and space, this necropolitical form of improvement—so central to what Laguna Pueblo writer Leslie Marmon Silko has called "white warfare"—would also lay the groundwork for the imagination of solidarity.[16]

In the early 1990s the Clinton administration, in a spirit of post–Cold War unipolar openness, established an advisory committee charged with investigating on a limited scale the covert human radiation experiments the United States had conducted, including on its own citizens and military personnel, in the name of national security in the lead-up to and long aftermath of its atomic bombings of Japan. In this rare window of national self-reflection, Congress held hearings touching on the secret U.S. human radiation research carried out on Marshallese bodies. The February 24, 1994, hearing on the U.S. Pacific nuclear tests clarified for the historical record the Marshall Islands' near-singular significance in the national security state's mobilization of radioactive fallout as a form of ecocide giving rise to slow death. Johnsay Riklon, a senator in the Marshall Islands, described the Rongelapese as a "highly unique class of Cold War casualties" who had "gained nothing and lost almost everything that gave our lives meaning" as a result of the nuclear tests the United States unilaterally imposed on them.[17] He elaborated: "The people of Rongelap were exposed to risks far greater, and we sustained injuries far more severe, than any other population except your enemy's population at Hiroshima and Nagasaki" (362). Yet unlike hibakusha whose exposure to fallout was relatively minimal, Marshall Islanders bore witness to "the killing power of lingering radioactive fallout" that in protracted, multigenerational, mutagenic effects, "far surpasse[d] the instant sledgehammer effect of the bomb's blast."[18] Pointing out that information gleaned from the human radiation experiments on the Rongelap people was vital to "the domestic well-being of the people of this country," Riklon concluded his testimony by driving home that the United States "got full value in the testing program, and arguably a good deal more" (362, 367).

Within a U.S.-centric developmental fiction of manageable, containable nuclear apocalypse, Hiroshima, Nagasaki, and the Marshall Islands thus sacrificially shielded the United States from what Riklon termed the atomic era's "future-shock" (361). The temporal implications of the cognitive mapping of the nuclear Pacific are worth considering. From the U.S. atomic bombings of Japan onward, nuclear devastation was cast in temporal terms unidentical with itself. Apocalypse was not recognized as *now* for the residents of Hiroshima and Nagasaki, the Bikinians, the Rongelapese, and other Marshall Islanders subjected to world-shattering nuclear violence, be it instantaneous or slow.[19] Instead, for the United States, as self-appointed global custodian and unleasher of near-unrivaled nuclear necropower, nuclear ruins were "never the end of the story . . . but always offer[ed] a new beginning" (Masco, *The Nuclear Borderlands*, 363). Indeed, in state accounts of U.S. security ties to its sites of nuclear devastation in the Pacific, disaster has perversely figured as precipitating democratization and bonds of friendship with the United States. Hiroshima and Nagasaki's annihilation was thus ideologically recuperated as the necessary grounds for Japan's rebirth as a peaceful nation, and the nuclear ruination of the Marshall Islands, which included the vaporization of entire islands and long-range human radiation experiments, was both deemed broadly beneficial to humankind and depicted as a step toward eventual Marshallese self-governance and "free association" with the United States. In this way Japan and the Marshall Islands were subordinated to the nuclear Pacific's militarized temporality. The perdurance of radiogenic communities in both sites bolstered the Cold War military-imperialist fantasy of (American) life after nuclear catastrophe.

The U.S. war machine's deliberate production of irradiated remnant life signaled a new global dispensation that Rey Chow has named "the age of the world target" in which "powers of terror are indistinguishable from powers of 'deterrence,' and technologies of war indissociable from practices of peace."[20] In a necropolitical world order in which ongoing total war was hegemonically framed as a time of amity and consent, the United States presented nuclear power as a means of achieving militarized "peace" rather than a deterritorializing end to life and modes of life-sustaining relations. Hiroshima, Nagasaki, and the Marshall Islands were enfolded into a neutralizing postwar narrative of what Native Hawaiian scholar Haunani-Kay Trask, following Frantz Fanon, has called "peaceful violence," which "kills without a sound, without a passing notice."[21] The Cold War marketing of nuclear power as "atoms for peace," in Dwight Eisenhower's phrase—indeed, the Janus-faced concept of "dual-use" nuclear technology with "civilian" and military applications—contributed to moral equivocation around nuclear violence.[22] At a time when newly developed nuclear weapons posed a threat of annihilation so vast as to make survival a pyrrhic prospect, the dual use of nuclear power, including peacetime "tests" whose consequences were impossible to distinguish from effects of war, was banalized as "the positive mechanism, momentum, and condition of possibility of society" (Chow, 34). Nuclear war and its redemptive corollary—in Eisenhower's lofty words, "the miraculous inventiveness" of nuclear technology "consecrated to . . . life"—thus normalized world-ordering visions of fascist futurity in which life could not be envisioned outside the militarized capacity to destroy. In a time of peaceful violence, the power to " 'make' live" relative to some lives was predicated on the power to " 'let' die" relative to others.[23] Against what Eisenhower called "the dark backdrop of the atomic bomb," the former presupposed the latter as its shadow.

Flying from Tinian in the Northern Marianas, the Enola Gay crew that dropped Little Boy on Hiroshima, weathered two shock waves, stuck around long enough to "[take] pictures," and only after growing "concerned that we better quit being sightseers . . . [got] out of there."[24] The atom bomber-cum-sightseer, in surveying the staggering devastation below, set a paradigm for GIs-cum-tourists to come. We might recall French filmmaker Chris Marker's apt observation: "The gaze of the victor . . . seems lacking in modesty."[25] In the nuclear Pacific this gaze would prove to be proprietary in its investment in the generative possibilities of ruin.[26] It would be encoded in the consumerism of post-1945 international tourism as a regional industry that, in the first instance, was born out of the business of militarized leisure. Indeed, GI tourism in Hiroshima would "deeply influence . . . how the bomb would be commemorated."[27] As part of "the material form of American victory," trophies of atomic devastation ideologically sutured democracy to the fearsome power of the American bomb. In so doing, they played a role in consolidating the Cold War shibboleth that the bomb was peace—the basis for both Japan's renewal and eventual Marshallese independence. The triumphalism in the phoenix-like arc of life emerging from ashes would imprint the bomb's transpacific culture, emplotting nuclear ruin into the romance of liberation, democratization, and bonds of friendship. Within this geopolitical framing, images of atomic apocalypse writ small and touristic "scene[s] of leisure" that displaced "the horror of the bomb" played to an American investment in violence.[28]

Beclouded Vision

In the scalar and temporal shift from expanses of scorched earth to scarred hibakusha flesh, Hiroshima, cast as a global symbol of nuclear devastation, emerged in the postwar years as arguably something less than an absolute "sign of terror" (Chow, 25). Gertrude Stein's 1946 prose piece "Reflection on the Atomic Bomb" offers a telling performance of zero affect: "They asked me what I thought of the atomic bomb. I said I had not been able to take any interest in it. . . . What is the use, if they are really as destructive as all that there is nothing left and if there is nothing there nobody to be interested and nothing to be interested about. If they are not as destructive as all that then they are just a little more or less destructive than other things. . . . If you are not scared the atomic bomb is not interesting."[29]

Whether sincere or ironic, Stein's breezy disregard for the atomic bombs' catastrophic consequences forecast the U.S. public's inoculation to nuclear horror *over there*. Insofar as nuclear violence failed to grip American political consciousness from the outset of the atomic age, it exemplified what Joseph Masco, in a nod to Hannah Arendt, has called "the banalization of . . . nuclear weapons in everyday American life."[30] If not with unconcern then with a spirit of triumph, Americans hailed the atomic decimation of Japanese civilian targets. In late 1945 a *Fortune* magazine survey revealed that just 5 percent of Americans polled opposed the atomic bombings and a significant minority would have supported the dropping of more bombs.[31] In 1948 George Marion, an early critic of the emerging U.S. empire of bases, satirized the casual violence of this apocalyptic position: "if, out of their moral backwardness, some peoples resist this *Pax Americana*, we can redeem them with atom bombs."[32]

The limits to U.S. historical consciousness regarding the atomic bombings of Japan—what cultural critic Kyo Maclear has punningly dubbed America's "beclouded vision"—have often been assumed to be an effect of the literal shortcomings of perspective as conventionalized in the aerial images of the mushroom cloud and scorched earth.[33] Anesthetizing and infinitely reproduced, these icons of the nuclear sublime signal a technologically triumphalist U.S. frame of reference. Against their alignment with U.S. war power there have been attempts to privilege narration from the other deictic position, the *here* of the target, so as to present the bombings' neglected human dimension. In keeping with the belief that "if the American people ever saw what the bomb had done to human beings they would demand an end to the arms race," ground-level images and hibakusha narration, both censored during the U.S. occupation, appear to intervene with the missing human side of an empyrean tale of the bomb.[34] It thus bears asking what valorizing such perspectives as the occluded other of America's beclouded vision has yielded. Have accounts enabling "a palpable . . . connection to these events and their direct sufferers" (Maclear, 83) negotiated transformative communicative ground with the audience nationally implicated in the mass death and suffering of noncombatants?[35] Have survivor tales of "the intentional targeting of great masses of people for instant, indiscriminate, and certain death" (Mitchell) succeeded in arguing that which is glaringly absent from technocratic accounts and military justifications of the bombings—namely, U.S. accountability?

Here it is worth turning to a pioneering visual account of the bombing of Hiroshima that first surfaced in underground American comics culture. If " 'Hiroshima' is now the name of a story," it has also been visualized in manga form as "a cartoon story," as the American subtitle of Nakazawa Keiji's *Barefoot Gen* (*Hadashi no Gen*) indicates, that has been in U.S. circulation for four decades.[36] A rare hibakusha account commanding a considerable transpacific readership, Nakazawa's fictionalized memoir revisits the nuclear annihilation of Hiroshima through the youthful perspective of his alter ego, Gen.[37] As a child survivor, Gen reanimates both "Little Boy," the U.S. military code name for the Hiroshima bomb, and the etymology of "atom," "child," "origin," "root," and "source" inhering in the Japanese term for atomic bomb, *genshi bakudan* (original child bomb). Nakazawa named his survivor-protagonist as such "in the hope that he would become a *root* or *source* of strength for a new generation of mankind."[38] As the manga's antinuclear poster child, Gen personifies the bomb's generative properties, so to speak, his function less to dwell on past injuries than to advocate for a nuclear-free future. His plight, in light of unabating global nuclear proliferation, is potentially our own. First published in a Japanese boys' periodical in the early 1970s and then serialized in a nearly two-thousand-page multivolume manga in Japan, Nakazawa's antinukes tale by the late 1970s surfaced in West Coast head shops and leftist bookstores as a corrective to uncritical U.S. treatments of nuclear power.[39] Founded in 1976 after a meeting between Japanese participants in the Continental Walk for Disarmament and Social Justice and Americans eager to learn about the atomic bombings of Japan, the volunteer organization Project Gen undertook as its first task the manga's translation so as to drive home its ban-the-bomb message to a U.S. audience. By foregrounding Hiroshima, which too often had been elided from U.S. antinuclear politics, *Barefoot Gen*'s U.S. publication signaled a shift away from Cold War atomic mutants to a sobering historical reflection on nuclear war's human toll.

Focalized partly via the ground-level lens of Gen as eyewitness, *Barefoot Gen* universalizes its no-nukes didactic by enabling its reader's vicarious presence in "Hiroshima." In an account of the ethical power of what she terms "prosthetic memory," Alison Landsberg has argued, "mass culture makes particular memories more widely available, so that people who have no 'natural' claim to them might nevertheless incorporate them into their own archive of experience."[40] American prosthetic memory of Hiroshima, however, has had as its dubious legacy the imaginative "'melting down' of difference" (Landsberg, 9) between historic perpetrators and victims. Attesting to the manga's mainstreaming for a U.S. audience, the 1990 Penguin and subsequent Last Gasp editions of *Barefoot Gen* give first word to *Maus* creator, Art Spiegelman. Of his encounter with "Hiroshima," he writes in his preface: "I've found myself remembering images and events from the *Gen* books with a clarity that make them seem like memories from my own life, rather than Nakazawa's."[41] The events Spiegelman recalls as though his own, images that "burned [their] way into [his] heated brain," are not, however, of a typical documentary nature. Rather, the form he credits with "blunt sincerity" is the comics image.[42]

By offering a dehistoricizing threshold into alterity, the comics strategies Nakazawa deploys to facilitate his readers' access to Hiroshima—visual reenactment, illusions of coextensive space, and appeals to intersubjectivity—have all too often in their U.S. reception fallen short of inciting reckoning with the criminality of the atomic bombings. Indeed, as with most hibakusha accounts, *Barefoot Gen* has not succeeded in repatriating Hiroshima onto U.S. terrain. Critics, including Robert Lifton, Greg Mitchell, and John Treat, have remarked the U.S. public's imperviousness to cultural accounts of the bombings. Although narratives of the bomb have in isolated cases been met with enthusiasm, they have mostly come and gone with little fanfare, their publication histories short and audiences seldom assured.[43] Japanese accounts from "the eyes of victims" have further been freighted with a fraught imperative, seeking to do their part in averting nuclear catastrophe even as they typically do not indict.[44] As paradigmatic cautionary tales of the nuclear age, survivor accounts may possess unique authority within an anodyne discourse of global peace, yet by refusing to identify the United States as historic perpetrator, they leave intact U.S. forward-facing rationales for nuclear violence. Ideologically conjoined more to the future than the past, Hiroshima thus functions as an atrocity tale that appears to require neither redress nor reparations. Always already contextualized against the economic rise of Japan, as exemplary Cold War U.S. client-state, the spectacularity of the bombing has been effectively canceled out.

Forward in propulsion, *Barefoot Gen* and other hibakusha accounts—as tales by those who survived the unsurvivable—have perversely served as incipient narratives of Japan's recovery in the face of cataclysmic adversity. Literally and symbolically leveled, with the ashes of the old cleared to make way for the new, Hiroshima has been scripted as a tragic but unavoidable prelude to the gift of American peace. *Barefoot Gen*, too, implies the eventuation of a catastrophic act of U.S. aggression against civilians in peacetime democracy. This exceptionalist thesis is essential to the manga's value as a wartime lesson for the postwar peace. Although Nakazawa stated his work was motivated by his desire "to fling my grudge at the U.S." ("Interview"), his manga is conditioned by the Pax Americana presumption that Japan's postwar democratization has rendered the material quest for justice for victims of the atomic bombings moot. Even as it bears witness to the human toll of U.S. total-war policies, *Barefoot Gen* thus offers an object lesson less in the pursuit of human rights than in Japan's exemplary posttraumatic recuperation and ascendancy in the geopolitical ambit of U.S. power.

Yet broad acceptance of Japan's reduction to ashes as necessary for its capitalist futurity has obscured the value of the atomic bombings of Hiroshima and Nagasaki for the United States. Theorizing necrocapitalism, Subhabrata Bobby Banerjee argues that for imperial states, war zones—as states of exception where killing can be done with impunity—serve as disciplinary arenas for the establishment of "behavioral and economic norms."[45] Predicated on Japan's defeat, the regional establishment of U.S. military empire facilitated the integration of a range of junior partners into the global capitalist economy. This system of dependent capitalism, or subimperialism, "transferr[ed] value to imperialist centres" while serving "the sub-imperialist country's capital reproduction."[46] Yet more than function as a "midwife," in Marx's phrase, that "hastens the process of transformation," be it corporate exploitation of disaster or the establishment of client regimes, military-imperial force in the nuclear Pacific demands contextualization within a Cold War U.S. national security calculus.[47] Within necrocapitalism, mass dispossession, destruction, and death are the predictable outcomes of the sovereignty-suspending practices of imperial accumulation. They are, as Naomi Klein has argued in her analysis of disaster capitalism, the basis of reconstruction as a form of colonialism.[48] Yet within the military-imperial framework of the nuclear Pacific, devastation—far more than an epiphenomenon—must be understood as itself the object of commodification. To the extent that the commodification of war ruin might be read as an allegory of primitive accumulation, the war target must be understood as a necrocapitalist enclosure—a demarcated arena of life, labor, and social reproduction rendered as *terra nullius*. The intended "product" is waste.

Tellingly, the U.S. national security state seized the remnants of life, land, and environs in Hiroshima and Nagasaki as critical evidence with regard to the technology of atomic devastation.[49] "Data," including rubble and victims' body parts, was classified as intelligence and deemed national security assets. Yet competing definitions over the value of war ruin portended diplomatic fissures in U.S.-Japan relations. Were irradiated human body parts military data or the remains of people to be mourned?[50] Cast in strategic rather than commemorative terms for most of the Cold War, the bomb's material archive would be the sole possession of the United States, electively shared with a handful of nations aligned under its nuclear umbrella. Here it is worth noting that in the historical juncture in which *Barefoot Gen* offered American readers a prophylactic foothold into Hiroshima's irradiated landscape, the United States belatedly repatriated human remains from

Hiroshima and Nagasaki that it had long claimed as state property. Against the backdrop of the Cold War, it justified custody of expropriated human body parts as vital to the battle against communism.[51] Having assumed a lien to such "data" but no responsibility for its deliberate destruction of life, the United States wielded these remains as "commodities that could be used in negotiations with the government of Japan" (Lindee, "Repatriation," 403). Covered widely in the Japanese press but scarcely mentioned in the U.S. media, the diplomatic wrangling over these depersonalized body parts culminated in their eventual return to Japan in the early 1970s. In other words, not long after these remains finally shifted into Japanese commemoration, *Barefoot Gen* crossed the Pacific in an antinukes effort to repatriate the story of Hiroshima within the United States.

This history is worth emphasizing insofar as the proprietary U.S. claim to the evidentiary archive of the bomb has had enduring categorizing implications for cultural narration, effectively ensuring that firsthand accounts, however moving in their own right, would be unevenly positioned in a realm marked as cultural relative to U.S. geopolitical dominance over Japan. As historian James Orr writes, "American policies set the framework in which the war was remembered in Japan."[52] The atomic bombings thus have as their legacy Hiroshima's ideological construction as both generic signifier for nuclear disaster *and* U.S. proprietorship over the disaster. What Peter Schwenger and John Whittier Treat dub "America's Hiroshima" accordingly marks a paradox. Censored, mobilized to ensure U.S. interests, and exploited for national security ends, Hiroshima has been critical to U.S. military-imperial ascendancy. Indeed, in a March 1, 1946, essay, "The Bomb and the Opportunity," Henry Stimson, secretary of war under Harry Truman, stated baldly: "By its sole possession of the bomb, at least for the present, the United States finds itself in a position of world leadership."[53] Yet in official U.S. and Japanese state discourse, the U.S. monopoly over Hiroshima-related research has been assiduously delinked from its accountability for the devastation. Promulgated as a matter of global security, more a future dilemma than an unredressed atrocity, "America's Hiroshima" may be recognized less by the degree to which it incriminates than the extent to which it shies away from doing so: "Hiroshima does not lie at the center of American national life, though some have suggested that it should. America, on the other hand, has been a constant presence—force—in Japanese life since 1945 and has been constantly 'represented' ... by the often heavy-handed demonstration of its national power" (Schwenger and Treat, 329). Even as the atomic bombings of Japan "might seem to demand obvious reference... to someone or something American" (Schwenger and Treat, 324), those ground-level narratives that have attempted to humanize the bomb's consequences have shied away from indicting the United States. Moreover, by implying that the United States, in laying Hiroshima to irradiated waste, planted democratizing seeds for Japan's peaceful recuperation, such accounts have played to a U.S. investment in violence.

Flash-Forward Democracy

Barefoot Gen is a markedly ex post facto rendering of the Hiroshima bombing, a revisitation of the nuclear cataclysm through a democratically "rehabilitated" lens. As a narrative of overcoming informed by its moment, the Gen series signaled the Japanese literary market's receptivity to hibakusha memoirs and reflected the post-Ampo (1960 revision of the U.S.-Japan Security Treaty) consolidation of Japan's identity as both "acknowledged mercantilist success" and "peace-loving nation" (Orr, 2). Hibakusha memoirs crystallized as a genre, that is to say, as Japan emerged on the global stage as a major export economy. Despite the fact its economic recovery depended on its production of war materiel for the United States in the Korean and Vietnamese theaters, Japan by the 1960s was internationally hailed as an exemplar of peace. Ironically, the "link between the bomb and peace" promoted by Occupation authorities to neutralize anti-American critique furnished the ideational basis for mass Japanese opposition to Japan's security alliance with the United States and its absorption under the latter's Cold War nuclear umbrella.[54] In an era typified by myriad contradictions of peace discourse, the democratic ideals of U.S. exceptionalism were thus translated into Japanese opposition to U.S. militarism yet to little avail. This backdrop furnishes insight into *Barefoot Gen* as an equivocal narrative that broadcasts pacifism and democracy as its ideals yet ultimately neglects a robust critique of the U.S. decision to use the bomb.

In a study of the entwined ideologies of collective victimization and peace in postwar Japan, Orr describes victim consciousness as a "transference of aggressive subjectivity" that "plac[ed] the now innocent Japanese people on the high ground of victimhood" while narrowly assigning the role of historic perpetrator to "the military [or] the militarist state" (3). Although critical in its portrait of the Japanese masses, *Barefoot Gen* adheres to this narrative of a military cabal that manipulated the people and through sheer recklessness made tragically unavoidable the U.S. recourse to the bomb. Indeed, Nakazawa's manga reproduces the tacit justification for the atomic bombings in the Allied leadership's July 26, 1945, declaration from Potsdam: "a new order of peace, security and justice will be impossible until irresponsible militarism is driven from the world."[55] Nakazawa captions his image of the late-war Allied conference by emphasizing that Japan was fairly warned "that further resistance would result in the annihilation of the Japanese Army and the destruction of the country" (206). The next frame reveals that "Japan's war leaders rejected the demand, vowing that the Japanese would fight to the last man" (206). Here, too, *Barefoot Gen* imbibes the Allied historiographical claim that war responsibility falls on the shoulders of "those self-willed militaristic advisers whose unintelligent calculations have brought the Empire of Japan to the threshold of annihilation" (Potsdam Proclamation). Depicted as "fooled" (13) by their leaders, the fear-driven, starving residents of Nakazawa's Hiroshima are ripe for liberation. In this otherwise grim setting, Gen's family stands as an undimmed beacon of hope. Even when mercilessly persecuted, Mr. Nakaoka, the manga's bearer of democratic tidings, does not falter in his conviction that "Japan has to walk the way of **peace**, not war" (34).[56] His dissident statements reinforce the manga's thesis that Japan's future depends on its demilitarization and democratization, neither of which appears likely given the "war fever" (13) gripping the nation. If motivated by Nakazawa's "grudge" against the United States, *Barefoot Gen* supports the notion that the atomic bombings were inevitable—actions that, however understandable in their moment, should never be repeated.

Commenting that hibakusha literature is remarkably free of blame toward the United States, Schwenger and Treat remind us that "speaking of America's 'Hiroshima' and Hiroshima's 'America' cannot ever mean speaking in compensatorily balanced equivalencies. As the target of nuclear war, and then as client state and proxy, the Japanese have never been as free to construe 'America' as vice versa" (329). Rarely overtly depicted, U.S. postwar dominance informs *Barefoot Gen*'s compulsion toward anachronism. The manga participates in "backshadowing" or "retroactive foreshadowing" of past events.[57] In this tale of atomic annihilation, Gen and his brother Shinji's speculative remarks about the future demand retroactive reading. His hands clenched in animated fists, Shinji declares, "I sure don't want Papa and Mama to get killed by a **bomb!**" (178). Yet it is this fate that conditions every moment leading to the blast. Through what might be called *flashforwarding*, Nakazawa's Hiroshima thus appears to assent to its fate in advance. Unmoved by the "people at the **top**" who attempt to brainwash the people into believing "that Americans and British are **demons**" (73), a handful of dissenting residents, the Nakaokas and the Korean Mr. Pak among them, represent prime material out of which future transpacific citizens in a U.S. sphere of influence might be salvaged. To his sons' incredulous queries, "You mean Japan's **not sacred** and the **Emperor's not God** and we're **not** going to receive **help** from the gods to win the war?" Mr. Nakaoka sets the record straight: "Even the schools, newspapers, radio stations, police, and the army of Japan today are under **control** of a military dictator. They're teaching you **lies**"—and here the narrative flash-forwards: "When the military grasps hold of **political power**, the world enters a dreadful darkness" (74). Despairing at the leaders who wield "military and police power to repress the growing dissatisfaction of the people," Mrs. Nakaoka ominously echoes her husband's views: "If **this** is what Japan is, it might as well be **wiped out!**" (176). Identifying the "people at the **top**"—the "**monsters** who started the war"—as the true victimizers of the Japanese people who bear "the blood of hundreds of thousands on their hands" (179), *Barefoot Gen* enables a flash-forward reading of Hiroshima's leveling as a necessary evil.

Liberated from the clutch of Japanese militarism, the pacifically inclined citizens of the new Japan were urged to assign democratic propulsion to the atomic bombings. The imprint of this postwar ideology can be discerned in the emplotment of Nakazawa's hibakusha tale. Opening with Mr. Nakaoka's lesson to his sons about "trampled wheat [that] sends strong roots into the earth, endures frost, wind, and snow, grows straight and tall . . . and one day bears fruit" (1), *Barefoot Gen* strains to realize the metaphor's naturalistic promise. As the manga's personification of a wheat-like ideal, Gen symbolizes the possibility of postnuclear rebirth. This theme of the child whose survival bespeaks the democratizing promise of "Little Boy" was vital to the Pax Americana portrait of nuclear ruins rehabilitated under U.S. guidance. Even as Nakazawa's manga dwells on the horror of the bomb, his survivor-protagonist gives the tale its resolute forward momentum. Hibakusha, as "deformed reminders of a miserable past," may not have been welcomed as "compatriots in the new Japan" (Dower, 128), but Gen represents less a war remainder than life sprung from irradiated ashes—in Nakazawa's words, "a root or source of strength for a new generation of mankind."

The Target and the Proving Ground

On March 1, 1954, the United States detonated a hydrogen bomb, Castle Bravo, at Bikini Atoll in the Marshall Islands. Castle Bravo's TNT-effect was one thousand times greater than the magnitude of the atomic bombs the United States dropped on Hiroshima and Nagasaki, yet the Bravo shot occurred outside war's parameters, and the Marshallese, previously colonized by Imperial Japan, were not a U.S. foe. In a late-war State Department blueprint anticipating U.S. trusteeship after Japan's defeat, the United States pointedly recognized that the "Islands clearly cannot be treated as conquered enemy territory."[58] In 1946, the year prior to its trusteeship, however, it commenced a series of devastating nuclear tests in Marshallese territory. Thereafter, for the duration of the Cold War, the Marshall Islands would be aligned under the U.S. nuclear umbrella in the sacrificial role of proving ground. Under the cover of the proving grounds concept, the United States zoned the Marshall Islands for death. As Robert Barclay writes in *Melal*, a novel about the U.S. nuclearization of the islands: "Death ruled the ocean. The ocean itself was not a dead thing, . . . but the life in it existed only as a byproduct of death."[59] In the Cold War nuclear Pacific, U.S. war power reached the dystopian limits of its necrocapitalist potential and in so doing bared its truth. It did not explode, harm, and kill in order eventually to make live. It did not rebuild from the ashes, did not opportunistically "grab hold of 'the terrible barrenness' . . . [to] fill it with the most perfect, beautiful plans" (Klein). It did not produce value in any conventional sense. Instead, it destroyed to destroy. Its product was death.

Tellingly, although weather reports before the Bravo blast indicated that Rongelap, Rongerik, and Utirik would be in the direction of radioactive fallout, the U.S. military did not evacuate the islanders for three days. In the ensuing decades the Rongelapese would find themselves transformed into permanent nuclear refugees, exiled from their ancestral home. Unbeknownst to them on March 1, 1954, they had already—since November of 1953—been designated by the U.S. national security state as human radiation test subjects.[60] Neisan Laukon, niece of John Anjain, Rongelap magistrate at the time, has recounted what he witnessed.[61] On the first day of the blast, having risen early to fish, he saw a bright light west of the atoll. The colors were extraordinary: yellow, green, blue, red. A gust of wind followed so powerful that people staggered. A smoke cloud then reached upward, booming louder than thunder. After the sound subsided, people resumed their activities, even though the sky was now strangely white. As they were catching fish, cooking, eating coconut, and sitting on the beach, powder began to fall, coating everything like snow. The next day, the water had turned yellow. A seaplane from Eniwetok arrived to survey the scene, staying under ten minutes and communicating nothing. For three days the people remained, consuming water and food. Their hair began falling out in clumps. Their skin displayed burn patterns. On the third day a plane and a ship finally arrived. The people were stripped naked and hosed down before being evacuated to Kwajalein.[62] As Anjain later stated of the Bravo blast: "That was the beginning of our demise."[63]

There were significant parallels between late-war U.S. nuclear strikes against Japanese civilian hubs and its nuclear violence in the Marshall Islands. If Hiroshima was strategically chosen, as Enola Gay pilot Paul Tibbets publicly admitted, for the purpose of conducting "bomb blast studies . . . on virgin targets" (*Atomic Café*), the Marshall Islands were also a "virgin target," albeit of a different kind. The colonial whiff of Tibbetts's phrase is worth noting. In contrast to the notion of virgin *territory* in settler-colonial ideologies—namely, inhabited lands imagined as void of people—virgin *targets*, as a designation of sites that could be turned into radioactive waste, did not signal the deterritorializing use of U.S. war power in order to enable the formation of "a new colonial society on the expropriated land base."[64] In the aftermath of nuclear ruination, the goal was not "land as [settler] life" (Wolfe, 387), nor was irradiated terrain envisioned as recoverable for conventional use. Rather, as its Cold War nuclear tests grew dirtier and more apocalyptic, the United States abandoned the quaint transwar fiction of atomic ruins as the basis of capitalist futurity. With no nonmilitary interests in the Marshall Islands, the United States left infamously unrehabilitated those areas it devastated.[65] What the media has referred to as the "nuclear coffin" on Runit Island, leaking plutonium-239 into the Pacific, is testament to the fact that the United States never finalized a solution for the storage of the radioactive waste it generated in the Marshall Islands.[66] Rather, it envisioned the islands solely through the crosshairs of its war machine. Indeed, to this day Kwajalein continues to serve as an ICBM test site for Vandenberg Air Force Base.

Roughly two months after the Bravo blast, in one of their earliest appeals to the world's conscience, the Marshallese lodged an April 20, 1954, complaint with the UN Trusteeship Council, seeking to counter the framing of their land as a virgin target: "*Land means a great deal to the Marshallese. It means more than just a place where you can plant your food crops and build your houses; or a place where you can bury your dead. It is the very life of the people. Take away their land and their spirits go.*"[67] The United States responded by arguing the value of Marshallese territory in Cold War strategic terms. It maintained that the 1947 UN designation of the islands as a "strategic trust territory" under U.S. administrative control implied its right to poison and to destroy Marshallese lands and oceans: *"from the outset, it was clear that the right to close areas for security reasons anticipated closing them for atomic tests"* (quoted in Johnston and Barker, *Consequential Damages*, 18 [italics in original]). The U.S. destructive right to enclose Marshallese lands and waters for death prevailed. To dispel any doubts, the United States, in the November 22, 1956, "Agreement in Principle Regarding the Use of Bikini Atoll," reaffirmed its militarized property right: "in order for the Trust Territory of the Pacific Islands to play its part in the maintenance of international peace and security it became necessary for the United States of America, the administrating authority for the said Trust Territory, to occupy and use, with the consent of the inhabitants, all of the atoll of Bikini located in the Marshall Islands . . . , thus depriving the owners of the use of said atoll."[68] Although the United States conducted its first nuclear test on the Marshall Islands in 1946, prior to assuming trusteeship, it exploited the "strategic trust" concept to develop its arsenal of weapons of mass destruction, disregarding Marshallese rights to their lands and ocean to sustain life. As Kimie Hara observes, "'Strategic trust' differed from other trusteeships, in that it allowed the administering authority to fortify and close any parts of the strategic area for 'security reasons.' The trusteeship agreement could not be altered or terminated without the administering authority's consent."[69]

The U.S. appropriation of the Marshall Islands for destructive use compels us to consider wartime targets and "peacetime" proving grounds along comparative lines. If the target signals the breachability of enemy sovereignty, the proving ground implies the domestic dependent nation's suspended sovereignty. These twinned concepts, both of which authorize the securitized enclosure of terrain and life for the purpose of destruction, prompt us to inquire into the logic of property specific to U.S. nuclear militarism's deterritorializing operations. We might retrieve Cheryl Harris's notion of property, "a delegation of sovereign power," to examine how the United States wielded the possessive right to destroy against wartime Asian enemy and peacetime indigenous ally alike.[70] From 1947 until it joined the Partial Test Ban Treaty in 1963, the United States enclosed the Marshall Islands as the principal site of its Pacific Proving Grounds, a vast oceanic nuclear testing arena it exploited with abandon. As Hara argues, "the greatest significance of the trusteeship was probably that it prevented enemies from using these islands' strategic potential. The general public, including Americans, were not allowed to visit the islands, and inhabitants' travel overseas was also restricted." If absorbed under the Department of the Interior and thereby "foreign in a domestic sense," the islands were off-limits.[71] Even though Operation Crossroads, the first U.S. nuclear test in the Marshall Islands in 1946, was, according to the Atomic Energy Commission (AEC), a "festive occasion attended by invited guests from many nations and a vast corps of reporters," the fanfare attending this "demonstration of the power of nuclear weapons" was specifically aimed at securing U.S. influence at an upcoming UN conference on atomic energy.[72] That this test rendered Bikini Atoll uninhabitable, transforming Bikinians into refugees, did not dampen U.S. resolve to maximize its use of the Marshall Islands. Rather, from 1946 to 1958, when the United States detonated the equivalent of 1.7 Hiroshimas and Nagasakis per day in the islands, this "virgin target" remained largely out of sight and out of mind of the American public.

Although the scale of U.S. nuclear destruction varied, the neologism *virgin target* implied both continuum with and contrast to the Four Corners region of the United States where it carried out the Trinity test a month prior to the Hiroshima and Nagasaki blasts. As a boundary-blurring total war waged by the United States on multiple fronts, World War II recalled U.S. war power's originary role in the deterritorialization of native sovereignty. Total war provided the rationale for securitizing native land, both for its uranium deposits and as the testing ground for the world's first nuclear detonation. Of the U.S. military's status as "one of the largest landowners in the United States," Winona LaDuke notes that "as weapons became more lethal—as harmful to those manufacturing, handling or storing these materials as they would be against an enemy—access to more isolated lands became a major military priority."[73] The government's seizure of public lands through emergency war powers in World War II—in essence, indigenous lands "withdrawn from the public domain and put under the control of military interests" for a spectrum of purposes, all contaminating in their effects—was a key first step in the launch of the journey of the atom in the Pacific as an arena of U.S. nuclear dominion.[74] The lands of the Diné, Pueblo, and Apache peoples would be mined for uranium, and they would be exploited as cheap disposable labor. The atom's destructive itinerary thus linked indigenous peoples and lands in the United States to the atomic ruination of Hiroshima and Nagasaki and the protracted nuclear horror perpetrated in the Marshall Islands—in effect, creating "an archipelago of contaminated sites."[75] In this way the bomb's sovereignty-asserting and -destroying capacity penetrated the peoples, atmospheres, and terrain of each node of the nuclear Pacific in world-altering ways.

Tellingly, each leg of the atom's crisscrossing journey across the Pacific marked a destructive advance in U.S. nuclear weapons research and development.[76] Unresolved "questions" from prior tests were "answered" in studies conducted at subsequent testing sites. In this regard nuclear war should be understood as a practice "perfected by Cold Warriors" (Johnston and Barker, *Consequential Damages*, 15). Their drive for lethal knowledge turned on the yoked function of the American Southwest, Hiroshima and Nagasaki, and the Marshall Islands as the apocalyptic underside to the American good life. Despite the fact that an estimated nineteen thousand people lived in a fifty-mile radius of the Trinity site in New Mexico, the U.S. government heedlessly viewed the surrounding region as vacant terrain, *terra nullius*, even in advance of the detonation. Only by denying the presence of native peoples could the government construe New Mexico's Jornado del Muerto Valley (now White Sands Missile Range) as a "virgin target."[77] Yet in subscribing to its own self-serving fiction of empty land, it missed a strategic opportunity to capitalize on the blast's biomedical value. As journalist Tanya Lee writes, the July 16, 1945, Trinity test generated considerable fallout: "both American Indian and government witnesses describe a light ash that rained down for four or five days. . . . It went everywhere—onto people's clothes and bodies and into their homes, into the cisterns they used to collect rainwater for drinking, on the crops they would feed their families, on the forage their animals would consume, and into the watershed from which the animals they hunted drank." Despite evidence pointing to the sizable radiation field created by the Trinity shot, the test lacked the extensive human-subject research component of radiogenic studies undertaken by the ABCC, AEC, and Department of Defense following U.S. nuclear detonations in Japan and the Marshall Islands.[78] Precisely because no such studies were pursued, indigenous communities harmed by Trinity's fallout have still not been recognized under the Radiation Exposure Compensation Act.

Most critically, the Trinity test left unaddressed U.S. nuclear technology's efficiency in actual war settings. It was therefore no coincidence that the U.S. military chose civilian sites for its nuclear strikes against Japan, interpreting Hiroshima and Nagasaki along total-war lines not just as targets to be destroyed but also, according to Tibbetts, as "a classroom experiment as far as being able to determine later the bomb damage." For U.S. war planners, these two cities were "virgin targets" precisely because they were densely populated and therefore "far more susceptible to demonstrating the upper ranges of the bomb's spectacular potential" (Chow, 27). Intimating more than that they had not yet been subjected to aerial bombing, "virgin targets," in application to urban civilian sites, suggested the violent conflation of land and people—at once inhabited terrain and sited life—whose strategic value resided in their capacity to be reduced to irradiated ashes or to survive with radiation sickness and in either case thereafter be subjected to scientific scrutiny.

Notwithstanding local speculation that "the soil on which Hiroshima stood would remain uninhabitable for one or two generations" (Jungk, 39), neither of the two atomic bombings of Japan resulted in sustained fallout. In his February 24, 1994, testimony before Congress on the secret human radiation experiments conducted on the Marshallese, Merril Eisenbud—director of the Health and Safety Laboratory (HASL) of the AEC, the federal agency that funded such experiments during the Cold War—argued that "data from the Japanese experience was much more meaningful" than that culled from the tests in the Marshall Islands "because the numbers of people were very much larger" (137).[79] Yet what distinguished the human radiation data retrieved following the Marshallese tests and made those tests so valuable was, he stated, fallout. Indeed, fallout's lingering impact prompted "reconceptualization of the atomic bomb—from a weapon that explodes and incinerates to a new tool in the chemical weapons arsenal" (Johnston, "More Like Us," 31). As legal counsel for the Bikinians, Jonathan Weisgall, asserted in the same hearing, U.S. nuclear tests in the Marshall Islands introduced "a weapon of terror called radioactive fallout that was really designed more for genocide than any kind of military purpose" (Weisgall, 12). It was precisely the U.S. government's anticipation of fallout's catastrophic perdurance, moreover, that governed its decision to test high-yield nuclear weapons not in Nevada but in the Marshall Islands. If unspectacular in its violence, the aftereffect of its high-yield tests was ineradicable radiation that contaminated the food chain, thereby providing "government scientists with the research opportunity to significantly expand their understanding of bioaccumulation and environmental sources of exposure in human beings" (Barker, *Bravo for the Marshallese*, 64) across generations. Central to U.S. government studies of fallout's radiogenic effects, the concept of bioaccumulation presumed the indivisibility of the Marshallese with the land, ocean, and air of their home. Under the elastic sign of the target, stretched to cover even Cold War allies, the United States thus again lethally conflated people and terrain.

If "life" was to be had in the necropolitical configuration of the nuclear Pacific, it was less native life—whose value resided in its proxy, degradable, and extinguishable function—than those distant lives secured, in theory, by this nihilistic pursuit of knowledge. As an epithet for zones of nuclear experimentation in a far-reaching geography of nuclear ruin, virgin targets bespoke an American possessive investment in ruin whose political telos cannot be assumed to be democracy. Robert Underwood, then-Guam delegate to the U.S. House of Representatives, stated the obvious during the same 1994 congressional hearing: "Human radiation testing sounds incongruous for democracy at best."[80] Little Boy, the relatively simple uranium bomb dropped on Hiroshima; Fat Man, the more complex plutonium bomb used on Nagasaki; Able and Baker, the atmospheric and submarine devices exploded in Bikini Atoll; and Bravo, the first of many hydrogen bombs detonated in the Marshall Islands—these progressively more catastrophic tests and their corresponding human studies have a key place in an undertold tale of American nuclear colonialism.

Yet this history also demands contextualization against the U.S. recuperation of the fascist science of vanquished Axis powers. Nuclearization, Haunani-Kay Trask reminds us, is "a unique kind of racism," "the kind that produced famous Nazi doctors and forced sterilization of Indian women in America" ("The Color of Violence," 13). Harnessed toward life that mattered, lives subjected to Cold War experimental predation were sacrificial lives; their value resided in their capacity to demonstrate the lethal efficacy of U.S. nuclear weapons technology. For comparison we might consider Yuki Tanaka's analysis of the notorious "Maruta" project of the Japanese Imperial Army's Unit 731, which performed germ warfare research in northeast China, reducing thousands of people, most of them local Chinese, to *maruta* (logs): "Maruta were no longer human beings but a means to the end of gaining knowledge. That knowledge was supposed to help save the lives of Japanese people. In sum, there was the conviction that *valuable lives* saved outweighed any concern that *worthless lives* might be lost—a conviction that made the process seem thoroughly justifiable. This, of course, means that the willingness to dispose of certain lives did, in fact, coexist with the desire to save the lives of others."[81] Rarely, however, are U.S. nuclear weapons and human-radiation research understood in relation to the amnesty the United States granted Nazi and Japanese scientists whose findings it recuperated. Yet throughout the Cold War the United States rationalized, in the name of national security, the subjection of "worthless lives" and lands to its war machine's imperatives. In the wake of the Castle Bravo test, AEC chair Lewis Strauss summarized its benefits to the United States as a global war power: "An enormous potential has been added to our military posture by what we have learned."[82] Even while conventionally historicized apart, this alienated, annihilationist dynamic, set in motion by the United States toward civilian populations in Asia and the Pacific, is impossible to distinguish from that put into play by early twentieth-century fascist science toward subject or marginalized peoples.

U.S. nuclear colonialism's profound racism animated the universalizing logic of sameness as much as it did the logic of difference. Documenting the arrival of Rongelapese in the United States for biomedical study, 1957 U.S. newsreel footage described John Anjain as "a savage, but a happy, amenable savage," whose "first visit to the white man's country meant the iron room."[83] Depicting the Rongelap men as tourists from a place "where hardly anybody lives," the voice-over narration emphasized the warm hospitality with which the islanders, clad in borrowed suits, had been received in the United States. In the recollection of one of their American medical examiners, "They were . . . awe-struck by the towering buildings" and "grateful" for the chance to relay "tales of their adventures to their fellow islanders."[84] Yet the underside of this story of a wide-eyed Marshallese encounter with American modernity lurked in communiqués in which U.S. researchers discussed the scientific bonanza of returning the Rongelapese to their home, "by far the most contaminated place on Earth" (Eisenbud, quoted in Johnston, "More Like Us," 25): "The habitation of these people on the island will afford most valuable ecological radiation data on human beings."[85] This mid-1950s window signaled a shift from early genetic studies in which fruit flies and mice had served as test subjects to human-population studies involving the Marshallese.[86] In an internal 1956 memorandum, HASL director Eisenbud noted the value of human uptake data extracted from the Rongelapese for American lives: "While it is true that these people do not live . . . the way Westerners do, civilized people, it is nevertheless true that these people are more like us than mice."[87] U.S. human radiogenic research thus turned on a postulate of near-sameness, with Marshallese bodies deemed analogous to American bodies and therefore model organisms for biomedical study. That the U.S. aim was scientific knowledge at any and all costs was evident in the peripheralization of care that typified these long-range U.S. biomedical studies, some of which extended over three decades.[88] Speaking before the UN, Marshallese foreign minister Tony deBrum described the brutality of U.S. human radiation experiments on the Marshallese: "Some of our people were injected with or coerced to drink fluids laced with radiation. Other experimentation involved the purposeful and premature resettlement of people on islands highly contaminated by weapons tests to study how human beings absorb radiation from their foods and environment" (*Nuclear Savage*). In a context of incessant illness, invasive medical tests, sample collections, and scant treatment, no Marshallese could sustain the illusion that near-likeness meant an assurance of their humanity. As Cold War proxies for American lives, they were even refused access to their own medical records.[89]

In a June 5, 1958, letter to Charles Dunham, head of AEC's biology and medicine division, Robert Conard, lead researcher of Brookhaven's government-sponsored studies of radiation-related illnesses in the Marshallese, commented on the intensification of resentment among the Rongelapese, who believed "we were doing too many examinations, blood tests, etc., which they did not feel necessary, particularly since we did not *treat* many of them."[90] Conard, whose career was founded on annual field excursions to the Marshall Islands, suggested a pacifying tactic: "next trip we should consider giving them more treatment or even placebos." Although the callous contents of Conard's 1958 letter to his colleague Dunham would not surface until the mid-1990s, when it was declassified as part of the Advisory Committee on Human Radiation Experiments documentary trove, the substance of this letter would be addressed in the mid-1970s by the Rongelapese. In an April 9, 1975, public letter to Conard, Rongelap magistrate Nelson Anjain, John Anjain's brother, rebuked the American scientist:

> I realize now that your entire career is based on our illness. We are far more valuable to you than you are to us. You have never really cared about us as a people—only as a group of guinea pigs for your government's bomb research effort. For me and for the other people on Rongelap, it is life which matters most. For you it is facts and figures. There is no question about your technical competence, but we often wonder about your humanity. We don't need you and your technological machinery. We want our life and our health. We want to be free.[91]

Anjain continued: "we do not want to see you again. We want medical care from doctors who care about us, not about collecting information for the U.S. government's war makers.... So we're going to invite doctors from hospitals in Hiroshima to examine us in a caring way." Three decades after the U.S. atomic bombings of Hiroshima and Nagasaki inaugurated the Cold War and a little more than two decades after U.S. thermonuclear testing forced the Rongelapese into permanent exile, the inhabitants of the wartime target and the peacetime proving ground—two nodes of the nuclear Pacific—sought to move together toward the possibility of life.

Radiogenic Solidarity

In Leslie Marmon Silko's *Ceremony* Tayo, an American Indian veteran, returns from the Pacific theater to the Laguna Pueblo reservation sick with war-fever. In flashbacks, the Japanese POWs whom his sergeant ordered his men to kill morph into his uncle Josiah. When his childhood friend and fellow soldier Rocky forces him to focus on a corpse, stating "'Tayo, this is a *Jap*! This is a *Jap* uniform!'" Tayo begins screaming because "it wasn't a Jap, it was Josiah" (7). As Tayo later maintains to the medicine man Old Betonie, Josiah, albeit "thousands of miles away, at home in Laguna . . . was there with those Japanese soldiers who died" (114) in the Philippines. In a novel that dwells on the links between uranium excavation in the Four Corners to "dismembered corpses and atomic heat-flash outlines" (34) in Japan, the nodes of the nuclear Pacific brutally converge, defying conventional limits of time and space. "White warfare," which "kill[s] across great distances without knowing who or how many had died" (33), disrupts the world's intricate web of interconnections. Evidence of this technologically alienated way of delivering death is on display in "target areas," monstrous enclosures of ruin where the dead, killed from afar, are scattered in fusion with "fallen jungle trees and muddy craters of torn earth" (33). Such warfare both perceives and renders the world dead:

> *When they look*
> *they see only objects.*
> *The world is a dead thing for them*
> *the trees and rivers are not alive*
> *the mountains and stones are not alive.*
> *The deer and bear are objects*
> *They see no life.* (125)

Yet Tayo understands that the *here* and *there* put into brutal motion by the destroyers who took "beautiful rocks from deep within earth . . . [laying] them in a monstrous design, realizing destruction on a scale only they could have dreamed," have "no boundaries" (129) in another important sense. Within a world torn asunder by white warfare, "human beings were one clan again, united by the fate the destroyers planned for all of them, for all living things united in a circle of death that devoured people in cities twelve thousand miles away, victims who had never known these mesas, who had never seen the delicate colors of the rocks which boiled up their slaughter" (128). Enclosed within "a circle of death" and condemned to premature death, the inhabitants of Japanese cities "twelve thousand miles away" and the peoples of the mesas whose extracted "rocks . . . boiled up their slaughter" are thereby "united." Against the deterritorializing logic that divides objects of settler colonial conquest from those of military-imperial defeat—American Indian from Japanese—placing them in lethal relations of enmity, Betonie discerns a connection suggestive of the shared possibility of life: "The Japanese . . . You saw who they were. . . . They were not strangers" (114–15).

This theme of misprision or conflation revealed to be unities, latent ties, and solidarities surfaces in other indigenous North American writing about the nuclear Pacific. In *Burning Vision* Métis playwright Marie Clements recounts a Dene seer's late 1880s prophecy: the "people they dropped this burning on . . . looked like us, like Dene."[92] Little Boy, her personification of uranium extracted from First Nations land as a native boy, states, "I want to go home," while the converging rhythm of "*Dene and Japanese drums submerg[es] in and out of the static of propaganda, the sound score of Western civilization*" (65). In an opening time line, Clements presents the mass incarceration of Japanese Canadians and the U.S. government order of sixty tons of Port Radium ore alongside the atomic bombings of Japan as linked events in the seer's burning vision. Although Dene miners who hauled the uranium that went into Little Boy suffered lethal radiation exposure, in 1998 a group of Dene elders traveled to Hiroshima to express remorse for the role they played.[93] In a play in which Fat Man, an "American test-dummy who man[s] his house," apologizes only when bombs hit close to home, the Japanese American Rose, whom he calls an "ungrateful alien," wryly notes the uneven geopolitics behind expressions of contrition: "Americans are Americans and everybody else is sorry": "Let's be honest, . . . you can't even apologize for the shit you did yesterday never mind fifty years ago. Indian residential schools, Japanese internment camps, hell, and this is just in your neighborhood" (1, 90–91).[94] In contrast to Fat Man's self-serving apologies, the dynamic between Dene and Japanese characters, as casualties of U.S. nuclear violence, is uncharted and supple. In the seer's songs, "children of incineration," "shadows of the dead," and "white bones of an empire war," to borrow Gerald Vizenor's language, engage in exploratory exchanges and musings.[95] Of Koji, the Japanese fisherman whose radiation-charred body lies beneath a cherry tree, the Dene widow of an ore miner asks, "Indian?" only for Rose to respond, "Indian enough from the other side" (96).

In the cultural archive of the nuclear Pacific, uncanny moments of recognition between and among American Indians, First Nations peoples, the Japanese, and the Marshallese bespeak the conjuncture of geographically far-flung radiogenic communities.[96] Harnessed in varying ways to the U.S. war machine's lethal operations, these miners, downwinders, hibakusha, radiation test subjects, and nuclear refugees have been cast in a world-historical tragedy with apocalyptic implications. They converge in vulnerability as "marginal and powerless groups in society" (Johnston, "Half-Lives, Half-Truths," 6). Yet by dint of direct experience, these "seasoned veterans of the nuclear era" possess "a more sophisticated understanding of the risks associated with nuclear science and technology than most Americans."[97] That uranium for Little Boy was derived chiefly from the Congo in addition to Dene, Diné, and Pueblo lands has brought Japanese and indigenous activists together in shared antinuclear cause within what Sasha Davis has called "networks of affinity."[98] In her poem "America Comes Out as the World's Top in Anything," Kurihara Sadako describes the power potential of unity on the underside of U.S. nuclear hegemony. If Kikkawa was Hiroshima's "Number One Atomic Bomb Sufferer" according to his ABCC designation, Lekoj Anjain, John Anjain's leukemia-afflicted son, was Rongelap's "Number One Hydrogen Bomb Sufferer" according to his tombstone. Kurihara describes the longing of Lekoj—transferred from a hospital in Hawai'i to another in Washington, DC—to return to "my dear Island." Of this "son" of the Marshall Islands, whose "life was sacrificed / As a guinea pig for nuclear testing," Kurihara concludes:

> Hiroshima, Nagasaki, and Bikini will one day
> Flow backward
> Across the [P]acific Ocean
> To become a massive surge of flame,
> Joining together with Nevada and Three-mile Island—
> So that together
> They may burn aflame
> As one
> In America.[99]

In 2015, on the seventieth anniversary of the U.S. bombing of Hiroshima and Nagasaki, Japanese, American Indian, and American antinuclear activists organized a Non-proliferation Treaty Peace Walk for a Nuclear-Free Future that began in Oakland, California, and ended at the United Nations. The impact of nuclearization, organizers made plain, was "not just on the residents of [Hiroshima and Nagasaki] but on places and people where the uranium was mined, the bombs tested, the waste stored."[100] Reflective of the far-reaching coordinates of the nuclear chain, the itinerary thus included stops at Diablo Canyon Nuclear Power Plant, which "stands on the sacred sites of the Chumash Tribe," the Nevada Test Site "on the lands of the Western Shoshone tribe," Diné and Hopi lands where uranium was extracted, and the West Valley nuclear dumping grounds that threaten "the land and people of the Seneca Nation." As these organizers vivified in practice, analysis of U.S. nuclear militarism calls for understanding how the U.S. war machine has created death zones not only in theaters of war but also within the flexible parameters of the settler-colonial state.

On June 8, 1957, three years after the Bravo test, the United States returned the Rongelapese to their atoll, proclaiming it safe for habitation despite knowing it had become a site of slow death, disability, and horror. For the next twenty-eight years the Rongelapese consumed contaminated water and food while U.S.-commissioned scientists studied their radioactive uptake. In this era of return, Rongelapese women describe birthing jellyfish, grape, turtle, and two-headed babies. The miscarriage rate was abnormally high and thyroid cancer endemic. Lijon Eknilang recounts: "When people in those years died on Rongelap, a seaplane would come and take the body away to Kwajalein to check it. My great-grandmother died and they came and cut her open and took her kidney, parts of her body and skin, and put it in a bottle. They took body samples and left her like an animal under a breadfruit tree. They treated her like an animal, like a dead animal" (*Nuclear Savage*).

By 1970, however, problems, as Conard recalled in his memoir, had "developed from an unexpected quarter: Japan" (38). According to Conard, the 1970s proved to be a "troublesome" decade for U.S. biomedical research teams because "Japanese anti-A and H-bomb groups became involved with the Marshallese politicians in criticizing the way the fallout victims were being handled" (45). Japanese antinukes activists invited Ataji Balos, the Micronesian congressional delegate for the Rongelap and Utirik peoples, to an August 1971 nuclear-bomb-testing symposium, in which John Anjain also took part. While there, Balos invited a team of Japanese reporters, a photographer, and doctors to carry out a fact-finding mission on Rongelap, only for the United States to deny them entry, leading to a firestorm of Marshallese criticism of unilateral U.S. authority.[101] Despite U.S. measures to thwart these transpacific antinuclear alliances, Rongelapese suspicions about the acute radioactivity of their atoll did not abate. In May of 1985, bypassing the U.S. refusal to evacuate them, the islanders called in Greenpeace to relocate them to Mejatto and Ebeye, an overcrowded ghetto where many still live.

In *Melal*, Noniep, a Marshallese helping spirit, "dreams of the legion of demons . . . feverishly intent in the service of their masters in wringing death from life, on replacing everything pure and natural and pleasurable with stinking rot and ruin, a living death" (14). In this *melal*, or "playground of demons," peace is "*the display of power to destroy mankind*" (283, 1 [emphasis in original]). As Julian Aguon, Chamoru legal counsel for the Marshallese people, has pointed out, "the sales pitch from the powerful" is that the "building up of armies, munitions, and weapons of mass destruction [will] lead to peace."[102] Against this demonic logic, the peoples of Japan, Okinawa, Korea, the Philippines, Guam, the Marshall Islands, and Hawai'i—all sites critical to the U.S. garrison state in the Pacific—must, he contends, expel the "US military presence from all our homes" (69). In the nuclear Pacific, where the Enola Gay flew from Tinian to Hiroshima in August of 1945; where the United States began conducting high-yield nuclear tests on the Marshall Islands just one year into the postwar "peace"; where the United States in its interventionist war in Korea contemplated creating a cobalt zone between North Korea and China where no life could live for a hundred years; where U.S. stealth bombers capable of carrying out nuclear strikes on North Korea are stationed on Guam; where ICBMs are routinely launched at Kwajalein Atoll from California; where the United States conducts the world's largest war exercises with regional allies that include dropping dummy nuclear munitions; and where nuclear aircraft carriers serve as mobile bases that encircle China—radiogenic solidarity is "not our best bet. It is our only one" (Aguon, 28).

5 People's War, People's Democracy, People's Epic
Carlos Bulosan, U.S. Counterintelligence, and Cold War Unreliable Narration

Words as Weapons

In "The Guerrilla Is like a Poet" (1968) Jose Maria Sison, founder of the Communist Party of the Philippines (CPP) in its Maoist reorganization and the New People's Army (NPA), the CPP's armed wing, famously likened guerrilla warfare tactics to poetics. One of the most celebrated works to emerge from the cultural front of the twentieth-century Philippine revolutionary struggle for democracy and national liberation, Sison's Vietnam War–era poem invokes what might be called a hermeneutics of counterinsurgency. It plays cannily to the militarized optics of asymmetrical warfare to confound the enemy's alienated practices of reading both the "people's war" and the "people's epic." Like the poet, the guerrilla plays on likeness, proximity, interchangeability. Whereas both anticipate interpretation, the guerrilla alone stages the world as a text whose elusive meanings tantalize from under the local environment's contours. More than draw sustenance from and seek refuge in the natural world, the guerrilla, the poem suggests, *is* nature. This visceral enactment of metaphor, the guerrilla's material unity with the milieu, bedevils counterinsurgent interpretation, catalyzing the war machine's total violence. From the view of the "armed eye," the human factor of the people's war cannot be distinguished from native terrain:

> He has merged with the trees
> The bushes and the rocks
> Ambiguous but precise
> Well-versed on the law of motion
> And master of myriad images.

Hidden in plain sight,

> He moves with the green brown multitude
> In bush burning with red flowers

> That crown and hearten all
> Swarming the terrain as a flood.¹

Wise to the "subtle rhythm of the greenery," its cloaked "inner silence" and "outer innocence," the guerrilla manipulates perception in ways aimed at "ensnar[ing] . . . the enemy." In what Sison elsewhere refers to as a double-edged "bladed poem," with its "well-versed weapon[s]" and "lea[ves] of steel," he gestures to insurgent lifeworlds and political visions that lurk below the play of surfaces.² If, as Paul Virilio has proposed, the "battlefield has always been a field of perception,"³ this poem implies dynamic movement beneath settled appearances.

The imperial war machine's spatial identification of guerrillas with the terrain they inhabit and social contexts in which they operate—their nativity with the land and "broad foundation in the people"—is the conflation that drives asymmetrical warfare's indiscriminate brutality.⁴ Structurally encoded in weapons of mass destruction, indistinction inheres in the logic of the target and lethal outcomes of area bombing. Not just anonymous and innumerable, the masses constituting the target are identified *as* their location. In the target, fleshly biopolitics and territorial geopolitics thus collide. We might recall Mao's Zedong's naturalistic aphorism: "The populace is for the revolutionaries what water is for the fish."⁵ Confronted with this blur, counterinsurgent violence is lawless, unbounded in its extermination. Arguing the genocidal nature of U.S. war in Vietnam, Jean-Paul Sartre described the Vietnamese as "reduced to the state of a formless mass, to the extremes of *vegetative existence*": "the population is subjected to massive and deliberately murderous bombardments, their cattle are killed, vegetation is ruined by defoliants, crops are sprayed with poisons and destroyed, machine-gunning is indiscriminate."⁶ Through the crosshairs the guerrilla is deemed indistinguishable from plant life, in essence, one and the same as the bushes, trees, and foliage below. Waging total war in sites far from the metropole, the imperial war machine makes superfluous legal distinctions between civilian and combatant, as well as categorical differences between humans and terrain. On the receiving end of all-out violence, the guerrilla discerns an exploitable logic. Indeed, people's war axioms turn on the fungibility of civilians as combatants and humans as terrain. In Eqbal Ahmad's analysis of revolutionary war, "At night, the loyal peasant turns into a guerrilla and all know him as such."⁷

Even when trained in the hermeneutics of counterinsurgency, the counterinsurgent figures as a distant thus bad reader. Confronted with myriad images arising from the "rebel infrastructure," theorists of counterinsurgency "surrender . . . to the pathology of bureaucratic perception" (Ahmad, 3, 38), unable to grasp what moves people to wage revolutionary struggle. Superiority of information and conviction is thus the guerrilla's home advantage. In a 1961 introduction to Mao Zedong's 1937 treatise on guerrilla warfare, retired U.S. Marine Corps brigadier general Samuel B. Griffith, a perceptive observer of the Chinese Civil War, identified intelligence as the "decisive factor" in interpreting "the guerrilla area."[8] Yet he deemed it to be an asset almost everywhere denied the counterinsurgent, who "is enveloped in an impenetrable fog" (23). Of the guerrillas' epistemological advantage in the people's war, Griffith emphasized the *sub-rosa* politicization of guerrilla strongholds, where "every person without exception must be considered an agent—old men and women, boys driving ox carts, girls tending goats, farm laborers, storekeepers, schoolteachers, priests, boatmen, scavengers" (22). In the shadow play of underground total war, the counterinsurgent enemy—conspicuous, outrageously brutal, lacking in political consciousness—"stands as on a lighted stage; from the darkness around him, thousands of unseen eyes intently study his every move, his every gesture. When he strikes out, he hits the air; his antagonists are insubstantial, as intangible as fleeting shadows in the moonlight" (Griffith, 23). Arguing the criticality of deploying guerrilla tactics "against the guerrillas themselves," Griffith, with an eye on Cuba and Vietnam, warned his readers in the U.S. military establishment of the interpretive challenges ahead: "Guerrillas are masters of the arts of simulation and dissimulation; they create pretenses and simultaneously disguise or conceal their true semblance" (33, 26).

In its teasing portrait of the perceptual limits of the Cold War anticommunist war machine, Sison's "The Guerrilla Is like a Poet" focuses on the fleeting traces of guerrillas in the material and social worlds they inhabit. In so doing, the poem underscores the alienation of the shadowboxing enemy, who, while perceived by all, perceives too little. In his poetic meditation on the vulnerabilities of counterrevolutionary modes of perception and interpretation, Sison predicted counterinsurgency doctrine's evolution, in particular its cultural turn. Notoriously tortured while imprisoned under the Marcos dictatorship and subsequently forced into exile in the Netherlands, Sison, in 9/11's wake, would be blacklisted by the U.S. government as a supporter of terrorism because of his ties to the CPP and NPA.[9] Secretary of State Colin Powell strained to justify the CPP and NPA as targets of the "War on Terror," yoking revolutionary violence and terrorism under the rubric of opposition to U.S. militarism: "The CPP, a Maoist group, was founded in 1969 [sic] with the aim of overthrowing the Philippine government through guerilla warfare. CPP's military wing, the New People's Army, strongly opposes any U.S. military presence in the Philippines and has killed U.S. citizens there."[10] Far from a thing of the past, U.S. Cold War anticommunism thus renovated itself under the doctrine of antiterrorism. Sison, exiled poet laureate of the Philippine people's war and long the Philippines' most wanted man, thereby moved into the limelight as U.S. public enemy in the same juncture in which the Pentagon, seeking to "build upon the lessons of Vietnam," implicitly drew on his poem's central insight by identifying interpretation of the foe as counterinsurgent warfare's main task.[11]

Central to the post-9/11 cultural turn in U.S. counterinsurgency doctrine was the idea of human terrain. Popularized by General David Petraeus, this crude portmanteau concept posited occupied peoples as counterinsurgency's "decisive terrain," a topography requiring interpretation "in the same way that we have always studied the geographic terrain."[12] Notwithstanding its genesis in the War on Terror, the idea derived from counterinsurgent conceptions of the "populace, host nation, and insurgents" (FM 3-24, 3-1) specific to Third World revolutions. Mobilizing the services of scholars with "on-the-ground cultural knowledge, linguistic competence, knowledge of local customs, traditional symbols and cultural history," the Pentagon sought to equip its fighting forces, strangers within the contexts to which they were deployed, with "interpretive acumen."[13] Far from humanistic, the knowledge presupposed by human terrain was of the order of intelligence—in Sun Tzu's terms *foreknowledge* or "the gathering of dependable information on the enemy."[14] Generated not for its own sake, this form of actionable knowledge was deployed to neutralize adversaries—to "deterritorialize the enemy" by "shattering his territory from within"—both on the battlefield and in the court of global public opinion.[15] Indeed, in the post-9/11 battle for hearts and minds, the Pentagon defined narrative as an operational arena in which the United States must prevail against unconventional foes. Theorizing terrorism as a "narrative" of insurgents and war as a matter of authorial supremacy, the 2006 U.S. Army/Marine Corps counterinsurgency field manual described narrative as the "most important cultural form for counterinsurgents to understand" (FM 3-24, 93).

That words might function as weapons and narrative serve as a battleground for rival claims to legitimacy has long been axiomatic to revolutionary struggle and counterinsurgency. Addressing the Philippine Congress on October 18, 2003, U.S. President George W. Bush, seeking to rally the Filipino people to his post-9/11 war agenda in the Middle East, hailed the Philippines as a model of democratization whose lessons might be usefully applied to the U.S. "liberation of Iraq."[16] Seeking to secure Filipino participation in the "Coalition of the Willing," he offered up a counterinsurgent tale of U.S. intervention in the Philippines. Framed as a democratizing force, the United States, "proud of its part in the great story of the Filipino people," had ushered in the Philippine's 1946 emergence as Asia's "first democratic nation," or so Bush claimed. He cast back to the Pacific War's late years, pointing to "Corregidor, Leyte, Luzon" as proof of the salutary U.S. role in "liberat[ing] the Philippines from [Japanese] colonial rule." Just as the United States had historically joined forces with the Philippines to defeat Japanese "militarists and fascists" in Asia and the Pacific, so, too, must both nations combine their military might to meet the "new totalitarian threat" of terrorism on the world stage. Unsurprisingly, this speech left to the side, as historian Alfred McCoy has observed, a long and brutal legacy of U.S. pacification and policing in the Philippines that extended back to the Philippine-American War—a sequence of remarkably dirty forgotten wars "marked by clandestine penetration, psychological warfare, disinformation, media manipulation, assassination, and torture" that established a pattern for U.S. interventionist wars to follow.[17]

Rippling below Bush's account of the United States working alongside Filipino allies to free their nation from the fascist yoke of Japanese rule was an insurgent history of the Filipino people's unceasing autochthonous struggle for democracy and national liberation—what Sison calls "the people's epic." Disrupting his narrative of U.S.-fostered democratization in the Philippines was, in other words, a potent counternarrative of people's democracy. Hints of this movement inhered in Powell's allusion to its decades-long resistance to the U.S. military presence in the Philippines. This history of militant revolutionary struggle did not, however, originate in the late 1960s. Rather, the meaning of March 29, 1969, the date the CPP founded the NPA as a "revolutionary army of the broad masses of the Filipino people against U.S. imperialists, the comprador bourgeoisie, the landlord class and the bureaucrat capitalists," drew from a legacy of armed Philippine opposition to U.S. military imperialism going back to the Pacific War, the era Bush would hold out as a shining moment of U.S.-Philippine collaboration.[18] To wit, on March 29, 1942, "in a clearing in the great forest that joins the corners of Pampanga, Tarlac and Nueva Ecija, the Hukbalahap was born."[19] Representing the armed wing of the CPP in its earlier incarnation, the Hukbo ng Bayan Laban sa Hapon (People's Anti-Japanese Army), or the Huks, were "the party's answer to

Japanese fascism in the military field" (Saulo, 30). In invoking Luzon, along with Bataan, Corregidor, and Leyte, as sites of joint U.S.-Philippine wartime heroism, Bush evacuated its significance as the historic bastion of the Huks, a guerrilla area so identified with Hukbalahap governance that international media dubbed it a "state within a state."[20] As Huk commander-in-chief Luis Taruc noted bitterly in his postwar memoir, *Born of the People*, "The credit due to the Hukbalahap for enabling [Central Luzon's liberation] to take place, has never been acknowledged, particularly by the American army" (188).

U.S. counterinsurgency doctrine in the Bush era may have proposed *knowing* U.S. foes in order to neutralize them, yet the United States thrust into the international arena a leader who stood "as on a lighted stage," striking out against antagonists "as intangible as fleeting shadows." In classic counterinsurgent fashion, the Bush administration wielded the rhetoric of terror to justify the U.S. war machine's roving crosshairs. More than "rage after the suspects it named" (Sison and Rosca, 220), it used 9/11 as an elastic justification for the projection of U.S. war and police power worldwide. Broadcasting its aim of "bring[ing] Abu Sayyaf to justice," the Bush administration, flouting the Filipino people's historic victory in closing Clark Air Base and Subic Naval Base, argued the urgency of renewed U.S. military expansion in the Philippines, in effect setting the stage to go after the New People's Army.[21] Lurking behind Bush's pitching of his war agenda were, in other words, the contradictions of postwar Philippines as a "democracy" under foreign domination.[22] Wielding a fork-tongued lexicon of friendship, freedom, liberation, sacrifice, and democracy, counterinsurgency proponents sanction extralegal violence in the form of special forces units, psychological warfare, and political terror.[23] Yet in the Philippines the protracted people's war has generated a vying idiom of popular resistance that demands being read against the hollow terminology of state propaganda. If revolutionary people's war is not synonymous with terrorism in the sense of "the willful and malicious infliction and threat of death and other physical harm on innocent civilians," people's democracy likewise is not "democracy," at least not as Bush wielded the term.[24]

Since the Philippines' emergence, in Bush's words, as "the first democratic nation in Asia," the shadow looming over official democracy discourse has been the unrealized promise of a people's democracy. In its December 26, 1968, "Programme for a People's Democratic Revolution in the Philippines," the CPP spurned "liberal democracy" as neocolonial jargon intended "to deceive the people."²⁵ Palpable in this rejection was bitter awareness of what in fact had arrived under the guise of U.S. liberation in 1946. In Huk leader Taruc's reflection: "As the 'liberation' progressed it became increasingly obvious that what [General Douglas] MacArthur wanted was a return to the status quo, that he was carrying out a colonial policy of an imperialist group" (*Born of the People*, 193). While formally recognizing Philippine independence, the United States, unwilling to cede its economic stranglehold over the nation, insisted on parity rights enabling Americans to own property and to exploit natural resources on par with Filipino citizens. Under the cover of electoral proceedings, it installed, most flagrantly in the office of the president, Filipino collaborators with the Japanese. In a mockery of Philippine national sovereignty, the United States secured extraterritorial military basing rights, transforming the Philippines into a launching pad for its anticommunist counterinsurgencies in the region. Having hitherto regarded the United States as a united-front ally, Taruc described his disillusionment: "The war was over, but the Philippines was still like a huge armed camp. The American army, in many places, outnumbered the Filipino civilians. San Fernando was teeming with American vehicles and GI's. They were a constant reminder that the liberation was like a new occupation" (*Born of the People*, 217). Democracy thus arrived in the Philippines in militarized American form—what journalist Hernando Abaya dubbed "Freedom in a Strait Jacket."²⁶ Far from speaking for or to the Filipino masses, much less its disenfranchised peasant base, it would, "under the shadow of American tanks and machine guns" (Taruc, 198), restore oligarchic interests—foreign capital, the landowning class, the comprador elite—that had exploited the Filipino people prior to the war. "The Americans," Taruc remarked, "had come back not to liberate us but to reclaim us" (206).

Signaling the betrayal of the Huks who had waged a people's war for genuine democracy, the "liberation" of the Philippines transformed their antifascist orientation. In a 1981 statement to the Permanent Peoples' Tribunal on the crimes of U.S. imperialism and white terror of the U.S.-backed Marcos regime, the NPA recalled U.S. perfidy toward its predecessors, the Huks: "the guerrilla forces had already broken the back of the Japanese resistance. Instead of treating the *Hukbalahap* as an ally in the anti-fascist struggle, however, the returning American forces quickly moved to destroy the people's army."²⁷ During the wartime occupation the lines of enmity were clear: the enemies of the people were the Japanese occupiers and those who collaborated with them. The postwar return of Filipino collaborators to power, backed by U.S. military might, however, necessitated reckoning with "the true meaning of imperialism"—namely, the fact that it "was the same, whether Japanese, American, British or Dutch" (Taruc, 206). Captured in a U.S. Army Counter Intelligence Corps (CIC) raid, a June 15, 1947, Huk directive demonstrated the shifting terms of the antifascist people's war, with U.S. imperialists and the collaborationist elite now the enemy: "in their military campaign against us, they employed fascistic terrorism. This resulted in great demoralization not only on the masses, but also to our comrades. . . . There can be no peace as long as there is the enemy that creates trouble."[28] During the war the unitary discourse around democracy may have papered over the contradictions of the tenuous united front between the Huks and the United States. Two years after "liberation," however, this alliance was irreparably fractured, and vying visions and narratives of democracy—one aligned with capital, the other against it—would emerge, both claiming legitimacy. "Our countries are joined by more than a market," Bush stated before the Philippine Congress. "We believe that democracy is the only form of government fully compatible with human dignity." With the CPP and NPA blacklisted as terrorist organizations, thus permissible targets of "preemptive" U.S. violence, Bush's invocation of democracy shimmered with past and present counterinsurgent violence.

Far from the last word on democracy in the Philippines, however, Bush's speech, if situated within the people's epic, amounts to a barbarous footnote. From the Huk archive, we have Taruc's postwar reflection on the Japanese occupation as a time of democratic praxis. As "Central Luzon now echoed with the indiscriminate gunfire of 'liberation,'" Taruc and his Huk comrades "looked back upon forest life under the Japanese with nostalgia, because there we had at least been able to practice democracy and live as free men" (*Born of the People*, 201). If the immediate goal had been to forge a wide anti-Japanese united front, the Huks also erected the infrastructure of a "functioning democracy through the development of people's councils at the grass-roots level" (Saulo, *Communism in the Philippines*, 31). As Taruc noted, "No de-facto government existed on Philippine soil [so] . . . we created one, putting the government into the hands of the people" (*Born of the People*, 116). With the landlords having fled for the war's duration, Central Luzon, although subjected to ceaseless Japanese military offensives, was a second world-of-sorts—a revolutionary democracy within occupied Philippines.[29] Taruc offers this portrait:

> Once fully organized under the BUDC [Barrio United Defense Corps], a barrio was a liberated island in the ocean of invaders and traitors. Within it, once spies

and betrayers had been liquidated, there was absolute unity and cooperation with our armed forces, and the people practiced self-rule, hidden from the eyes of the enemy. In accordance with the demands of a people's war, the BUDC's had three main channels of activity: the most important, aid to the military struggle; second, the development of an economic program that would both supply the army and keep food products from the enemy; and third, the putting forward of new political perspectives for the people that would be a factor in a democratic Philippines at the end of the war. (*Born of the People*, 119–20)

Construed not as a goal on the horizon, people's democracy was realized by the Huks as an organizing principle in their ranks as well as implemented on the ground.

Imperial Justice

In *Born of the People* Taruc described the astonishing turn of events characterizing the U.S. "liberation" of the Philippines. Of the inversion of wartime categories of friend and enemy evident in the late-war period, Taruc, thrown into jail on February 22, 1945, by U.S. military intelligence, wryly remarked that the Americans seemed to have "forgotten the Japanese and considered the Communists their main enemy" (197). Far from embraced as Philippine patriots, the Huks were criminalized as "lawless elements" and hunted down as "dangerous Reds" (196). Taruc incredulously recounted: "For 22 days we sat in an imperialist prison in our own country, which we had fought for three years to free. Outside the 'liberation' was in progress. This was the day of victory for which we had struggled" (198). In the San Fernando jail where the Huk high command was interrogated and held incommunicado, a fellow Huk leader "used a nail to cut a bitter phrase into the wall of his cell: 'Democracy in the hands of the U.S. Army'" (197).

In *All the Conspirators*, Carlos Bulosan's early Cold War tale of the volatile postwar "peace" in the Philippines, Guyo, a local character, advises the American protagonist: "Don't forget: the war may be over but not the terror."[30] For the Huks the war's end did not signal the cessation of fascist brutality. Of the invisible war that arose from the ashes of the liberation, what Taruc described as "the horror, the terror, and the persecution . . . to follow," the Huks were caught off guard, forcibly disarmed, incarcerated, rooted out, massacred: "We trusted the Americans. . . . In our united front frame of mind, we thought of them as allies in a war against a fascist enemy. We had not even considered that our allies themselves would turn to using fascist methods" (Taruc, 190). Blacklisted by the CIC, the front-line political-policing force of the liberation, and subjected to a "mailed fist policy" by the collaborationist Roxas regime while MPs and civilian guards perpetrated gross abuses against the people, including "murder, tortur[e], burning, looting, and rap[e]," the Huks soon came to realize that the Pax Americana was a "peace of slaves" (Taruc, 246, 245).[31] On February 7, 1945, north of Manila in Malolos, "with the full knowledge of the American CIC, the men of [Adonais] Maclang dragged the Huks of Squadron 77 into the courtyard, forced them to dig their graves, and there shot and clubbed them all to death" (Taruc, 191). Instead of being brought to justice for slaughtering 109 Huks, Maclang, on the CIC's orders, was appointed mayor of Malolos.[32]

With the Pacific War drawing to a close, the "ruins of Japan's empire," Tessa Morris-Suzuki states, "were being refashioned into contours determined by the geopolitics of the hot/cold war, but the process was neither instant nor neat, and many lives were caught in the fissures of the shifting tectonic plates."[33] Wartime resistance struggles against Japanese occupation may have eventuated in national autonomy for North Koreans, Indonesians, Chinese, and Vietnamese, thus reshaping the political topography of Asia.[34] Yet for many Asian and Pacific Islander peoples, self-determination was not forthcoming. As Kim Dong-choon, former standing commissioner of South Korea's Truth and Reconciliation Commission, observes: "As part of its efforts to restrain Russia and China from communizing, the United States not only white washed Japan's colonial and war responsibilities, but even upgraded Japan's status to that of a trustful partner in order to maintain hegemony in East Asia."[35] Although 984 Japanese and Japanese colonials were executed for war crimes and 3,419 more received sentences as harsh as life imprisonment in the immediate aftermath of the war, the U.S. recuperation of Japan as its premier Cold War client-state within its expanding military empire meant, for all intents and purposes, Japan's exculpation from its war crimes. In the Pax Americana order, not only was Japan rehabilitated as an anticommunist bulwark, but also, regional collaborators with Imperial Japan were restored to power. Utsumi Aiko points out that this license to erase "memories of colonialism" enabled the postwar Japanese government to avoid "experiencing the pain or sense of loss that should have accompanied postcolonial normalization and reparations."[36] Yet the effect was regional. Bringing to view Japanese imperial training on an entire generation of postwar Asian leaders, Han Suk-jung remarks: "Simply recall the fact that Indonesia's Sukarno and Suharto, Burma's Aung San, and [South Korea's] Park

[Chung Hee] . . . , to name a few, were trained in Japanese schools, military academies, mass organizations or government offices."[37]

The collaborationist elite in the Philippines likewise inherited the newly independent nation, with forty-five collaborators elected to the Philippine Congress. In sharp contrast leftist guerrilla groups that in theory had worked in antifascist league with the United States against Japanese imperialism suddenly found themselves targets of brutal U.S.-backed counterinsurgency campaigns. If, in theory, wartime collaboration with the Japanese meant the "betrayal of the American war effort in general," the postwar "peace" signaled an inversion of this logic.[38] Having entered an upside-down postwar world, Hassim, a Huk character in Bulosan's novel *The Cry and the Dedication*, asks in bewilderment, "Where is the peace? . . . The real freedom? The equality among men? The democratic ideal?" (223). In his 1949 memoir Taruc describes how this profound betrayal impelled the Hukbalahap to return to arms: "The plain below changes hands at night; in the daytime, it is an oppressed area, ruled by MP's and civilian guards, but when night falls it becomes a liberated region, where the people receive our soldiers with open arms" (280). Central Luzon was once again transformed into an arena of fierce guerrilla war, only this time against U.S.-backed forces.[39] Driven by U.S. national security imperatives, the Cold War containment system in the Philippines gave rise to a sustained period of counterinsurgent reaction that might be viewed as a "long twilight war."[40]

For U.S. client-states in Asia and the Pacific, independent in name alone, the anticommunist "peace that [was] no peace" delayed the decolonization process.[41] Shaped not by rule of law but by rule without law, as militarism must be understood, the region was reconfigured according to what critics have dubbed "victor's justice."[42] Conjuring the pre-1945 colonial mapping of Asia and the Pacific, the International Military Tribunal for the Far East (IMTFE) allowed imperial powers-cum-Allied victors to present separate indictments against Japan. Neglecting the atrocities Japan had perpetrated against Asian and Pacific Islander civilian populations and turning a blind eye to those committed by the United States against civilian populations in Japan, these U.S.-dominated trials delivered a strategic "justice" that, far from being postcolonial in nature, reinforced European and U.S. imperial interests in the region. By leaving the U.S. atomic bombings of Japan unaddressed, thereby building U.S. immunity from war crimes into the postwar order, they anticipated what Mark Selden has referred to as U.S. "security imperialism."[43] Moreover, by overlooking the grievances of colonized peoples, the "other Nuremberg," as the IMTFE has been called,[44] sanctioned a realpolitik in which collusion with the U.S. war machine emerged as the central avenue of economic reconstruction for regional allies, thus leaving suspended the matter of justice—and, with it, decolonization. Within U.S. military empire, the peoples of the region would thus be harnessed to U.S. military imperatives, instrumentally construed as "objects of policy" (Ahmad, 41) rather than sovereign subjects.

In *Asia as Method* Taiwanese scholar Kuan-Hsing Chen argues a complex geopolitical truth with regard to "postwar" Asia: "third-world decolonization has not unfolded as it could have because deimperialization movements did not take place in the homelands of the former empires."[45] As history-grappling processes of moving forward, decolonization and deimperialization require, he states, dynamic mutuality. Yet because empires, both past and present, "have not actively thought through the history of their imperialism," their reckoning with "living historical issues in the former colonies" (200) is limited. They, moreover, have little cause to undertake the implosive task of historical self-reflection, much less to initiate redress or to accept prosecution for their crimes. In Chen's prescription the Third World accordingly must be "mobilized to drive the next round of deimperialization" (200). In Asia and the Pacific, a region penetrated by U.S. war and police power following Japan's defeat, however, deimperialization and decolonization have been difficult to disentangle as political projects because of the collusive entanglements that knit the United States and its client-states into a lethal "grid of operations and surveillance."[46] Often obscured from view, the United States has stood "at the supply end of a pipeline of repressive technology."[47] Seeking to indict the United States and Ferdinand Marcos, the NPA, testifying before the Permanent Peoples' Tribunal during the era of martial law, offered a pithy critique of this subfascist dynamic: "Marcos shoots the gun and Washington provides the bullets."[48]

The specter of suspended justice shadowing the reconstructed ruins of Japan's empire thus has its origins in the betrayal of the antifascist struggle, specifically the refusal of the United States and its client-states to grapple structurally with the problem of collaboration. This corruption is at the heart of postwar U.S. military empire in Asia and the Pacific. Indeed, the failure to enact justice broadly produced a regional order in which Cold War politics, far from neatly bipolar, took on an ambivalent cast—militantly anticommunist yet distorted with regard to the foundations of postwar authority. Having returned in the garb of antifascist liberator, the United States erected a formidable extraterritorial garrison state, unleashing catastrophic violence throughout the region and placing the Asian communist opponents of Japanese fascism in its war machine's crosshairs. By contrast rarely prosecuted for their crimes, collaborators were rehabilitated into the repressive apparatuses of subfascist U.S. client-states, where they proved indispensable to U.S. foreign-policy objectives. As Kim points out, "In the name of the war against communism, the pro-Japanese collaborators, who were allowed by the United States to flood the ranks of the police, military, and government, set out to 'eradicate leftists'" ("Korea's Movement," 161). As drivers of U.S. anticommunist policy, collaborators thus played a defining role in Asia's postwar twilight wars. Counterinsurgent accounts of these informal wars that emphasize the "valiant but unsuccessful U.S. effort to protect freedom against Communist terror and subversion" (Chomsky and Herman, 30) are therefore hounded by questions of legitimacy. As a closeted truth, the restoration of collaborators taints the pretext of democratization behind both triumphalist narratives of U.S. liberation and claims to legitimate rule by U.S. allies.[49]

The absence of formal justice would beget a cultural legacy in the former Pacific theater of World War II, whose difference from the aesthetic deliberation on violence in the former European theater demands consideration. If the staggering human ruin consequent to Nazism prompted cultural reflection positing a decisive postwar break from fascist violence—art *after* Auschwitz—the cultural archive of the postwar Pax Americana in Asia and the Pacific, by contrast, has implied less rupture with that which came before than shadowy continuity. Despite the war's world-shattering violence for Asian and Pacific Islander peoples, there is no identifiable region-specific oeuvre shaped by ethical deliberation on the war's profound human toll. There is, this is to say, nothing comparable to what Adorno called "lyric poetry after Auschwitz" or what Elie Wiesel theorized as "literature of testimony."[50] Haunted by the barbarism of Nazism yet informed by the Holocaust's layered legal legacy, including the Nuremberg, Eichmann, Zundel, and Demanjuk trials, Holocaust testimonial literature arguably possesses a "juridical unconscious."[51] In stark contrast, transpacific culture after the atomic bomb demands contextualization within a geopolitical setting fundamentally conditioned by the glaring lack or failure of formal mechanisms of justice. What emerges is not just a question of comparative humanity but also a question of comparative geopolitics. How, after all, do we account for the apparent inconsequentiality of the tens of millions of Asian and Pacific Islander civilians who died in that same war, those colonial casualties Aimé Césaire deemed the "dead weight" of history?[52] How do we reckon with the sweeping Cold War counterrevolutionary violence that shattered the region in the aftermath of World War II? Insofar as the "hazy perception of reality" of counterinsurgent worldviews takes the form of "incredible acts of inversion" (Ahmad, 41), thus destabilizing truth itself, then how, moreover, do we read cultural works distorted by U.S. counterrevolutionary violence?

Often set against neocolonial backdrops tarnished by anxieties about the legitimacy of state authority, transpacific Pax Americana writings muddle lines of Cold War enmity, refusing the reader neutral or innocent ground. Written in the early Cold War era, in his words a time of "false peace," Bulosan's novella *All the Conspirators* and his novel *The Cry and the Dedication* engage counterinsurgency's armed eye, blurring distinctions between friend and foe. Both narratives feature collaborators we come to realize have reinvented themselves in the postwar era: an expatriate American woman who switched sides during the Japanese occupation and a Catholic priest who conspired against the very people he was meant to serve. In both works the narrative tension derives from these obscured legacies of wartime collaboration with the Japanese. The narratives are clouded, moreover, by their mediation by first-person narrators or third-person focalizers whose function as impartial observers is compromised by their complicity in histories of unredressed fascist violence. The epistemological instability of these narratives can be attributed to the perceptual limits of the narrators who serve as vehicles into the worlds they inhabit. More pointedly, however, hampered perception in these works reflects the weaponized securitization of information in the Philippines circa the early Cold War.

Revealingly, *All the Conspirators* and *The Cry and the Dedication* obscure questions of guilt in their diegetic present, an opacity typical of transpacific Pax Americana fictions. In his classic 1961 account of unreliable narration Wayne Booth dubs the narrator "an 'I' who becomes involved in the action so deeply that he produces the catastrophe."[53] Although itself ahistorical, Booth's analysis of unreliable narrators as flawed reflectors complicit in the ruin they describe calls for contextualization in the Cold War moment in which he was writing. Insofar as unreliable narration underreports the historical—indeed, typically features a limited narrator that enacts a seemingly clueless, innocent, or insouciant remove from history—it invites readerly historicization as a stabilizing act. With their "hazy perception of reality," in other words, counterinsurgent fictions performatively enact historical distortion and in so doing not only confound their readers but also challenge them to determine reliability if not facticity as part of the interpretive process. With regard to counterinsurgent narratives in which the perpetrators of—or collaborators in—imperialist brutality serve as narrators or focalizers of the social terrain distorted by that violence, they invite being read through a deimperializing lens.

In a landscape distorted by asymmetrical violence in which national sovereignty is subjected to foreign manipulation, truth thus emerges as a site of contestation, albeit deformed by brute politics. Set in the unsettled wake of the U.S. "liberation" of the Philippines, Bulosan's early Cold War fiction performs unreliability, challenging not only his readers' interpretive capacity but also their political alignment. In *All the Conspirators* and *The Cry and the Dedication* the United States initially appears as neutral backdrop or bystander. Yet insofar as U.S. war power deforms their settings, these narratives testify to U.S.-sponsored counterrevolution in the Philippines. They do so, moreover, in ways that mirror the imperial war machine's counterinsurgent strategies. Here, it bears noting that Cold War U.S. military counterintelligence required evaluating "native informants" along a spectrum of reliability before operationalizing the information they produced in "pacifying" enemy territory. Read alongside declassified U.S. military counterintelligence files in which a range of informants in liberated or pacified areas of the Philippines were tasked with generating insider information about the "enemy," Bulosan's early Cold War fiction performs *as intelligence*. More than an effect of authorial intention, the unreliability of his writings cannot be untangled from the context they reference and ultimately critique—namely, a counterrevolutionary framework shaped by an epistemology of enmity.[54]

Reading the Enemy

Unpublished during his lifetime, *The Cry and the Dedication*, Bulosan's novel about the postwar Huk guerrilla struggle, was in multiple ways written "in the language of the enemy."[55] With inset texts that read as intelligence about the guerrilla underground, it plays to counterinsurgent interpretation. In this way the novel enacts what might be called *enemy consciousness*, a self-reflexive awareness of being surveilled through military-imperial power's lethal lens. Focalized from shifting subjective centers, a decentralized narrative mode reflective of underground Huk collectivist politics and organizing, the novel engages with the counterinsurgent politics of the written record with regard to the postwar people's war. Information about the Huks, the cadres know all too well, can be weaponized against them. In a setting in which information is wielded as a tool of war, the Huks in the novel, all of whom operate under aliases, anticipate the militarized scrutiny of the CIC, MPs, civilian guards, and the Philippine Constabulary, taking pains not to leave material traces behind.[56]

Dramatizing Huk vigilance, Bulosan describes Hassim, the cell's counterintelligence chief, burning a communiqué detailing their next mission: "when nothing remained but ashes, he crushed the black remnants with the heel of a shoe" (33). Not intended for posterity, much less the enemy's invasive eyes, these instructions have been transferred to their only repository, Hassim's memory. As Griffith states in his account of people's war, guerrillas must "deny all information of themselves to their enemy" (23), strategically rendering themselves inscrutable. In counterrevolutionary settings, decolonization hinges on this subterranean war of intelligence and counterintelligence. Both Huks *and* the U.S.-backed Philippine Constabulary must know their adversary: "Where is the enemy? In what strength? What does he propose to do? What is the state of his equipment, his supply, his morale? Are his leaders intelligent, bold, and imaginative or stupid and impetuous? Are his troops tough, efficient, and well disciplined, or poorly trained and soft?" In the context of a shadowy war these questions, aimed at producing "all conceivable information" (Griffith, 22, 23), are essential to victory. Both the insurgent and the counterinsurgent—in a word, the enemy—thus must be *read*.

As the cell's counterintelligence chief, Hassim has two main commissions: the acquisition of "details concerning the operations of the enemy" and the gathering of "information relating to the atrocities and brutalities committed upon the people by the enemy and the mercenary police of the landlords, and the *tulisanes* [bandits]" (Bulosan, *The Cry and the Dedication*, 10). The purpose of logging the latter information is to deliver swift revolutionary justice against enemies of the people.[57] In Bulosan's rendering of this informal war, the cell must know the enemy in order to preempt the latter's tactics, strategies, and methods, including counterrevolutionary propaganda. In highlighting the criticality of Huk counterintelligence, Bulosan thematizes a core aim of guerrilla warfare: victory on the terrain of information. As CIC-captured Huk documents at the National Archives disclose, during the Japanese occupation Huks instructed their members to wage an incessant "murmuring campaign," a propaganda offensive intended to proceed "from mouth to mouth from day to day until nobody believes the Japs, their Puppets and their press but only in the authority of the honesty and truthfulness of the underground."[58] As this directive suggests, even as guerrillas must be "masters of the arts of simulation and dissimulation" (Griffith, 26), their mission relative to the rebel infrastructure is dissemination of revolutionary truth.

Set in the counterrevolutionary aftermath of Japan's expulsion from the Philippines, *The Cry and the Dedication* grapples indirectly with the role of the United States in supplanting Japan, through both flunkies and outright military terror, as the Huks' principal foe. In Bulosan's novel U.S. planes fly in V-formations in an attempt, as the Huks speculate, "to locate our camps and photograph . . . the whole terrain for future destruction" (110). In a time of "peace between wars" that was a time of "preparation for the actual armed conflict" (58), in Bulosan's assessment, the Philippine Air Force flew no less than twenty-six hundred sorties against Huk targets, unleashing more than a million rounds of ammunition and a quarter-million pounds of explosives.[59] Although the United States initially turned to the Philippine Constabulary to neutralize the Huk resistance, it subsequently intervened to the tune of more than a billion dollars as Asian communism reared its head in China and North Korea. By late 1951 the United States was waging two simultaneous Cold War "police actions." Embroiled in all-out war in Korea, where it was carrying out incendiary strikes against alleged red regions, the United States equipped the Philippine Air Force with napalm to obliterate suspected Huk strongholds.[60] As E. San Juan Jr. notes: "U.S. armed aggression against the Korean people under the banner of the United Nations . . . , and by proxy against Filipino workers and peasants, was then in full blast" (xiv). In 1952, while writing *The Cry and the Dedication*, Bulosan, as editor of the International Longshoremen's and Warehousemen's Union, Local 37, yearbook, described terrorism as "rid[ing] the Philippines."[61] Speaking for Filipino workers in the United States, he called for "friendship with the People's Democratic Republic of China and . . . strongly protest[ed] against the rearming of Japan, and against aggression in Korea" (27). In an allusion to U.S. counterrevolution in Asia he argued that only the "unity of all workers" could challenge "the evil designs of imperialist butchers and other profiteers of death and suffering [aimed at] . . . plung[ing] humanity into a new world war.'"[62]

Bulosan's novel demonstrates the lethal susceptibility of information to instrumentalization in a time of anticommunist terror. In a key scene Dante, a Huk historian of the people, grills Father Bustamante, a Catholic priest and collaborator with the enemy who is, in fact, Dante's own brother, about his sources: "'I suppose your organization has all our pictures and dossiers. It didn't take you long to recognize us'" (279). Extracting a pamphlet from his desk drawer, the priest throws it down for Dante and other cell members to view. Its title reads:

KNOW THE ENEMY:
THEIR BACKGROUND, PICTURES, CHARACTERISTICS. (279)

Startled, Dante and Hassim, who like all Huk cadres have operated under aliases, must ponder: "The church had all that information about them? If they had, how did they get it? If they got it, who did the work?" (279). This fatal encounter between brothers, now on opposing sides of a twilight war, is further conditioned by the paradoxical incommensurability yet convergence of their understanding of the people. By shooting his brother dead, Bustamante snuffs out the life of a people's historian who "trac[ed] our history from the revolutionary viewpoint" (5). Meant to serve as political primer for the people, Dante's *Tales of My Own People* holds a mirror up to his underground Huk comrades, furnishing political biographies, including what was previously a word-of-mouth account of Old Bio's participation in the armed opposition against the Spanish.

Their incompatible politics notwithstanding, the similarity of these two inset histories in Bulosan's novel—the one a rightist pamphlet and the other a revolutionary history-from-below—illuminates a defining feature of Cold War–era studies: the potential of human-sourced information to be securitized as counterinsurgent knowledge.[63] Viewed via a military-imperial lens as "human intelligence" (HUMINT), such information about the so-called enemy could be sourced from both the collaborationist figure of the native informant *and* guerrilla-produced materials, including those aimed at mass political education. In an era when the U.S. national security state weaponized area studies in order to fill "the vacuum of knowledge about a vast hegemonic and counterhegemonic global space," the lines of difference between a police-state pamphlet like "Know the Enemy" and an underground history like *Tales of My Own People* would have been functionally immaterial. Both might conceivably be mined for information that could be preemptively deployed against the enemy. Just as the postwar race novel, as Jodi Melamed has argued, "functioned as a privileged tool" for "white Americans . . . to get to know difference—to learn the supposed inside stories of people of color," so could *Tales of My Own People*, or even *The Power of the People*—the title under which *The Cry and the Dedication* was published in the Philippines in 1986—be marshaled as intelligence toward lethal ends.[64]

Whether from a source "friendly" or "hostile," intelligence, in theory, was subjected to a hermeneutics of suspicion. Typically appending U.S. military counterintelligence records was the investigator's assessment of the source's reliability. As the "eyes and ears of the Occupation" in the Pacific theater, the CIC, as a militarized political police, played a decisive role in orchestrating the transition of authority from the Japanese to the Americans. Deployed with frontline combat troops to secure "Japanese" territory, the CIC scooped and sifted through tons of Imperial Army paperwork—documents central to the formation of the U.S. archive of World War II's Pacific theater. As one Imperial Japanese holding after another fell into U.S. hands, the CIC's primary task was *to read* the on-the-ground situation and on that basis to effect political transition.[65] Relative to Central Luzon, derisively referred to as "Huklandia" by the U.S. media and the Philippine collaborationist state, the CIC "did more than interfere in the selection of public officials in Central Luzon villages."[66] From February of 1945, the CIC actively targeted the Huk leadership. According to the June 1945 306th CIC Detachment Report, as historian Ronald Edgerton notes, it "became the responsibility of CIC to determine the identity of . . . individuals who were, 'for one reason or another, unsympathetic to the United States,' to apprehend them, to investigate their activities, and, when justified by evidence, to intern them pending action by the Philippine Commonwealth Government" (437–38).

Significantly, CIC files on the Huks—their organizational structure, key players, political activities, and associations—date back to World War II. The United States mobilized its wartime intelligence on the Huks as a then-"friendly" organization to neutralize them as a postwar "enemy." Information on the Huks was thus reread in the light of the dawning Cold War. We might recall the Huks' sobering lesson in the perils of sharing information with the U.S. "liberators": the roster of Huk fighters that Taruc assisted the CIC in compiling as part of the Hukbalahap application for the backpay the United States promised anti-Japanese guerrillas was transformed into "a blacklist to persecute and murder our comrades" (Taruc, 217). Although it abandoned the Philippines during the war, the United States maintained occupation-era intelligence files on literally hundreds of anti-Japanese Filipino guerrilla groups that spanned the political spectrum from left to right and were warily construed, through a united-front lens, as "friendly." In *The Cry and the Dedication* Bulosan remarks the bewildering landscape of guerrilla insurgency during the war: "there were many kinds of guerrillas: one for the landlords, another for the people, and still another for themselves" (132). Taken as a whole, the U.S. Army Forces in the Far East (USAFFE) guerrilla-recognition files offer a capacious portrait of the wartime insurgent landscape of the Philippines, a mere 30 percent of which the Japanese managed to pacify.

In charge of determining which locals had collaborated with the Japanese, which might serve in administrative capacities, and which posed a present threat, the CIC, as a central player in the American "liberation" of key sites in Asia and the Pacific, inaugurated a reticulated structure of surveillance, intelligence, and counterintelligence, which would evolve in the Cold War into a repressive, anticommunist architecture. Military historians John Finnegan and Romana Danysh contend that, Imperial Japan's defeat notwithstanding, U.S. "victory did not bring security."[67] As they observe, "It was now the task of the U.S. Army and its Intelligence component to help keep the uncertain peace" (99). Yet the CIC's covert intelligence operations throughout the former Pacific theater were quickly enfolded into "a wider secret war" that would be prosecuted on a far-reaching, if logistically chaotic, basis during the Cold War.[68] Even as its late-war mopping-up missions signaled a shift to investigations, security surveys, and security clearances, the CIC was critical to the emergence of a subimperial system geared for counterinsurgency, a mode of "warfare where armies depend almost exclusively on intelligence for successful operations."[69] With regard to Micronesia, the CIC referred to this budding surveillance, intelligence, and counterintelligence structure as a "native police-boy system." Reliant on "youths [who] contacted village chiefs, led reconnaissance patrols, helped interrogate native suspects, and assisted in special investigations and in maintaining an informant network," the CIC extracted and compiled "information of a tactical and counterintelligence significance" (*Counter Intelligence Corps*, 73). In other words, in the process of investigating and dismantling a political infrastructure of indigenous collaborators who had aided the Japanese, the CIC was instrumental in assembling one of its own that likewise relied on "native informants," "police boys," and "indigenous interpreters" as indispensable fixers for the U.S. occupation forces.[70]

Hampered by their inability to speak local languages and to assess local terrain on their own, U.S. occupation authorities required the services of intermediaries, functionaries instrumental to the consolidation of the emerging postwar U.S. military empire. Their labor would lay the groundwork for the anticommunist violence—hot wars, counterinsurgencies, low-intensity conflicts—ahead. In the Philippines the CIC compiled a vast Huk archive with the aim of eradicating the organization. While some documents were captured, others attest to an informant network, including a "Who's Who" personality index amplified by insider details, which was distributed to CIC agents prior to U.S. landing operations in the Philippines. Not only was this information used to dismantle the Huk infrastructure, including through the capture, arrest, and murder of Huk leaders, all in the same juncture the Japanese surrendered, but also, the United States installed *"reliably* pro-American officials" drawn from the prewar ruling class, many of whom had collaborated with the Japanese.[71] In rehabilitating the empire it succeeded, the Pax Americana, as a military-imperial regime in its own right, strategically gave new life to subfascist figures who had served under the Japanese, thus thwarting the process of decolonization.

Fog of Twilight War

Bulosan's *All the Conspirators*, like his novel *The Cry and the Dedication*, takes as its backdrop postwar political upheaval in the Philippines. This 1950s novella shifts locale, moving between expatriate lairs in war-devastated Manila and active guerrilla operations in the mountains of Baguio in northern Luzon. Unlike *The Cry and the Dedication*, which is focalized through members of a Huk cell, *All the Conspirators* is narrated by a white American, Gar Stanley, who has returned to Manila, the city where he was born and raised, after completing college in the United States and a tour of duty in Europe. Back in the Philippines to search for a childhood friend, Clem Mayo, who appears to be in league and possibly hiding out with Filipino guerrillas, Gar, now thrust into the role of an amateur gumshoe, must navigate the dizzying social terrain of the city he once called home, now teeming with shady characters in the wake of the war. Slow on the uptake and prone to being knocked unconscious, Gar makes for a notably unreliable narrator, unable to interpret a city whose prewar social contours had made manifest sense to him.

The colorful dramatis personae of Bulosan's novella, like moving puzzle pieces, confound Gar's—and the reader's—capacity to construe the governing context: from Clem's wife and Gar's ex–love interest Candy, a cool and collected American expatriate who somehow survived the war unscathed; to the pockmarked and scrawny Goyo; to the husky-voiced Agna, who sings at the nightclub El Cairo; to the Chinese Filipino femme fatale Rosa Linkhow, the "slant eye[d]" (67) lover of the banker Montalvo; to the ubiquitous mestizo Pepe Gonzalez, scion of a wealthy Manila family; to Damyan, the mute Igorot with one earring. Attempting to figure out who's who, Gar dimly deduces that there must be multiple "conspirac[ies] of collaborators" (52) at play: "Whoever they were, they had a terrific stake. They were desperate" (35). He discerns that present in the baffling scene before him is "an underground of unimportant little people ... allied against another group of whom they were in mortal terror" (32). Yet Gar's fuzzy apprehension of who the key players might be in this twilight war and what they hope to gain or thwart ultimately leaves him poorly equipped to make sense of a topsy-turvy world whose signs appear before him as ciphers. Struggling "to stand on neutral ground," he remarks, "Ordinarily, the system of things doesn't change that fast in the tropics," before concluding that "only the war could have accomplished this radical social change" (25, 43).

For all his ineptitude, Gar's postwar "homecoming" to Manila in the role of inadvertent sleuth dramatizes the challenges bedeviling Americans, despite their significant colonial history in the Philippines, in their return as occupation forces following Japan's defeat. Here, Gar's nationality and race surface as more than mere details. Goyo, who for a price assists Gar in his quest to locate Clem, points out the obvious: "You are an American and too conspicuous on the street" (56). As a white American who has come back to a country where his family settled and established a gold-mining operation prior to the Japanese takeover and whose investigation ends up leaving many dead, Gar invites being read as an allegory for the United States in its overdetermined role as colonizer, occupier, and investigator vis-à-vis the Philippines. In particular, his gumshoe work references the far-from-neutral mission of the CIC, which, as the U.S. occupation's investigative arm, was in charge of interrogating locals, determining who among them had collaborated, and recommending punitive charges. Indeed, the U.S. Army, anticipating the cultural illiteracy of its investigators in the Philippines, set up a wartime CIC academy in Brisbane, Australia, offering instruction in basic Tagalog; classes on "language, customs, habits, character and traits of the natives, names of geographical locations, local laws, ... secret societies, etc."; and training in investigative methods—preparation aimed at circumventing "those problems facing an American investigator in the Philippines" (*Counter Intelligence Corps*, 77). These measures notwithstanding, the CIC's work, like Gar's, turned on the on-the-ground aid of local intermediaries. In Bulosan's portrait, when left to his own devices, Gar stumbles badly. By the novella's end, three people have died "needless deaths" (34) because of his poor judgment. "A man like yourself," Gar is cautioned, "is apt to be mistaken in his sympathies because he is unacquainted with the whole structure of the case" (74).

Compromising Gar's claims to neutrality is his complicity in the scenes of suffering before him. He functions less as a dispassionate finder of facts than as an agent whose own interests and entanglements demand closer scrutiny. As a direct beneficiary of profits reaped under U.S. colonial rule, Gar lets it be known, as a cover for his investigation, that he must settle family-related property matters. In intimating the murkiness of Gar's motivations, Bulosan's novella departs from the genre of detective fiction and begins to resemble Cold War geopolitical fiction driven by U.S. global intrigue. Like the CIA operative Alden Pyle in Graham Greene's *The Quiet American* (1955), whose pretext for being in Vietnam is plastics, a key ingredient in bomb construction, Gar is an "innocent" American who manages to leave a trail of destruction in his wake.[72] Time and again, he presents himself as a "friend" to whoever might furnish him with information, yet the reader is left uncertain as to his ultimate agenda. Frustrated at Gar's vague description of his mission to find an "American who fought the enemy," Agna retorts: "Do we have the same enemy? For people like you it doesn't really matter who wins. You are safe and secure. But for little people like us—" (25). In Bulosan's depiction of the early postwar period as a time of acute epistemological uncertainty in the Philippines, the Cold War evacuation of the war-forged distinction between "friend" and "enemy" comes to light. The clarity wartime antifascism gave those terms has evaporated. Gar muses to Pepe, "A man in this country doesn't know his enemies any more," to which Pepe responds, "Sometimes . . . a man doesn't recognize his friends either" (94). After Agna's murder, a death for which he is directly responsible, Gar muses over who might have killed her: "These were thugs in the pay of someone, some individual or group of individuals, so ruthless that human life meant nothing" (35). Deflecting culpability, Gar fixates on the riddle of Agna's last words: "She had kept talking about some enemy—the enemy who had served the invaders during the war" (35). These confounding last words, more than the weight of her death, impel him forward in his investigation: "What in the Sam Hill did she mean?" (32). Looking for "information" that would do him "good," Gar seeks out another informant who might confirm his suspicions of "a diabolical conspiracy" (35) underfoot.

In a setting where the lines of enmity are blurred, the pursuit of truth—and, by extension, any commitment to historical justice—appears a fool's errand. Constrained by the limited perspective of its narrator, who voraciously consumes hearsay, catalogs any and all observations, and interrogates everyone, *All the Conspirators* performatively assails its reader with unsifted intelligence. In this respect Bulosan's novella mirrors the CIC's early postwar "Counter Intelligence Summary," distributed on a semimonthly basis, which compiled "lists of wanted persons, suspects, information desired on individuals and organizations, a report of the guerrilla situation, and a general summary" (*Counter Intelligence Corps*, 80). From a summary generated by the 1135th CIC detachment and dated April 16–30, 1947, we have the following bewildering composite portrait of "the recent activities of the more prominent members of Manila's Alien Community":

a. RAY AUBURN, whose activities have long been of interest to this office, is currently reported to be running a bit-time, by invitation only, gambling game at his home. The gamblers are primarily white businessmen in Manila.
b. ZOYA MONKOVA VALDEZ, attractive young widow of dubious associations, is reported as attempting to arrange entry into the Philippines for her sister in Shanghai. ZOYA is seen frequently in Manila with MICHAEL ZASLAWKY and JENNY VEINERMAN although she is apparently making her home in Baguio at the present time.
c. NICHOLAS S. DRAPIN, who claims to be a naturalized American citizen, has attracted interest in Leyte by his attacks upon U.S. policies and his fraternization with known Chinese Communist supporters and collaborators. DRAPIN is under continued lose [sic] surveillance.
d. The *Blue Elephant* night club [sic], once a center for the Manila Russian Community, has lost its last white hostesses and appears to be losing money for the owners.
e. VERA VERONICA COHEN, formerly with the Blue Elephant, has transferred to YE OLDE MANSION. VERONICA is currently considering a trip to Hongkong [sic] to secure a divorce from JACK COHEN, of the EL CAIRO club. The incentive for this move appears to be an American Army Ordnance Captain.[73]

Even as intelligence gleaned from the CIC's informant network was cross-checked where possible and rated according to reliability, these voyeuristic sketches of suspect foreigners read like lurid fiction. We might recall Clausewitz's uneasiness about the operational value of intelligence: "Many intelligence reports in war are contradictory; even more are false, and most are uncertain." Thus, he writes, the "difficulty of *accurate recognition* constitutes one of the most serious sources of friction in war."[74] In Bulosan's novella, confusion around who the enemy might be in the many underworlds of postwar Manila compounds the problem of recognition.

Early postwar intelligence files like this one, preoccupied in scattershot ways with an array of petty criminals and expatriates and their possible political, business, or heritage ties to China and the Soviet Union, demonstrate that the CIC's original mission of rooting out and bringing to justice pro-Japanese collaborators had been abandoned. Characters in the novella routinely invoke "the War Crimes court" (37), implying that punishment will be meted out to Candy the American, Montalvo the banker, and others who collaborated with the Japanese. "Every country had its Quislings, every nation its collaborators," Gar comments; "that is what War Crimes Trials were for—to make the world free from traitors and selfish opportunists" (75). Historically, even as some U.S. Justice Department officials advised establishing a war crime tribunal with "Filipino judges and prosecutors but . . . American support" to tackle the "basic and gigantic problem of collaborationism," the U.S. president, on MacArthur's advice, demoted the pursuit of justice to a low priority.[75] MacArthur, who wielded near-unilateral authority in the postwar U.S. occupation, made fatefully clear that collaboration was "not a legal question."[76] He led by example, exonerating Manuel Roxas, head of the collaborationist regime's Economic Planning Board and supervisor of its much-despised rice procurement agency. In the end the CIC turned over its evidence to the U.S.-installed late Commonwealth leadership, which formed a feeble People's Court, which in turn found a handful of Filipinos guilty of collaboration. After gaining the Philippine presidency in 1948, with MacArthur's full-throated endorsement, Roxas granted blanket amnesty to Filipino collaborators while declaring the Huks, who had fought valiantly against the Japanese, to be an illegal organization.[77]

Written not long after the treacherous postwar reinstatement of the collaborationist elite, *All the Conspirators* offers a counterfactual portrait. Working underground "to round up the collaborators," Damyan, the mute Igorot whose tongue was cut out by "the Japs," assures his fellow guerrillas that "the Americans were putting on trial those who had betrayed us during the war" (82, 113). Also imprisoned and tortured during the occupation, Goyo maintains that although "the people who played with the enemy want us to forget what they did," these pro-Japanese collaborators now fear "being arrested and tried by the War Crimes court" (37). For this reason "they have organized themselves. They punish anyone who speaks against them. We are all afraid" (37). The novella permits the trim reading that the "Montalvo gang" (135) represents the sum total of the "conspiracy of collaborators" who strike fear into the antifascist underground that fought against the Japanese. Yet Bulosan's unreliable narrative impels readers to counterconstruct the facts according to the historical record—namely, that the conspiring collaborators were, in point of fact, the United States and the postwar ruling oligarchy in the Philippines. That is, even as the driving U.S. role in creating a postwar culture of impunity is obscured in the novella, its flagrant counterfactuality demands against-the-grain historicization. As with other Pax Americana fiction, justice in this postwar novella has become spectral.

The Last Word

During the years when Bulosan was writing *The Cry and the Dedication* and *All the Conspirators*, the Cold War turned spectacularly hot in Asia, and U.S. police power cast its spotlight on him. On the FBI's Security Index for most of the last half decade of his life and subjected to a coordinated investigation on the part of the FBI, the CIA, Naval Intelligence, and the Philippines government, Bulosan was surveilled, his associates interrogated, and his known writings and statements pored over.[78] With the U.S. "police action" in Korea raging in the background, he fell under FBI scrutiny for linked reasons: his alleged membership in the Communist Party in the United States, his alleged ties to the Hukbalahap, and his alleged foreknowledge about a wave of looming communist insurgencies that promised to shake Asia's Cold War political topography. Indeed, particularly troubling to the agency was a report by an informant that Bulosan, on the basis of direct intelligence from Taruc, not only predicted that the Korean War would occur within the same month of its actual outbreak but also stated that on the heels of "the Korean affair," a region-wide strike against the U.S. containment regime in Asia would ensue. The agency thus zeroed in on correspondence between Taruc, whom it identified as "the leader of the Communist Party in the Philippine Islands," and Bulosan, whom it worried was "the 'number one man' among the Filipinos in the Communist Party in America."[79] In a July 31, 1950, memo to J. Edgar Hoover, the Special Agent-in-Charge (SAC) at the Seattle field office paraphrased the informant's account of the content of Taruc's letters, which he claimed Bulosan permitted him to view: "TARUC had forecast to BOULSON [sic] that the Korean revolution would occur" and "that within 16 months from June of 1950," communist uprisings in Formosa and Japan would occur, with a "revolution in the Philippine Islands" to follow.[80]

Of Bulosan's imagined involvement in a region-wide communist conspiracy in Asia, his FBI dossier reveals that U.S. intelligence officials regarded him as having "collaborated in the preparation of communist propaganda" (quoted in Baldoz) that was then circulated in the Philippines. According to Rick Baldoz, intercepted correspondence to Taruc revealed that "Bulosan praised the Huk political program and ... planned to write a book about the peasant movement to popularize their struggle among progressive American audiences," averring that he was "not afraid of the *fascist* bastards at home." Whatever the actual degree of his involvement, Bulosan, while carrying out research for *The Cry and the Dedication*, communicated with key figures in the Huk leadership.[81] In May of 1955, however, after a five-year investigation in which no evidence was uncovered that he had "taken an active or leading part in front organizations" (Alquizola and Hirabayashi, 40), the Seattle SAC advised that Bulosan be removed from the Security Index. His "compromising contacts" (Alquizola and Hirabayashi, 40), as the SAC explained, were deemed to reflect in part the concerns of his literary research. Yet Bulosan's early Cold War writings, absent from his FBI case file and posthumously published, were more than mere fiction. They pointed damningly to the persistence of fascism in the postwar era and the role of U.S. intelligence and military violence in the counterinsurgent terror that typified the American "peace" in Asia. Characters like the Huk revolutionary Old Bio in Bulosan's *The Cry and the Dedication* were lifted from the pages of *Born of the People*, a guerrilla memoir Taruc described not as an autobiography but rather "a chapter in the biography of the Filipino people" (278).[82] If the postwar Philippines, shattered and remade through U.S. war power, were meant to be "America's showcase of democracy in Asia after independence," a semisovereign nation where "the world would be asked to judge the efficacy of the American way," Bulosan's *The Cry and the Dedication* and *All the Conspirators* offered, in contrast, narratives of insurgent democracy.[83]

Remarking the "low estimate of the masses" inherent in counterinsurgent worldviews, Eqbal Ahmad, writing in the Vietnam War era, commented on the boomerang effect of U.S. wars of aggression abroad—the "ways in which the practice of counter-insurgency erodes the democratic processes and institutions of metropolitan countries" (41). Although COINTELPRO had not yet been exposed, Ahmad noted that the militarized disregard for the peoples on the receiving end of U.S. foreign policy—their lives, needs, aspirations, and histories—domestically translated into the enhanced "power of the secret services of government over which parliamentary institutions can exercise little or no control and whose activities public organs (press, political parties, etc.) are normally unable to report and censure" (44). Bulosan's accounts about U.S. counterinsurgencies in Asia were also part of a Cold War tale, as his FBI file suggests, of invisible wars at home. Yet in the war of narrative typifying this two-front twilight war, his early Cold War fiction, by illuminating the Filipino people's revolutionary struggle for democracy, battled for the last word.

The Enemy at Home
Urban Warfare and the Russell Tribunal on Vietnam

Criminalizing U.S. Military Empire

In May of 1967, as the International War Crimes Tribunal on Vietnam was convening for its inaugural session, James Baldwin, writing from Istanbul, announced his disaffiliation with Bertrand Russell's "people's tribunal" in *Freedomways*, the "central theoretical journal of the Black Freedom Movement."[1] Of his little-known involvement as uneasy fellow traveler to what is commonly called the Russell Tribunal—a pioneering anti-imperialist human rights project that audaciously "propose[d] to apply to capitalist imperialism its own laws," in Jean-Paul Sartre's words—Baldwin offered a slender account, "The War Crimes Tribunal."[2] Compelled to clarify his position, he argued the tribunal's pursuit of justice must dialectically engage the black freedom struggle in the United States for its inquiry into U.S. aggression in Southeast Asia to have broad legitimacy. Despite the fact that tribunal organizers had been stymied in trying to secure a location for the proceedings, going to the governments of Great Britain, France, and Algeria before finally prevailing with Sweden and Denmark, "such a trial," Baldwin maintained, "should really be held in Harlem, USA."[3] His reasoning: "A racist society can't but fight a racist war—this is the bitter truth. The assumptions acted on at home are also acted on abroad, and every American Negro knows this, for he, after the American Indian, was the first 'Viet Cong' victim" (244). Suspicious, too, of an endeavor in which a consortium of intellectuals dominated by Europeans arrogated to itself the right to pass judgment on U.S. military-imperial violence while leaving to the side "crimes [Europeans] are now committing in Rhodesia, Angola, [and] South Africa," Baldwin simultaneously made plain his desire to "go on record" as "having no part" in the American "criminal endeavor" (242, 244) in Vietnam.[4]

Baldwin's essay brings into view an unexamined shadow infrastructure of human rights critical of U.S. war and police power that would find expression in the innovative North-South civil-society initiative of the international people's tribunal.

Following the Russell Tribunal, a series of markedly anti-imperialist people's tribunals would proliferate in Asia and the Pacific, most driven by Global South movements and enlivened by international solidarity. The paradoxical measure of the independence of these endeavors was, as Sartre stated of the Russell Tribunal, their powerlessness: unbeholden to imperialist authority, "we cannot receive orders," but "we will name the guilty."[5] Wielding human rights and international humanitarian law, such people's courts have sought to criminalize the unilateral violence of U.S. intervention in Asia, U.S. nuclear testing in the Pacific, U.S. wars against its own citizenry, anticommunist white terror perpetrated by regional U.S. client-states, and unredressed Japanese war crimes. Modeled after the Russell Tribunal, these undertakings include the 1980 Permanent Peoples' Tribunal on the Philippines, the 1990 International Tribunal on Political Prisoners and Prisoners of War in the United States, the 2000 Women's International War Crimes Tribunal on Japanese Military Sexual Slavery, the 2001 Korea International War Crimes Tribunal, and the 2014 Republic of the Marshall Islands lawsuit against the United States and other nuclear powers, to name a few. On the whole these left-legal initiatives have garnered negligible media coverage and scholarly attention. If dominant post–Cold War human rights politics have all too often been complicit in a hegemonic U.S. global agenda—making the case for rather than against U.S. intervention—the human rights trajectory signaled by these people's tribunals suggests linked efforts, across time, to reckon with the counterrevolutionary violence of post-1945 U.S. militarism in the Asia-Pacific region and at home.

In a juncture when the global spotlight was cast on U.S. aggression in Southeast Asia, the Russell Tribunal condemned U.S. war violence in the language of international humanitarian law. In arguing the lawlessness of the U.S. war in Vietnam, it more broadly indicted the brutality of the U.S. "peace" regime in a region where post-1945 reconstructive opportunity entailed complicity with U.S. wars and where justice in the wake of mass violence was serially deferred.[6] Unlike the Nuremberg Trials, the International Military Tribunal for the Far East adjudicating Japan's defeat was unabashedly strategic, not moral, in nature, helping to lay the grounds for U.S. "security imperialism" in the former Pacific theater.[7] Those European colonial powers unseated by Japanese expansion, including France, whose Indochinese wars the United States would inherit, exercised individual prosecutorial authority. The only justice out of eleven with international legal experience, Bengali jurist Radhabinod Pal, dissented from the majority judgment, noting that "in the Pacific War under our consideration," the most egregious act of state terrorism against civilian populations was "the decision coming from the allied powers to use the ATOM BOMB," a crime whose nonjusticiability paved the way for unbridled U.S. bombing campaigns in Korea, Vietnam, and Laos.[8] Aware that the Japanese Imperial Army set up "comfort" stations in the Pacific theater, yet recognizing injury to solely Dutch women, the Tokyo Trials perpetrated, in Ustinia Dolgopol's words, a grave "legacy of omission."[9] In contrast to the Nuremberg judgment, which established common knowledge about the Holocaust's horrors, the Tokyo trials, by turning a blind eye to colonial victims of Japanese brutality, affirmed an "existing international division of humanity."[10] Their nonredressive nature ensured that subimperial collusion with the U.S. war machine would be a key pathway to economic modernization for regional allies like South Korea, Japan, Thailand, the Philippines, Australia, and New Zealand—all nations named in the Russell proceedings as accomplices to U.S. war violence in Vietnam.

To challenge U.S. immunity, the Russell Tribunal invoked the mostly fallow precedents of crimes against the peace (wars of aggression), war crimes, crimes against humanity, and genocide—all international legal norms the United States had applied to Germany and Japan at World War II's end—as well as the 1907 Hague Convention, the 1928 Kellogg-Briand Pact, the 1945 UN Charter, the Nuremberg Statute, the 1954 Geneva Agreements, and the U.S. Army manual *The Law of Land Warfare*.[11] The salient question was whether the U.S. war in Vietnam could be deemed criminal by the same laws by which Nazism was indicted. Committed to reanimating "the spirit of Nuremberg," the Russell Tribunal alighted on the possibility, explored in an eruption of left and mainstream legal scholarship, that the novel laws the United States had framed in response to the Holocaust and Japanese militarism might be visited on the framer.[12] As Sartre stated in the *New Left Review*, the Russell Tribunal was not intent on "demonstrating the indignant disapproval of a group of honest citizens, but of giving a juridical dimension to acts of international politics, in order to combat the tendency of the majority of people only to judge the conduct of . . . a government in expedient or in moral terms." For Sartre, the tribunal's radicality thus resided not in the creation of new laws but rather (in a global arena deformed by asymmetrical power relations) in "reintroducing the legal notion of international crime" ("Imperialist Morality," 5, 6). While acknowledging that "as imperialists always do, the US considers itself above the law," Italian socialist jurist and tribunal participant Lelio Basso argued the significance of insisting on international legal impartiality by animating the "paralysed" "organs" of the international penal code: "We . . . shall pass our judgement on the basis of the very principles used in the judgement by the United States of the Japanese war criminals."[13] The U.S. "claim that the victims have only to comply with American conditions to have a better life" (334) was belied, Basso contended, by the systematic, deliberate nature of its exterminationist campaign in Southeast Asia. It was, he pointed out, a bald "violation of international law to make any person or group of people choose between submission to the domination of an unwanted foreign power and slavery or death in a concentration camp" (334).

Through the "anti-fascist" (Tynan, 135) forum of the international people's tribunal, the Russell Tribunal thus sought to rectify the legal illegibility of U.S. violence in Vietnam by classifying it as a war of aggression, or a crime against peace—a crime retroactively established at the Nuremberg and Tokyo Trials.[14] At its Stockholm session the tribunal found the United States responsible for "commit[ing] a crime of aggression against [Vietnam], a crime against peace."[15] With this finding it challenged a key feature of the Pax Americana, the militarized "peace" regime that reconfigured the Asia-Pacific region as a U.S. security zone after Japan's 1945 defeat—namely, the U.S. prerogative to thereafter wage "informal" war with impunity. Of the world's greatest military power wielding its might against a peasant people—what he deemed the colonizer's war of example—Sartre maintained that "the only possible relationship between an overindustrialized country and an underdeveloped country" was genocide, "the only relationship, short of picking up and pulling out."[16] In public statements Ho Chi Minh likewise drove home the criminality of U.S. violations of Vietnam's "sovereignty, independence, unity and territorial integrity," pointing as well to the aggressive U.S. campaign to turn "South Vietnam into a U.S. colony and military base, which would be permanently incorporated into the sphere of activity of the South-East Asian aggressive organization (S.E.A.T.O.)."[17] In a February 15, 1967, letter to Lyndon Johnson, he spelled out Vietnam's charges:

> The U.S. Government has committed war crimes, crimes against peace and against mankind. In South Vietnam, half a million U.S. and satellite troops have resorted to the most inhuman weapons and the most barbarous methods of warfare, such as napalm, toxic chemicals and gases, to massacre our compatriots, destroy crops, and raze villages to the ground. In North Vietnam, thousands of U.S. aircraft have dropped hundreds of thousands of tons of bombs, destroying towns, villages, factories, roads, bridges, dykes, dams, and even

churches, pagodas, hospitals, schools.... May I ask you: Who has perpetrated these monstrous crimes? It is the U.S. and satellite troops. The U.S. government is entirely responsible for the extremely serious situation in Vietnam.[18]

In a message to Bertrand Russell prior to the tribunal's commencement, Ho Chi Minh underscored the severity of U.S. crimes in Vietnam, describing them as "more odious than [those of] the Hitlerite fascists."[19] By weighing whether the methods of extermination the United States deployed in Vietnam were systematic and deliberate, the tribunal identified a broad pattern of war crimes that subsequent revelations—including Seymour Hersh's investigation of the Son My massacre, the Pentagon Papers, and Robert McNamara's disclosures—would affirm in fuller detail.[20]

Yet as Samir Amin has stated, "Imperialist powers... will never be held accountable for their violations of international law, even when these violations are irrefutable."[21] Albeit prioritized as "the supreme international crime"—in fact placed in magnitude above crimes against humanity and war crimes in the postwar Nuremberg and Tokyo tribunals and enshrined as crimes of aggression in the Rome Statute of the International Criminal Court—crimes against peace, the legal category for aggressive war, have revealingly become a dead letter in international law. Even so, salvoes against U.S. aggression from the margins of "law's empire" (Bartholomew, 2) have sought to establish a precedential record of U.S. criminality and to incite the court of public opinion in order to forge an anti-imperialist united front. These quasi-legal undertakings have not been without impact. Tariq Ali, an investigator for the Russell Tribunal, discerned in his findings patterns of brutality that resurfaced in later U.S. interventionist wars.[22] For Basso the Russell proceedings served as a procedural model for the Permanent Peoples' Tribunals (PPT), established in 1979, in that they advanced the cause of decolonization through anti-imperialist interpretations of international law. Assembled roughly forty times since its inception, the PPT, as a radical foil to the international courts associated with the UN, has honored its Russell bequest by issuing bold verdicts on the consequences of U.S. neocolonialism and militarism in the Asia-Pacific region.[23] With regard to the Philippines, for example, the PPT in 1980 condemned the U.S.-backed Marcos dictatorship, in 2007 found the Arroyo regime guilty of crimes against humanity, and in 2015 convened in Washington, DC, finding Barack Obama guilty for "the increasing US political, economic and military intervention in the Philippines that is at the root of the intensifying poverty and repression in the country."[24]

If the Russell Tribunal held far-reaching critical import for participants such as Basso and Ali, Baldwin, as his *Freedomways* essay reveals, was unpersuaded by its effectiveness as a vehicle of political critique. His retreat from the proceedings raises questions of why he found the tribunal wanting and what alternative he envisioned.[25] His public disengagement suggests a critical difference between the internationalism of his antiwar stance—with its dialectical focus on American ghettoes as a battlefront in a multisited U.S. war—and that of the tribunal. Rather than articulate the black freedom struggle in the language of international law, he cast human rights in the insurgent idiom of the black freedom struggle, exposing the continuum between U.S. police power and war power. Without question, the violence of the U.S. war in Vietnam—which left more than three million dead, exposed millions across generations to the devastating effects of Agent Orange, destroyed Vietnam's civilian infrastructure, and poisoned its ecology—calls for reckoning in its own right. Yet Baldwin's argument that the Russell Tribunal must engage the black freedom struggle alighted on a militarized truth. If situated on opposing sides of a war machine that increasingly harnessed nonwhite life to target nonwhite life, black Americans and Vietnamese civilians were located on the receiving end of U.S. war policy, if in incommensurate ways, and in this regard, to borrow from Lisa Lowe, "intimate parts of the same imperial conjuncture."[26]

Reflecting on a decade of lethal race riots, William Patterson, in a 1970 foreword to the 1951 Civil Rights Congress petition *We Charge Genocide*, noted their linkages to U.S. interventionist wars in Asia: "the wantonly murderous and predatory racist attacks on Korea, Vietnam and Cambodia ... are inseparably related to the *equally criminal* murders of rebellious black youth in Chicago, Illinois, New Haven, Connecticut, Augusta, Georgia, and Jackson, Mississippi."[27] If the Russell Tribunal is mostly unremembered today and Baldwin's essay, along with his larger body of commentary on the Vietnam War, not located alongside his novels and major essays, his manifesto-like critique of its proceedings places him in an undertheorized black radical human rights genealogy that warrants closer examination for the complexity of its two-fronted critique of U.S. war power. His brief tribunal membership speaks to a Cold War legacy of black radical recourse to international human rights as a means of contesting counterrevolutionary war at home.

Dark Crimes without a Name

At recurring Cold War intervals key figures in the black left in the United States turned to what Malcolm X dubbed "the human-rights tree" as a revolutionary alternative to "the civil-rights tree."²⁸ Although their politics were not homogeneous, they marshaled the idiom of human rights to indict the United States for systematic racist violence, and they did so before a global audience.²⁹ Recentering the history of Cold War black freedom struggles on the human-rights tree brings into view a genealogy of black radical petitions to the UN that, taken as a small yet significant body of post-1945 political literature, have gone largely unexamined. Submitted to the UN prior to the codification of genocide, W. E. B. Du Bois et al.'s 1947 NAACP petition *An Appeal to the World: A Statement on the Denial of Human Rights to Minorities in the Case of Citizens of Negro Descent in the United States of America and an Appeal to the United Nations for Redress* helped foster a vernacular rather than doctrinal, emergent rather than dominant, paradigm of human rights. It offered a radical reading of human rights as inextricable from resource claims, Nuremberg as decolonizing precedent, and individuals empowered via the public sphere to level criminal charges against states.³⁰ Following the example of Du Bois, who drafted petitions to the UN for the National Negro Congress in 1946 and the NAACP in 1947, subsequent petitioners to the UN—Patterson and Paul Robeson for the Civil Rights Congress in 1951, Malcolm X as chairman of the Organization of Afro-American Unity in 1964, Huey Newton and Bobby Seale on behalf of the Black Panther Party for Self-Defense in the late 1960s—all sought to advance the black freedom struggle in the language of human rights.³¹ These Cold War petitions tested the limits of the instruments in the midcentury human rights canon—the 1945 UN Charter, the 1948 Universal Declaration, and the 1948 Genocide Convention—by insisting on their applicability to black repression in the United States. Adducing material from the ruptured archives of the black American experience to argue the systematic nature and genocidal intent of U.S. racial violence, they framed the interests of black people in the United States "not [as] the private affair of Americans, but the concern of mankind everywhere."³²

Even as human rights accrued legal identity immediately following World War II, black radical articulations of human rights, as an emancipatory language from below, demand theorization within a longer genealogy of black revolutionary discourse that both predated and in unorthodox ways intersected with the emergence of the midcentury UN-centric international human rights regime. The appeal of human rights for black radical petitioners resided in their theoretical unity with a revolutionary anticapitalist vision of economic and social justice that exceeded national borders to find common cause with anti-imperialist struggles around the globe—"a vision of the future," Robin Kelley observes, "sorely lacking in most contemporary arguments for reparations."[33] By insisting on insurgent interpretations of post-1945 human rights doctrine at odds with Cold War realpolitik, such negotiations of human rights did not simply hover, quixotic and illegible, on the periphery of the dominant human rights regime. Their varying politics notwithstanding, in their shared argument for the supersession of U.S. state authority—indeed the criminalization of the United States—black radical human rights expressions attest to a demotic lineage of human rights originating with the publication of slave and ex-slave writings.

It bears recalling that the rights of which Frederick Douglass so powerfully spoke in *My Bondage and My Freedom* were not civil but human rights, rights conceived not negatively as freedom from harm but as "the universal and unconditional emancipation of my race."[34] Douglass anticipated the logic of crimes against humanity nearly a century before the category's recognition: "Slavery is a crime, not against Englishmen, but against God, and all the members of the human family; and it belongs to the whole human family to seek its suppression" (379). Assailing slavery as a system whose inhumanity and moral corruption were evident in its refusal to treat the "killing [of] a slave, or any colored person" as an incontrovertible crime, he evocatively referred to "outbreaks of atrocious cruelty" that were "openly perpetrated on the plantation" as "dark crimes without a name" (124, 148). In so doing, Douglass augured Winston Churchill's 1941 reference to the Nazi slaughter of Russians as "a crime without a name," a pattern of state-sponsored violence that in 1944, relative to the systematic and deliberate destruction of European Jewry, gained the name of genocide.[35] That "dark crimes without a name" might be nominated *as crimes* and the United States recognized as a perpetrator under the Genocide Convention galvanized Cold War black radical human rights politics. Yet the international community's reluctance to endorse this emancipatory interpretation of human rights makes plain that, far from being identical, the trajectories of Douglass's "dark crimes without a name" and Churchill's "crimes without a name" would remain separate and unequal. Black radical human rights politics, even when engaged with the United Nations, thus has a place in a vernacular legacy shaped less by institutional realpolitik than by a vision of black liberation conjured by figures like Douglass and David Walker, who rose from below to contest their people's oppression.

Although the establishment of the UN gave rise to black radical appeals addressed to the General Assembly, the petition has a distinctive American trajectory whose major nodes—abolition, antilynching, and Jim Crow—reflect defining battles in the black freedom struggle. Of the petition as a long-standing instrument of the black left, Du Bois clarified the historical record: "From the very beginning of this nation, ... the Negroes of the United States have appealed for redress of grievances, and have given facts and figures to support their contention" (*An Appeal*, 12). As a Cold War human rights genre, the petition would go global. Aimed at advancing black self-determination, black radical human rights petitions to the UN sought to access a higher law that, in the words of the 1951 Civil Rights Congress petition, not only "supersedes, negates, and displaces all discriminatory racist law on the books of the United States" (xii) but also criminalized the United States. Hoping to challenge the dominion of the national frame from within which they were writing—indeed, at times refusing recognition as U.S. nationals—black radicals wielded the human rights petition not as a mode of entreaty to power but as a manifesto. In their refusal to submit to U.S. state authority, we can detect something of the latent insurgency, "the nascent fury embodied in the form," or what Malcolm X presented as a choice between "the ballot or the bullet."[36]

If the petition has served as "a potent instrument through which minority political causes and people denied the full rights of republican citizenship" have fashioned "alternative routes to the polis," its Cold War black radical mobilization recalled David Walker's 1829 *Appeal to the Colored Citizens of the World*, which called for slaves to overthrow the tyranny of bondage with violence, if necessary.[37] In the 1960s the overtly anticolonial Third World alignment of human rights petitions to the UN by black radicals and their belief in just resort to self-defense indicated that recourse to the diplomacy of words was compatible with advocacy of revolutionary deeds. Neither mistakable with supplications to U.S. authority nor in any way construed as such by the latter, the petitions drafted by Du Bois and others who followed in his stead might have sought, in the first instance, "to bring about a revolution without violence and bloodshed."[38] They were not averse, however, to the "use of organized political violence as a necessary (and ethical) response to the struggle against the racist ... state" (Williams, *The Divided World*, xxi). In this regard these petitions were part of a broad and flexible strategy of international revolutionary struggle during the Cold War, one in which human rights were envisioned as a weapon against imperialism.

Much as the participation in the Russell Tribunal by National Front for the Liberation of the South (NLF) members—for example, Nguyen Van Dong, the North Vietnamese ambassador to the Soviet Union and a witness from South Vietnam, and Nguyen Thi Tho, an NLF activist—was consistent with their commitment to militant anti-imperialist revolutionary struggle, so, too, were Cold War black radical human rights petitions just one dimension of a capacious revolutionary politics.[39]

Equal parts appeal, referendum, and manifesto, these Cold War petitions exposed—before an international audience—the racist brutality of the world's foremost democracy, demonstrating, in the global arena, the falsity of its promise of full political participation through citizenship: "Let the world know how bloody his hands are," Malcolm X urged his fellow blacks in the United States in his 1963 "Ballot or the Bullet" speech: "Let the world know the hypocrisy that's practiced over here" (35). In his 1964 "The Black Revolution" speech, Malcolm X advocated that black people in the United States bypass "the American stage" of civil rights for the world stage of human rights: "When you go to Washington, D.C., expecting those crooks down there—and that's what they are—to pass some kind of civil-rights legislation to correct a very criminal situation, what you are doing is encouraging the black man, who is the victim, to take his case into the court that's controlled by the criminal that made him the victim. It will never be solved that way" (50, 53).

On the Cold War's cusp, in his 1947 UN petition, Du Bois anticipated this argument, stating the time had come for "the question . . . , which is without doubt primarily an internal and national question," to become "an international question" (13). The Black Panthers would follow suit. As Huey P. Newton and Bobby Seale stated in their late 1960s "Petition to the United Nations": "The racist planned and unplanned terror suffered by more than 40 millions of black, brown, red and yellow citizens of the United States cannot be regarded solely as a domestic issue" (55). Seeking if not legal remedy from a world court, then backing from the court of global opinion, Cold War black radical petitions cannily elicited the power of international censure, aiming to secure consensus in excess and pointed defiance of U.S. jurisdictional authority.[40] The United States might be "the dominant nation in the United Nations," Patterson conceded, yet in an era of global decolonization movements, he exploited the political chasm between the General Assembly and the United States: "The General Assembly of the United Nations, by reason of the United Nations Charter and the Genocide

Convention, itself is invested with power to receive this indictment and act on it" (Patterson, foreword, xii, xiii).[41] Calling on that body to act in the interests of "the establishment of a people's democracy on a universal scale" (Patterson, foreword, xiii), these petitions, drafted in the wake of World War II, at the onset of the Korean War, and during the Vietnam War, put the international community's human rights commitments to the test.

Aimed not at reforming the state but overcoming its authority, these petitions protested U.S. racist violence in supranational terms yet in historical junctures in which U.S. unilateral violence on the global stage—most spectacularly evident in its serial wars in Asia—was impossible to ignore. In this sense black radicals seized human rights as a potentially dialectical discourse, enabling analysis of "the civil-rights struggle ... from another angle—from the inside as well as from the outside" (Malcolm X, "The Ballot," 31). Published in key "hot war" moments during the Cold War, these petitions insisted on the structural correlation between U.S. domestic and foreign policy, construing racism within the United States to be the domestic expression of a global pattern of U.S. imperialism. Tenaciously, they reasoned that racist violence and economic exploitation in the United States would beget more of the same as it projected its war power abroad: "We solemnly declare that continuance of this American crime against the Negro people of the United States will strengthen those reactionary American forces driving towards World War III as certainly as the unrebuked Nazi genocide against the Jewish people strengthened Hitler in his successful drive to World War II" (Civil Rights Congress, *We Charge Genocide*, 7). Central to the legal briefs in these petitions were concerted efforts to compare U.S. state criminality to that of the Third Reich yet in political tone and tenor, to move beyond the Holocaust's legal legacy. Not singular to or narrowly defined by policies and practices of Nazi rule, genocide, war crimes, and crimes against humanity described systematic U.S. violence against black people domestically and Asian peoples abroad. In *An Appeal to the World* Du Bois syllogistically argued the global implications of American racism: "the disfranchisement of the American Negro makes the functioning of all democracy in the nation difficult; and as democracy fails to function in the leading democracy in the world, it fails in the world" (6). Similarly, the Korean and Vietnam Wars would furnish Patterson and Malcolm X, respectively, with evidence to bolster their claims that racist imperial violence begins at home.[42]

The "wanton murder of Negroes," Patterson contended, "had been a dress rehearsal for the murder of Koreans and Chinese."[43] Published a year into the Korean War, the 1951 Civil Rights Congress petition *We Charge Genocide: The Historic Petition to the United States for Relief from a Crime of the United States Government against the Negro People*, principally authored by Patterson, conjured visceral links between the murderous effects of "the lyncher and the atom bomber" to illustrate their structural continuity:

> We, Negro petitioners whose communities have been laid waste, whose homes have been burned and looted, whose children have been killed, whose women have been raped, have noted with particular horror that the genocidal doctrines and actions of the American white supremacists have already been exported to the colored peoples of Asia. We solemnly warn that a nation which practices genocide against its own nationals may not be long deterred, if it has the power, from genocide elsewhere. White supremacy at home makes for colored massacres abroad. Both reveal contempt for human life in a colored skin. Jellied gasoline in Korea and the lynchers' faggot at home are connected in more ways than that both result in death by fire. The lyncher and the atom bomber are related. The first cannot murder unpunished and unrebuked without so encouraging the latter that the peace of the world and the lives of millions are endangered. (7)

Vigorously suppressed by the U.S. State Department, which revoked Patterson's passport, *We Charge Genocide*—published as the Korean War was raging and the 1948 Genocide Convention, absent U.S. ratification, entered into force—marshaled the harrowing example of U.S. interventionist war in Korea, which left four million Koreans dead, to illuminate a less visible war at home. The U.S. police action in Korea, this petition asserted, had a corollary in a rising domestic police state. In asserting that napalm and "the lynchers' faggot" were "connected in more ways than that both result in death by fire," *We Charge Genocide* implied that unofficial U.S. war had persisted, at home and abroad, long after World War II had come to an end. This insistence on a structural link between "Negro petitioners" and "colored peoples of Asia" enabled a radicalizing shift of human rights away from a line of legal defense against state-sponsored harm to common ground for coalitional offense by peoples subjected to terror and "racial murder" (12).

As one aspect of a "wider, more ambiguous legacy of post–World War II decolonization" (Singh, 53), black radical human rights petitions were animated by a vision of black freedom that imperfectly corresponded to the politics of anticolonial national liberation movements. In their appeals for international solidarity, the collective speaking subject of these petitions only rarely assumed citizenship as the basis of an insurgent argument against U.S. jurisdictional authority. As Malcolm X declared in his April 3, 1943, human rights speech, "The Ballot or the Bullet": "Those Hunkies [sic] that just got off the boat, they're already Americans; Polacks are already Americans; the Italian refugees are already Americans. Everything that came out of Europe, every blue-eyed thing, is already an American. And as long as you and I have been over here, we aren't Americans yet" (25–26). Wrestling with "the anomalous position of Black Americans who were neither . . . bearers of national rights nor of human rights,"[44] Malcolm X maintained that the "entire civil-rights struggle needs a new . . . broader interpretation" ("The Ballot," 31). Pointing out that civil rights gains had not guaranteed blacks in the United States the most basic rights—and that "your dumb vote . . . put in an administration in Washington, D.C., that has seen fit to pass every kind of legislation imaginative, saving you until last" (27)—Malcolm X sought to bypass the limitations of black citizenship for nascent black or Third World nationalism.[45]

Yet if black people in the United States were not the intended subjects of rights, throughout the Cold War, they were not self-evident wielders of anticolonial nationalist critique either. Even as black radical UN petitions argued that the "unpunished and unrebuked" brutality of slavery and Jim Crow must be recognized as the basis for the impunity with which the United States waged its wars abroad, the articulation of black resistance to domestic U.S. hegemony, in the years after World War II, increasingly took the form of the "colonial analogy." Animated by the possibility of inclusion in "a global majority, rather than a national minority," black anticolonial critique ran as a common thread through the petitions submitted to the UN in each successive Cold War decade.[46] In a 1947 editorial, Du Bois maintained that blacks in the United States were "quasi-colonial [in] status" (quoted in Roark, 261). In "The Black Revolution" Malcolm X similarly argued: "America is a colonial power. She has colonized 22 million Afro-Americans by depriving us of first-class citizenship, by depriving us of civil rights, actually by depriving us of human rights" (50). If the NAACP "draped itself in the flag" (Anderson, 107) as the Cold War loomed—forcing Du Bois out, repudiating his UN petition, and forsaking its human rights agenda—by contrast, Cold War black radicals embraced a language that estranged their politics from a rigidly national context while insisting on the applicability of the colonial paradigm to the domestic arena.

Whether summoning the interwar CPUSA "nation within a nation" thesis, invoking the concept of internal colonialism, or referencing black nationalist politics, black radical human rights petitions tussled with the problematic concept of a nascent black nation. Du Bois mounted his argument along strained lines: "The United Nations surely will not forget that the population of this group makes it in size one of the considerable nations of the world" (*An Appeal*, 13–14). The spirit of anticolonialism that infused the human rights speeches and petitions of Cold War black radicals—the very spirit moving former colonies in Africa and Asia toward independence—could not similarly resolve into nationhood for blacks in the United States. Of the "flaw in the idea of the ghetto as an internal colony," Nikhil Pal Singh notes that "its prospects for liberation were always slim."[47] In seeking to bring the colonial metaphor home, Malcolm X identified "land" as the basis for insurgent claims against the brutal sovereignty of the United States yet in doing so came up against the limitations of anticolonialism as a framework for black freedom ("The Black Revolution," 50). Whereas former colonies might, and indeed did, resolve into autonomous states, the emancipation of oppressed minorities in a settler colonial state presented a problem the UN was ill-equipped to address. Ultimately, these petitions were restricted by the imperial sovereignty they sought to overcome.[48] Unlike Third World states that successfully pressed for self-determination after World War II or even U.S. client-states that exercised semisovereignty, black Americans, presented as a people in the petitions, inhabited a territorial space defined by the "totalizing authority" (Byrd, 188) of the United States. The issue of political geography cannot be underestimated. Unlike indigenous tribal nations whose sovereignty had been violated by the United States, black Americans, although a dispossessed minority, were hard-pressed to assert collective sovereign right over the land they inhabited.

If Du Bois's petition lost momentum as the Cold War dawned, Patterson's *We Charge Genocide* faltered as the Cold War turned hot and red-baiting in the United States took on a fevered pitch. Countercharged as communists, these black radicals were ruthlessly persecuted by U.S. federal authorities. Despite tacit support from small, mostly postcolonial states, *We Charge Genocide* did not garner robust international backing. At a November 1951 meeting of the General Assembly in Paris, Patterson "approached first the Indian, then the Ethiopian,

Egyptian, Haitian, Dominican, and finally Liberian delegations": "These diplomats assured him how sympathetic they were, but let him know that, due to anticipated development aid from the United States, championing such a petition, no matter how valid, would not be diplomatically prudent" (Anderson, 100). Far from offering a clear alternative to what Malcolm X in 1964 dubbed the "civil-rights tree," the UN "human-rights tree"—more realistically a thorny thicket—could not be extricated from global terrain shaped by U.S. power. Any account of black radical human rights as an oppositional politics thus must theorize U.S. dominance in the Cold War international system, the very institutional basis for human rights that emerged out of World War II's ashes. Just four years before the Asian African Conference at Bandung, the vacillation of the UN delegations to which Patterson appealed, all representing nations that would declare themselves nonaligned by the early 1960s, largely proved fatal to black radical human rights politics in the United States. Contingent on the General Assembly as a site of global solidarity "where our African brothers can throw their weight on our side, where our Asian brothers can throw their weight on our side, where our Latin-American brothers can throw their weight on our side, and where 800 million Chinamen are sitting there waiting to throw their weight on our side" (Malcolm X, "The Ballot," 35), black human rights, as the historical record reveals, could not surmount the realpolitik of the Cold War world order. It thus bears inquiring into how the vision of black radical human rights exceeded the limits of UN internationalism.

The Enemy at Home

On April 3, 1964, less than a year before he was assassinated, Malcolm X opened a speech later known as "The Ballot or the Bullet," by wryly acknowledging his host and various members of the audience at Cleveland's Cory Methodist Church. "Mr. Moderator, Brother Lomax, brothers and sisters, friends and enemies," he began, and then paused to clarify, "I just can't believe everyone in here is a friend and I don't want to leave anybody out" (24). For Malcolm X the state's surveillance and racial counterintelligence operations were nothing new. In his experience the long arm of the police state dated back to the total-war measures of the U.S. government on the home front during World War II. Loath to being drafted into the Jim Crow military in 1943 and well aware that "Army Intelligence soldiers, those black spies in civilian clothes, hung around in Harlem with their ears open for the white man downtown," Malcolm X played on the wartime state's fears regarding black demoralization and color-line alignment with the Asian enemy. He let it be known, in the right quarters, that he was "frantic to join . . . the Japanese Army."[49]

The home front that the World War II total-war state dubbed the "Zone of the Interior" (ZI) had evolved into what the Cold War national security state referred to as an arena of "civil defense."[50] If the ZI during World War II corresponded to a geostrategic mapping of roughly the continental United States in which a Jim Crow military prepared for both national defense and deployment abroad, it was also a covert site of political warfare—of overlapping domestic and military racial counterintelligence programs that sought to root out political subversion, sabotage, and sedition by profiling, surveilling, and neutralizing disaffected minorities (especially blacks) and communists.[51] By the Cold War, urban areas were reimagined as vulnerable to Soviet nuclear attack.[52] To the extent that the national security state envisioned U.S. cities in the enemy's crosshairs, civil defense served as the "defensive counterpart of strategic bombing doctrine. U.S. strategists began to see national territory from the vantage of an enemy in a total war—as a space of potential targets."[53] By the 1960s, the "practice of training Americans to see themselves as targets" (Galison, 30) went far beyond atomic-era bomb shelters and duck-and-cover exercises. As a form of Cold War imperialist consciousness, the imagination of the domestic arena as susceptible to external threats extended to the imagined enemy at home. By the time Malcolm X spoke at Cory Methodist Church, he had been a target for almost a decade of the FBI Counterintelligence Program (COINTELPRO), whose aim, according to Chicano activist Ricardo Romero, was to "eliminate, intimidate, incarcerate, and terrorize" organizations and individuals deemed subversive.[54] Not only were his enemies in the house but also as an enemy of the state, he would become a casualty of a covert home-front war waged during a time of brutal interventionist war abroad.[55]

In a few years' time, Martin Luther King Jr. would be assassinated after declaring his independence from the U.S. war in Vietnam and agitating across the color line for economic justice as a necessary phase of the civil-qua-human rights struggle. Malcolm X was tellingly assassinated in a juncture when he had embraced revolutionary human rights politics, broadcast his views that guerrilla warfare was the "next step in the civil rights struggle," and, under the newly formed Organization of Afro-American Unity, was fostering ties to the leadership of African postcolonial nations.[56] Speaking to the press at New York's Park-Sheridan Hotel on March 12, 1964, he declared his intention to "be very active in every phase of the American Negro struggle for Human Rights" ("FBI HQ file 23, part 2"). Forecasting that 1964 would be an "explosive year on the racial front," he urged the public to be "peaceful, law abiding" while making clear the time had come for "the American Negro to fight back in self-defense whenever and wherever he is being unjustly and unlawfully attacked" ("FBI HQ file 23, part 2"). Describing the LAPD as "a 'Ku Klux Klan police force' which uses Gestapo tactics against Negroes," warning the NYPD that "there are probably more armed Negroes in Harlem than in any spot on earth," calling for African aid to blacks in the United States, and condemning the "criminal action of the United States government in conjunction with Belgium in the Congo" ("FBI HQ file 23, part 2"), Malcolm X, as his FBI file reveals, was articulating human rights in unmistakably insurgent terms during the final two years of his life.[57] Central to the internationalism particular to his human rights vision—and that of other Cold War black radicals—was more than a repudiation of U.S. sovereignty. In aligning with anti-imperialist forces abroad and refusing to renounce revolutionary violence against "the greatest purveyor of violence in the world," they inevitably came up against an image of themselves projected by the U.S. national security state: domestic enemy.[58] In his *Freedomways* essay Baldwin intimated the global solidaristic potential of such enemy consciousness: black Americans, "after the American Indian, [were] the first 'Viet Cong.'"

Central to U.S. domestic intelligence operations around the time of the Vietnam War—COINTELPRO, the CIA's Operation CHAOS, and the U.S. Army's civil-disturbance intelligence program—was a covert politics of enmity that blurred distinctions between inside and outside, home front and war front, U.S. national and foreign enemy. The national security juggernaut unleashed against Americans perceived to be enemies, so-called internal security measures, proceeded from the idea that "within the civilian body politic lurks an enemy that one day the military might have to fight, or at least be ordered to fight."[59] The methods deployed by U.S. racial intelligence and counterintelligence programs against black radicals, antiwar protestors, Puerto Rican independence fighters, American Indian sovereignty activists, student organizers, and others on the New Left spectrum uneasily mirrored, though by no means on the same scale, U.S. strategies of pacification and neutralization in Vietnam. In Vietnam the United States aimed to decimate the organized basis of anti-imperialist insurgency, decapitate its leadership via targeted assassination, establish comprehensive security index files, develop networks of native informants and local elites, and demoralize the mass base into submission—all goals that translated into domestic racial counterintelligence operations. As then–State Department adviser Samuel Huntington argued in the policy journal *Foreign Affairs*, the Viet Cong "cannot be dislodged from its constituency as long as the constituency continues to exist" (quoted in Chomsky, 32–33). This genocidal prescription speaks to scalar differences between permissible margins of indiscriminate death in U.S. war zones and political repression and violence in the imperial center. In Vietnam the CIA undertook counterrevolutionary measures to obliterate "the Viet Cong Infrastructure (VCI)," an operational plan that, for all its rhetoric of precision, sweepingly targeted the Vietnamese masses for death.[60] Central to the Phoenix Program, which the CIA established in 1967, the Vietnamese secret police "functioned like the FBI in America, establish[ing] a nation-wide informant network to identify VCI and their sympathizers" (Valentine, 148). This program had a home-front correlate in Operation CHAOS, which was also launched in 1967 to gather political intelligence on race-radical and other revolutionary organizations in a context of pitched urban warfare in the United States.[61]

Racial counterintelligence, as a method of neutralizing the enemy, was central to the informal war the United States was waging in Vietnam and the war it was prosecuting at home. By deciding which groups and individuals endangered national security, the state's police arm actively intervened in the domestic political landscape. True to its counterrevolutionary purpose, it fulfilled "the classic role of a secret political police" by targeting political opposition and dissent.[62] Predictably, each author of black radical human rights petitions to the UN—Du Bois, Patterson, Newton, and Seale—as well as key affiliates like Robeson, would be subjected to counterintelligence investigation. Excerpts from Baldwin's *Freedomways* essay were placed in his FBI file.[63] In the late Vietnam War era, evidence of the scale of this repressive apparatus would surface. In a 1976 study of the U.S. police state David Wise gave some sense of the magnitude of this "invisible government": "From 1955–1975, the FBI investigated 740,000 'subversive' targets. The CIA indexed 300,000 names in its 'Hydra' computer during Operation CHAOS and compiled separate files on 7,200 Americans. The Army kept files on some 100,000 Americans, including members of Congress and other civilians. The FBI as late as 1972 had 7,482 'ghetto informants' on its payroll.... The IRS had more than 465,000 Americans in its IGRS intelligence files, and another 11,500 in the basement files of the Special Service Staff."[64] By the mid-1970s, COINTELPRO was revealed to have "employed agent provocateurs, conducted burglaries, engaged in black propaganda (disinformation), fraud, and perhaps in the case of Dr. Martin Luther King Jr. and several other black leaders outright assassination."[65] In violation of the CIA's 1947 charter prohibiting domestic operations, Operation CHAOS spied on U.S. citizens in the United States and infiltrated a range of politically left organizations.[66] In contravention of the 1878 Posse Comitatus Act, proscribing the use of the military as domestic police, the federal government deployed the U.S. military to suppress black people in the 1965 Watts and 1967 Detroit riots.

The illegality of these operations demands contextualization against the criminality of the U.S. war in Vietnam, yet if international humanitarian law might be applied to the latter, by contrast, the war at home lacked a ready framework in which its significance might be understood. Albeit not comparable in scale to the U.S. wars in Korea and Vietnam that resulted respectively in upward of four and three million dead, the war at home was not dismissible as hyperbole. The vast military-industrial complex and intelligence apparatus that emerged from World War II paved the way for "the militarization of the police and the inculcation of a national security ideology that allowed for the rationalization of gross human rights violations" throughout U.S. military empire, including at its imperial core.[67] During the Vietnam War era, radical criminologists strove to offer a macrological account of U.S. criminality by casting light on the "interdependency of policing the homefront and policing the empire."[68] As Tony Platt of the Union of Radical Criminologists argued, "The state and legal apparatus, rather than directing our investigations, should be a central focus of investigation as a criminogenic institution, involved in corruption, deception, and crimes of genocide."[69] Noting that U.S. armed forces committed an "overwhelming number of killings in the 1960's," the authors of *The Iron Fist and the Velvet Glove* remarked that "the police did not arrest the men who planned and directed the U.S. aggression in Southeast Asia; they arrested the people who protested against that aggression." Moreover, "in the ghetto revolts of Harlem, Watts, and Newark, the police did not use tear gas and shotguns on slumlords or on merchants who sold shoddy and overpriced goods; they used them on the Black people who rebelled against that victimization."[70]

If black radicals during World War II wielded the term *fascism* to expose the illegitimacy and counterrevolutionary nature of the racial capitalist state, including its waging of domestic war, in the late 1960s, with an eye to forging a broad anti-imperialist united front, the Black Panther Party gave new life to antifascist critique as a way to indict both the U.S. government's domestic repressive apparatus and its war machine in Southeast Asia.[71] Such insurgent efforts to expose state criminality, however, came up against a countervailing "Law and Order" initiative. As Ruth Wilson Gilmore has argued, the ascendant right campaigned that it could contain social unrest by "using already existing, unexceptionable capacities: the power to defend the nation against enemies foreign and domestic": "And so the contemporary US crime problem was born. The disorder that became 'crime' had particular urban and racial qualities and the collective characteristics of activists (whose relative visibility as enemies was an inverse function of their structural lack of power) defined the face of the individual criminal."[72]

Proposing to neutralize radical international movements through the application of police power, the federal government acted to quell revolution under the rubric of criminal law, putting away the targets of its militarized counterintelligence campaigns as criminals. It exploited the 1970 Racketeer Influence and Corrupt Organizations (RICO) Act, a law intended to prosecute organized crime, for its elastic counterterrorism provision in order to lock up anti-imperialist revolutionaries. If, at the height of the U.S. "police action" in Korea, "the policeman's bullet" had supplanted the lyncher's rope—indeed, "the killing of Negroes ha[d] become police policy in the United States" (Patterson, 8, 9)—domestic counterrevolutionary warfare would be recoded in the ensuing decades as the work of law and order in "keeping the peace"—in other words, as routine police work. "Police," Mark Neocleous argues, "has thus become a central feature of the discursive trope through which the war power is now simultaneously invoked and elided."[73] By the late Cold War era, what this effectively meant was that key figures in the black freedom struggle were behind bars, in exile, dead, or otherwise "neutralized."

In December of 1990—roughly two decades after the racial uprisings of the 1960s, fifteen years after the U.S. withdrawal from Vietnam, and as the Cold War era was drawing to a close—a people's tribunal convened in New York City that focused on the human costs of the invisible war at home. Modeled after the Russell Tribunal, the Special International Tribunal on the Human Rights Violations of Political Prisoners and Prisoners of War in the United States made recourse to an anticolonial idiom of international humanitarian law and human rights in order to indict the illegal U.S. incarceration of "over 100 Political Prisoners and Prisoners of War within its own prisons" under the pretext "they are 'terrorists.'"[74] If the Russell Tribunal shone a light on the U.S.

war in Vietnam, the New York tribunal examined how the counterrevolutionary war at home persisted in the form of the domestic carceral regime. Finding on behalf of a range of incarcerated black, Puerto Rican, American Indian, Chicano, and white radical activists, most targeted by COINTELPRO in the 1960s and 1970s, and against George H. W. Bush, as well as his attorney general, FBI and CIA directors, and Bureau of Prisons head, the verdict identified the petitioners as either political prisoners "incarcerated as a result of activity in opposition to injustices perpetrated by the United States government" or POWs "incarcerated because of [their] actions as combatants in movements seeking liberation from the United States" (49). Identifying the latter not as U.S. nationals subjected to the sovereignty of the United States but as "anti-colonial combatants captured in the course of their struggle for national liberation," the verdict referenced UN resolutions protecting the right of "colonial people to struggle by all necessary means at their disposal against colonial powers which suppress their aspiration for freedom and independence" and affirming the status of "combatants struggling against colonialism" (48, 51). Finding that the U.S. "denial of the existence of Political Prisoners and Prisoners of War in its jails, and its consequent deprivation of the protection internationally offered by these laws constitute[d] . . . outright violation of human rights," it further found "that captured combatants in a legitimate national liberation movement are entitled to the special protected status of Prisoner of War and should not be tried and imprisoned by the US government as criminals" (48, 56).

As the Russell Tribunal's home-front counterpoint, the Special International Tribunal on the Human Rights Violations of Political Prisoners and Prisoners of War in the United States sought to cast light on the criminality of U.S. police power in neutralizing "the state's political opponents."[75] COINTELPRO's "final goal," as J. Edgar Hoover stated in an internal March 4, 1968, memo, was "to prevent the long-range growth of militant black nationalist organizations, especially among youth" (quoted in Bloom and Martin, *Black against Empire*, 202). Seeking to annihilate the "freedom dreams" of black radicals by subjecting them to erasure, up to the point of death, Cold War counterintelligence programs—FBI, CIA, and U.S. Army—endeavored to "crush the people's war" by "eliminat[ing] the people" (Chomsky, 33). Yet as this late Cold War tribunal demonstrated, those who had been discarded as criminals sought to expose, through insurgent readings of human rights, COINTELPRO as a mode of warfare and to clarify their relationship to the state to be that of prisoners of war.

Revolutionary Humanity

Moving beyond critique, Baldwin's essay "The War Crimes Tribunal" hinted at a powerful vision of racial justice that might arise with the liberation of the "Viet Cong" not only in Vietnam but also in the United States. Less orientalist than it might appear, his invocation of the epithet *Viet Cong*, a U.S. counterintelligence construction in the first place, functioned as a flexible placeholder for the enemy relative to the U.S. war machine, a figuration of both the target *and* insurgent power, brutalized but not subdued. On the fungibility of blacks targeted by myriad forms of state violence on a daily basis and reduced to subsistence in U.S. ghettoes, on the one hand, and the Vietnamese forced from lands and families, herded into concentration camps, and vulnerable to the U.S. war machine's predations, on the other, there was no ready terminology—at least none that captured the difference in history and scale yet revealed the structural continuum. Insofar as the U.S. war in Vietnam was imprinted by earlier and ongoing genocides, its violence, Baldwin maintained, thus demanded location in a home-front genealogy of the dispossession, pacification, and neutralization of American Indians and blacks. Black people in 1960s urban America, he intimated, were at war, located both within and on the receiving end of the U.S. war machine.[76]

In 1967, the year Baldwin disengaged publicly from the Russell Tribunal, violence shattered urban America like never before, with one contemporaneous study suggesting that there were up to 249 race riots across the country.[77] In the first nine months alone there were more than 160 disturbances in 128 cities. Triggered by antiblack police brutality, these were part of a pervasive pattern of uprisings that would in turn be pacified through the state's war and police power. From 1965 to 1968 there were more than three hundred riots that resulted in roughly two hundred dead and several thousand businesses destroyed in Harlem, Watts, and other sites across the nation.[78] If race riots until this time had largely been "battles instigated by white people against people of colour," from the 1965 Watts riots onward, "urban uprising became a means by which Black and other people held court in the streets to condemn police brutality, economic exploitation and social injustice" (Gilmore, 175). If informal, war in the streets of urban America was no metaphor. In a study of the shifting state tactics toward urban security Jennifer Light notes: "No official wars were fought in the continental United States during the twentieth century. But urban rioting in the 1960s came perilously close" (608). With urban unrest erupting on the heels of the deployment of U.S. combat troops to Vietnam, "quelling urban riots became a domestic job for military troops" (Light, 609). From 1965 to 1968, 184,133 troops were mobilized primarily to crush civil unrest.[79] Although post-1960s U.S. military blueprints advised "Commanders and their personnel" to "avoid appearing as an invading, alien force," the image of thousands of combat-ready military units "equipped with M-16s and patrolling in jeeps and tanks" in U.S. cities was emblazoned in the memories of witnesses and participants.[80] Of the spectacle of state force unleashed in U.S. cities, military historian Roger Beaumont was compelled to ask: "should uniformed military forces in a democracy be encouraged to wage a low-level version of *la guerre révolutionnaire* on their people?"[81]

Established by Lyndon Johnson on July 29, 1967, the National Advisory Commission on Civil Disorders (Kerner Commission) cautioned against "moves to equip police departments with mass destruction weapons, such as automatic rifles, machine guns and tanks," pointing out that arms "designed to destroy, not to control, have no place in densely populated urban communities."[82] Yet the militarization of urban policing took fearsome institutional form in the Vietnam War era. Reliant on the surveillance and infiltration of black America for the "evidence" it presented in its report, the Kerner Commission generated recommendations that assumed, rather than questioned, the military's entrenched role in domestic affairs.[83] On the local level it recommended that intelligence units rely on undercover police and informants to anticipate potential civil disorders.[84] Frank Morales argues: "Although the Kerner Commission has over the years become associated with a somewhat benign, if not benevolent character, codifying the obvious, 'we live in two increasingly separate Americas' etc., the fact is that the commission itself was but one manifestation of a massive military/police counter-insurgency effort directed against U.S. citizens, hatched in an era of emergent post-Vietnam 'syndrome' coupled with elite fears of domestic insurrection" (62).

By mid-1968 the Directorate of Civil Disturbance Planning and Operations was renamed the "Directorate of Military Support." Housed in the Pentagon's basement (dubbed the "domestic war room"), the directorate had 150 officials responsible for twenty-four-hour monitoring of civil disorders, coordinating intelligence from military data banks located in major U.S. cities, as well as overseeing deployments of federal troops.[85] Invested in more than riot suppression, the military-industrial complex viewed 1960s urban unrest as a lucrative market for defense contracts. Government officials and Department of Defense–subsidized think-tank analysts identified the task before them as "'civil defense' of a new variety: maintaining domestic urban security by continuing to apply defense and aerospace innovations and ideas to city planning and management" (Light, "Urban Security," 609–10).

Deployed to quell insurrection in Los Angeles and Detroit, the U.S. Army was involved in formulating domestic counterinsurgency doctrine.[86] In his account of civil disturbance planning, Morales locates the "roots of militarized efforts to suppress domestic rebellion" in "the U.S. Army's master plan, Department of Defense Civil Disturbance Plan 55-2" (65), an operational plan known as Garden Plot. Aimed at anticipating civil unrest and pacifying urban areas, Garden Plot was a blueprint for the militarized profiling of cities according to various criteria— "population by race," "poor economic and sociological conditions," "concentrated unemployment," presence of "militant racial, leftist (anti-war and anti-draft), and extreme right-wing groups," "existence of wide-spread sense of injustice," and access to weaponry.[87] Of the military's role in domestic counterintelligence operations, U.S. Army historian Paul Scheips notes the Vietnam War era had an unacknowledged "darker side" in that "military intelligence activities proliferated in the domestic arena under the lash of both civilian and military officials who sought information on all those they deemed a threat to national security with little regard for the cost to individual rights" (451). As he argues, "In some ways the Army's tendency to apply foreign intelligence-gathering methods to domestic situations reflected its earlier error of applying the standards of foreign war to the control of domestic disturbances. The basic problem was a mind-set in the intelligence community that saw conspiracy in protest and the threat of revolution in disorder" (299).

Through the lens of counterinsurgency doctrine, American cities were envisioned as arenas to be pacified. Vietnam War–era studies likened "high-crime areas" to "enemy territory" where "guerrillas live off the civilian population by exacting food and shelter" and "blend into the civilian population when under close surveillance or pursuit," making it "difficult for the pursuing army to distinguish between the enemy and the civilian population."[88] According to one analysis: "As in the war in Vietnam, where an American soldier finds it difficult to distinguish among Vietnamese ('*They all look alike*'), so the white American policeman finds it difficult to distinguish among Negroes, the predominant population in high-crime areas" (Black and Labes, 667).

It was precisely because of this raging domestic war that Baldwin maintained that the Russell Tribunal should be held in Harlem: "No one, then, could possibly escape the sinister implications" ("War Crimes Tribunal," 243) of the racist home-front corollary to the U.S. war in Vietnam. Although implausible, with the State Department unwilling to grant entry to foreign tribunal members intent on indicting the United States for war crimes, much less National Front for the Liberation of the South (NLF) witnesses, Baldwin's insistence on Harlem as the most apposite venue illuminated the political stakes of where justice is imagined and performed.[89] In criticizing the tribunal, Baldwin neither joined the chorus of conservative and liberal critics who dismissed the proceedings as a kangaroo court nor rejected the urgency of pursuing justice.[90] Rather, he insisted that the viability of any external condemnation of the U.S. war in Vietnam depended on its translation into internal terms, thus the significance of his voice as a critical "witness" to a nation that demanded he "pledge allegiance to a flag which had pledged no allegiance to [him]."[91] At issue was that "what Americans were doing in Asia in the name of democracy they had done for generations to their black compatriots" (Leeming, 277). An indictment that failed to recognize the domestic corollary of U.S. counterrevolutionary war in Vietnam would accordingly be one-sided at best. If, by the mid-1960s, "Vietnam had replaced American race relations" in the global spotlight, Baldwin, by contrast, sought to center U.S. race relations as vital to deliberations on Vietnam.[92] Whereas figures like Du Bois, Robeson, and Patterson at different Cold War moments marshaled human rights petitions to expose Jim Crow violence in a world forum and Malcolm X likewise urged urban black audiences to "take the case of the black man in this country before the nations in the UN," Baldwin essentially argued the reverse. Rather than bring the case of black people before a world court, the Russell Tribunal, he argued, ought to be brought before Harlem. If Sartre viewed the tribunal's dialectical force as residing in its animation of Nuremberg, Baldwin by contrast underscored the structural homology between black people in U.S. ghettoes and the Vietnamese.

Having initially enthusiastically written to and met with Russell in early 1965, two years prior to the tribunal, Baldwin emphasized "the need for American intellectuals to see the war in the context of the racial war raging in America" (Leeming, 277). In a 1965 meeting with Russell in London, Baldwin—advocating for Stokely Carmichael, another designated tribunal member, and himself—urged the aging activist-philosopher to invite prominent civil rights figures such as James Forman,

Fannie Lou Hamer, and Rosa Parks to take part in the proceedings.[93] Not merely symbolic, the participation of black civil rights leaders could galvanize draft-age men to refuse military service, as would be borne out when Martin Luther King Jr. spoke out against the war. Indeed, an initial activist intention of the tribunal was to furnish draft-resisters with a legal basis for refusing to serve. Of a nation that would send to Vietnam a black American who had "never seen the nation his uniform was meant to represent" (Baldwin, *Price of the Ticket*, xvi), Baldwin was plain: "to ask Negro soldiers to die there, while one is busily destroying their kinsmen at home—is of an impertinence so arrogant, and immorality so flagrant, as to take one's breath away."[94] No longer at the vanguard of a Double-V campaign, the enlisted black man was a slave in a system that wished to "keep him in his place," a slave who must daily reckon with the question, "*Was it worth his life*?" (Baldwin, *Price of the Ticket*, xv [emphasis in original]). His fight in no way a struggle against fascism on two fronts, the black soldier in Baldwin's Vietnam War–era writings could go to the other side yet commit no treachery.

In "Appeal to the American Conscience," a 1966 radio broadcast in which he urged an end to U.S. aggression in Vietnam, Russell described what "the papers have called the 'Vietcong'" to be "a broad alliance, like the popular fronts of Europe," and identified the "Negro struggle in Harlem, Watts, and the American South" and the American antiwar movement as critical to an international revolutionary stance against U.S. aggression.[95] Yet even as Russell sought to draw attention to parallels between the violence the United States visited on black Americans and the war it was waging against the Vietnamese, the civil rights figures Baldwin had pressed him to invite were not numbered among the left luminaries and cosmopolitan intellectuals, Sartre, Simone de Beauvoir, Isaac Deutscher, Gunther Anders, Lelio Basso, Tariq Ali, and others, who took part in his people's tribunal.[96] Though the report on U.S. bombing raids in North Vietnam by Julius Lester and Charlie Cobb Jr., Student Nonviolent Coordinating Committee members, was entered into evidence and Stokely Carmichael made a brief appearance, Baldwin's dialectical vision of hearings in Harlem did not come to pass.[97]

In light of how Harlem figures as Vietnam's domestic counterpart in Baldwin's *Freedomways*, it bears considering the obduracy with which he yoked "Harlem" with the Holocaust. As late as 1984, Baldwin reverted to this comparison: "The American Jew, if I may say so—and I say so with love, whether or not you believe me—makes the error of believing that his Holocaust ends in the New World, where mine begins" (xix). Variously dubbed "ghetto," "gas oven," "concentration camp," and "occupied territory," Harlem surfaced in Baldwin's early essays as a site of lingering enslavement and horror for "captive[s] in the promised land."[98] In a 1972 televised exchange with the conservative British journalist Peregrine Worsthorne, Baldwin insisted on this comparison, even as Worsthorne charged him with polemicizing the grim economic reality of black "slum[s]" by invoking "the emotive terms of ghetto":

> You talk about black ghettos. It's a totally inappropriate word to use. A ghetto ... was the area imposed in central Europe on the Jews, ... where rich and poor Jews were forced to live by law. There is no law in America ... that makes rich Negroes live in the New York as-you-call-it "ghetto."[99]

Baldwin rejoined:

> A man, who is strapped in, I repeat, a ghetto, who makes 27 dollars a week and can't make any more, not because he's stupid, who worked life away in a factory all of his life to support 9 children and cannot get out of the ghetto and cannot get out of the factory his only refuge is in Jesus Christ and this is not my father's fault, that man is a slave.[100]

Faint echoes of Baldwin's unapologetic conflation of black and Jewish Holocausts can be detected in his *Freedomways* essay. Yet the shifting terms of his comparison of the black American experience from the Holocaust to the Vietnam War suggests a working-through of the "small and stubborn possibility" of a "future" beyond "racial war" ("War Crimes Tribunal," 244).

In conjuring "the spectre of Auschwitz in seeking a parallel for the tribulation of American blacks" (Campbell, 183), Baldwin's rhetoric converged with the Russell Tribunal's rhetoric and aims, though not its quasi-legalistic orientation. In his 1966 "Appeal to the American Conscience" and his later "Postscript" Russell argued that Nazism's "unconscionable criminality" in occupied Europe served as precedent for the genocidal illegality of U.S. intervention in Vietnam: "in order to suppress a national revolution, such as the great historic uprising of the Vietnamese people, the United States is obliged to behave as ... the Nazis behaved in Eastern Europe. This is literally true."[101] Russell's perception that U.S. conduct in Vietnam was the same as that of the Nazis in Eastern Europe would be reflected in the tribunal's application of international humanitarian laws crafted in response to the Holocaust to the U.S. war in Vietnam. Yet unlike

Russell, Baldwin professed no faith in law's neutrality, much less in the prospects of it being marshaled, on the basis of compelling interpretation alone, against a powerful transgressive state. In a 1970 interview he contrasted the founding documents of U.S. democracy to the terror being waged by the United States in Southeast Asia: "It doesn't make any difference what one says about the Declaration of Independence, the Bill of Rights, the Magna Carta, when ... the Vietnamese are being killed on their own soil by American bombs."[102] From Baldwin's earliest essays we can perceive his distrust of liberation framed legalistically or as the select project of "the Western world" ("War Crimes Tribunal," 242). He deemed formal equality under the law an expedient ruse of Western nations, "the lie of their pretended humanism" that "coldly exclude[s] a considerable part of humanity."[103] He pointedly described human freedom as that "which cannot be legislated."[104] As he later elaborated: "To respect the law, in the context in which the American Negro finds himself, is simply to surrender his self-respect."[105] With its legal horizons, the civil rights struggle thus "contained within itself something self-defeating."[106] In *Freedomways* Baldwin further identified the fallacy of democratization to be "freedom" through "imposition" (243).

Spurning legal humanism's abstract universality, Baldwin turned to revolutionary humanity's material prospects. Unpersuaded by the returns of juridical enterprise even when the legal tools were international rather than domestic, he shifted, in his late 1960s writings, from an insistence on the Holocaust as an interpretive framework for the black experience in the United States to a focus on revolutionary struggle in Vietnam as a corollary for black freedom. His conceptual itinerary from the Holocaust to Vietnam and from Vietnam to Harlem marked a trajectory toward an imagination of humanity predicated on a genealogy of U.S. counterinsurgency. Tracing U.S. state terror from the American Indian to the black American to the insurgent "Viet Cong," he located in the latter black political possibility—what he called the "small and stubborn possibility" of a future beyond "racial war" ("War Crimes Tribunal," 244). If international human rights have been invoked in terms of safeguards against harm for powerless victims, Baldwin, by contrast, envisioned a politicized black subject whose dignity inhered not in protection from injury but in a chance at a future. Delving beneath the canonical literature of the "American idea of freedom" ("War Crimes Tribunal," 243) to unearth its obverse—foundational racial violence—he exhumed a revolutionary politics: "Long ... before the Americans decided to liberate the Southeast Asians, they decided to liberate me: my ancestors carried these scars to the grave, and so will I. A racist society can't but fight a racist war—this is the bitter truth. The assumptions acted on at home are also acted on abroad, and every American Negro knows this, for he, after the American Indian, was the first 'Viet Cong'" ("War Crimes Tribunal," 244). As a reference to the People's Liberation Armed Forces, the NLF's military arm, the American neologism *Viet Cong* has long since lost the radical resonance it once possessed. Yet for Baldwin and other committed leftist writers and thinkers in the 1960s, the Vietnam War was more than an unjustified war of "economic strangulation and foreign military rule," as Russell put it.[107] It was a revolutionary challenge to U.S. hegemony.

In "Many Thousands Gone," the title of which evokes black genocide in America, Baldwin wrote of the black man who "breaks our sociological and sentimental image of him" and therefore "stands in the greatest danger."[108] We might turn, here, to Maurice Merleau-Ponty's *Humanism and Terror* (1947), a work that, akin to Baldwin's war-crimes tribunal essay, critiqued the liberal humanist trappings of a procedural forerunner to the Russell Tribunal, the Dewey Commission. In this early Cold War essay Merleau-Ponty dared to raise the possibility of revolutionary justice outside the "judicial dream of liberalism."[109] In assessing the Dewey Commission, an international citizens' commission of inquiry formed in response to the global outcry over the Moscow Trials, Merleau-Ponty's philosophical argument makes no apology for Stalinism. Yet he distinguishes between "the operation of conservative societies" (34) founded on settled law and the workings of revolutionary justice, which can be evaluated only in retrospect. As he put it, "bourgeois justice adopts the past as its precedent," whereas "revolutionary justice adopts the future" (27). In the late 1960s Baldwin conceded that "in our image of the Negro breathes the past we deny," yet he cautioned that it was an error "to believe that the past is dead" ("Many Thousands Gone," 68). In the "Negro" as the "first 'Viet Cong,'" he located the insurgent prospect of black freedom. In a 1967 interview he stated:

> The ghetto is more heavily policed than it has ever been before, more brutally and more blatantly oppressed. After all those prayers and petitions and bombings, neither the Negro child nor the Negro parent has anything resembling a future.... Black Power means the recognition that neither the American government nor the American people have any desire, or any ability, to liberate Negroes or—which comes to exactly the same thing—themselves. Well, the job must be attempted, we *must* save ourselves if we can; and if we can save our-

selves, we can also save the country; it is now absolutely and literally true that the . . . Negro is America's only hope. (61)

"A revolution," he observed, "can fail long before it gets off the ground if it isn't understood."[110] Of the symbiosis between the poet and the people with regard to the revolution, he stated: "A change, a real change is brought about when the people make a change. The poet or the revolutionary is there to articulate the necessity, but until the people themselves apprehend it, nothing can happen. When the people have taken the necessity, when the movement starts moving, then the world moves. Perhaps it can't be done without the poet, but it certainly can't be done without the people."[111]

In *No Name in the Street*, a chronicle of the 1960s and early 1970s, Baldwin played the poet's part, noting that "for a policeman, all black men, especially young black men, are probably Black Panthers and all black women and children are probably allied with them, just as, in a Vietnamese village, the entire population, men, women, children, are considered as probable Vietcong" (131). Not reducible to targets of police brutality or a domestic figuration of the "victimized Third World," the "native Vietcong," the epithet Baldwin reserved for the Black Panthers, encoded the possibility of a future beyond racial abjection.[112] In their mission to bring "land, bread, housing, education, clothing, justice, and peace"— in a word, self-determination—to "the ghetto," they bore the revolutionary promise of turning the ghetto into "a village" (Baldwin, *No Name in the Street*, 167).

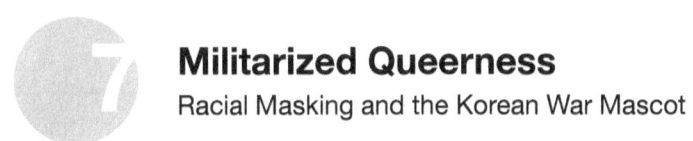

Militarized Queerness
Racial Masking and the Korean War Mascot

Coming Out in Uniform

On December 19, 2011, more than a year and a half after his discharge under the "Don't Ask, Don't Tell" (DADT) policy, which barred openly gay, lesbian, and bisexual military personnel from serving in the U.S. armed forces, Dan Choi, a West Point–trained Arabic linguist and former army infantry officer who had signed up for service in the wake of 9/11, sought once again to report for duty. Although DADT was by now defunct, Choi's reenlistment efforts had been stymied by his ongoing legal battles with the U.S. government over his protests against the policy. Defiantly clad in full military regalia and accompanied by Daniel Ellsberg of Pentagon Papers' fame, Choi attempted to be seated at Chelsea Manning's hearing in Ft. Meade, Maryland, in a show of support for the embattled former army intelligence analyst. His stated purpose a duty to defend the Constitution, as he recounted on national media, Choi was initially detained at the base entrance for wearing his uniform. On gaining access, he was thrown to the ground by military police. Adding insult to injury, they ripped the rank off his uniform before expelling him from the premises.

Having come out on *The Rachel Maddow Show* in 2009, Choi, arguably the most prominent advocate against—and casualty of—the infamous DADT policy, repeatedly thereafter publicly presented himself in military uniform. Speaking with Keith Olbermann after having been ejected from Manning's hearing, Choi, again in military dress, greeted the political commentator by stating it was "an honor to be with you in the uniform of my country."[1] Yet Choi's sartorial fidelity to his country was met repeatedly with rebuffs and, as he eventually put it, "betray[al]" by U.S. officials and fellow service-members who, like him, had pledged to defend the nation yet refused to grant him recognition. Somewhere in the course of his public struggle to hold the U.S. military to a higher moral standard, it appeared the former lieutenant had become ill-suited for the uniform, or it had ceased to represent him. Eventually, he stopped wearing it altogether. In his increasing alienation from the institution in which he had once so proudly served, he had, in his words, "become the other."[2] In starker language to the *Huffington Post* in late March 2013, Choi stated: "It's hard to know that all of a sudden, I'm the terrorist. [In the army] we called activists very bad names . . . and now, I'm them" (Bennett-Smith).[3] No longer formally aligned with the fighting forces of the world's chief military-imperial power, he had not simply reverted to civilian status but theoretically had become the enemy. Once inside the U.S. war machine, Choi was now, by his account, externalized as its target.

Yet Choi's dissentient relationship to what journalist Chris Hedges called "the public lie" (11) of U.S. interventionist war often came across as inadvertent or unintentional—more an effect of having come out while DADT was still in full force than an oppositional stance against the U.S. war machine. Indeed, more than merely challenging DADT's assumption that LGBT identity was not consonant with military form, Choi contended it was synonymous with exceptional moral courage and thus ideally suited to the nation's defense. Far from being potentially treasonous or "susceptible to blackmail by enemy agents"—the "homosexual menace" argument behind the U.S. government's Cold War persecution of gays and lesbians as national security threats—the "gay community," he declared, was "the only community in the world that bases its membership on one thing, integrity."[4] By "stand[ing] for transparency," coming out was consistent, he maintained, with patriotic values aimed at "guard[ing our] country and our way of life."[5] In numerous speeches and interviews before and after his effort to attend Manning's hearing, Choi likened her leaking of classified material to the act of coming out. At a rally at the entrance to Ft. Meade, where the hearing was held, Choi called for full disclosure as vital to the public interest and America's global reputation as a democracy: "They told us under 'Don't Ask, Don't Tell' that certain information about us should be classified and hidden from other people because they said good order and discipline would be compromised" (Becker). Assailing the "wall of separation between the American people and the American truth," Choi, in Reagan-esque terms, challenged Barack Obama to "tear down this wall!" His passionate exhortation, "It is time that we unclassify the truth that we deserve to know!" registered his trajectory from credulous poster child for LGBT military integration to his painful realization that the Iraq War, in which he served in a combat role, was unjust and "illegal."[6]

Choi thus emerged as an unlikely comrade-in-arms for Manning. Although careful not to ascribe Manning's whistleblowing to either sexual orientation or gender identity in the way her defense team would, Choi imputed a kind of gay virtue to her actions while making a case for the U.S. war machine's moral recuperability: "What Bradley Manning did, as a gay [sic] American, as a soldier, a good soldier—in fact, the only soldier in his entire chain of command who did the right thing . . . —there's no choice but for patriotic Americans to . . . support Bradley Manning in the dignity and full honor of the uniform of service."[7] Charged with aiding the enemy for having transmitted military and diplomatic intelligence to WikiLeaks, a capital offense, Manning had opened the military closet, in her words, "some server stored in a dark room in Washington DC," to out its crimes.[8] Seeking to expose "the true nature of twenty-first century asymmetrical warfare"—namely, "how the first world exploits the third, in detail, from an internal perspective"—she had broadcast the U.S. military's dark secrets, its criminal disregard for civilian life, for all the world to see, and in so doing, challenged the institution's very authority.[9] By contrast, Choi's act of coming out was aimed at the institution's reform; in the early days of his anti-DADT advocacy he approached the military as a structure of civil rights recognition rather than an engine of devastation and terror.[10] If Choi's alliance with Manning recalled something of the late 1960s tension between suits and queers, his support also signaled ambivalence toward a unilateral invasion he had once eagerly signed up for.[11]

In the process Choi inadvertently called attention to a queer legacy of militarized racial inclusion specific to U.S. interventionist war in the Asia-Pacific region. That the steps in his agonizing political itinerary, from would-be military insider to forcibly ejected outsider, were fodder for the news cycle makes it possible to trace his dawning disillusionment. One seed of his later defense of Manning was conceivably planted during an October 22, 2010, *Democracy Now!* debate on the question of whether opposing DADT bolstered U.S. militarism.[12] Squaring off with queer antiwar activist Mattilda Bernstein Sycamore, he defended LGBT military integration as a matter of both equal opportunity and life chances. Insisting that "the military is sometimes the only option," Choi depicted enlistment as the sole pathway to a future for some gays, lesbians, "undocumented immigrants [and] Muslim Americans," each of whom he identified as a "stigmatized minority." Refuting this logic, Sycamore argued that the only defensible stance toward "the US war machine" was a destructive one: "if we need to support any soldiers," they should be (in reference to Manning) those "releasing classified documents to bring down the US war machine." Seeking to reenlist at this point, Choi countered with a portrait of the U.S. military as an institution with a long history of promoting peace, a legacy stretching back to the Korean War. Citing his mother's experiences as "an orphan of the war," he paraphrased her advice: " 'Your job in the military is not to create havoc, but . . . to create peace.' " He added, "This is going to sound like fingernails on the chalkboard to some of your viewers, but war is a force that gives us meaning." Invoking the title of Hedges's *War Is a Force That Gives Us Meaning* yet misreading its critique, Choi insisted "war is a force that teaches us lessons of humanity."

Yet surfacing faintly in Choi's revelation that his mother was a Korean War orphan was an obscure history of Cold War racial securitization. Indeed, race shadowed Choi's account of the Korean War, a catastrophic interventionist war whose humanitarian face was "orphan" rescue yet whose obverse was the indiscriminate U.S. targeting of civilian infrastructures.[13] Early Cold War U.S. practices of racial securitization in this way linked two forms of racialized humanity: on the one hand were those nonwhite bodies targeted and collateralized by the U.S. war machine *and* those incorporated into it—otherwise put, "orphans, widows, the disabled, the homeless" whom Hosu Kim and Grace Cho have dubbed "biopolitical excess"; and on the other hand were the soldiers of color that North Korean war propaganda deemed "cannon fodder."[14] Semiotically uniting Korean orphans and GIs of color, as "stigmatized minorit[ies]," was the U.S. military uniform. Betokening the prospect of full national inclusion, the uniform Choi donned postdischarge suggested its ideological potency as a nationalist shield, a form of cover that in theory neutralized difference. If, as Leti Volpp notes, people of color, in the wake of 9/11, "drape[d] their dwellings, workplaces, and bodies with flags in an often futile attempt at demonstrating their loyalty," the act of doing so reinforced their racial vulnerability, with the flag serving as nationalist skin-of-sorts.[15] The urgency with which Choi appeared in uniform postdischarge likewise indicates that the act of coming out for him did not correspond to "the story of the uncovered self."[16] Rather, race persisted as something requiring concealment. Rarely, however, has Choi's coming out in uniform been understood as a story about *race* under the sign of war or a story demanding theorization of the military uniform's postracializing work. Of its power to disrupt the theoretical identity of racialized subjects with U.S. enemies, we might recall the early Cold

War remarks of Dwight Palmer, a member of Truman's Fahy Committee tasked with overseeing military desegregation: "Along with the uniform goes a halo of bravery and good Americanism."[17]

Choi's precipitous slide from military officer to vulnerable enemy, at least in his perception, raised the specter of race some six decades after Truman recommended the desegregation of the U.S. armed forces. In this regard, as Chandan Reddy has argued, "we ought to see the military fixation on and pursuit of homosexuals in the era of 'don't ask, don't tell' through a genealogy of race."[18] This insight enables us to consider how Choi, following his discharge under DADT policy, was effectively outed again, only this time as racially queer. However drastic his assessment of his fall may have been—"all of a sudden, I'm the terrorist"—it implied the precarious fungibility of status for historically marginalized demographics in wartime. On a domestic register his reasoning appeared to echo the binary logic of George W. Bush's post-9/11 ultimatum to nations worldwide: "Either you are with us or you are with the terrorists."[19] Yet scrutinized more closely, Choi's casting of his demilitarized self in enemy terms suggested a discomfiting blurring of the friend-enemy distinction with regard to race-marked subjects. Even as U.S. wars have served as the ideological impetus for expanded national unity, with opposition to various enemies catalyzing broad multiracial configurations of "what it means to be American" (Volpp, 151), race unsettled Choi's act of coming out as a gay American soldier. Insofar as it had to be covered, it remained obstinately queer.

Here, a longer view permits the tracing of U.S. militarism's racially queer genealogy in Asia and the Pacific. Against their more obvious interpretation as militarized spaces, deterritorialized wastelands, and forms of unfreedom, the U.S. concentration camp, the bombed-out cityscapes of Hiroshima and Nagasaki, the front lines of U.S. interventionist wars, and the U.S. military uniform were coded as sites of democratic opportunity for racialized subjects, both foreign and American. Integrated into the U.S. war machine as an arena of provisional life possibility, race-marked subjects were thereby securitized. Their chance at a future required the neutralization of the threat they were imagined to pose. By bringing into view constellated forms of militarized humanity during the Korean War—orphans, military mascots, desegregated troops—I pose questions casting forward to our post-DADT moment: how might investigation into Cold War–era war trash, biopolitical excess, and cannon fodder permit queerness to reenter the jingoistic narrative into which the gay or lesbian soldier has been assimilated?[20] Might excavation of the former shed critical light on what lurks below the U.S. military's framing as an incorporative engine of social equality—namely, the war machine's illiberal violence? Regarding state projects that "fold ... [queers] into life," Jasbir Puar has posed the question, does "securitization of queers entail deferred death or dying for others, and if so, whom?"[21] Casting back to the Korean War not as a watershed of racial liberalism but as a paradigmatic project of racial securitization, how might we retrieve a nontriumphalist account of militarized queerness?

Dogs of War

In the Obama era the unresolved Korean War would be resurrected as a civil rights victory. Activists and scholars demanding DADT's reversal invoked as precedent Truman's Executive Order 9981, which called for an end to racial discrimination in the armed forces in 1948 but was broadly operationalized two years later in the Korean theater.[22] That the Korean War spurred Jim Crow's federal dismantlement, enabling black Americans to serve on the front lines of an institution that had relegated them to World War II's labor battalions, "helped point the way," Barack Obama declared at a 2013 commemoration at the Korean War Memorial, "toward the ideas of equality and opportunity."[23] Observing that on Truman's orders, "our troops served together in integrated units," Obama argued that "the heroism of African Americans in Korea—and Latinos and Asian Americans and Native Americans—advanced the idea: If these Americans could live and work together over there, surely we could do the same thing here." Having signed DADT's repeal in 2010, he referenced the Korean War's blurring of the color line as a durable lesson in national unity: "Korea taught us that, as a people, we are stronger when we stand as one." Representing a rainbow swath of society, the memorial's composition drove his point home. Three of the nineteen steel figures are black, two Latino, one Asian, one American Indian, and the rest white, as the National Parks description discloses. That their ethnicities are impossible to discern, much as uniforms in theory mask racial difference, contributes to their ideological effect: militarized colorblindness.

More than marking the U.S. war machine's "democratic" renovation on battlefields *over there*, the Korean War was held out as a civil rights milestone *here*. With some Nisei and black soldier "retreads" who had served in World War II's segregated forces, the war was distinguished as the first U.S. conflict to be fought with integrated units. A 1954 government-backed report, *Breakthrough on the*

Color Front, was quick to frame the Korean War as a salutary social "experiment," hailing military desegregation as a "living example of democracy in action" that had "changed the complexion" of the armed forces and betokened, by extension, the transformation of U.S. civil society.[24] If fought to a bitter draw, the war, this report maintained, was a social engineering triumph: "On the battlefields of Korea, on America's fighting ships and planes and at its bases at home and abroad, a victory has been forged in one of the most significant social wars in the nation's history."[25] Propagated in this way as a pioneering advance toward full minority inclusion, the Korean War, notwithstanding its profoundly dirty asymmetrical nature, was heralded as a staging ground for civil rights reform and the military championed as a leveler of unequal social relations.

Published a year prior to Obama's 2013 address, Toni Morrison's novel *Home* dilates the Jim Crow home front, offering a sobering counter to redemptive Korean War narratives: "An integrated army is an integrated misery. You all go fight, come back, they treat you like dogs. Change that. They treat dogs better."[26] Featuring a freshly demobilized black soldier, Frank Money, *Home* explores the toll of black participation in a U.S. interventionist war that left an estimated four million Koreans dead, the majority civilians. It does so by moving back and forth between what Morrison portrays as intersecting sites of racist violence: a United States denuded of vital color and a Korea saturated with blood. Confined to a West Coast mental asylum as the novel opens, Frank escapes only to be confronted by hostile terrain as he makes his way home to Lotus, Georgia. Against the mythos of the 1950s as a time of war-fostered plenty, *Home* exposes the United States as "worse than any battlefield" (83), at least for the protagonist. Structured along merging tracks of space and recollection, Frank's travels back to the segregated South are overlaid by flaring screen memories. One is of fighting "horses"—one "rust-colored, the other deep black"—which he, as a child, had seen rising inexplicably "like men" (4, 5, 134). Another is of a "wee" Korean girl whom he observed pawing "like a tiny starfish" (95) for edible scraps in U.S. military garbage. As Frank recalls, the scavenging child offers sex to GIs and is killed by a fellow soldier. The first memory a sublimation of a lynching—a lethal "dog fight" (95) pitting a black father and son against each other for white entertainment—and the second a displacement of his murder of a Korean child who aroused him sexually, Frank's surfacing recollections expose the closeted racial costs of a two-front war. "How he had covered his guilt and shame with big-time mourning for his dead buddies," the novel reveals: "Day and night he had held on to that suffering because it let him off the hook, kept the Korean child hidden" (135). Bound by tropes of trash, animality, and secrecy, the casualties of U.S. war in Korea also include the repatriated black soldier who struggles to stand "like a man."

In Morrison's novel Frank's sister muses on his strangeness as she gazes at his army portrait, in which he appears as a "smiling warrior in a uniform, holding a rifle, ... look[ing] as though he belonged to something else, something beyond and unlike Georgia" (53). The uniform's ideological function as a neutralizer of difference may be central to the Korean War's civil rights returns, so to speak. Yet *Home* provocatively ascribes to the black man in uniform the home-front brutalization of the black man racialized as dog, suggesting that informal U.S. war, both in the Jim Crow United States and in Korea's "bleak landscape" (93), generated neither peace nor equality but rather degraded life. Inquiring with local Lotus men, all veterans of prior U.S. wars, about the stud farm where he once saw horses "*bit[e] each other like dogs*" but rear up "like men" (3), Frank, himself just discharged from an army that treated black soldiers "like dogs," is met with a terse reply: "They graduated from dogfights. Turned men into dogs" (139). Described as "men-treated-like-dog fights" (138), the lethal battle royals Frank strains to recall placed father against son. The local men describe the father urging his son to kill him, with the result an existence shattered by parricide. Bookending a tale of the Korean War, itself a fratricidal conflict, this scene of intrafamilial combat incited from without suggests that ruptured kinship is a racial cost of informal U.S. war. In this way *Home* dramatizes what it means to be mobilized to kill and to die in a situation not of one's making or choosing.

Described in Cold War black radical critique, as well as in North Korean, Chinese, and North Vietnamese propaganda, as "cannon fodder," black soldiers fighting in counterrevolutionary U.S. wars in Asia were reminded by figures like Paul Robeson that the "place for the Negro people to fight for their freedom is here at home."[27] "No one," Robeson remarked in 1953, with an eye on both Korea and Vietnam, "has yet explained to my satisfaction what business a black lad from a Mississippi or Georgia sharecropping farm has in Asia shooting down the yellow or brown son of an impoverished rice farmer" (357). Insofar as U.S. military desegregation in Korea affirmed the operational value of black soldiers in a "killing business" against Asian peoples, thereby heightening their own exposure to death, it signaled a dubious civil rights advance at best.[28] The dismantling of Jim Crow on Korea's battlefields meant less a guarantee of eventual assimilation into the national body politic than black labor's immediate incorporation into the U.S. war machine.[29] The military's biopolitical inclusivity thus superficially belied the U.S. war machine's brute geopolitics and antihumanism. In this regard the Korean War was "shadowed by uneasy racial consciousness."[30]

Contesting U.S. efforts to exhibit black soldiers in the desegregated armed forces as proof of the nation's democratic commitments, North Korean and Chinese propaganda identified them as disposable life, with little to gain but everything to lose. Spurning Cold War lines of enmity, North Korean propaganda leaflets, scattered across battlefronts, read as rare exchanges between target and cannon fodder, subjects yoked by firsthand experience of indiscriminate brutality from the United States. Addressed to "Negro Soldiers," one six-page pamphlet cites *We Charge Genocide*, the 1951 Civil Rights Congress petition to the United Nations, to drive home the homology between "lynching at home" and "jellied gasoline in Korea": "Both reveal contempt for life in a colored skin."[31] Listing by name black Americans lynched during the war and pointing to the disproportionate court-martialing of black soldiers, the dearth of black officers, and the ongoing struggle against Jim Crow, the pamphlet asks: "What do you think this means to you? Don't you see that this war against the colored people of Korea is the same kind of dirty business as discrimination against you—that it's based on the idea that colored people have no right to exist unless they bow down to someone?"

Writing in exile from China in the late 1960s, Korean War veteran and proponent of black self-defense Robert Williams would continue this provocative line of reasoning. In *Listen, Brother!*, a polemic rendered in the second person, he referred to black soldiers in Vietnam as dogs of war defined by their instrumentality on the battlefield: "You cuddle in your foxhole like a vicious but obedient dog. . . . Like all of the black veterans before you, you are at war, cannon fodder and trained killer dogs in a white man's crusade to safeguard ruthless white power."[32] Harnessed to the U.S. war machine for purposes other than their own liberation, such soldiers, Williams argued, were more domesticated animal than human, more weapon than self-realized man. If, almost a century earlier, Frederick Douglass had exhorted black men to don the Union uniform by pointing to the prospect of full humanity on the horizon—"The opportunity is given to us to be men"—Williams warned that dehumanization, by contrast, was the toll of serving in wars of aggression against colonial peoples struggling for their freedom.³³ By "trick[ing] black people into winding up on the wrong side of the fence . . . fighting the wrong cause against the wrong people" in a war not their own, U.S. intervention in Southeast Asia had made "Vietnam the Mississippi of Asia" (21). It transformed the black man, he maintained, into "a white man's killer dog to be sicked at will on colored humanity": "He can do anything to you and all you do is tuck your tail and take the spite out on colored Vietnamese" (26, 15).³⁴

Wielding a freighted image of white supremacist terror to illustrate its reanimation in U.S. interventionist war, Williams invoked the predatory canines mobilized by slave patrols, Jim Crow lynch mobs, and modern police: "Deadly planes, loaded with rockets and napalm, zoom through the sky. The hunt, the pogrom is on. The screaming eagles of death are vicious, like mad dogs, in their crazed desire to burn, maim and kill the colored flesh of the . . . Vietnamese" (22). Yet "dogs of war" had a literal referent in the context of the U.S. counterrevolutionary war in Vietnam. Four thousand dogs were deployed to lead "jungle" patrols, not simply to sniff out landmines but also to root out "enemies." Against Vietnamese nativity to or superior familiarity with local terrain, U.S. war dogs, Ryan Hediger writes, "mitigated some of the Viet Cong's advantages by adding information with a very different regime of sensory abilities, from acute scenting to sharp hearing."³⁵ In tandem with the aerial application of Agent Orange, scout dogs positioned on the ground uncovered what were otherwise "neatly camouflaged positions and base camps."³⁶

If vaunted as obedient heroes, these canine forces were abandoned as "expendable equipment" (56) upon U.S. withdrawal.³⁷ Category flipping, Hediger argues, was endemic to the war, with its exigencies amplifying "the fickle reversibility, the fluidity, of the categories 'human,' 'animal,' and 'machine'" (56). Best friends, lethal instruments, and ultimately war trash, these discarded dogs signaled the precariousness of socially denigrated life integrated into the war machine. In this sense dogs of war in Vietnam represented the "inclusion of the inassimilable remnant, which still remains the target of sovereign violence."³⁸ As an index of what some scholars have dubbed the posthuman military, the working animal was not just another element in what might be viewed as a hybrid "assemblage of humans, non-humans and things"; rather, in the military as an institution of social domination structured by multiple hierarchies, "few animals are lucky and most are exploited, often to further human ends that make light of all forms of life."³⁹

Wolf Children

Revisionist attempts to recuperate the Korean War as a pioneering civil rights advance have left to the side the U.S. war machine's flexible incorporation of Korean "orphans" and other forms of nonnormative life, even though such examples of GI "humanitarianism" were widely propagated in their moment. As the last conflict in which the U.S. military tacitly permitted child mascotry, the Korean War generated "spaces of beings-in-encounter" (Cudworth and Hobden, 525), fostering the emergence of war-contingent communities. If multiracial and multinational, such war-forged associations were not "co-constituted in a context of equality" (Cudworth and Hobden, 525). Rather, human and animal mascots moved in hazardous milieus in which "limited personhood for nonhuman animals emerge[d] geographically alongside human populations subjected to death," as Neel Ahuja theorizes in other contexts.[40] Indeed, some animal mascots were elevated to the status of honorary citizens while Korean "waifs" and "urchins," although typically framed in U.S. media accounts as objects of charity, were phobically cast in news reports as wolves "preying on kind-hearted GIs."[41]

The child mascot looms large in recent research on the Cold War origins of South Korea's adoption industry, yet within such scholarship, the mascot's continuum with associated forms of nonnormative life, both animals and "cannon fodder," as well as the mascot's status fluidity, have gone largely unremarked.[42] The fungibility of the mascot merits closer consideration insofar as both the Korean War's sheer brutality *and* its progressive value turned on the human-animal conflation. In *Home* Morrison depicts Jim Crow brutality as blurring the species divide, with horses standing like men and black men fighting like dogs. More than literary device, the likening of one species to another reflects the racial logic of U.S. war violence in this era. In war's mutable settings, mascots inhabited an unstable threshold between human and animal. In newspaper articles about desegregated troops, the war was also framed as an occasion to extend humanity on a tokenistic basis to indigenous life, including animals. Selective humanization was nowhere more quixotically on display than in the legend of Reckless. Few mascots, human or animal, gained more laurels than Reckless, a Korean mare with the First Marine Division that "ate our food and drank our beer," "slept in our tents and bunkers," and, on earning sergeant's chevrons, transferred to California, where she was declared an honorary citizen in recognition of combat bravery.[43] "After all, she wasn't a horse—she was a Marine!" biographer Robin

Hutton writes.[44] Accounts of Reckless highlighted her preternatural humanity: the men in her platoon "sensed a person was looking back at them."[45] Ultimately, however, in a setting conditioned by lethal force, Reckless was valued for her front-line function. Previously called "Ah Chim Hai" (Morning Flame or Sun) by her Korean owner, she was renamed after the weapon she carried time and again into battle, the recoilless rifle.[46]

Although presented as objects of rescue, mascots were likewise mobilized in dangerous roles that marked their militarized collusion and recalled their original status as permissible targets of war violence. Yet in human-interest stories in the U.S. military newspaper *Stars and Stripes* and stateside publications, smiling mascots were marshaled to evince war's humanitarian face in Korea.[47] In emphasizing how the U.S. war machine rehabilitated the most vulnerable survivors of its indiscriminate violence, this hearts-and-minds media angle obscured the devastating human costs of asymmetrical war. As Bernd Hüppauf states about modern war photography, "An iconography based on an opposition between the human face and inhuman technology oversimplifies complex structures."[48] Insofar as child mascots "attached" to or "adopted" by U.S. units represented indigenous life spectacularly salvaged by the U.S. war machine, they bore an inverse relationship to area bombing and civilian massacres—two defining features of the war.[49] The brutality of the Korean War's racial biopolitics and territorial geopolitics nonetheless lurked behind the war mascotry. War may have been the force that destroyed the child mascot's family, yet by according the mascot a token place—and temporary life—in U.S. military units, it gave the mascot meaning. By dint of defying the odds, mascots were mystified as talismans of life, and the U.S. military, an engine of necropower, was refashioned not as a generator off mass death but as an agent on the side of life.

It is no coincidence that the roundup of Korean children "found wandering aimlessly" by GIs, "taken back to camp, where they became mascots or house boys," and thereafter dispatched to orphanages that facilitated their overseas adoption was dubbed "Operation Mascot."[50] Christina Klein argues that early Cold War international adoption was part of U.S. "world-ordering projects of containing communism and expanding American influence."[51] By "saving" Asian children from the supposed perils of communism and transforming them into Americans, international adoption fostered the "multiracial, multinational family" as a sentimental national ideal; this recasting of U.S. interventionist policy in a "familial language of political obligation" (Klein 153, 187) enabled the United

States to disavow the profound racism of its war machine. It is crucial to recognize, however, that a necessary prior stage in the international adoption process for Korean "orphans" was the militarized socialization of remnant enemy life. Korean mascots occupied the same symbolic register as war "trophies, remnants from a kill, [and] longingly kept reminders of past glory," all "signs of prowess and superiority" over a vanquished people.[52] Defined by nativity on occupied territory, mascots signaled the recoding of enmity. The premise for their provisional inclusion in occupation army ranks was the domestication of their foreignness and the deterritorialization of native terrain.

Although propagated as proof of the U.S. military's colorblind humanitarianism, the Korean War mascot, as indigenous life made over as potential adoptee, thus demands theorization as an object of colonial conquest. In the mascot we might discern a logic common to the deterritorializing operations of U.S. militarism and U.S. settler colonialism—namely, eclipsed sovereign right. "Indian" sports mascots, as Philip Deloria contends, encode native defeat and U.S. triumph on the symbolic field of battle: "mascots celebrated 'Indian' ferocity and martial (read also athletic) skill," yet they were also "trophies of Euro-American colonial superiority: 'Indians were tough opponents, but 'we' prevailed. Now we 'honor' them (and in doing so, celebrate ourselves).'"[53] In a settler culture that trademarks "Indianness" in war, sports, and consumer cultures, sports mascots bear the "refractory imprint of the native counter-claim."[54] Yet that "fighting spirit" is harnessed in ways that affirm and reproduce the erasure of native sovereign right. Pointing to outsized American Indian representation in the armed forces, Winona LaDuke has pointedly asked: "How did we move from being the target of the US military to being the US military itself?"[55] Her question extends beyond military overrepresentation. As LaDuke and others note, native peoples are enshrined in the nomenclature of "the machinery of war" (LaDuke, xvii), with aircraft of today's cavalry named after the "tribes it once subdued: Black Hawk, Kiowa Warrior, Chinook, Iroquois, Sioux Scout, Cheyenne, and Comanche."[56] As a generator of new social order, the U.S. war machine has refashioned native life-forms by severing them from their origins, disrupting their social meaning in prior lifeworlds. Critical to the violence of both U.S. settler colonialism and U.S. interventionist war, indigenous life's identity with war's terrain, its nativity, thus emerges as a site of contestation itself. By rendering mascots socially dead *as Korean*, militarized mascotry, as a Korean War practice of racial securitization, thus must be theorized alongside aerial bombing as complicit in the destruction and remaking of the enemy's lifeworld. Critical here is the deterritorialization of native sovereignty that relegates "animals *and* humans perceived as having no world-making effects" to the tenuous occupation of space, thus affirming the occupying power's sovereignty in lands not its own.[57]

As a war remnant, a singularity whose obverse was the mass casualty, the Korean mascot hovered in a gray zone between friend and enemy as a form of queer life. In an August 25, 1951, *Chicago Tribune* article, war correspondent Walter Simmons cautioned against what he claimed were the predatory schemes of "thousands of 'wolf children,'" some of whom "spied for the North Koreans": "In their shoe-shine boxes some carry poison liquor which has already killed 12 Americans in Seoul alone within the last few weeks." To such "trained urchins," the tenderhearted GI was "a marked man." Revealingly, U.S. military counterintelligence worried about the access granted to child mascots, framing them as figures whose allegiances could not be assured. The Army Counter Intelligence Corps (CIC) delivered lectures to troops, instructing them not to fraternize with "indigenous" subjects, including South Korean employees with security clearances, and underscored "the dangers of allowing children the free run of all positions."[58] Although some media accounts praised mascots like Chocoletto, an honorary Marine sergeant, for furnishing his unit with vital intelligence on enemy guerrilla forces, the CIC warned that Korean children could be used "as low level agents by the North Koreans" (117).[59] In the context of a war experienced as total on the Korean end, their anxieties were not wholly unfounded. In North Korea's Victorious Fatherland Liberation War Museum in Pyongyang, for example, an exhibit is dedicated to the contributions of children who participated in the guerrilla struggle—to the point of death—against U.S. occupation (figs. 7 and 8).

Few, if any, Korean War historical accounts, however, emphasize that South Korea and the United States also mobilized children as military labor. In 2012, after six decades of denial, South Korea's Defense Ministry finally admitted the U.S.-backed Syngman Rhee regime had drafted nearly thirty thousand child soldiers, more than three thousand of whom would perish in combat.[60] Unsurprisingly, poor children constituted the vast majority. Also a source of anxiety for Occupation authorities was the covert U.S. deployment of Japanese combatants, including mascots and houseboys, insofar as those killed or captured in battle could be propagandized by North Korea or China as proof of postwar Japan's belligerent role in the Korean theater.[61] U.S. military records confirm that a handful of the Japanese sent into the Korean theater were children. The United States armed

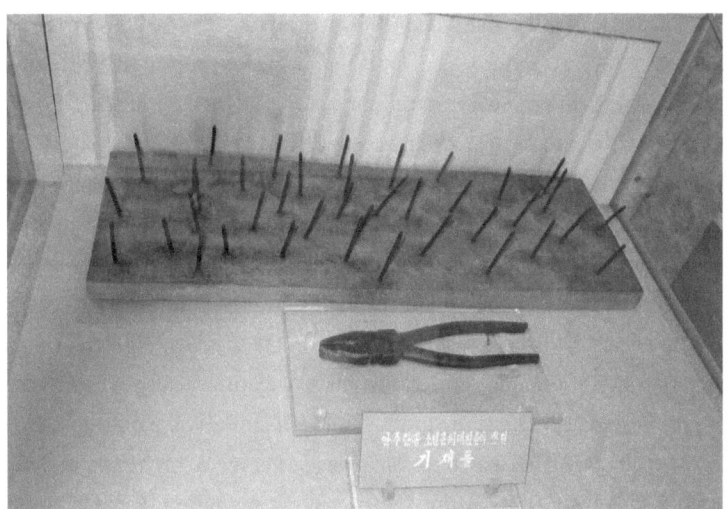

Figure 7. Display of a nail-board and pliers used by North Korean children to puncture the tires of U.S. military vehicles during the late-1950 occupation of North Korea. Placard reads: "Tools used by Anju Coal Mine Youth Guards." Fatherland Liberation War Museum, North Korea. Photo by author.

Figure 8. Photo of North Korean youth guards in display at the Fatherland Liberation War Museum, North Korea. Placard reads: "Anju Coal Mine Youth Guards who fought to the death to protect their home village." Photo of display by author.

nearly a third of these "invisible allies," and even among those who were unarmed, one houseboy "was given the task of carrying mortar ammunition, while another joined his American employer on military patrols" (Morris-Suzuki, "Post-War Warriors"). Media photos of armed mascots decked out in military gear thus cannot be dismissed as quixotic. If, "to be counted a civilian," you must "refrain completely from contributing in any way to the war effort, and put significant distance between yourself and all important target areas," child mascot proximity to and location on battlefronts, compounded by their donning of uniforms, placed them squarely in enemy crosshairs.[62] Tucked amid reports depicting Korean orphans as beneficiaries of GI humanitarianism are, moreover, disquieting accounts of U.S. forces processing all refugees, including children, as POWs. An August 8, 1950, *Pacific Stars and Stripes* dispatch reads: "The youngest PW of the war to date was admitted to an advanced PW camp recently when an 11-month-old baby, on the back of its four-year-old brother, was entered on the stockade books."[63]

Possibly abandoned or separated from family, likely displaced and homeless, yet generically construed as orphaned, Korean War mascots, who bore nicknames like Sergeant Yo-Yo, Killer, Chocoletto, and Baby-san, indexed "the in-between status of most civilians during the seesaw Korean War—men, women, and children who were put into compromised positions and forced to take sides."[64] With Korean relatives erased in U.S. media accounts of "waifs of war," as Eleana Kim remarks, "the benevolent American soldier" moved to the fore "as a parental figure, ... crossing racial and cultural moats ... to provide for and 'clothe' the needy third-world child."[65] Yet this spotlight on individual acts of GI kindness mystified the nature of social relations between the invading army and native populations. Produced by war violence, child mascots rarely solely occupied the beneficiary status of fictive offspring of specific GI fathers. Rather, "adopted" by entire units, they entered into queer kinship relations with the U.S. war machine, their insider status contingent on the war's chaos. Insofar as "ambiguous forms of intimacy ... emerged out of the neocolonial encounter between South Korea and the U.S." (Kim, 8), the mascot's function as surrogate kin was fraught with peril. As Tessa Morris-Suzuki states, the "line between fraternization and infantilization, camaraderie and exploitation was thin."[66]

Imagined as without kin and stripped of prior social bonds, mascots, as deracinated forms of life, were made over in the occupiers' image. News photos routinely featured them in scaled-down fatigues (fig. 9). By disrupting a "semiotics of disloyalty" connecting them to the enemy from whom they were otherwise indistinguishable and performing fidelity to the occupying power, their visual transformation was key to their racial securitization.⁶⁷ Even while demarcating its wearers as targets in combat, by assigning them right-of-place behind the line, the uniform performed a shared *esprit de corps* with the occupiers. In a memoir describing his hard-scrabble existence below the thirty-eighth parallel as an unaccompanied child refugee from North Korea, Link White, a Korean War mascot later adopted by American parents, recalled that procuring fatigues was his first task in the business of survival: "if I wanted to become a mascot, then I had also better look like one."⁶⁸ Taking stock of how other mascots were attired, he "was able to finagle a pair of the smallest-sized khakis and a cunt-cap from the unit's supply room" (81). Although White lacked identity papers, his "altered G.I. uniform" (79) served as his visual passport to safety.

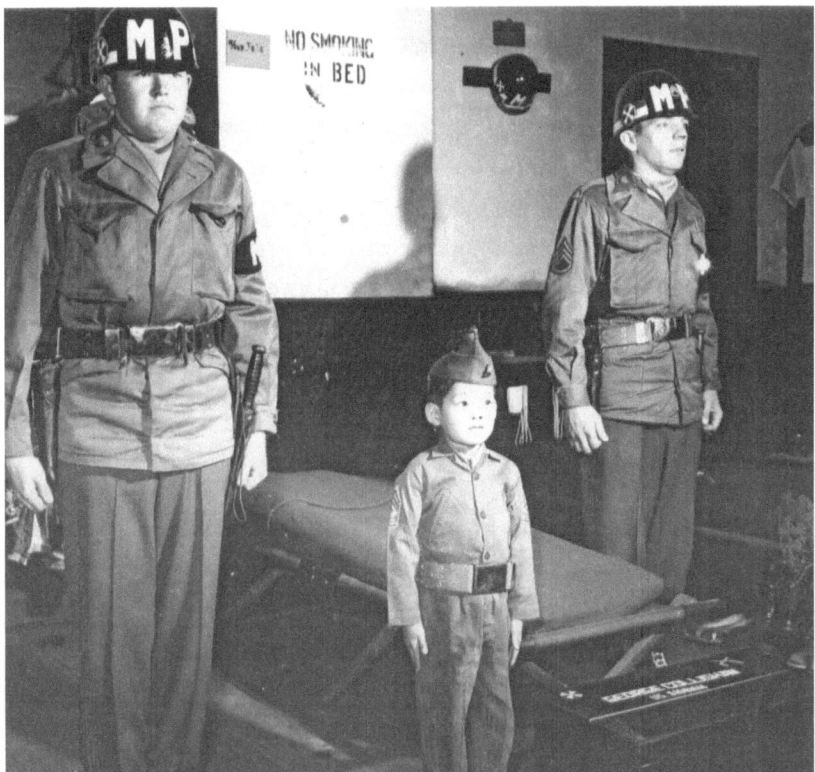

Figure 9. "Sergeant Yo-Yo," with members of the Fifty-Fifth Military Police Company. Original article subheading reads: "Youth Found in Gutter 'True' Unit Member." *Pacific Stars and Stripes*, March 29, 1953. Frank Praytor /©1953, 2019 *Stars and Stripes*, All Rights Reserved. Reprinted with permission.

In a world in which the killing of civilians, racialized as undifferentiated masses, was the norm, the mascot's life-giving "mask" was a pint-sized version of adult military fatigues. In the Korean theater the target was perceived via a "racial colonial optics."[69] Militarized practices of undifferentiated viewing relative to civilians meant their indiscriminate extermination. Shadowed by the specter of mass death, U.S. military uniforms thus served as racial cover for child mascots, "a surrogate for flesh" (Nguyen, 792), inoculating them against predation by the U.S. war machine. Not safe in their own skin, uniformed mascots were thereby securitized, in the sense of momentary "deferral of future harm" (Ahuja, 136), in the chaotic and hazardous context of asymmetrical war.

Queering the Military Archive

Neither civilian nor soldier, human nor animal, kin nor stranger, child nor adult, American nor Korean, friend nor foe, beneficiary nor victim, alive nor dead, plaything nor labor, object of love nor object of sexual desire—the Korean War mascot indexed the U.S. war machine's production of biopolitical slippages between these categories. The story of the mascot, as an enemy war remnant recuperated by and into the occupation forces, is a tale of the Cold War securitization of race and indigeneity by the imperial U.S. war machine. If traced back to the practice of military mascotry specific to the U.S. war in Korea, former Lt. Dan Choi's postdischarge insistence on donning full U.S. military regalia suggests that several decades following the battle phase of the as-yet-unresolved Korean War, race, for the gay soldier of color, remained that requiring militarized masking.[70]

That the Cold War blurring of the color line was spurred by the imperatives of the U.S. war agenda in Korea suggests that American multiculturalism must be understood as a tale of race in the confines of militarism. Insofar as it furthered an agenda geared toward the mass annihilation of nonwhite peoples, militarized multiculturalism—as a significant origin and not simply a variant of U.S. racial liberalism—requires reckoning with the extraction of "necropolitical labor" from securitized outsiders-turned-insiders who had been domesticated under the sign of war.[71] Yet more than domesticated, Korean War child mascots undertook labor crucial to the overseas reproduction of the U.S. military. Often one and the same as houseboys in the units to which they were attached, they were typically assigned housekeeping duties, the province of black servicemen relegated to U.S. labor battalions during World War II as messmen, janitors, and stevedores. Mascots took on a range of tasks, including, as Link White details, "making beds, which required just straightening out their [GIs'] sleeping bags and covering them with the Army blankets, shining their shoes and belt buckles, taking and bringing back their clothes for the wash, sweeping the tent's dirt floor, and making sure the tent's stove was always fueled and the water cans were always filled" (81).

Geared toward the needs of the occupation forces, this necropolitical labor— or "the extraction of labor from those 'condemned' to death" (6), to draw from Jin-kyung Lee's analysis of militarized labor—was aimed at fostering the lives of U.S. military personnel in the distant and hazardous milieus to which they were deployed, generating for U.S. troops a sense of home away from home. Not dissimilar in this regard to the so-called comfort women stationed during the Pacific War on Japan's Imperial Army front lines or military prostitutes in post-1945 camptowns around U.S. bases in Asia, Korean War mascots were vital to a nonnormative imaginary of care and filiation in a context of industrialized domination and death. They were critical to U.S. militarism's social reproduction.

Organized according to hierarchy and unit division, U.S. military archives militate against a broad portrait of the Korean War mascot's biopolitical significance. Memoirs, news articles, records from orphanages and children's charities, government studies of Cold War intercountry adoption, and cultural representations constitute the default archive from which traces of the history of the Korean War mascot might be gleaned. This wealth of material culture notwithstanding, few documents disclose the potency of mascots' affective labor and the ambivalence of their status more than GI photos. In Korea, as American cartoonist Bill Hume noted, "cameras [were] almost a standard part of the [soldier's] uniform."[72] The result was a vast unofficial archive of veterans' photos of the war. Conceivably shared with friends and family back home, these images of GIs and their mascots in settings "beyond and unlike Georgia" (Morrison) were at the same time often uncannily homelike in nature. In pictures of camp life that routinely show up in personal photo albums, the mascot's presence shifts the affective register of distant war scenes in ways that point to the significance of indigenous labor in the reproduction of military imperialism. In some cases archived online or sold as war memorabilia following the original owners' deaths, anonymous photo collections of long-concluded tours of duty typically offer few biographical clues and just a smattering of historical details. Yet even as such images demand interpretive practices that extend beyond the ambit of private memory, their intimate recollection by American veterans stands as testament to the mascot's affective labor.

Enigmatically surfacing in veterans' photos, mascots act as more than surrogates for the familiar. In early Cold War Korea's war-decimated landscape they register the queerness and malleability of deterritorialized indigenous life. Often uncaptioned, photos of child mascots prompt unanswerable yet lingering questions. In some, the eroticization of the mascot's vulnerability is palpable (figs. 10 and 11). The erotic, Sharon Holland reminds us, is the "glue" (32) for racist order. Conditioned by asymmetrical violence, such images imply uncertain and unsettling "'feelings' across the color line."[73]

As historian Tessa Morris-Suzuki remarks, "In a world full of homeless and abandoned children, the individuals and units which adopted child 'mascots' may have done so with the best of intentions, but the potential for abuse is also glaringly obvious."[74] A February 26, 1951, *Pacific Stars and Stripes* article describes the makeover of a four-year-old refugee, "Chun Jea Lee," a.k.a. "Miss 57th Field Artillery": "The battalion sweetheart is wearing GI clothes, but a collection was taken to buy her a complete feminine wardrobe."[75] Two GIs, serving as "emergency mothers," helped to "bathe her, feed her, and dress her every morning." Yet the media emphasis on the GIs' role as paternal surrogates or "emergency mothers" to these "waifs of war" disclosed only part of the tale, leaving untold the mascot's affective and reproductive labor relative to the imperial war machine, both in the form of kin work for soldiers stationed abroad and other modes of "service." Tellingly, other U.S. military units "adopted" girls they nicknamed "Baby-san," a generic term indissociable from militarized prostitution during the Korean War.[76] In an account of the "gendered, racialized, sexualized, and colonial processes" shaping GI relations with Korean children, Soojin Pate observes that female mascots were at times cast "in the image of the *gijichon* [South Korean camptown] woman" (45, 59). More than just representational continuum, however, the identity of military mascot and military sex worker theoretically dovetailed in the same figure. Indeed, "the earliest prostitutes were camp followers of troops," women widowed or girls orphaned by the war who were disparagingly referred to as "blanket squads."[77] In this emerging shadow economy of war, the complement to first the tour of duty and thereafter the "hardship tour" would be the sexual trafficking and labor exploitation of Korean women and children (fig. 12)—and the illegibility of their human rights.[78]

Figure 10. Photo of Korean child mascot and American serviceman at camp, ca. early 1950s. From author's personal collection.

Figure 11. Photo of Korean child mascot at camp, ca. early 1950s. From author's personal collection.

Figure 12. Photo from author's personal collection, ca. early 1950s. The reverse side reads: "boys and Bob. These kids do steal, cheat and pimp off there [sic] sisters to earn money. You can tell just by looking at them. Dirty, lousy and ignorant."

In its realization as an infrastructure of ongoing U.S. occupation in South Korea, the unending Korean War corresponds to a discomfiting biopolitical genealogy of U.S. militarism within South Korea's internal margins, which liberal American attempts to claim the war as an underrecognized civil rights watershed must disavow. Giving the lie to the Cold War U.S. military's multicultural veneer, the camptown counters home-front U.S. recuperations of the Korean War as an "equalizing moment in which racial and national identity were reconciled."[79] Such selective focus on the racial integration of the U.S. armed forces necessarily disregards the racially undemocratic form that U.S. militarism took on the Korean peninsula. Virtually overnight, the U.S. military camps and tent cities erected during the war's battle phase gave way to fixed bases, one marker among many of South Korea's semisovereign status relative to the United States. Casting back to the mascot's role in socially reproducing a sense of home away from home for GIs, the establishment of *gijichon* ("camptowns" around U.S. bases) formalized a South Korean affective economy geared toward U.S. military clientele. Throughout much of the Cold War, camptowns served as arenas of overlapping U.S. and South Korean biopolitical intervention, including the forcible monitoring of military prostitutes for sexually transmitted diseases in order to safeguard the "fighting strength" of U.S. forces. If indelibly associated with R&R for successive generations of U.S. soldiers, these ghettoes around U.S. bases—with their Americanized nightclubs, restaurants, bars, and brothels—appear in South Korean literature as a site of internal exile, "an island between Korea and the U.S." where "temporary sweethearts," "nameless 'honeys' for the GIs," and "whores for Westerners" form a cast of abject figures "ignored by our motherland."[80] As zones of transaction between notoriously disposable Korean labor and U.S. military personnel shielded by extraterritorial rights, camptowns have predictably loomed large in Korean people's struggles for self-determination because of the glaring contradiction they pose to democracy on the peninsula.

Unthinkable outside the geopolitics of the unending Korean War, the South Korean camptown, as a liminal biopolitical space between nations, has historically produced figures deterritorialized as Korean yet not nationalized as American, including children internationally marketed as war orphans long after the Korean War's active hostilities had ceased. Not just a site of sexual exploitation, however, the camptown also demands interpretation as a racially queer space. Indeed, decades after Truman's military desegregation order, the camptown evinced Jim Crow's mapping onto the unincorporated margins of the U.S. garrison state in Asia and the Pacific. In Heinz Insu Fenkl's semiautobiographical novel *Memories of My Ghost Brother*, the narrator recalls the Vietnam War–era camptown in which he came of age as a ghetto where Jim Crow politics lethally shaped social realities. Not just spatially realized, with some bars and strip clubs marked "black" and others "white," Jim Crow's militarized extension to South Korea demarcated the bodies of local women—those Korean military prostitutes and GI brides who "went black" versus those who "went white"—on opposing sides of an imposed black-white color line and positioned their mixed-race children on the precarious threshold between host and occupying nation. Of the war power that alienated him from his father, a white soldier in the U.S. Army, Fenkl's narrator reflects on his father's military insignias as more than "*symbols of power*"; they were "*totems of the clan that kills people whose skin is the color of mine*."[81] Marked by race and thus the war trash of U.S. interventionist war, the narrator moves in the underworlds of the camptown's shadow economy. As the narrator recalls of his childhood: "I had walked down alleys where girls not much older than me would suck a GI's penis for a few dollars, where boys my age would let a man fuck them. . . . We were all doing our best to get money from the yellow hairs, the long noses, the Yankees" (249). Largely closeted, camptown biopolitics are part of the queer racial legacy of the Korean War. War is the force that gives the camptown its meaning.

EPILOGUE

On the eve of the Trump era the spectacle of race in militarized form occupied center stage before receding, at least for a time, from view. At the 2016 Democratic National Convention (DNC) in Philadelphia, a photo of U.S. Army captain Humayun Khan was projected onto the giant screen as a stark and poignant example of liberal American values. The significance of his life as a South Asian immigrant who was born in the United Arab Emirates, arrived in the United States as a child, came of age in Maryland, and died twelve years earlier in the U.S. war in Iraq was keyed to Hillary Clinton's 2016 presidential campaign slogan, "Stronger Together." In a short video prefacing his father's DNC speech, a solemn Clinton, standing at a podium with U.S. flags in the background, narrated the fateful moments that led up to the young soldier's death. Spliced footage of a rapt audience representing a cross-section of multicultural America—a black woman in hijab, a woman of color clasping her hands in prayer, and a white man wearing a yarmulke comforting an older man overcome with emotion—modeled the greater message: the urgency of national unity in the face of a common enemy.

Seeking to counter her opponent's white nationalist appeal by demonstrating the multiethnic and multifaith character of her support base, the Clinton campaign capitalized on the populist draw of multiracial democracy by casting the national spotlight on a Muslim American soldier who risked and ultimately forfeited his life in a multifronted U.S. "war on terror." Over the course of subsequent presidential debates, Clinton would make plain that both Muslim Americans and "majority Muslim nations" had indispensable roles to play against other Muslims in the blurred zone between warfront and home front: "We need American Muslims to be part of our eyes and ears on our front lines. I've worked with a lot of different Muslim groups around America. I've met with a lot of them and I've heard how important it is for them to feel that they are wanted and included and part of our country, part of our homeland security, and that's what I want to see. It's also important . . . to defeat ISIS, to do so in a coalition with majority Muslim nations."[1]

In the *longue durée* of the war on terror Muslim Americans, positioned as ceaselessly obligated to prove their allegiance, have been instrumentally identified as an exploitable pool of counterinsurgent labor for the national security state.[2] In Clinton's geostrategic vision of U.S. global dominance, their value derived from their racialized intelligence function as the "eyes and ears" of U.S. deterritorializing operations against "terrorism"—in other words, from their operational collusion with U.S. police and war power. Leaving to the side any critical reflection on the unilateral nature of U.S. counterinsurgent violence and its production of mass death, social upheaval, and environmental ruin, this securitized framing of Muslim Americans as vital strategic assets in the U.S. war on terror was presented as both a *democratic* contrast to Trump's exclusionary proposals and a *democratizing* pathway to insider status within the United States. In keeping with the war on terror's Manichean sorting of targeted demographics into alignment with or against the U.S. war machine, military-imperial complicity was imagined as an engine of national inclusion—of the progressive, if at times posthumous, enfolding of outsiders, neutralized of any danger, into the national body politic.

Extolling Khan as the "best of America," a soldier who ordered his troops to stay back while he inspected a suspicious vehicle, Clinton exhorted her listeners to reap the dividends of his sacrifice by inviting them into the unifying patriotic space of a nation at war: "It's time to stand up and say, 'We are Americans. We will not turn on each other or turn on our principles.' "[3] As this video and Khan's father's ensuing speech implied, even the most suspect denizens of post-9/11 multicultural America, Muslims, had demonstrated loyalty in the crucible of U.S. interventionist war in the Middle East. Khan had realized the promise of inclusion that the United States proffered to outsiders in its most sacrosanct form: death in service. The securitizing impact of his death, moreover, rippled outward, granting his family instant membership in that unassailable demographic the U.S. military refers to in hallowed terms as "Gold Star survivors."[4]

With his son's larger-than-life image behind him and his wife, Ghazala, by his side, Khizr Khan took to the stage to make the case for multiculturalism's centrality to U.S. national security. Introducing himself and his hijab-clad wife as "patriotic American Muslims with undivided loyalty to our country," Khan was met by a roaring response that swept the conventional hall, "USA! USA!

USA!"—the same chant first responders had shouted three days after 9/11, when George W. Bush paid a visit to Ground Zero.[5] Yet if Muslims were interpellated as the chant's "terrorist" exterior when Bush warned that "the people who knocked these buildings down will hear all of us soon," Khan and his wife, by dint of their son's death, were located not as the implied target of "USA! USA! USA!" but rather under the shield of its military-imperial formation. If momentarily jarred, Khan regained his rhetorical momentum, singling out one listener in particular, Trump, in order to school him in the basics of American democracy. Denouncing Trump's proposed Muslim ban, Khan offered, to thunderous applause, to lend the Republican presidential candidate his pocket copy of the Constitution, pointing to the Fourteenth Amendment's promise of the law's equal protection. As he reminded Trump, those "who died defending [the] United States" were of "all faiths, genders, and ethnicities." Clad in the mantle of his son's service, Khan drove home his stinging critique: "You have sacrificed nothing and no one."

Yet even as these words were meant expressly for Trump, referencing his serial draft deferments from the mid-1960s to the early 1970s and his children's privileged inoculation from the risks of war, they more broadly extended to most Americans following the U.S. military's transformation in the late Vietnam War years to all-volunteer forces. From that point forward, as the American Homefront Project notes, the "burdens of war," far from democratically distributed, "began falling on fewer shoulders."[6] By 2017, of the 33.4 million Americans of prime enlistment age, just 9.7 million were regarded as qualified to join the army; of the latter category, only an estimated 136,000, according to the U.S. Army Recruiting Command, were deemed to have any interest in doing so.[7] As the number of active military personnel has dipped well below 1 percent of the total U.S. population, the shoulders on which the yoke of military service has fallen have been increasingly nonwhite.[8] Acknowledging the "difficult recruiting environment" after 9/11, *Non-citizens in Today's Military*, a 2005 think-tank report cited in advocacy for the DREAM Act, bluntly predicted that "much of the growth in the recruitment-eligible population will come from immigration."[9] In 2008, in accordance with such findings, the Bush administration authorized Military Accessions Vital to the National Interest (MAVNI), a recruitment initiative that aimed to enlist noncitizens with medical training or critical "language and cultural capabilities"—all skills deemed "vital to the national interest"—by promising them a fast track to citizenship.[10] In 2012, when the Obama administration implemented Deferred Action for Childhood Arrivals (DACA), MAVNI became the sole portal through which DACA recipients could sign up for service.[11] Although the Trump administration, citing security concerns, suspended MAVNI in 2016, the Pentagon—with an eye to boosting enlistment—has actively continued to "tinker at the margins," in the phrase of a Rand analyst, including by offering bonuses, disregarding poor test scores, and granting waivers to recruits convicted of minor drug charges.[12]

This targeted recruitment of poor, undocumented, and migrant youth has reinforced the notion that even if it comes at the cost of their lives, "the poorest people, regardless of citizenship or immigration status, should feel lucky to be exploited."[13] In the post–Cold War era, as the military budget of the United States has taken on ever-more unrestrained dimensions, dwarfing the military spending of the next nine countries combined—indeed surpassing the military expenditures of its former foes and current rivals, China and Russia, fourfold and tenfold, respectively—the labor that sustains the U.S. war machine and its hubristic vision of full-spectrum global dominance draws heavily from its most vulnerable populations.[14] According to 2018 data, 43 percent of enlisted men and 56 percent of enlisted women are "Hispanic or a racial minority."[15]

The minoritization of U.S. military service personnel has been by long historical design. What historian Melani McAlister, in reference to post–Cold War U.S. wars of intervention in the Middle East, has called "military multiculturalism"—or "a militarized national construct" that incorporates racial difference "in order to forge a new unity"—derives from a Cold War playbook.[16] On the level of geostrategic logic Truman's 1948 Executive Order 9981, which called for the desegregation of the Jim Crow armed forces, worked in tandem with the National Security Act, which authorized the consolidation of the national security state just a year prior. In that early Cold War juncture the national security state, with an eye to the U.S. war machine's efficiency, exploited the domestic democratic promise of racial integration in its military ranks. Military multiculturalism thus arose out of the same context that gave rise to the U.S. national security state and the consequent militarization of U.S. foreign policy.

Writing during World War II, the Caribbean historian Eric Williams cautioned that "no peace terms perpetuating foreign overlordship under any guise whatsoever can be reconciled with the democratic principle."[17] Yet throughout the Cold War and beyond, U.S. military empire's expansion, if associated around the globe with the fascism of U.S. war power, has proceeded domestically under the sign of racial liberalism. In the long peace-that-is-no-peace that has succeeded the Cold War's catastrophic brutality, integration into the U.S. war machine for structurally excluded or minoritized subjects has been framed as a mode of uplift and a vehicle for civil rights.[18] In terms of domestic returns—codified in the 1990 amendment of the Immigration and Nationality Act extending posthumous citizenship to noncitizen service personnel who died while on duty in a time of U.S. war, the 2008 establishment of MAVNI, the Obama-era repeal of Don't Ask, Don't Tell, and the DREAM Act's military option—post–Cold War U.S. interventionist wars have been ideologically rehabilitated through their promise of a multicultural war dividend—namely, the prerogatives of insider status as compensation for wartime service and its attendant risk of death.[19] All told, from 2001 to 2017, 125,452 noncitizen service members were naturalized.[20]

In retrospect the 2016 transformation of Humayun Khan into an object lesson of American multicultural democracy—if positioned against the Trump administration's resolve to implement a Muslim ban, to roll back DACA, to suspend MAVNI and initiate the deportation of some participants, as well as to ban transgender people from serving in the military—may have appeared, to some, to have been liberalism's last act before it unceremoniously exited stage left. Former secretary of state Madeleine Albright, who notoriously justified the death of five hundred thousand Iraqi children as an acceptable "price" of U.S. sanctions, has encouraged just such a periodization.[21] Sounding the alarm about the twenty-first-century resurgence of fascism, she has stated: "If we think of fascism as a wound from the past that had almost healed, putting Trump in the White House was like ripping off the bandage and picking at the scab."[22] Yet this partisan attack discloses little about the political nature of U.S. military-imperial violence from the Korean War–era integration of the armed forces onward. Conceiving of U.S. fascism in ad hominem terms, it fails to indict an imperial system geared overtly and covertly for perpetual warfare that has donned domestic liberal trappings, deploying the "use of military form to give the individual compensation for inequality."[23]

In this regard the story of race in U.S. militarized form requires us to contend with the total-war origins of and military-imperial impetus behind early Cold War–era integrationist ideology. It entails locating federal desegregation against a backdrop of the global ascendancy of the United States following its overwhelming military victory in World War II. The commemoration of World War II as a global battle against the forces of fascism may have imparted to that war the veneer of both a "good fight" and a people's war, yet the typical focus on the "Rome-Berlin-Tokyo axis" has left to the side both the wartime and the postwar race-radical critique of the fascism of U.S. war and police power. By disavowing the latter, accounts like Albright's render inexplicable the structures and duration of imperial violence for those positioned on the receiving end of U.S. interventions. Of the subterranean lines of continuity linking the informal wars the United States prosecuted throughout the Cold War to the 9/11 attacks, Arundhati Roy, writing in September of 2001, pointed to the plausibility of blowback: "The September 11 attacks were a monstrous calling card from a world gone horribly wrong. The message may have been written by Bin Laden . . . but it could well have been signed by the ghosts of the victims of America's old wars," those who suffered at the hands of "all the terrorists, dictators and genocidists whom the American government supported, trained, bankrolled and supplied with arms."[24] Inhering, however, in the hubristic imperial insistence on blowback as just cause for new interventions is the imperial refusal to contextualize blowback as the consequence of past interventions, much less as sobering evidence of the unfinished nature of "America's old wars" for peoples around the globe. In this way, blowback, beyond its somewhat benign CIA definition as "the unintended consequences" of U.S. foreign policy, has been strategically enfolded into the logic of permanent war and its authorization of continuous violence.[25]

To no small degree, the prosecution of permanent war relies on the illegibility of the penetrating reach of U.S. war and police power—and the latter's dematerialization of any distinction between *over here* and *over there*. The total-war concept of the U.S. "homeland" as an arena of American life to be defended against enemies, both foreign and domestic, without question came of age after 9/11. The blurring of the front line—and with it the indiscriminate expansion of the battlefield—was operationalized, however, during World War II in the Zone of the Interior (ZI) and throughout the Cold War under the rubric of civil defense. If the ZI signaled the securitization of the continental United States, where a Jim Crow army prepared for national defense and deployment to foreign combat zones, it also reconfigured national terrain in durable ways as "a consciously secured rear area," a site of subterranean political warfare in which racial counterintelligence programs sought to root out subversion, sabotage, and sedition by neutralizing disaffected minorities and communists—an agenda that extended well into the postwar period.[26] This perception of U.S. terrain through its own war machine's crosshairs gave rise to a preemptive Cold War structure of "relentless resilience" that fundamentally unsettled the conventional boundaries and definitions of warfare.[27] Beyond traditional approaches to perimeter defense, homeland security *avant la lettre* turned on what U.S. war planners identified as the enemy within, putting into motion the covert transformation of U.S. domestic policy along counterinsurgent lines.[28] World War II accordingly demands interpretation less as a race war whose contradictions were resolved in the postwar shift to racial liberalism than as a multifronted military-imperial war of racial intelligence and counterintelligence whose long reach into the twenty-first century calls for careful analysis.

Far from specific to the post-9/11 era, the concept of homeland security dates back to the informalization of U.S. wars in the wake of World War II and the centrality of racial intelligence and counterintelligence to the prosecution of those wars. If, during World War II, industrialized capitalist societies gave "birth to the monster of total war," as Jean-Paul Sartre argued, the United States, by producing, dropping, and testing atomic weapons, rendered the distinctions between civilians and combatants, home front and battle front, as well as peace and war superfluous.[29] More than prompt questions of temporal duration, the Cold War inauguration of permanent war extended war to sites not conventionally understood as arenas of combat. It gave rise to the unbounding of war. Central to Cold War U.S. domestic counterintelligence campaigns, as well as the multiplicity of wars-by-other-names—police actions, proxy wars, irregular wars, and low-intensity conflicts—was the militarized incorporation of operatives able to maneuver undercover, so to speak, within racialized target populations.[30] In this regard the Cold War U.S. war machine blurred racial difference and dispersed the battlefield in both spectacular and covert ways.

As a tale of a hegemonic U.S. global agenda aimed at ensuring the lethality of its hybrid human-nonhuman killing technology, race in militarized form demands theorization against the fascism of U.S. war and police power. It has a central place within the legacy of what antifascists identified during World War II as the fascism of appeals to military-imperial war unity, or the "noneconomic harmony of the nation in arms" (Lauterbach, *Economics in Uniform*, 195). In contrast to the black-and-white composition of the Union Army during the Civil War, which lent that conflict its democratizing promise, the multiethnic transformation of the U.S. war machine, from the Cold War era onward, cannot simply be understood as a democratic reflection of changing national demographics. Rather, it calls for analysis as a counterinsurgent mirroring, within the composition of U.S. fighting forces, of U.S. foes.[31] To the extent that it does, the war of racial counterintelligence has never ended. In the wake of 9/11 the "racialization of counterterrorism," as Sahar Aziz has argued, has turned on "the assumption that the diverse Muslim communities across the country" have privileged insight into terrorism.[32] The donning of the U.S. military uniform may have been held out as a second skin of sorts, a neutralizer of racial or religious difference for potentially suspect Asians, Pacific Islanders, Latinos, Africans, and Muslims. Tellingly, however, it is the diversity within U.S. military ranks—"not just racially and ethnically, but also linguistically and culturally"—that U.S. war planners have deemed "particularly valuable as the United States faces the challenges of the Global War on Terrorism" (Hattiangadi et al., *Non-citizens in Today's Military*, 1). Reliant in this way on racial intelligence and counterintelligence, permanent war must therefore be understood as the biopolitical prosecution of informal war in a geographically unbounded battle zone.

The theater of U.S. interventionist war has long commandeered the globe as its stage. Throughout the Cold War and well into the post–Cold War era, the history of the embattled military-imperial state has been emplotted as a multisited drama of democratization. Yet the compositional elements of this aestheticized war politics—namely, race within militarized form—betray their origins in the early twentieth-century fascist assemblages that sutured humanity to the war machine, with a difference in emphasis. By placing racialized humanity center stage, dramas of democratization thereby have disavowed the shattering impact of military-imperial violence, minimizing the structures in which race was targeted, captured, and mobilized in the first place.

A cognitive mapping of the Pax Americana as a military-imperial regime, however, exposes far more than the integuments of power. On the capillary level, sites of top-down dramas of democratization are spaces in which democracy has been imagined otherwise—as insurgent visions of justice, the shared prospect of life, and the forging of relations beyond those sanctioned by the war machine.

Notes

Introduction

1. Ruth Wilson Gilmore, *The Golden Gulag* (Berkeley: University of California Press, 2007), 28.

2. Fred J. Cook, *The Warfare State* (New York: Collier, 1964), 106.

3. On the "iron first and velvet glove" analysis of the role of policing in American democracy see Tony Platt et al., *The Iron First and the Velvet Glove: An Analysis of the U.S. Police* (Berkeley, CA: Center for Research on Criminal Justice, 1975).

4. Martin Luther King Jr., "Declaration of Independence from the War in Vietnam," *Ramparts* 5, no. 11 (1967): 37, 36.

5. Ho Chi Minh, "Appeal on the Anniversary of the Geneva Agreements," in *Against U.S. Aggression for National Salvation* (Hanoi: Foreign Languages Publishing House, 1967), 84–85.

6. King, "Declaration," 33 (emphasis in original).

7. See John Lewis Gaddis, "The Long Peace: Elements of Stability in the Postwar International System," *International Security* 10, no. 4 (1986): 99–142.

8. For a description of the Pacific Command (PACOM) see Winona LaDuke, with Sean Aaron Cruz, *The Militarization of Indian Country* (East Lansing: Michigan State University Press, 2013), 48.

9. The phrase "empire of bases" is Chalmers Johnson's. See Chalmers Johnson, *The Sorrows of Empire: Militarism, Secrecy, and the End of the Republic* (New York: Metropolitan Books-Henry Holt, 2004), 5.

10. See Howard Winant, "The Modern World Racial System," in *Transnational Blackness: Navigating the Global Color Line*, ed. Manning Marable and Vanessa Agard-Jones (London: Palgrave MacMillan, 2008), 41–54.

11. "Initial Recommendations by the President's Committee on Equality of Treatment and Opportunity in the Armed Services," May 24, 1949, Armed Services, Record Group 220: Records of the President's Committee on Equality of Treatment and Opportunity in the Armed Services, Truman Library, www.trumanlibrary.gov/library/research-files/initial-recommendations-fahy-committee?documentid=NA&pagenumber=2 (emphasis added).

12. Rey Chow, *The Age of the World Target: Self-Referentiality in War, Theory, and Comparative Work* (Durham, NC: Duke University Press, 2006), 31.

13. Quoted in Barbara Dianne Savage, *Broadcasting Freedom: Radio, War, and the Politics of Race, 1938–1948* (Chapel Hill: University of North Carolina Press, 1999), 140.

14. C. Vann Woodward, *The Strange Career of Jim Crow* (1955; Oxford: Oxford University Press, 2002), 219–20.

15. See Barack Obama, "Remarks by the President at 60th Anniversary of the Korean War Armistice," July 27, 2013, Office of the Press Secretary, www.whitehouse.gov/the-press-office/2013/07/27/remarks-president-60th-anniversary-korean-war-armistice.

16. Daniel Widener, "Seoul City Sue and the Bugout Blues: Black American Narratives of the Forgotten War," in *Afro Asia: Revolutionary Political and Cultural Connections between African Americans and Asian Americans*, ed. Fred Ho and Bill Mullen (Durham, NC: Duke University Press, 2008), 78.

17. Bruce Cumings, *War and Television* (London: Verso, 1992), 215; see also Sahr Conway-Lanz, *Collateral Damage: Americans, Noncombatant Immunity, and Atrocity after World War II* (New York: Routledge, 2006), 20.

18. Chris Marker, *Coréennes*, trans. Brian Holmes (1959; Columbus, OH: Wexner Center for the Arts, 2009), https://chrismarker.org/coreennes-english-text.

19. Lisa Lowe, *The Intimacies of Four Continents* (Durham, NC: Duke University Press, 2015), 107.

20. Toni Morrison, "In Toni Morrison's 'Home,' Soldier Fights War Abroad, Racism at Home," interview by Jeffrey Brown, *PBS News Hour*, May 29, 2012, www.pbs.org/newshour/show/in-toni-morrison-s-home-soldier-fights-war-racism.

21. Ralph Ellison, "Airman Novel," Box 115, Folder 1, ms. and ts., Papers of Ralph Ellison, Library of Congress, Washington, DC.

22. The phrase "race-radical" is Jodi Melamed's. See Jodi Melamed, *Represent and Destroy: Rationalizing Violence in the New Racial Capitalism* (Minneapolis: University of Minnesota Press, 2011), xix.

23. Harold Black and Marvin J. Labes, "Guerrilla Warfare: An Analogy to Police-Criminal Interaction," *American Journal of Orthopsychiatry* 37, no. 4 (1967): 666–70.

24. D. Marvin Jones, *Dangerous Spaces: Beyond the Racial Profile* (Santa Barbara, CA: Praeger, 2016), 41.

25. Patrisse Khan-Cullors and Asha Bandele, *When They Call You a Terrorist: A Black Lives Matter Memoir* (New York: St. Martin's, 2017), 134.

26. Brandon C. Davis, "Defending the Nation, Protecting the Land: Emergency Powers and the Militarization of American Public Lands," in *Proving Grounds: Militarized Landscapes, Weapons Testing, and the Environmental Impact of U.S. Bases*, ed. Edward A. Martini (Seattle: University of Washington Press, 2015), 35.

27. See LaDuke, *Militarization of Indian Country*, 37.

28. See Traci Brynne Voyles, *Wastelanding: Legacies of Uranium Mining in Navajo Country* (Minneapolis: University of Minnesota Press, 2015), 7.

29. Eqbal Ahmad, "Revolutionary War and Counter-Insurgency," *Journal of*

International Affairs 29, no. 1 (1971): 41. See also David Wise, *The American Police State: The Government against the People* (New York: Random House, 1976), 401–2.

30. William L. Patterson, foreword to *We Charge Genocide: The Historic Petition to the United Nations for Relief from a Crime of the United States Government against the Negro People* (New York: Civil Rights Congress, 1951), 8.

31. Claudia Jones, *Jim-Crow in Uniform* (New York: New Age, 1940), 8.

32. Chester Himes, *If He Hollers Let Him Go* (Cambridge, MA: Da Capo, 1945), 38.

33. Ralph Ellison, "Employment—WPA, Federal Writers Project, Reports—'The Negro and the War,'" unpublished Federal Writers' Project essay, circa 1940, Box 20, Papers of Ralph Ellison, Library of Congress, Washington, DC. Hereafter "The Negro and the War." See Bernhard J. Stern on this same point: "Identification with the nation is offered as a form of compensation for economic insecurity." Bernhard J. Stern, "Alternative Proposals to Democracy: The Pattern of Fascism," *Journal of Negro Education* 10, no. 3 (1941): 378.

34. Robert K. Chester, "'Negroes' Number One Hero': Doris Miller, Pearl Harbor, and Retroactive Multiculturalism in World War II Remembrance," *American Quarterly* 65, no. 1 (2014): 36.

35. "Steelworkers Hit Military Bias," *The Militant*, Oct. 25, 1941; J. R. Johnson [C. L. R. James], "Why Negroes Should Oppose the War," in *Fighting Racism in World War II*, ed. Fred Stanton (New York: Pathfinder, 1980), 45.

36. Neda Atanasoski, *Humanitarian Violence: The U.S. Deployment of Diversity* (Minneapolis: University of Minnesota Press, 2013), 5 (emphasis in original).

37. For a discussion of multiculturalism as "a militarized national construct," see Melani McAlister, *Epic Encounters: Culture, Media, and U.S. Interests in the Middle East since 1945* (Berkeley: University of California Press, 2001), 259.

38. See V. I. Lenin, "Imperialism and Imperialist War," in *Selected Works*, vol. 5, trans. Marx-Lenin Institute (New York: International Publishers, 1943), 112.

39. See Ernest Allen Jr., "Waiting for Tojo: The Pro-Japan Vigil of Black Missourians, 1932–1943," *Gateway Heritage* 16 (Fall 1995): 48.

40. T[akashi] Fujitani, *Race for Empire: Koreans as Japanese and Japanese as Americans during World War II* (Berkeley: University of California Press, 2013), 10.

41. Theodore Bassett et al., *Is Japan the Champion of the Colored Races? The Negro's Stake in Democracy* (New York: Workers Library, 1938).

42. Quoted in Mary L. Dudziak, *Cold War Civil Rights: Race and the Image of American Democracy* (Princeton, NJ: Princeton University Press, 2011), 8, 9.

43. See Allen, "Waiting for Tojo," 43.

44. See also John Dower, *War without Mercy: Race and Power in the Pacific War* (New York: Pantheon, 1996), 174.

45. George Lipsitz, "'Frantic to Join . . . the Japanese Army': The Pacific War in the Lives of African American Soldiers and Civilians," in *The Politics of Culture in the Shadow of Capital*, ed. Lisa Lowe and David Lloyd (Durham, NC: Duke University Press, 1997), 326–27.

46. Bassett et al., *Is Japan the Champion*, 10.

47. Ralph Ellison, "Comments on War Propaganda, Fascism, Negro Participation in the War Effort, Japanese Propaganda n.d.," Box 60, ms. and ts., Papers of Ralph Ellison, Library of Congress, Washington, DC.

48. George Marion, *Bases and Empire: A Chart of American Expansion* (New York: Fairplay, 1948), 130, 62.

49. Christopher Sandars, *America's Overseas Garrisons: The Leasehold Empire* (Oxford: Oxford University Press, 2000), 25.

50. See Christine Wing, "The United States in the Pacific," in *The Sun Never Sets . . . : Confronting the Network of Foreign Military Bases*, ed. Joseph Gerson and Bruce Birchard (Boston: South End, 1991), 125. On the Korean War increase of U.S. overseas bases see David Vine, *Base Nation: How U.S. Military Bases Abroad Harm America and the World* (New York: Metropolitan, 2015), 40.

51. Roland G. Simbulan, *A Guide to Nuclear Philippines: A Guide to the US Military Bases, Nuclear Weapons, and What the Filipino People Are Doing about These* (Manila: Ibon Primer Series, 1989), 210.

52. Walden Bello, *People and Power in the Pacific: The Struggle for the Post–Cold War Order* (London: Pluto Press, 1992), 7.

53. Harry Magdoff, *Imperialism without Colonies* (New York: Monthly Review, 2003); Michael T. Klare, *War without End: American Planning for the Next Vietnams* (New York: Alfred A. Knopf, 1972), 9; Sandars, *America's Overseas Garrisons*; Steven Hugh Lee, *Outposts of Empire: Korea, Vietnam, and the Origins of the Cold War in Asia, 1949–1954* (Montreal: McGill-Queen's University Press, 1995), 7. See also "U.S. Military Bases and Empire," *Monthly Review* 53, no. 10 (2002): http://monthlyreview.org/2002/03/01/u-s-military-bases-and-empire/#seven.

54. Mathias Luce, "Sub-imperialism, the Highest Stage of Dependent Capitalism," *BRICS: An Anti-capitalist Critique*, ed. Patrick Bond and Ana Garcia (Auckland Park, South Africa: Jacana Media, 2015), 29.

55. Noam Chomsky and Edward S. Herman, *The Washington Connection and Third World Fascism: The Political Economy of Human Rights*, vol. 1 (Boston: South End, 1979), 15, 41.

56. Jeremy Kuzmarov, *Modernizing Repression: Police Training and Nation-Building in the American Century* (Amherst: University of Massachusetts Press, 2012), 21.

57. Japanese Commission, "Report of the Japanese Commission on the Complicity of Japan," in *Prevent the Crime of Silence: Reports from the Sessions of the International War Crimes Tribunal, Founded by Bertrand Russell*, ed. Ken Coates et al. (London: Allen Lane-Penguin, 1971), 320; for an account of the forty "Free World countries" that aided the U.S. intervention in Vietnam, see Stanley Robert Larsen and James Lawton Collins Jr., *Allied Participation in Vietnam* (Washington, DC: Department of the Army, 1975).

58. Frank Baldwin et al., *America's Rented Troops: South Koreans in Vietnam* (Philadelphia: American Friends Service Committee, c. 1975), 2.

59. Larsen and Collins, *Allied Participation in Vietnam*, 6. The suicide note of the seventeen-year-old suicide bomber Nguyen Van Troi condemned Vietnamese collaboration

with the United States: "The greatest tragedy, he wrote, was that 'U.S. imperialists had made Vietnamese kill Vietnamese'" (Kuzmarov, *Modernizing Repression*, 141).

60. As Frank Baldwin writes, "Manpower—providing [General William] Westmoreland the men he needed without increasing the U.S. draft or mobilizing the reserves—was a paramount objective for U.S. war planners" (Baldwin et al., *America's Rented Troops*, 5). Larsen and Collins also note that "the U.S. commander in Korea did not favor combat duty pay [for South Korean troops in Vietnam]—especially at the same rate paid to U.S. troops—but was in agreement with the payment of an overseas allowance" (*Allied Participation in Vietnam*, 126).

61. As the study further notes, "The U.S. commander was to have operational control over the Vietnamese Army forces also, but this control was to be exercised under the guise of 'operational co-ordination' to avoid offending the sensibilities of the Vietnamese" (Larsen and Collins, *Allied Participation in Vietnam*, 21).

62. Donald Duncan, "The Whole Thing Was a Lie," *Ramparts* 4, no. 10 (1966): 14.

63. Lelio Basso, "Summing-Up of the Second Session," in *Prevent the Crime of Silence: Reports from the Sessions of the International War Crimes Tribunal, Founded by Bertrand Russell*, ed. Ken Coates et al. (London: Allen Lane-Penguin, 1971), 335.

64. See Bruce Cumings, *The Korean War: A History* (New York: Modern Library, 2010), 243.

65. Hosu Kim and Grace Cho, "The Kinship of Violence," *Journal of Korean Adoption Studies* 1, no. 3 (2012): 12.

66. Roland G. Simbulan, *The Bases of Our Insecurity: A Study of the US Military Bases in the Philippines* (Manila: BALAI Fellowship, 1985), 13.

67. Kimie Hara, "Micronesia and the Postwar Remaking of the Asia Pacific: 'An American Lake,'" *Asia-Pacific Journal* 5, no. 8 (2007): http://apjjf.org/-Kimie-Hara/2493/article.html.

68. See Lee, *Outposts of Empire*, 7.

69. Karl Liebknecht, *Militarism and Anti-militarism* (Montréal: Black Rose, 2012), 13.

70. Theodor Adorno, "Commitment," trans. Francis McDonagh, in *The Essential Frankfurt School Reader*, ed. Andrew Arato and Eike Gebhardt (Oxford: Blackwell, 1978), 312; Elie Wiesel, "The Holocaust as Literary Inspiration," in E. Wiesel et al., *Dimensions of the Holocaust: Lectures at Northwestern University* (Evanston, IL: Northwestern University Press, 1977), 9.

Chapter 1. "Democracy within the Teeth of Fascism"

1. Ralph Ellison, "Twentieth-Century Fiction and the Black Mask of Humanity," in *Shadow and Act* (New York: Vintage International, 1995), 28. By his account written in 1946 yet published in 1953, this essay is prefaced by Ellison's note: "When I started rewriting this essay it occurred to me that its value might be somewhat increased if it remained very much as I wrote it during 1946." Signs of the essay's revision, however, are evident in a brief Korean War reference. See Ellison, "Twentieth-Century Fiction," 22, 27, 29.

2. Lee Nichols, *Breakthrough on the Color Front* (New York: Random House, 1954), 177.

3. Assistant Secretary of Defense Anna Rosenberg, quoted in Nichols, 179; Nichols, 53 (emphasis added).

4. Daniel Widener, "Seoul City Sue and the Bugout Blues: Black American Narratives of the Forgotten War," in *Afro Asia: Revolutionary Political and Cultural Connections between African Americans and Asian Americans*, ed. Fred Ho and Bill Mullen (Durham, NC: Duke University Press, 2008), 78.

5. Ellison's unpublished essay "The Negro and the War" is not to be confused with his untitled 1943 *Negro Quarterly* editorial, which Eric Sundquist subsequently titled "The Negro and the Second World War." See Ellison, "Employment—WPA, Federal Writers Project, Reports—'The Negro and the War,'" Box 20, Papers of Ralph Ellison, Library of Congress, Washington, DC. Hereafter "The Negro and the War."

6. John O. Killens, review of *Invisible Man*, *Freedom* (June 1952): 7.

7. Ralph Ellison, "Novels—Invisible Man, Drafts—Preface to Franklin Library Edition," Box 150, Folder 5, Papers of Ralph Ellison, Library of Congress, Washington, DC. Hereafter "Drafts—Franklin Library Preface."

8. Ralph Ellison, *Invisible Man* (New York: Vintage International, 1995), xvii.

9. Black militias and black ownership of land were central to radical Reconstruction. On the counterrevolutionary disarming of blacks, which Ellison's protagonist's grandfather alludes to, see James S. Allen, "Prologue to the Liberation of the Negro People," *The Communist* 12 (1933): 158, 164, 167.

10. Ellison, "Airman Novel," Box 115, Folder 1, ms. and ts., Papers of Ralph Ellison, Library of Congress, Washington, DC. Hereafter "Airman Novel."

11. Mark Neocleous, *War Power, Police Power* (Edinburgh: Edinburgh University Press, 2014), 82 (emphasis in original).

12. Barbara Foley contends, for example, that "*Invisible Man* is, unequivocally, a text of the Cold War, manifesting a thoroughgoing antipathy to the organized Left and participating fully in the discourse of anti-communism." Barbara Foley, "From Communism to Brotherhood: The Drafts of *Invisible Man*," in *Left of the Color Line: Race, Radicalism, and Twentieth-Century Literature of the United States*, ed. Bill V. Mullen and James Smethurst (Chapel Hill: University of North Carolina Press, 2003), 164. Arguing that Ellison's evolving anticommunist politics must be understood as distinct from the repressive politics of the Cold War policy establishment, Cathy Bergin maintains *Invisible Man* is "not rooted in McCarthyite anti-Communism." Cathy Bergin, *Bitter with the Past but Sweet with the Dream: Communism in the African American Imaginary* (Leiden: Brill, 2015), 122.

13. The Double-V slogan encompassed a spectrum of politics. The Socialist Workers' Party critiqued Double V as "far from a radical or antiwar slogan" and "a cover for unqualified support of the war." See Albert Parker [George Breitman], "Why the Communist Party Attacks 'Double V,'" in *Fighting Racism in World War II*, ed. Fred Stanton (New York: Pathfinder, 1980), 197.

14. Other than Ellison's two biographers, Lawrence Jackson and Arnold Rampersad, who give spare coverage to "Airman Novel," the only critics that address this early draft account are Michel Fabre and Barbara Foley. Fabre uncovered a copy of Ellison's Rosenwald application in Yale University's Richard Wright Archive and devotes just a page of analysis to it. See Michel Fabre, "From *Native Son* to *Invisible Man*: Some Notes on Ralph Ellison's Evolution in the 1950s," in *Speaking for You: The Vision of Ralph Ellison*, ed. Kimberly W. Benston (Washington, DC: Howard University Press, 1987), 205. Foley offers a synopsis in her book, *Wrestling with the Left: The Making of Ralph Ellison's "Invisible Man"* (Durham, NC: Duke University Press, 2010), 146–49.

15. Arnold Rampersad, *Ralph Ellison: A Biography* (New York: Knopf, 2007), 194. In a 1955 *Paris Review* interview, Ellison offered what became his standard account of *Invisible Man*'s inception: "In the summer of 1945, I had returned from the sea, ill, with advice to get some rest. Part of my illness was due, no doubt, to the fact that I had not been able to write a novel for which I'd received a Rosenwald Fellowship the previous winter. So on a farm in Vermont where I was reading *The Hero* by Lord Raglan and speculating on the nature of Negro leadership in the United States, I wrote the first paragraph of *Invisible Man*." Ralph Ellison, "The Art of Fiction: An Interview," *Shadow and Act* (New York: Vintage International, 1995), 176. Hereafter "The Art of Fiction."

16. Ellison, "The Art of Fiction," 176. A decade later, during a television interview, Ellison again referred to this project as "a failure." See "The Novel—Ralph Ellison on Work in Progress," National Education Television, New York, YouTube video, www.youtube.com/watch?v=LgCozZ3okh8.

17. Ralph Ellison, introduction to *Invisible Man* (New York: Vintage International, 1995), vii, xi–xii.

18. See Ellison, "Airman Novel." On Ellison's research method see Rampersad, *Ralph Ellison*, 180. It is unclear whether Ellison was familiar with the story of Luther Smith, a Tuskegee airman held as a POW in Stalag 18. Smith's testimony is typical of the statements of repatriated POWs featured in Ellison's saved clippings: "The German people are very militaristic. They recognize rank and they respect it. Since I was an officer, although I was black, they treated me how they treated their own people." Luther H. Smith, "Luther H. Smith, Air Force Captain, 1942–1947," in *We Were There: Voices of African American Veterans, from World War II to the War in Iraq*, ed. Yvonne Latty (New York: Amistad, 2004), 18.

19. Intriguingly, given *Invisible Man*'s damning portrait of such a figure, the Julius Rosenwald Fund's eponymous founder was both colleague and friend to Booker T. Washington and sat on the Tuskegee Board of Directors until his death in 1932, a year prior to Ellison's matriculation at Tuskegee.

20. Edwin R. Embree, *American Negroes, a Handbook* (New York: John Day, 1942), 79.

21. In a study of black experiences under Nazism and the contested number of black POWs, Clarence Lusane states, "The experience of black POWs is one of the least-researched areas of World War II." Clarence Lusane, *Hitler's Black Victims: The Historical*

Experiences of Afro-Germans, European Blacks, Africans, and African Americans in the Nazi Era (New York: Routledge, 2002), 147, 148.

22. Clippings collected in Ellison, "Airman Novel" folder (see note 10 above).

23. On job opportunities opened up by the war for black workers, see Stephen Tuck, *We Ain't What We Ought to Be: The Black Freedom Struggle from Emancipation to Obama* (Cambridge, MA: Belknap Press of Harvard University Press, 2010), 213.

24. Gordon Parks, *A Choice of Weapons* (1965; St. Paul: Minnesota Historical Society, 2010), 265.

25. Charles R. Sims, "Armed Defense," in *The Black Soldier: From the American Revolution to Vietnam*, ed. Jay David and Elaine Crane (New York: William Morrow, 1971), 197.

26. Ralph Ellison, "An American Dilemma: A Review," in *Shadow and Act* (New York: Vintage International, 1995), 310; and Ralph Ellison, "Remembering Richard Wright," in *Going to the Territory* (New York: Vintage International, 1995), 206.

27. See Ralph Ellison, "Hidden Name and Complex Fate," in *Shadow and Act* (New York: Vintage International, 1995), 162; and "Remembering Richard Wright," 201.

28. Lawrence Jackson, *Ralph Ellison: Emergence of Genius* (New York: John Wiley, 2002), 170.

29. André Malraux, *Days of Wrath*, trans. Haakon M. Chevalier (New York: Random House, 1936), 120.

30. Waldo Frank, foreword to *Days of Wrath*, by André Malraux, trans. Haakon M. Chevalier (New York: Random House, 1936), xiv.

31. See also Jackson, *Ralph Ellison*, 170.

32. Malraux dedicated *Days of Wrath* to "German Comrades who were anxious for me to make known what they had suffered and what they had upheld."

33. On the politics of black surrealism akin to Ellison's argument regarding an emancipatory literary aesthetics bringing together Freud and Marx, see Robin D. G. Kelley, foreword to *Black Marxism: The Making of the Black Radical Tradition*, by Cedric J. Robinson (Chapel Hill: University of North Carolina Press, 2000), xxi.

34. Burke cites these same three lines from *Hamlet* in his "Psychology and Form," *The Dial* 79 (1925): 35.

35. See Ellison, "Twentieth-Century Fiction," 26.

36. See Cedric J. Robinson, *Black Marxism: The Making of the Black Radical Tradition* (Chapel Hill: University of North Carolina Press, 2000), 200.

37. J. R. Johnson [C. L. R. James], "Why Negroes Should Oppose the War," in *Fighting Racism in World War II*, ed. Fred Stanton (New York: Pathfinder, 1980), 44.

38. Ralph Ellison, "Editorial Comment," *Negro Quarterly* 1, no. 4 (1943): 296. Also published under the title "The Negro and the Second World War," in *Cultural Contexts for Ralph Ellison's "Invisible Man*," ed. Eric Sundquist (Boston: St. Martin's, 1995), 234–40.

39. See Barbara Dianne Savage, *Broadcasting Freedom: Radio, War, and the Politics of Race, 1938–1948* (Chapel Hill: University of North Carolina Press, 1999), 112.

40. Theodore Bassett et al., *Is Japan the Champion of the Colored Races? The Negro's Stake in Democracy* (New York: Workers Library, 1938), 26.

41. On Ellison's interactions with James see Jackson, *Ralph Ellison*, 211; and John Wright, *Shadowing Ralph Ellison* (Jackson: University Press of Mississippi, 2006), 163.

42. Savage, *Broadcasting Freedom*, 107.

43. Siegfried Kracauer, *The Mass Ornament: Weimar Essays*, trans. and ed. Thomas Y. Levin (Cambridge, MA: Harvard University Press, 1995), 81.

44. See Jin-kyung Lee, *Service Economies: Militarism, Sex Work, and Migrant Labor in South Korea* (Minneapolis: University of Minnesota Press, 2010), 38.

45. Ellison's excoriation of the Tuskegee training program furnishes insight into his portraits of both the Tuskegee-like black educational institute in *Invisible Man* and the Golden Day filled with mentally disabled black veterans. See also William H. Hastie, *On Clipped Wings: The Story of Jim Crow in the Army Air Corps* (New York: National Association for the Advancement of Colored People, 1943).

46. Ralph Ellison, "Editorial Comment," *Negro Quarterly* 1, no. 2 (1942): i (emphasis in original).

47. Sven Lindqvist, *A History of Bombing*, trans. Linda Haverty Rugg (New York: New Press, 2000).

48. Charles A. Lindbergh, "Aviation, Geography, and Race," *Readers Digest* 35 (1938): 64. On Lindbergh as "the lawful spouse of the fortune of Morgan ... and friend of Field Marshal Goering," see Claudia Jones, *Jim-Crow in Uniform* (New York: New Age, 1940), 8.

49. In early June of 1934, a year after Ellison arrived in Tuskegee, two black pilots, Cornelius Coffey and John Robinson, founders of the Illinois Brown Eagle Aero Club, planned a trip from Decatur to Tuskegee. Their crash onto a southern farmer's cotton field possibly served as inspiration for Ellison's short story "Flying Home." For an account see Lawrence P. Scott and William M. Womack, *Double V: The Civil Rights Struggle of the Tuskegee Airmen* (East Lansing: Michigan State University Press, 1998), 45, 48.

50. In Ellison's burlesque tale Todd, flying above the land of Jim Crow, crashes midair into a buzzard, which sends him hurtling down onto a white southerner's field. Norma Jean Lutz writes: "Albert Murray was stationed at the Tuskegee Army Air Field during the war.... Murray happened to read 'Flying Home' in *Cross Section* and was amused by an incident in the story where an airman had to crash-land a plane after flying into a buzzard. Murray sat down to write to Ralph that one of their planes had actually flown into an Alabama buzzard—after the story had been published." See Norma Jean Lutz, "Biography of Ralph Ellison," in *Ralph Ellison*, ed. Harold Bloom (Philadelphia: Chelsea House, 2003), 34.

51. Georgia Writers' Project (Savannah Unit), Works Progress Administration, *Drums and Shadows: Survival Studies among the Georgia Coastal Negros* (Westport, CT: Greenwood, 1940), 18.

52. Civil Rights Congress, *We Charge Genocide: The Crime of Government against the Negro People*, ed. William L. Patterson (New York: Civil Rights Congress, 1951), 4.

53. The number, I believe, derives from Offlag 369, the POW camp in "Airman Novel."

54. Of Ellison's "That I Had Wings," Jackson writes: "Borrowing his central motif of flight from the thwarted dream of Wright's antihero Bigger Thomas, Ellison made it

an extended analogy about the Negro's desire for full participation in American life." See Jackson, *Ralph Ellison*, 286.

55. Ellison stated he envisioned his narrator's submerged location as an "area of American experience lying between the Revolution and the end of Reconstruction." See "Draft—Franklin Library Preface." He also describes *Invisible Man* as "really a memoir written underground." See Ellison, "The Art of Fiction," 178. On Ellison's symbolic understanding of "the Negro" as "the man lowest down and the mysterious, underground aspect of human personality," see Ellison, "Brave Words for a Startling Occasion," in *Shadow and Act* (New York: Vintage International, 1995), 104. Hereafter "Brave Words."

56. Ellison, "Richard Wright's Blues," in *Shadow and Act* (New York: Vintage International, 1995), 94.

57. Raymond Williams, *Marxism and Literature* (Oxford: Oxford University Press, 1977), 123.

58. The emergent, Lisa Lowe writes, refers to "the incomplete, still unfolding meanings, practices, and relationships" of "not yet fully articulated emergent social worlds." See Lisa Lowe, *The Intimacies of Four Continents* (Durham, NC: Duke University Press, 2015), 19.

59. Truman's 1948 Executive Order 9981 recommending U.S. military desegregation would be realized in the 1950–53 U.S. "police action" in Korea.

60. Martin Luther King Jr., "Declaration of Independence from the War in Vietnam," *Ramparts* 5, no. 11 (1967): 37, 36.

61. Bernhard J. Stern, "Alternative Proposals to Democracy: The Pattern of Fascism," *Journal of Negro Education* 10, no. 3 (1941): 378.

62. See Stern on this point: "Identification with the nation is offered as a form of compensation for economic insecurity" (375).

63. Peter F. Drucker, *The End of Economic Man: A Study of the New Totalitarianism* (New York: John Day, 1939), 195. See also Daniel Woodley, *Fascism and Political Theory: Critical Perspectives on Fascist Ideology* (London: Routledge, 2010), 58.

64. In an untitled 1918 *Crisis* editorial—later referred to as "Close Ranks"—W. E. B. Du Bois controversially urged black Americans to "forget our special grievances and close our ranks shoulder to shoulder with our own white fellow citizens and the allied nations that are fighting for democracy." Although Du Bois abandoned this position with regard to World War II, Ellison and other black writers referenced his earlier accommodationist views as counter to their own. See W. E. B. Du Bois, "Editorial," *The Crisis* 16, no. 5 (1918): 111.

65. Robert A. Hill, introduction to *The FBI's RACON: Racial Conditions in the United States during World War II*, comp. and ed. by Robert A. Hill (Boston: Northeastern University Press, 1995), 27.

66. On the writer as "manipulator of blood, brains, heart, and bowels which, while we sleep, dictate the mould of our desires," see Burke, "Psychology and Form," 40. Appointed civilian aide to the secretary of war in 1940, Hastie contextualized Roosevelt's decision against "tremendous bitterness and vocal expression of dissatisfaction

in the black community as to the result of the exclusion of blacks both from rapidly developing defense industrial mobilization, and from the rapidly expanding Army." See William H. Hastie, "Oral History Interview," by Jerry N. Hess, Jan. 5, 1972, www.trumanlibrary.org/oralhist/hastie.htm#transcript, 14. Hereafter "Oral History Interview."

67. Executive Order 8802, June 25, 1941, General Records of the United States Government, Record Group 11, National Archives, www.ourdocuments.gov/doc.php?flash=true&doc=72.

68. Goodwin Watson, *Civilian Morale: Second Yearbook of the Society for the Psychological Study of Social Issues*, ed. Goodwin Watson (Boston: Reynal and Hitchcock, 1942), v.

69. "Historical Background of the American Negro in Aviation" (ca. 1945), 15, Air Force, Record Group 220, Records of the President's Committee on Equality of Treatment and Opportunity in the Armed Services, www.trumanlibrary.gov/library/research-files/historical-background-american-negro-aviation?documentid=NA&pagenumber=16.

70. Roscoe E. Lewis, "The Role of Pressure Groups in Maintaining Morale among Negroes," *Journal of Negro Education* 12, no. 3 (1943): 473.

71. Quoted in Savage, *Broadcasting Freedom*, 114.

72. Lee Finkle, "The Conservative Aims of Militant Rhetoric: Black Protest during World War II," *Journal of American History* 60, no. 3 (1973): 701. J. J. Butts notes: "In addition to general editorial work, most of Ellison's tasks [as 1938–42 FWP staff] fell into two categories: research and reporting for the Negro History subunit and its project *The Negro in New York*; and interviews and research on urban folklore for Nicholas Wirth's Living Lore subproject." J. J. Butts, "Pattern and Chaos: Ralph Ellison and the Federal Writers' Project," *American Studies* 54, no. 3 (2015): 37.

73. Jerre Mangione, *The Dream and the Deal: The Federal Writers' Project, 1935–1943* (Syracuse, NY: Syracuse University Press, 1996), 305.

74. "The Way It Is," *New Masses*, Oct. 20, 1942, 11.

75. See Parker, "Why the Communist Party Attacks," 197.

76. On the army's disavowal of any basis to black grievances about the Jim Crow armed forces see Stanley Sandler, "Homefront Battlefront: Military Racial Disturbances in the Zone of the Interior, 1941–1945," *War and Society* 11, no. 2 (1993): 105, 109.

77. See Stern, "Alternative Proposals to Democracy," 377–78.

78. *Counter Intelligence Corps History and Mission in World War II* (Fort Holabird: Counter Intelligence Corps School, 1959), 14.

79. Lewis, "Role of Pressure Groups," 472. Cf. Chester Himes, *If He Hollers Let Him Go* (Cambridge, MA: Da Capo, 1945), 3.

80. See Fred Stanton, introduction to *Fighting Racism in World War II*, ed. Fred Stanton (New York: Pathfinder, 1980), 22.

81. "Initial Recommendations by the President's Committee on Equality of Treatment and Opportunity in the Armed Services," May 24, 1949, Armed Services, Record

Group 220: Records of the President's Committee on Equality of Treatment and Opportunity in the Armed Services, Truman Library, www.trumanlibrary.gov/library/research-files/initial-recommendations-fahy-committee (emphasis added).

82. During World War II the Western Defense Command, which comprised coastal Washington, Oregon, California, and the southernmost portion of Arizona, was regarded as a war theater. See *Order of Battle of the United States Land Forces in the World War: Zone of the Interior: Organization and Activities of the War Department*, vol. 3, pt. 1 (Washington, DC: Center of Military History, United States Army, 1988), originally published Washington, DC: U.S. G.P.O, 1931–49, 1. Hereafter "Order of Battle."

83. The term *morale operations* was institutionally specific to the OSS, yet during World War II its realization extended beyond this agency. In Elizabeth McIntosh's definition: "There was also Morale Operations (MO), which today is often called disinformation. Wartime MO was 'black' propaganda, as distinguished from 'white' or official news provided by the Office of War Information, now the Voice of America. MO was subversive, its sources disguised and its product disowned by our government if an operation backfired." Elizabeth P. McIntosh, *Sisterhood of Spies: The Women of the OSS* (Annapolis, MD: Naval Institute Press, 1998), 15.

84. George Lipsitz, "'Frantic to Join . . . the Japanese Army': The Pacific War in the Lives of African American Soldiers and Civilians," in *The Politics of Culture in the Shadow of Capital*, ed. Lisa Lowe and David Lloyd (Durham, NC: Duke University Press, 1997), 324.

85. Ellison, "Editorial Comment (1943)," 299. On the peril of being labeled a "fifth columnist" for agitating against lynching during the war years, see James Ford, introduction to *Jim-Crow in Uniform*, by Claudia Jones (New York: New Age, 1940), 2–4.

86. Gunnar Myrdal, *An American Dilemma: The Negro Problem and Modern Democracy*, vol. 1 (New Brunswick, NJ: Transaction, 2005), 421.

87. Sandler, "Homefront Battlefront," 101–2.

88. Quoted in Tuck, *We Ain't What We Ought to Be*, 220.

89. Roscoe Lewis writes: "Whether at Bataan or on Beale Street, the spirit of 'do or die' constitutes good morale; whether it be freedom for oppressed peoples of the world or only those of America, morale builds on belief in the rightness of the cause. . . . Just as national morale is stimulated by the catch-phrase, 'the Four Freedoms,' so is minority morale reassured by pressure campaigns for a 'Double Victory' and for 'Victory at Home as well as Abroad'" (Lewis, "Role of Pressure Groups," 472).

90. Sandler, "Homefront Battlefront," 101. Sandler acknowledges only the *documented* instances of black rebellions. He writes that "violent, racially provoked confrontations" occurred at military bases across the nation, including "Camp Van Dorn (Mississippi), Camp Stewart (Georgia), March Field (California), Fort Bliss (Texas), Camp Phillips (Kansas), Camp Breckinridge (Kentucky), Camp Shenango (Pennsylvania), Las Vegas, Phoenix, and Lake Charles (Louisiana), to name only the worst" (106). On official suppression of such information see Maggi M. Morehouse, *Fighting in the Jim Crow Army: Black Men and Women Remember World War II* (Lanham, MD: Rowman and Littlefield,

2000), 113. On the reasons for concentrating military training centers in the South, see Hastie, "Oral History Interview," 16.

91. See Kryder, *Divided Arsenal*, 3. Nat Brandt observes: "In cities as diverse as Newark, New Jersey; Mobile, Alabama; Los Angeles, California; Chester, Pennsylvania; and Beaumont, Texas, the violence often brought an abrupt halt to defense manufacturing. All work shut down when whites protested the hiring or promoting of blacks, when blacks were placed in production departments or made plant guards, or when white workers demanded separate toilet facilities." Nat Brandt, *Harlem at War: The Black Experience in WWII* (Syracuse, NY: Syracuse University Press, 1996), 137.

92. On the substantial resources the army and army air forces wasted "to find proof of communist or even Nazi subversion behind military racial violence," see Sandler, "Homefront Battlefront," 108.

93. Roy Wilkins, "The Harlem Riot," *The Crisis* 50, no. 9 (1943): 263.

94. Civil Rights Congress, *We Charge Genocide*, 4, 8.

95. Hill, *The FBI's RACON*, 4.

96. U.S. Army, *The History of the Counter Intelligence Corps in the United States Army, 1917–1953*, vol. 8 (Fort Holabird: U.S. Army Intelligence Center, 1959), 38.

97. Toni Morrison, "Racism and Fascism," *Journal of Negro Education* 64, no. 3 (1995): 384.

Chapter 2. Revolution from Above

1. Quoted in *Mark Twain's Weapons of Satire: Anti-imperialist Writings on the Philippine-American War*, ed. Jim Zwick (Syracuse, NY: Syracuse University Press, 1992), 5.

2. Major Waller, quoted in Mark Twain, "A Defense of General Funston," in *Mark Twain's Weapons of Satire*, 131.

3. Sven Lindqvist, "Bombing the Savages," trans. Linda Haverty Rugg, *Transition* 87 (2001): 48.

4. Charles A. Lindbergh, "Aviation, Geography, and Race," *Readers Digest* 35 (1939): 64.

5. Ruth Wilson Gilmore, *The Golden Gulag* (Berkeley: University of California Press, 2007), 28.

6. Bernd Hüppauf, "Experiences of Modern Warfare and the Crisis of Representation," *New German Critique* 59 (1993): 65.

7. Theodore Cohen, *Remaking Japan: The American Occupation as New Deal*, ed. Herbert Passin (New York: Free Press, 1987), 6, 5.

8. See Ashley Smith, "The Occupation of Japan," *International Socialist Review*, no. 29 (May-June 2003): www.isreview.org/issues/29/japan_occupation.shtml.

9. Karl Liebknecht, *Militarism and Anti-Militarism* (1907; Montréal: Black Rose, 2012), 13.

10. Yoneyuki Sugita, *Pitfall or Panacea: The Irony of U.S. Power in Occupied Japan, 1945–1952* (New York: Routledge, 2003), 6.

11. W. E. B. Du Bois, *Black Reconstruction in America, 1860–1880* (New York: Free Press, 1998), 345.

12. Jeremy Kuzmarov, *Modernizing Repression: Police Training and Nation-Building in the American Century* (Amherst: University of Massachusetts Press, 2012), 59. On the Occupation of Japan as paradigm "for the militarist and anti-popular character of American intervention in Asia," see Edward Friedman and Mark Selden, introduction to *America's Asia: Dissenting Essays on Asian-American Relations*, ed. Edward Friedman and Mark Selden (New York: Vintage, 1971), xi.

13. Chalmers Johnson, "America's Empire of Bases," *TomDispatch*, Jan. 15, 2004, www.tomdispatch.com/post/1181/chalmers_johnson_on_garrisoning_the_planet.

14. See Jodi Kim, *Ends of Empire: Asian American Critique and the Cold War* (Minneapolis: University of Minnesota Press, 2010), 104.

15. On Reconstruction as a form of "liberation from the top," see Howard Zinn, *A People's History of the United States, 1492–Present* (London: Routledge, 1980), 171.

16. James S. Allen, "Prologue to the Liberation of the Negro People," *The Communist* 12 (1933): 166.

17. Moon-Ho Jung, "*Black Reconstruction* and Empire," *South Atlantic Quarterly* 112, no. 3 (2013): 467.

18. Quoted in Michael Cullen Green, *Black Yanks in the Pacific: Race in the Making of American Military Empire after World War II* (Ithaca, NY: Cornell University Press, 2010), 39; see also Toshio Nishi, *Unconditional Democracy: Education and Politics in Occupied Japan, 1945–1952* (Stanford, CA: Stanford University Press, 1982), 245.

19. See Chalmers Johnson, "The People Who Invented the Mechanical Nightingale," in "Showa: The Japan of Hirohito," ed. Stephen R. Graubard, special issue, *Daedalus* 119, no. 3 (1990): 75–76.

20. *The History of the Counter Intelligence Corps in the United States Army, 1917–1953*, vol. 28, *CIC in the Occupation of Japan (August 1945–June 1950)*, ed. Ann Bray (Fort Holabird: U.S. Army Intelligence Center, 1959), 72, RG 319, Box 8, National Archives at College Park, MD. Hereafter CIC in the Occupation.

21. Quoted in Nishi, *Unconditional Democracy*, 248.

22. See Steven Hugh Lee, *Outposts of Empire: Korea, Vietnam, and the Origins of the Cold War in Asia, 1949–1954* (Montreal: McGill-Queen's University Press, 1995), 7.

23. See Michael Cullen Green, *Black Yanks in the Pacific: Race in the Making of American Military Empire after World War II* (Ithaca, NY: Cornell University Press, 2010), 147.

24. See Eiji Takemae, *The Allied Occupation of Japan*, trans. and adapted by Robert Ricketts and Sebastian Swann (New York: Continuum, 2002) 75; and Green, *Black Yanks*, 41.

25. See Daniel Widener, "Seoul City Sue and the Bugout Blues: Black American Narratives of the Forgotten War," *Afro Asia: Revolutionary Political and Cultural Connections between African Americans and Asian Americans*, ed. Fred Ho and Bill Mullen (Durham, NC: Duke University Press, 2008), 78.

26. Robin D. G. Kelley, *Freedom Dreams: The Black Radical Imagination* (Boston: Beacon, 2002), 6.

27. See Michael C. Robinson and Frank N. Schubert, "David Fagen: An Afro-American Rebel in the Philippines, 1899–1901," *Pacific Historical Review* 44, no. 1 (1975): 69; Martin Luther King Jr., "Declaration of Independence from the War in Vietnam," *Ramparts* 5, no. 11 (1967): 33.

28. Paul Gilroy, *The Black Atlantic: Modernity and Double-Consciousness* (London: Verso, 1993), 16 (emphasis added).

29. See Jin-kyung Lee, *Service Economies: Militarism, Sex Work, and Migrant Labor in South Korea* (Minneapolis: University of Minnesota Press, 2010), 6.

30. See Sina Najafi and Peter Galison, "The Ontology of the Enemy: An Interview with Peter Galison," *Cabinet*, no. 12 (Fall/Winter 2003): 64.

31. Jennifer C. James, *A Freedom Bought with Blood: African American War Literature from the Civil War to World War II* (Chapel Hill: University of North Carolina Press, 2007), 146.

32. Referring to breeding in the sense of animal husbandry, "*Shiiku*" has been translated as "The Prize Stock" and "The Catch." See Kenzaburo Oé, "Prize Stock," trans. John Nathan, in *A Personal Matter: The Silent Cry; Teach Us to Outgrow Our Madness* (New York: Book-of-the-Month Club, 1995), 111–68; and Ōe Kenzaburō, "The Catch," trans. John Bester, in *"The Catch" and Other War Stories*, ed. Shōichi Saeki (Tokyo: Kodansha International, 1981), 15–60. Of the two versions, John Nathan's translation is more faithful to the original. On John Bester's bowdlerized translation see Reiko Tachibana, "Structures of Power: Ōe Kenzaburō's 'Shiiku' ('Prize Stock')," *World Literature Today* 76, no. 2 (2002): 46. Bester's English translation of *Shiiku* first appeared in *Japan Quarterly* in 1959. See Ōe Kenzaburō, *The Catch, Japan Quarterly* 6, no. 1 (1959): 60–93. In citing Ōe's writings and scholarship on his writings, I have maintained the variations in the transliteration and sequencing of his name specific to those publications.

33. See Carol Gluck, "The Idea of Showa," in "Showa: The Japan of Hirohito," ed. Stephen R. Graubard, special issue, *Daedalus* 119, no. 3 (1990): 3–4.

34. John Nathan, introduction to Kenzaburo Oé, *A Personal Matter: The Silent Cry; Teach Us to Outgrow Our Madness*, trans. John Nathan (New York: Book-of-the-Month Club, 1995), n.p.

35. Oe, "The Day the Emperor Spoke in a Human Voice," *New York Times*, May 7, 1996, www.nytimes.com/1995/05/07/magazine/the-day-the-emperor-spoke-in-a-human-voice.html. Hereafter "Day the Emperor Spoke."

36. On Ōe's take on the ruling Liberal Democratic Party's exploitation of the imperial form's flexible properties, see Ōe Kenzaburō, "Speaking on Japanese Culture before a Scandinavian Audience," trans. Kunioki Yanagishita, in *Japan, the Ambiguous, and Myself: The Nobel Prize Speech and Other Lectures* (Tokyo: Kodansha International, 1995), 36–37. Hereafter "Speaking on Japanese Culture."

37. "Imperial Rescript Renouncing Divinity," Jan. 1, 1946, ww2db.com/doc.php?q=464.

38. Public Relations Office, General Headquarters, United States Army Forces,

Pacific, "Gen. MacArthur Sees Liberalism in Imperial Rescript," press release, Jan. 1, 1946, Shoshireibu Shirei Oboegaki Rui, National Diet Library, www.ndl.go.jp/constitution/e/shiryo/03/056shoshi.html.

39. Gavan MacCormack, *Client State: Japan in the American Embrace* (London: Verso, 2007), 2.

40. On MacArthur's canny manipulation of Hirohito as crucial to the "political reshaping of Japan," see John Curtis Perry, *Beneath the Eagle's Wings: Americans in Occupied Japan* (New York: Dodd, Mead, 1980), 66. On the infrastructural pragmatism of the decision to retain Hirohito, see Naoko Shibusawa, *America's Geisha Ally: Reimagining the Japanese Enemy* (Cambridge, MA: Harvard University Press, 2006), 111.

41. Hiroshi Masuda, *MacArthur in Asia: The General and His Staff in the Philippines, Japan, and Korea*, trans. Reiko Yamamoto (Ithaca, NY: Cornell University Press, 2009), 204.

42. Hisaaki Yamanouchi, quoted in Maya Jaggi, "In the Forest of the Soul," *The Guardian*, Feb. 4, 2005, https://amp.theguardian.com/books/2005/feb/05/featuresreviews.guardianreview9. Tachibana argues the black soldier ("a black horse") is a substitution of Hirohito on a white horse, another wartime imperial emblem. See Tachibana, "Structures of Power," 45.

43. Ōe Kenzaburō, "An Attempt at Self-Discovery in the Mythic Universe of the Novel," *World Literature Today* 76, no. 1 (2002): 7. Hereafter "An Attempt." Historically, the Tuskegee airmen flew solely over the European theater and North Africa. Yet black airmen served, from 1943 to 1945, with the 1345th Air Transport Command in Dacca, India, and "flew 'The Hump,' the famous air route from India to China that kept Generalissimo Chiang Kai-shek's Kumintang [sic] forces supplied during WWII." "A Chronology of African American Military Service," web.archive.org/web/20091002220527/http://www.ufphq.com/aams.htm/WWI. Tachibana offers a different take on Ōe's recollection, which has the black soldier imprisoned, not murdered: "Ōe remembered—correctly or incorrectly—that a teacher at school had told his class about an enemy plane that had crashed on the southernmost main island of Japan. The teacher told the children that two soldiers were captured, one a man who was then killed with bamboo spears, the other a black man who became a prisoner of war." See Tachibana, "Structures of Power," 37.

44. On "the catch" as an allusion "to the fact that the village makes its living by hunting," see Tachibana, "Structures of Power," 39. By contrast, Ōe maintains the villagers are mostly farmers. See Ōe, "An Attempt," 7.

45. See Mikhail Bakhtin, *Rabelais and His World*, trans. Helene Iswolsky (Bloomington: Indiana University Press, 1984), 11.

46. See Mark Selden, "A Forgotten Holocaust: US Bombing Strategy, the Destruction of Japanese Cities and the American Way of War from World War II to Iraq," *Asia-Pacific Journal* 5, no. 5 (2007): http://apjjf.org/-Mark-Selden/2414/article.html.

47. See Green, *Black Yanks*, 32; and Associated Press, "Deadly WWII U.S. Firebombing Raids on Japanese Cities Largely Ignored," *Japan Times*, March 10, 2015, www.japantimes.co.jp/news/2015/03/10/national/deadly-wwii-u-s-firebombing-raids-on-japanese-cities-largely-ignored.

48. Ōe Kenzaburō and Kim Chi-ha, "An Autonomous Subject's Long Waiting, Coexistence," *Positions* 5, no. 1 (1997): 292.

49. Kuan-Hsing Chen, *Asia as Method: Toward Deimperialization* (Durham, NC: Duke University Press, 2010), vii.

50. On Japan as a "peripheral, marginal, off-centre country," see Kenzaburo Oe, "Nobel Lecture: Japan, the Ambiguous, and Myself," Dec. 7, 1994, www.nobelprize.org/nobel_prizes/literature/laureates/1994/oe-lecture.html.

51. Oe Kenzaburo, "Being a Writer," interview by Harry Kreisler, "Art and Healing: Conversation with Kenzaburo Oe," April 16, 1999, http://globetrotter.berkeley.edu/people/Oe/oe-con2.html.

52. Ernest Allen Jr., "Waiting for Tojo: The Pro-Japan Vigil of Black Missourians, 1932–1943," *Gateway Heritage* 16 (1995): 48. As Tachibana notes, Japan "declared war against the U.S. and England on 8 December 1941 under the slogan 'Down with White Imperialism' in Asia." Seizing on "the cruel treatment by the Allied forces of black members of the American army, and, implying a natural alliance among people of color," Japan "called upon blacks to help drive out the white devils from Asia." See Tachibana, "Structures of Power," 38.

53. Tachibana, "Structures of Power," 124.

54. Ōe draws his examples from Chester Himes's 1945 novel *If He Hollers Let Him Go.* See Ōe Kenzaburō, "Huckleberry Finn and the American Dream in the Shadow of the Vietnam War," trans. Hiroaki Sato, *Asia-Pacific Journal* 13, no. 43.1 (2015): http://apjjf.org/-Hiroaki-Sato/4390. Hereafter "Huckleberry Finn and the American Dream."

55. Michiko Wilson, *The Marginal World of Ōe Kenzaburō: A Study in Themes and Techniques* (Armonk, NY: East Gate, 1986), 23.

56. Ōe Kenzaburō, "The Art of Fiction," *Paris Review* 183 (2007): 43.

57. Ōe Kenzaburō, "From the Beginning to the Present, and Facing the End: The Case of One Japanese Writer," in *On Politics and Literature: Two Lectures by Kenzaburô Ôe, Occasional Papers of the Doreen B. Townsend Center for the Humanities*, no. 18, ed. Christina M. Gillis (1999): 45.

58. Lindsley Cameron and Kenzaburō Ōe, "Starting from Zero at Hiroshima: An Interview with Kenzaburo Oe," *VQR* 95, no. 3 (Fall 2019): www.vqronline.org/web-exclusive/starting-zero-hiroshima-interview-kenzaburo-oe (originally published June 24, 2005). Hereafter "Starting from Zero."

59. Tsuyoshi Ishihara, *Mark Twain in Japan: The Cultural Reception of an American Icon* (Columbia: University of Missouri Press, 2005), 72.

60. Mark Twain, *Adventures of Huckleberry Finn* (Berkeley: University of California Press, 2001), 362.

61. Descriptions of Ōe's earliest encounter with Twain's novel vary, with some accounts suggesting he first read a translation when Occupation authorities propagated the novel as exemplary of American democracy. Nathan maintains Ōe first read Twain's novel after the war: "Ōe's first actual encounter with America was in the fall of 1945, when the Occupation jeeps drove into the mountain village where he lived. . . . His

second decisive encounter with America occurred four or five years later, when he read for the first time a Japanese translation of *Huckleberry Finn*." See Nathan, introduction, n.p. On Ōe's "secondary education under what was actually American occupation, following curricula devised by education specialists at the American GHQ and accumulating knowledge from books censored by them," see Emiko Sakurai, "Kenzaburō Ōe: The Early Years," *World Literature Today* 58, no. 3 (1984): 370. By contrast, Ōe claims his first encounter with Twain's novel occurred during World War II: "In the midst of the Second World War, at a time when I was seeking to avoid being consumed by feelings of enmity, loathing, contempt, and terror of everything American, *Adventures of Huckleberry Finn* first came to my attention. And in no time Huckleberry became the first hero I acquired through literature. I cannot remember who my benefactor was who gave me the Iwanami paperback edition of *Adventures of Huckleberry Finn*, translated by Nakamura Tameji, but thinking that it was my late father allowed me to have the best memory of him." Ōe, "Huckleberry Finn and the American Dream," 5. Elsewhere, Ōe offers this variation: "Toward the end of the war, even when circumstances did not allow many books to be published, [my mother] used to spend a whole day traveling from the village to a regional town to barter, in exchange for rice, books for me such as *The Wonderful Travels of Nils Holgerson* or *The Adventures of Huckleberry Finn*." Ōe, "An Attempt," 16.

62. On Huck's "decision 'forever, betwixt two things'" as Ōe's central moral dilemma, see Wilson, *The Marginal World of Ōe Kenzaburō*, 34.

63. See Eric J. Sundquist, *To Wake the Nations: Race in the Making of American Literature* (Cambridge, MA: Belknap Press of Harvard University Press, 1993), 232. The phrase "second slavery" is Twain's. See Sundquist, 232. See also Mary A. Knighton, "'Was Huck *Burak(k)u*?': Reading and Teaching Twain in Asian Pacific World Literature," *Mark Twain Studies* 1, no. 1 (2004): 95. For Ōe's reading of the evasion sequence as a narrative loophole in his essay "Huckleberry Finn and the Problem of the Hero," see Wilson, *The Marginal World of Ōe Kenzaburo*, 34.

64. See, e.g., Neil Schmitz, "The Paradox of Liberation in Huckleberry Finn," *Texas Studies in Literature and Language* 13, no. 1 (1971): 125–36; Sundquist, 228–44; and Neil Schmitz, "Twain, *Huckleberry Finn*, and the Reconstruction," *American Studies* 12 (1971): 60.

65. On slavery, in Du Bois's account, as "not an aberration of liberal democracy in the United States but its central contradiction . . . constitutive of U.S. democracy, and of the extension of American power around the world," see Lisa Lowe, *The Intimacies of Four Continents* (Durham, NC: Duke University Press, 2015), 167.

66. In numerous public statements and essays, including his Nobel Prize acceptance speech, Ōe has acknowledged a debt to Twain.

67. On the idea of the frontier, conjured by the term *territory* within the rationale for multiple forms of U.S. empire, including "the call for open doors abroad," see Amy Kaplan, *The Anarchy of Empire in the Making of American Culture* (Cambridge, MA: Harvard University Press, 2002), 96.

68. On Frog as potentially *burakumin* and *Shiiku* as a tale of Japan's "outcastes in dialogue with America's," see Knighton, 101. On the analogy mid-nineteenth-century Japanese envoys to the United States made between slaves and *burakumin*, see John Russell, "Race and Reflexivity: The Black Other in Contemporary Japanese Mass Culture," *Cultural Anthropology* 6, no. 1 (1991): 20.

69. Knighton and Victor LaValle are notable exceptions. Knighton writes of Ōe's racialization of the POW: "Numerous characters, even some children, refer to him as 'nigger' (*kurombo*). Physically, he is said to have 'thick rubbery lips' and 'smell like an animal'—among other derogatory, stereotypical images as [John] Russell points out; what Russell fails to note, however, is that the Japanese who capture the black soldier and control his destiny are also depicted as debased, weak, dirty animals, yet never praiseworthy like their 'prize stock'" (Knighton, 95). LaValle likewise comments, "Oe does not use the language of revulsion only when it comes to the black airman. In fact, Frog and the rest of the townspeople see the villagers as 'dirty and smelly.' They treat the villagers 'like dirty animals.' In return, the villagers hate the townspeople, who use their power . . . to keep their rural counterparts in a constant state of subordination" (Victor LaValle, "Admiring Oe's Talent for Discomfort," interview by Chris Lehmann, *NPR*, August 3, 2006, www.npr.org/templates/story/story.php?storyId=5613311.

70. Tachibana, 37. Sanroku Yoshida contends that Ōe's reputation as an "international writer" has contributed to his critical neglect in Japan. See Sanroku Yoshida, "The Burning Tree: The Spatialized World of Kenzaburō Ōe," *World Literature Today* 69, no. 1 (1995): 16.

71. Theodore Bassett et al., *Is Japan the Champion of the Colored Races? The Negro's Stake in Democracy* (New York: Workers Library, 1938), 15, 12, 13.

72. Cf. Nishi, *Unconditional Democracy*, 286: "According to MacArthur, . . . this control was not difficult at all. 'Measured by the standards of modern civilization,' he informed the US senators, 'they [the Japanese] would be like a boy of twelve compared with our development of forty-five years.'"

73. "Japan's Capabilities as Democratic Nation Tested: Kenzaburo Oe," *Europe solidaire sans frontières*, Sept. 29, 2012, www.europe-solidaire.org/spip.php?article26507.

74. Arasaki Moriteru, "The Struggle against Military Bases in Okinawa—Its History and Current Situation," *Inter-Asia Cultural Studies* 2, no. 1 (2001): 103.

75. See Oguma Eiji, *The Boundaries of "the Japanese,"* vol. 1, *Okinawa 1818–1972—Inclusion and Exclusion*, trans. Leonie R. Stickland (Melbourne: Trans Pacific Press, 2014), 3.

76. See Lisa Yoneyama, *Cold War Ruins: Transpacific Critique of American Justice and Japanese War Crimes* (Durham, NC: Duke University Press, 2016), 44.

77. See Nozaki Yoshiko, "Educating the Public about the Damage Caused by the U.S. Military Bases in Okinawa," *Critical Asian Studies* 33, no. 1 (2001): 97.

78. See Laura Hein and Mark Selden, "Culture, Power, and Identity in Contemporary Okinawa," in *Islands of Discontent: Okinawan Responses to Japanese and American Power*, ed. Laura Hein and Mark Selden (Lanham, MD: Rowman and Littlefield, 2003), 3.

79. International Movement against All Forms of Discrimination and Racism, "Japan: Violation of Human Rights of Indigenous Peoples of Ryukyus in Okinawa," June 3, 2012, http://imadr.org/wordpress/wp-content/uploads/2013/12/Written-Statement_HRC-20th-session_Indigenous-Peoples-in-Okinawa-2012.pdf. See also Oguma, *The Boundaries*, 1.

80. "The Talk of the Town," *New Yorker*, June 8, 1968, 26.

81. Quoted in Michael Shaller, *Altered States: The United States and Japan since the Occupation* (New York: Oxford University Press, 1997), 196.

82. Japanese Commission, "Report of the Japanese Commission on the Complicity of Japan," in *Prevent the Crime of Silence: Reports from the Sessions of the International War Crimes Tribunal, Founded by Bertrand Russell*, ed. Ken Coates et al. (London: Allen Lane, 1971), 320.

83. Against ultranationalist claims of democracy's foreignness to Japan, Ōe has maintained a complex position, contending U.S.-sponsored democracy enabled "the first actualization of democracy in Japan," while in his praxis consistently "opposing American policies in Japan." See Ōe, "From the Beginning," 42; and Ōe, "Starting from Zero." Cf. Yoshida, "The Burning Tree," 16.

84. On Okinawa's separation from the mainland in terms of Occupation policies, see Toriyama Atsushi, "Okinawa's 'Postwar': Some Observations on the Formation of American Military Bases in the Aftermath of Terrestrial Warfare," *Inter-Asia Cultural Studies* 4, no. 2 (2003): 401.

85. On the number of civilian dead see Aniya Masaaki, "Compulsory Mass Suicide, the Battle of Okinawa, and Japan's Textbook Controversy," trans. Kyoko Selden, *Asia-Pacific Journal* 6, no. 1 (2008): http://apjjf.org/-Aniya-Masaaki/2629/article.html. Historian Saburō Ienaga estimates civilian casualties at up to 160,000. See Saburō Ienaga, *The Pacific War, 1931–1945: A Critical Perspective on Japan's Role in World War II*, trans. Frank Baldwin (New York: Pantheon, 1978), 199.

86. Ōe was the object of an ultimately unsuccessful lawsuit accusing him of libel for stating in *Okinawa Notes* that the Imperial Army was culpable for the deaths of Okinawan civilians forced to commit suicide.

87. On the No Gun Ri–like massacres perpetrated by U.S. forces in Okinawa, see Arasaki, "Struggle against Military Bases," 101.

88. See Shaller, *Altered States*, 196. See also Jon Mitchell, "Vietnam: Okinawa's Forgotten War," *Asia-Pacific Journal* 13, no. 16.1 (2015): http://apjjf.org/Jon-Mitchell/4308.html.

89. Ōe Kenzaburō, "Misreading, Espionage and 'Beautiful Martyrdom': On Hearing the Okinawa 'Mass Suicides' Suit Court Verdict," trans. Scott Borba, *Asia-Pacific Journal* 6, no. 10 (2008): http://apjjf.org/-Oe-Kenzaburo/2915/article.html.

90. "Japanese Nobel Laureate Kenzaburo Oe on 70th Anniv. of US Atomic Bombings of Hiroshima and Nagasaki," *Democracy Now!* August 6, 2015, www.democracynow.org/2015/8/6/japanese_nobel_laureate_kenzaburo_oe_on.

91. On the Osprey's "assault support capability . . . needed to fight and win on tomorrow's battlefield," see "MV-22 Osprey," *U.S. Marine Corps Concepts and Programs*,

www.candp.marines.mil/Portals/216/documents/CNP%20Publications/CNP_2014.pdf?ver=2018-03-08-090028-247: 190.

92. Andre Vltchek, "Okinawa: Notes from the 'Evil Island,'" *Counterpunch*, Dec. 28, 2012, www.counterpunch.org/2012/12/28/notes-from-the-evil-island.

93. Ron Berler, "Saving the Pentagon's Killer Chopper-Plane," *Wired*, July 1, 2005, www.wired.com/2005/07/osprey. Nicknamed the "Widowmaker," the Osprey was part of President Obama's fleet, but because of "its habit of falling out of the sky," he was not permitted to ride in it. See Andrew Tarantola, "The President Gets a Personal Osprey He's Not Allowed to Use," *Gizmodo*, August 13, 2013, http://gizmodo.com/the-president-gets-a-personal-osprey-hes-not-allowed-t-1108783801.

94. In their post-9/11 operation in Afghanistan, Ospreys suffered accidents at a rate of 40–1 compared to all other U.S. Marine Corps aircraft. See Ayako Mie, "Nonfatal Osprey Crash in Okinawa Brings Safety Fears to Fore," *Japan Times*, Jan. 9, 2017, www.japantimes.co.jp/news/2017/01/09/reference/nonfatal-osprey-crash-okinawa-brings-safety-fears-fore.

95. The Pentagon downplayed this crash as a "mishap." See Justin McCurry, "US Grounds Osprey Fleet in Japan after Aircraft Crashes off Okinawa," *The Guardian*, Dec. 17, 2016, www.theguardian.com/world/2016/dec/14/us-osprey-mv22-fleet-grounded-japan-okinawa-aircraft-crash-military.

Chapter 3. A Blueprint for Occupied Japan

1. The government name for the camp was the "Central Utah Relocation Center." On the inaccuracy of "relocation center" and other euphemisms used to describe the American concentration camp, see "Terminology," in *Densho Encyclopedia*, https://densho.org/terminology/. On the inaccuracy of *internment* to describe the mass incarceration of Japanese Americans, see Roger Daniels, "Words Do Matter: A Note on Inappropriate Terminology and the Incarceration of Japanese Americans," in *Nikkei in the Pacific Northwest: Japanese Americans and Japanese Canadians in the Twentieth Century*, ed. Louis Fiset and Gail M. Nomura (Seattle: University of Washington Press, 2005), 190.

2. Deborah Calkins to Miné Okubo, Oct. 5, 1943, telegram, Miné Okubo Papers, Center for Social Justice and Civil Liberties, Riverside Community College District, Riverside, CA.

3. In an interview Okubo described her time at Topaz as "always busy": "In the daytime I went around sketching. There wasn't any photographing allowed so I decided to record everything. Observing. I went around doing all these minute sketches of people and events. I didn't sleep much. I worked all night at the newspaper. It was lunacy to work all night, going twenty-four hours a day. I was art editor for the daily newspaper and art editor for *Trek* literary magazine." Deborah Gesensway and Mindy Rosemen, *Beyond Words: Images from America's Concentration Camps* (Ithaca, NY: Cornell University Press, 1987), 69.

4. Robert Vanderlan, *Intellectuals Incorporated: Politics, Art, and Ideas Inside Henry Luce's Media Empire* (Philadelphia: University of Pennsylvania Press, 2010), 82; Michael

Augspurger, *An Economy of Abundant Beauty: "Fortune" Magazine and Depression America* (Ithaca, NY: Cornell University Press, 2004), 137.

5. *Fortune*, Dec. 1943, 121.

6. See Gesensway and Roseman, *Beyond Words*, 74.

7. Miné Okubo, "Preface to the 1983 Edition," in *Citizen 13660* (Seattle: University of Washington Press, 1983), ix. Hereafter "Preface."

8. In *Trek*'s profile of Okubo, Jim Yamada describes her furious productivity: "Since evacuation, Mine [sic] has made from 1500 to 2000 rough sketches. Later she intends to develop some of them into finished paintings. Her last extended creative effort was at Tanforan when she completed approximately 50 paintings in a month." Jim Yamada, "Portrait of an Artist," *Trek* 1, no. 1 (1942): 22.

9. With the bulk of her post-1945 artwork uncatalogued in her lifetime, a diachronic account of Okubo's career, including what Elena Tajima Creef describes as "the breadth and immensity of the paintings she produced in the last fifty years of her life," has yet to emerge. See Elena Tajima Creef, "Following Her Own Road: The Achievement of Miné Okubo," in *Miné Okubo: Following Her Own Road*, ed. Greg Robinson and Elena Tajima Creef (Seattle: University of Washington Press, 2008), 5.

10. Larry Tajiri, "Secret Role of the Nisei," *NOW*, Second Half December 1945, reproduced in *Pacific Citizens: Larry and Guyo Tajiri and Japanese American Journalism in the World War II Era*, ed. Greg Robinson (Urbana: University of Illinois Press, 2012), 107.

11. On the Nisei role as "'experts' on Japanese culture'" relative to the occupation, see John Curtis Perry, *Beneath the Eagle's Wings: Americans in Occupied Japan* (New York: Dodd, Mead, 1980), 173.

12. "War Relocation Authority Application for Leave Clearance," Jan. 4, 1943, Miné Okubo evacuee case file, Record Group 210, stack area 18W3, row 8, compartment 27, shelf 5, National Archives Building, Washington, DC.

13. This report was also published in anonymous abridged form in *Harper's Magazine*'s October 1942 issue.

14. K. D. Ringle, "On the Japanese Question in the United States," Miscellaneous WRA Publications, Office File of Commissioner John Collier, 1933–1945, Records of the Bureau of Indian Affairs, Record Group 75, stack area 11E–Z, row 30, compartment 9, shelf 5, National Archives Building, Washington, DC.

15. "The Citizen-Subject . . . Tightens His Belt and Wipes Off His Smile," in "Japan and the Japanese: A Military Power We Must Defeat, a Pacific Problem We Must Solve," special issue, *Fortune*, April 1944, 147.

16. Larry Tajiri writes: "unconstitutional, undemocratic procedures against any one minority can prove the opening wedge for such action against all other minorities" (Robinson, *Pacific Citizens*, 73).

17. Henry Luce, "The American Century," *Life*, Feb. 17, 1941, repr. at www-personal.umich.edu/mlassite/discussions261/luce.pdf.

18. See Bruce Cumings, *The Korean War: A History* (New York: Modern Library, 2010), 243.

19. Nikhil Pal Singh, "Culture/Wars: Recoding Empire in an Age of Democracy," *American Quarterly* 50, no. 3 (1998): 478.

20. *Fortune*, Dec. 1943, 125.

21. See Larry Tajiri, "The Loaded Weapon," *Pacific Citizen*, Feb. 25, 1950 (reproduced in Robinson, *Pacific Citizens*, 210); Larry Tajiri, "Secret Role of the Nisei," 105.

22. On *imaginators* see Augspurger, *Economy of Abundant Beauty*, 210.

23. Takashi Fujitani, "The Reischauer Memo: Mr. Moto, Hirohito, and Japanese American Soldiers," *Critical Asian Studies* 33, no. 3 (2001): 393.

24. See Brian Hayashi, *Democratizing the Enemy: The Japanese American Internment* (Princeton, NJ: Princeton University Press, 2004), 204.

25. Henry Stimson, Memorandum for the President, Dec. 13, 1944, President's Secretary's File, Franklin Delano Roosevelt Library.

26. Miné Okubo to Isamu Noguchi, Sept. 1942, repr. in *Amerasia Journal* 30, no. 2 (2004): 20.

27. Quoted in Robert J. Maeda, "Isamu Noguchi: 5-7-A, Poston, Arizona," in *Last Witnesses: Reflections on the Wartime Internment of Japanese Americans*, ed. Erica Harth (New York: Palgrave MacMillan 2001), 156. According to Maeda, "Noguchi was provided with an official WRA letter precisely spelling out his status as a volunteer, 'not an evacuee,' who would not require a permit to travel outside of the restricted military zone," yet "the freedom granted by this letter would prove illusory" (158). Having entered Poston on May 8, 1942, Noguchi wrote repeatedly to Collier, appealing for release, yet not until "November 12, 1942, some seven months after he arrived in Poston, ... was [he] finally released from camp, but only on a 'temporary basis'" (162).

28. Isamu Noguchi, interview by Paul Cummings, Nov. 7–Dec. 26, 1973, Smithsonian Archives of American Art, www.aaa.si.edu/download_pdf_transcript/ajax?record_id=edanmdm-AAADCD_oh_216546. On Collier's belief that Japanese American labor could be productively deployed to improve indigenous agricultural lands managed by the Department of the Interior, see Karen J. Leong and Myla Vicenti Carpio, "Carceral Subjugations: Gila River Indian Community and Incarceration of Japanese Americans on Its Lands," *Amerasia Journal* 42, no. 1 (2016): 103–20.

29. Isamu Noguchi, "I Become a Nisei," May 1942, Isamu Noguchi Archive, https://archive.noguchi.org/Detail/archival/50830.

30. See Ansel Adams, *Born Free and Equal: Photographs of the Loyal Japanese-Americans at Manzanar Relocation Center, Inyo County, California* (New York: U.S. Camera, 1944); Maisie Conrat and Richard Conrat, eds., *Executive Order 9066: The Internment of 110,000 Japanese Americans* (San Francisco: California Historical Society, 1972); and Dorothea Lange, *Impounded: Dorothea Lange and the Censored Images of Japanese American Internment*, ed. Linda Gordon and Gary Y. Okihiro (New York: Norton, 2006).

31. "Loyalty and Character Report on Mine [sic] Okubo," Sept. 23, 1943, Miné Okubo evacuee case file. See also Evelyn K. Johnson, assessment of Miné Okubo, Jan. 30, 1943, Miné Okubo evacuee case file; and Miles E. Cary to E. R. Fryer, memorandum, August 25, 1942, Miné Okubo evacuee case file.

32. Marita Sturken, "Absent Images of Memory: Remembering and Reenacting the Japanese Internment," in *Perilous Memories: The Asia-Pacific War(s)*, ed. Takashi Fujitani et al. (Durham, NC: Duke University Press, 2001), 46.

33. Norman Thomas, *Democracy and Japanese Americans* (New York: Astoria, 1942), 24.

34. Greg Robinson also observes this feature of *Citizen 13660*. See Greg Robinson, "What I Did in Camp: Interpreting Japanese American Internment Narratives of Isamu Noguchi, Miné Okubo, Jeanne Wakatsuki Houston, and John Tateishi," *Amerasia Journal* 30, no. 2 (2004): 53.

35. These reviews are collated in a Columbia University Press press-packet archived in the Miné Okubo Materials at the Rivera Library at the University of California, Riverside. See "Excerpts from Comments on 'Citizen 13660' by Miné Okubo," Miné Okubo Materials, History of California Collections, UC Riverside Library.

36. Richard Drinnon writes: "The men who ran America's concentration camps were liberals of the genus New Deal." Richard Drinnon, *Keeper of Concentration Camps: Dillon S. Myer and American Racism* (Berkeley: University of California Press, 1987), 4.

37. Jodi Melamed, *Represent and Destroy: Rationalizing Violence in the New Racial Capitalism* (Minneapolis: University of Minnesota Press, 2011), xvi.

38. Melamed, xxvi, xxviii.

39. Carey McWilliams, *Prejudice: Japanese-Americans, Symbol of Intolerance* (Boston: Little, Brown, 1944), 298.

40. The phrase "the world republic of letters" comes from Pascale Casanova, *The World Republic of Letters*, trans. M. B. DeBevoise (Cambridge, MA: Harvard University Press, 2007).

41. "The Job before Us," in "Japan and the Japanese," 121.

42. Table of Contents, in "Japan and the Japanese," 1.

43. "Fortune's Wheel," in "Japan and the Japanese," 2.

44. Caroline Chung Simpson, *An Absent Presence: Japanese Americans in Postwar American Culture, 1945–1960* (Durham, NC: Duke University Press, 2001), 44, 49.

45. "Fortune's Wheel," 4. The editors did not mention that Kuniyoshi was a WPA artist who had been active in the antifascist American Artists' Congress in the 1930s or that Yashima (Jun Atsushi Iwamatsu) served in the U.S. Army and worked for the OSS.

46. Shirley Sun, *Miné Okubo: An American Experience* (San Francisco: East Wind, 1972), 11. Though the answers to her leave-clearance form must be taken with a grain of salt, on the January 4, 1943, form, Okubo indicated that she did speak Japanese but "poorly." Her response to "Do you read Japanese?" was "not at all." See Miné Okubo evacuee case file.

47. The article "Issei, Nisei, Kibei" would be reprinted, along with nine of Okubo's line drawings, as an American Council on Public Affairs pamphlet. See *The Displaced Japanese-Americans* (Washington, DC: American Council on Public Affairs, 1944).

48. "Japan and the Japanese," 62, 66–67, 70, 95.

49. See John Dower: "Some, like the Hearst newspapers, warned of a 'Yellow Peril' led by Japan as early as the 1890s, and maintained an unwavering editorial policy of

anti-Oriental polemics over the next half century." John Dower, *War without Mercy: Race and Power in the Pacific War* (New York: Pantheon, 1986), 7, 157.

50. See Hayashi, whose "study does not find that the United States government treated enemy aliens relatively well because of a 'liberal' tradition. Rather, the American concentration camps did not become oppressive because of the need to ensure humane treatment of over twenty-one thousand American servicemen and fourteen thousand civilians in Japanese hands by 1942." Hayashi, *Democratizing the Enemy*, 11.

51. See Okubo on why the *Fortune* editors wrote this article: "When the *Fortune* magazine people saw the vast collection of drawings that I had on the evacuation, they were surprised and excited, and when they learned that American citizens were evacuated, they were ashamed, and they decided to look into the matter more, and they wrote an article called 'Issei, Nisei, Kibei.' It's one of the first illustrated articles that came out in one of the largest periodicals of the time, because anything Japanese was not quite known in the East yet." Miné Okubo, "Statement of Miné Okubo before the Congressional Committee on Wartime Relocation and Internment (1981)," in "A Tribute to Miné Okubo," ed. Greg Robinson and Elena Tajima Creef, special issue, *Amerasia Journal* 30, no. 2 (2004): 16. Hereafter "Statement."

52. Drinnon writes: "Technically, the inmates were free to walk to the barbed wire and be killed, as happened to James Hatsuaki Wakasa at Topaz, Utah, on April 11, 1943. At the time and still several decades later, [Milton] Eisenhower tried to shield himself and his readers from the simple truth that enclosures where people, most of them citizens, have been penned without being charged with crimes and without being sentenced by ordinary process of the law, and then shot if they try to leave, are enclosures correctly called concentration camps." Drinnon, *Keeper of Concentration Camps*, 6. Consider, too, the insistence of Harold L. Ickes, Roosevelt's secretary of the interior, on the term *concentration camp*, even in 1946: "Crowded into cars like cattle, these hapless people were hurried away to hastily constructed and thoroughly inadequate concentration camps, with soldiers with nervous muskets on guard, in the great American desert. We gave the fancy name of 'relocation centers' [to] . . . these dust bowls, but they were concentration camps nonetheless, although not as bad as Dachau or Buchenwald." Harold L. Ickes, "Man to Man," *New York Post*, Sept. 23, 1946.

53. McWilliams, *Prejudice*, 102.

54. As explained in *Fortune*'s April 1944 issue: the "WRA has a lexicon of its own: Caucasian is the term for appointed administrative personnel, to distinguish them from the '*évacuées*,' sometimes called 'colonists'; beyond the gate is 'the outside.'" "Issei, Nisei, Kibei," 74.

55. *Fortune* dovetailed, on this point, with Justice Murphy's "concurrence" (originally a dissent) in the Supreme Court's 1943 Hirabayashi decision: "To say that any group cannot be assimilated is to admit that the great American experiment has failed, that our way of life has failed." Hirabayashi v. United States, 320 U.S. 81 (1943).

56. In his 1944 study of prejudice against Japanese Americans, McWilliams remarks: "If the race bigots have their way, all the [recently released] evacuees will be

rounded up, before the war is terminated, relodged in concentration camps (not relocation centers), and deported to Japan at the end of the war"; possibly alluding to incarcerated Japanese Latin Americans, he adds, "This possibility is closely related to a possible fate which may be in store for Japanese people throughout the world." McWilliams, *Prejudice*, 324.

57. Dillon S. Myer, "Japanese American Relocation: Final Chapter," *Survey Graphic*, 1945, 61–62.

58. Quoted in Deborah K. Lim, *Research Report Prepared for Presidential Select Committee on JACL Resolution No. 7*, 1990, Conscience and the Constitution, June 5, 2007, https://resisters.com/learn-more/jacl/the-lim-report-part-ii-b/. Lim gleans this excerpt from an April 2, 1942, letter, housed in the JACL archives, written by Mike Masaoka to then-WRA director Milton Eisenhower.

59. Dorothy Swaine Thomas, *The Salvage: Japanese-American Evacuation and Resettlement* (Berkeley: University of California Press, 1952), 89.

60. Under the Foreign Morale Division of the Office of War Information, English social anthropologist Geoffrey Gorer spun theories about Japanese behavior that were then popularized by the wartime press, including an August 7, 1944, essay, "Why Are Japs Japs?" in *Time* magazine that pathologized "Japanese" "concern with ritual and tidiness." For an overview of Gorer's theories see Dower, *War without Mercy*, 124–28.

61. See Galen M. Fisher, "Japanese Colony: Success Story," *Survey Graphic*, .1943, 41–43.

62. Sandra C. Taylor, "Japanese Americans and Keetley Farms: Utah's Relocation Colony," *Utah Historical Quarterly* 54 (1986): 334.

63. William Petersen, "Success Story, Japanese-American Style," *New York Times Magazine*, Jan. 9, 1966, 21.

64. Stuart Davis, quoted in Nicolas Lampert, *A People's Art History of the United States* (New York: New Press, 2013), 171.

65. *Survey Midmonthly* republished this image with the caption "Christmas in a Relocation Center" in its December 1944 issue. See "Christmas in a Relocation Center," *Survey Midmonthly* 80, no. 12 (1944).

66. See *Common Ground* editor Margaret Anderson's follow-up advice in an April 7, 1943, letter to Okubo, having earlier urged her to create an illustrated story of camp life: "I hope you'll emphasize the very human situations in which the evacuees find themselves—which are the basic human situations anywhere. That was what was so good about your Christmas scene and the mess hall one, too. We all have so much more in common than we have in differences, though many of us don't have our eyes open to see it" (Miné Okubo Papers).

67. Richard B. Finn, *Winners in Peace: MacArthur, Yoshida, and Postwar Japan* (Berkeley: University of California Press, 1992), 113.

68. I adapt the phrase "domesticate the foreign" from Amy Kaplan, "Manifest Domesticity," *American Literature* 70, no. 3 (1998): 589.

69. Miné Okubo, "The Trend Is Toward Assimilation," *Pacific Citizen*, Dec. 24–31, 1976, 4 (emphasis added).

70. Okubo's statement concerning the simultaneous publication of "Issei, Nisei, and Kibei" in a Japanese edition of *Fortune* is uncorroborated by the latter's publication record. According to "History of Magazines in Japan: 1867–1988," *Fortune Japan*, the forerunner to *President*, was established in 1963, long after Okubo's illustrations were published in *Fortune*'s April 1944 issue in the United States. On the history of *Fortune Japan* see "History of Magazines in Japan: 1867–1988," Web Kanzaki, July 7, 1996, www.kanzaki.com/jpress/mag-history.html. Cullen Wheeler of *Fortune*'s Letters Department speculates Okubo's statement reflected "confusion on her part." According to Wheeler, although "there were some TIMELIFE publications that were reproduced in 'Armed Forces Editions [AFEs],'" which circulated in Japan, the chief archivist for TIMELIFE is "not aware of FORTUNE being reproduced in such a manner." Yet Wheeler notes that Okubo's work "could've been published in one of the AFEs . . . [which] later grew into International editions of TIME and LIFE." Cullen Wheeler, email to author, March 9, 2007.

Chapter 4. Possessive Investment in Ruin

1. Bill Hume, *Babysan: A Private Look at the Japanese Occupation* (Columbia, MO: American Press, 1953), 12.

2. "When Atom Bomb Struck—Uncensored," *Life*, Sept. 29, 1952, 24.

3. M. Susan Lindee, *Suffering Made Real: American Science and the Survivors at Hiroshima* (Chicago: University of Chicago Press, 1994), 26.

4. Ienaga Saburō, *The Pacific War, 1931–1945*, trans. Frank Baldwin (New York: Pantheon, 1978), 200.

5. John Bugher, quoted in Lindee, *Suffering Made Real*, 134.

6. Kurihara Sadako, "America Comes Out as the World's Top in Anything," trans. Ohara Miyao, *Atlantis* 12, no. 2 (1987): 16–17.

7. Robert Jay Lifton, *Death in Life: Survivors of Hiroshima* (New York: Random House, 1967), 95.

8. Robert Jungk, *Children of the Ashes: The Story of a Rebirth*, trans. Constantine Fitzgibbon (1959; New York: Harcourt, Brace, and World, 1961), 40.

9. In 1949 the British physicist P. M. S. Blackett described the atomic bombings as "not so much the last military act of the second World War, as the first major operation of the cold diplomatic war with Russia now in progress." P. M. S. Blackett, *Fear, War and the Bomb: Military and Political Consequences of Atomic Energy* (New York: Whittlesey, 1949), 139.

10. Joseph Masco, "'Survival Is Your Business': Engineering Ruins and Affect in Nuclear America," *Cultural Anthropology* 23, no. 1 (2008): 363.

11. As Barbara Rose Johnston notes, "Civil defense programs were largely meant to pacify public concerns over nuclear weapons tests" and were premised on the fiction Americans could purchase products and undertake actions that might safeguard them

from fallout. Barbara Rose Johnston, "Half-Lives, Half-Truths, and Other Radioactive Legacies of the Cold War," in *Half-Lives and Half-Truths: Confronting the Radioactive Legacies of the Cold War*, ed. Barbara Rose Johnston (Santa Fe, NM: School for Advanced Research, 2007), 7.

12. Elizabeth M. DeLoughrey, "The Myth of Isolates: Ecosystem Ecologies in the Nuclear Pacific," in *Postcolonial Studies: An Anthology*, ed. Pramod K. Nayar (West Sussex: John Wiley, 2016), 565.

13. The United States carried out 105 atmospheric and underwater nuclear tests in the Pacific Proving Grounds—an area encompassing the Marshall Islands and a few other sites in the Pacific. In 1962, before the passage of the partial nuclear ban treaty, the United States also conducted devastating nuclear tests on Kiritimati (Christmas Island) without evacuating the islanders.

14. Traci Brynne Voyles, *Wastelanding: Legacies of Uranium Mining in Navajo Country* (Minneapolis: University of Minnesota Press, 2015), 9, 10.

15. See John Locke, *Second Treatise of Government*, ed. C. B. McPherson (1690; Indianapolis, IN: Hackett, 1980), sec. 32, www.gutenberg.org/files/7370/7370-h/7370-h.htm. On wastelands as "undesirable, unproductive, or unappealing" indigenous territories see Voyles, *Wastelanding*, 1–26.

16. Leslie Marmon Silko, *Ceremony* (1977; New York: Penguin, 2006), 33.

17. "Statement of Senator Johnsay Riklon, Member—Marshall Islands Nitijela, before the Committee on Natural Resources Subcommittee on Oversight and Investigations, U.S. House of Representatives," Feb. 24, 1994, in *Radiation Exposure from Pacific Nuclear Tests* (Washington, DC: U.S. Government Printing Office, 1994), 362.

18. "Statement of Jonathan M. Weisgall, Legal Counsel to the People of Bikini, before the House Natural Resources Committee," in *Radiation Exposure from Pacific Nuclear Tests* (Washington, DC: U.S. Government Printing Office, 1994), 12. Hereafter "Weisgall."

19. On slow violence see Rob Nixon, *Slow Violence and the Environmentalism of the Poor* (Cambridge, MA: Harvard University Press, 2011).

20. Rey Chow, *The Age of the World Target: Self-Referentiality in War, Theory, and Comparative Work* (Durham, NC: Duke University Press, 2006), 32.

21. Haunani-Kay Trask, "The Color of Violence," *Social Justice* 31, no. 4 (2004): 10.

22. Dwight D. Eisenhower, "Atoms for Peace Speech," Dec. 8, 1953, International Atomic Energy Agency, www.iaea.org/about/history/atoms-for-peace-speech.

23. Michel Foucault, *Society Must Be Defended: Lectures at the Collège de France, 1975–76*, trans. David Macey (1976; New York: Picador, 2003), 241.

24. Paul Tibbetts, quoted in *Atomic Café*, dir. Jayne Loader, Kevin Rafferty, and Pierce Rafferty (1982; New York: Docurama, 2008).

25. Chris Marker, *Coréennes*, trans. Brian Holmes (1959; Columbus, OH: Wexner Center for the Arts, 2009), https://chrismarker.org/coreennes-english-text.

26. My conception of a possessive investment in ruin is indebted to George Lipsitz's notion of a "possessive investment in whiteness," which he theorizes as a structural consequence of not only chattel slavery and Jim Crow but more pointedly as

"the putatively race-neutral liberal social democratic reforms of the past five decades." Whereas Lipsitz's critique of welfare capitalism enables him to examine the dispossessive racializing effects of liberal reforms within the United States, my focus is on the Pacific as an arena of U.S. military-imperial dominion in which the United States commodified nuclear ruin. See George Lipsitz, "The Possessive Investment in Whiteness: Racialized Social Democracy and the 'White' Problem in American Studies," *American Quarterly* 47, no. 3 (1995): 372.

27. Stefanie Schäfer, "From Geisha Girls to the Atomic Bomb Dome: Dark Tourism and the Formation of Hiroshima Memory," *Tourist Studies* 16, no. 4 (2016): 357.

28. Teresia K. Teaiwa, "Bikinis and Other S/Pacific N/Oceans," *Contemporary Pacific* 6, no. 1 (1994): 93, 92.

29. Gertrude Stein, "Reflection on the Atomic Bomb," in *Reflection on the Atomic Bomb*, ed. Robert Haas (Los Angeles: Black Sparrow, 1973), 161.

30. Joseph Masco, *The Nuclear Borderlands: The Manhattan Project in Post–Cold War New Mexico* (Princeton, NJ: Princeton University Press, 2006), 5.

31. See Paul Bower, "Exotic Resonances: Hiroshima in American Memory," in *Hiroshima in History and Memory*, ed. Michael J. Hogan (Cambridge: Cambridge University Press, 1996), 145.

32. George Marion, *Bases and Empire* (New York: Fairplay, 1948), 186.

33. See Kyo Maclear, *Beclouded Visions: Hiroshima-Nagasaki and the Art of Witness* (Albany: State University of New York Press, 1999).

34. Greg Mitchell, "A Hole in History: America Suppresses the Truth about Hiroshima," *The Progressive*, August 1995, www.thefreelibrary.com/A+hole+in+history%3A+America+suppresses+the+truth+about+Hiroshima.-a017367812.

35. The population of wartime Hiroshima was not exclusively Japanese. It was home to sizable populations of Korean and Chinese forced laborers, as well as small numbers of American POWs and Japanese Americans.

36. Peter Schwenger and John Whittier Treat, "America's Hiroshima, Hiroshima's America," in *Asia/Pacific as Space of Cultural Production*, ed. Rob Wilson and Arif Dirlik (Durham, NC: Duke University Press, 1995), 324.

37. See Nakazawa Keiji, *Barefoot Gen: A Cartoon Story of Hiroshima*, vol. 1, trans. Project Gen (San Francisco: Last Gasp, 2003).

38. Quoted in Nakazawa Keiji, "About Barefoot Gen," in *Barefoot Gen: A Cartoon Story of Hiroshima*, n.p. (emphasis added). In the first-person seed narrative, *I SAW IT*, the narrator is identified autobiographically as "Keiji."

39. See Leonard Rifas, "Cartooning and Nuclear Power: From Industry Advertising to Activist Uprising and Beyond," *PS: Political Science and Politics* 40, no. 2 (2007): 255–60. The manga first appeared in limited English-language release as *Barefoot Gen* in the late 1970s and in small-press distribution as *I SAW IT* and *Gen of Hiroshima* in the early 1980s through the public-interest comics label EduComics.

40. Alison Landsberg, *Prosthetic Memory: The Transformation of American Remembrance in the Age of Mass Culture* (New York: Columbia University Press, 2004), 49.

41. Art Spiegelman, "Barefoot Gen: Comics after the Bomb," introduction to *Barefoot Gen: A Cartoon Story of Hiroshima*, by Nakazawa Keiji (San Francisco: Last Gasp, 2003), n.p.

42. On the efficacy of comics in conveying Hiroshima's horror, Nakazawa contended "manga offers the best access." See Nakazawa Keiji, "Barefoot Gen, the Atomic Bomb and I: The Hiroshima Legacy," interview by Asai Motofumi, trans. Richard Minear, *Asia-Pacific Journal* 6, no. 1 (2008): https://apjjf.org/-Nakazawa-Keiji/2638/article.html. Hereafter "Interview."

43. Who recalls or still reads, for example, Nagai Takashi's landmark 1951 compilation *We of Nagasaki*? See Nagai Takashi, *We of Nagasaki: The Story of Survivors in an Atomic Wasteland*, trans. Shirato Ichiro and Herbert B. L. Silverman (New York: Duell, Sloan, and Pearce, 1951).

44. See also "When the Atom Bomb Struck—Uncensored," *Life*, Sept. 29, 1952, 19–25.

45. Subhabrata Bobby Banerjee, "Necrocapitalism," *Organization Studies* 29, no. 12 (2008): 1549.

46. Mathias Luce, "Sub-imperialism, the Highest Stage of Dependent Capitalism," in *BRICS: An Anti-capitalist Critique*, ed. Patrick Bond and Ana Garcia (Auckland Park, South Africa: Jacana Media, 2015), 29, 31–32.

47. Karl Marx, *Capital: A Critique of Political Economy*, vol. 1, trans. Ben Fowkes (London: Penguin, 1976), 916, 915.

48. The phrase "disaster capitalism" is Klein's. See Naomi Klein, "The Rise of Disaster Capitalism," *The Nation*, April 14, 2005, www.thenation.com/article/rise-disaster-capitalism.

49. See Marita Sturken, "Absent Images of Memory: Remembering and Reenacting the Japanese Internment," in *Perilous Memories: The Asia-Pacific War(s)*, ed. T[akashi] Fujitani, Geoffrey M. White, and Lisa Yoneyama (Durham, NC: Duke University Press, 2001), 46.

50. For a discussion of the diplomatic wrangling over body parts see M. Susan Lindee, "The Repatriation of Atomic Bomb Victim Parts to Japan: Natural Objects and Diplomacy," *Osiris* 13 (1998): 376–409. Hereafter "Repatriation."

51. Lindee, "Repatriation," 382.

52. James J. Orr, *The Victim as Hero: Ideologies of Peace and National Identity in Postwar Japan* (Honolulu: University of Hawai'i Press, 2001), 16.

53. Henry L. Stimson, "The Bomb and the Opportunity," *Harper's Magazine*, March 1946, 204.

54. Lisa Yoneyama, *Hiroshima Traces: Time, Space, and the Dialectics of Memory* (Berkeley: University of California Press, 1999), 20.

55. "Proclamation Defining Terms for Japanese Surrender Issued, at Potsdam," July 26, 1945, Atomic Heritage Foundation, www.atomicheritage.org/key-documents/potsdam-declaration. Hereafter "Potsdam Proclamation."

56. The first Last Gasp reissues of *Barefoot Gen* are hand-lettered with words boldfaced for emphasis and rendered entirely in capitals. I have maintained just the boldface.

57. Quoted in Roger Chickering and Stig Förster, "Are We There Yet? World War II and the Theory of Total War," in *A World at Total War: Global Conflict and the Politics of Destruction, 1937–1945*, ed. Roger Chickering et al. (Washington, DC: German Historical Institute; Cambridge: Cambridge University Press, 2005), 5.

58. Quoted in Kimie Hara, "Micronesia and the Postwar Remaking of the Asia Pacific: 'An American Lake,'" *Asia-Pacific Journal* 5, no. 8 (2007): https://apjjf.org/-Kimie-Hara/2493/article.html.

59. Robert Barclay, *Melal: A Novel of the Pacific* (Honolulu: University of Hawai'i Press, 2002), 214.

60. See Tony deBrum's comments about Project 4.1 in *Nuclear Savage: The Islands of Secret Project 4.1*, dir. Adam Jonas Horowitz (Honolulu: Pacific Islanders in Communications, 2011).

61. John Anjain and four of his children subsequently suffered thyroid cancer. His son Lekoj, just a year old when exposed to fallout from Castle Bravo, died of leukemia as a teenager. Thyroid cancer also plagued the generation of grandchildren.

62. Neisan Laukon, "Nuclear Zero Lawsuits: Why the Tiny Marshall Islands Took on the Nuclear Nine," Women's Action for New Directions (WAND) webinar, August 6, 2014, account based on author's notes.

63. Horowitz, *Nuclear Savage*.

64. Patrick Wolfe, "Settler Colonialism and the Elimination of the Native," *Journal of Genocide Research* 8, no. 4 (2006): 388.

65. See Robert C. Kiste, *The Bikinians: A Study in Forced Migration* (Menlo Park, CA: Cummings, 1974), 196.

66. See, e.g., Kyle Swenson, "The U.S. Put Nuclear Waste under a Dome on a Pacific Island. Now It's Cracking Open," *Washington Post*, May 20, 2019, www.washingtonpost.com/nation/2019/05/20/us-put-nuclear-waste-under-dome-pacific-island-now-its-cracking-open.

67. Barbara Rose Johnston and Holly M. Barker, *Consequential Damages of Nuclear War: The Rongelap Report* (Walnut Creek, CA: Left Coast Press, 2008), 18 (italics in original).

68. Trust Territory of the Pacific Islands, "Agreement in Principle Regarding the Use of Bikini Atoll," Nov. 22, 1956 (repr. in Kiste, *The Bikinians*, 199).

69. Hara, "Micronesia and the Postwar."

70. See Cheryl Harris, "Whiteness as Property," *Harvard Law Review* 106, no. 8 (1993): 1724.

71. The status of the Marshall Islands resembled that of the Philippines, Guam, and Puerto Rico, all U.S. unincorporated territories that early twentieth-century Supreme Court justices argued were "foreign in a domestic sense." See "'Foreign in a Domestic Sense,' 1898–1945," History, Art and Archives: United States House of Representatives, https://history.house.gov/Exhibitions-and-Publications/HAIC/Historical-Essays/Foreign-Domestic/.

72. Atomic Energy Commission, "Studies of Radioactive Fallout," in *Radiation Exposure from Pacific Nuclear Tests* (Washington, DC: U.S. Government Printing Office, 1994), 75.

73. Winona LaDuke, with Sean Aaron Cruz, *The Militarization of Indian Country* (East Lansing: Michigan State University Press, 2013), 37, 38.

74. Brandon C. Davis, "Defending the Nation, Protecting the Land: Emergency Powers and the Militarization of American Public Lands," in *Proving Grounds: Militarized Landscapes, Weapons Testing, and the Environmental Impact of U.S. Bases*, ed. Edward A. Martini (Seattle: University of Washington Press, 2015), 35.

75. Masco, *The Nuclear Borderlands*, 311; see also LaDuke, *Militarization of Indian Country*, 37.

76. On the massive increase in lethality of the U.S. nuclear tests in the Marshall Islands see Johnston and Barker, *Consequential Damages*, 19. Barker also notes "the total yields of Nevada were 1 percent of the yields of the Marshall Islands." Holly M. Barker, "From Analysis to Action: Efforts to Address the Nuclear Legacy in the Marshall Islands," in *Half-Lives and Half-Truths: Confronting the Radioactive Legacies of the Cold War*, ed. Barbara Rose Johnston (Santa Fe, NM: School for Advanced Research, 2007), 236.

77. See Tanya H. Lee, "H-Bomb Guinea Pigs! Natives Suffering Decades after New Mexico Tests," *Indian Country Today*, March 5, 2014, https://newsmaven.io/indiancountrytoday/archive/h-bomb-guinea-pigs-natives-suffering-decades-after-new-mexico-tests-jpZAFe1gFEmRCGfiq42BDg.

78. None of the U.S. Public Health Service radiation-impact studies of uranium miners focused on American Indian populations. See Barbara Rose Johnston, Susan E. Dawson, and Gary E. Madsen, "Uranium Mining and Milling: Navajo Experience in the American Southwest," in *Half-Lives and Half-Truths: Confronting the Radioactive Legacies of the Cold War*, ed. Barbara Rose Johnston (Santa Fe, NM: School for Advanced Research, 2007), 104.

79. At the same time, post-Bravo American scientists recognized the value of the Rongelapese as "a very small population exposed to a very high dose of radiation ... an ideal situation [for] genetic study. It is far more significant than anything you could ever get out of Hiroshima and Nagasaki." Quoted in Barbara Rose Johnston, "More Like Us Than Mice," in *Half-Lives and Half-Truths: Confronting the Radioactive Legacies of the Cold War*, ed. Barbara Rose Johnston (Santa Fe, NM: School for Advanced Research, 2007), 40 (emphasis added).

80. Robert A. Underwood, "Statement of Hon. Robert A. Underwood," in *Radiation Exposure from Pacific Nuclear Tests* (Washington, DC: U.S. Government Printing Office, 1994), 2.

81. Yuki Tanaka, *Hidden Horrors: Japanese War Crimes in World War II* (Boulder, CO: Westview Press, 2006), 162 (emphasis added).

82. Quoted in Keith M. Parsons and Robert A. Zaballa, *Bombing the Marshall Islands: A Cold War Tragedy* (Cambridge: Cambridge University Press, 2017), 70.

83. Horowitz, *Nuclear Savage*.

84. Robert A. Conard, *Fallout: The Experiences of a Medical Team in the Care of a Marshallese Population Accidentally Exposed to Fallout Radiation* (Upton, NY: Brookhaven National Laboratory, 1992), 26.

85. Conard et al., quoted in Holly M. Barker, *Bravo for the Marshallese: Regaining Control in a Post-Nuclear, Post-Colonial World* (Belmont, CA: Wadsworth, 2013), 45.

86. Johnston, "Half-Lives, Half-Truths," 13.

87. Quoted in Johnston, "More Like Us," 25.

88. Brookhaven National Laboratory conducted government-sponsored studies of irradiated Marshall Islanders from 1954 until 1998.

89. Johnston and Barker, *Consequential Damages*, 23.

90. Robert Conard to Charles Dunham, June 5, 1958, 2, www.osti.gov/opennet/servlets/purl/16364942.pdf (emphasis in original).

91. Nelson Anjain to Robert Conard, April 9, 1975, Department of Energy, Box 128, Folder "Bio-Med Dr. Conard 01 thru 06/1975," www.osti.gov/opennet/servlets/purl/16366706.pdf.

92. Marie Clements, *Burning Vision* (Vancouver, BC: Talonbooks, 2003), 111.

93. See Dennis Riches, "Canada & the First Nations in the Manhattan Project," *Mint Press News*, Oct. 16, 2014, www.mintpressnews.com/MyMPN/canada-manhattan-project.

94. On September 22, 1988, timed with Ronald Reagan's apology to Japanese Americans, Canadian prime minister Brian Mulroney apologized to Japanese Canadians for their mass removal and incarceration during World War II. On June 11, 2008, six years after *Burning Vision* opened on the stage, Prime Minister Stephen Harper apologized to former students of Indian residential schools.

95. Gerald Vizenor, *Hiroshima Bugi: Atomu 57* (Lincoln: University of Nebraska Press, 2003), 2.

96. The phrase "radiogenic communities" is Barbara Johnston's. See Johnston, "Half-Lives, Half-Truths," 2.

97. Howard L. Hills, "Statement of Howard L. Hills before the Subcommittee on Oversight and Investigations Committee of Natural Resources, U.S. House of Representatives," in *Radiation Exposure from Pacific Nuclear Tests* (Washington, DC: U.S. Government Printing Office, 1994), 170.

98. Sasha Davis, *The Empires' Edge: Militarization, Resistance, and Transcending Hegemony in the Pacific* (Athens: University of Georgia Press, 2015). On the concentration of uranium resources on indigenous lands globally, see LaDuke, *Militarization of Indian Country*, 36.

99. Kurihara, "America Comes Out," 17.

100. "Peace Walk Beginning Friday March 20 in Richmond CA," Corrina Gould to author, email, March 18, 2015.

101. Conard, 39.

102. Julian Aguon, *The Fire This Time: Essays on Life under U.S. Occupation* (Tokyo: Blue Ocean, 2006), 50.

Chapter 5. People's War, People's Democracy, People's Epic

1. Jose Maria Sison, "The Guerrilla Is like a Poet," 1968, https://josemariasison.org/the-guerrilla-is-like-a-poet-2.

2. Jose Maria Sison, "The Bladed Poem," 1982, https://josemariasison.org/the-bladed-poem.

3. Paul Virilio, *War and Cinema: The Logistics of Perception*, trans. Patrick Camiller (London: Verso, 1989), 20.

4. Mao Tse-tung, "What Is Guerrilla Warfare?" in *On Guerrilla Warfare*, vol. 9 of *Selected Works of Mao Tse-tung* (1937), Mao Tse-tung Reference Archive, Maoist Documentation Project (2000), www.marxists.org/reference/archive/mao/works/1937/guerrilla-warfare/ch01.htm.

5. Quoted in Eqbal Ahmad, "Revolutionary War and Counter-Insurgency," *Journal of International Affairs* 25, no. 1 (1971): 2. See also Griffith's translation: "The former [the people] may be likened to water and the latter [the troops] to the fish who inhabit it" (93). Mao Tse-tung, *On Guerilla Warfare*, trans. Samuel B. Griffith (1961; Urbana: University of Illinois Press, 2000), 93.

6. Jean-Paul Sartre, "Genocide," *New Left Review* 48 (1968): 20 (emphasis added).

7. Ahmad, "Revolutionary War and Counter-Insurgency," 10.

8. Samuel B. Griffith, introduction to *On Guerrilla Warfare*, by Mao Tse-tung, trans. Samuel B. Griffith (1961; Urbana: University of Illinois Press, 2000), 22.

9. Since 1961, Sison has been continuously under U.S. blacklist. See Ninotchka Rosca, "Introduction: A Biographical Sketch," in *Jose Maria Sison: At Home in the World, Portrait of a Revolutionary*, by Jose Maria Sison and Ninotchka Rosca (Greensboro, NC: Open Hand, 2004), 12.

10. Colin L. Powell, "Designation of a Foreign Terrorist Organization," August 9, 2002, U.S. Department of State, https://2001-2009.state.gov/secretary/former/powell/remarks/2002/12542.htm. The CPP was founded in 1968, not 1969. The New People's Army, the CPP's armed wing, however, was founded in 1969.

11. John A. Nagl, "The Evolution and Importance of Army/Marine Corps Field Manual 3-24, *Counterinsurgency*," *The U.S. Army/Marine Corps Counterinsurgency Field Manual*, 2006 (Chicago: University of Chicago Press, 2007), xiv. Hereafter FM 3-24.

12. David Petraeus, "Learning Counterinsurgency: Observations from Soldiering in Iraq," *Military Review*, Jan.-Feb. 2006, 51.

13. David H. Price, *Weaponizing Anthropology* (Oakland, CA: AK Press, 2011), 3; Vanessa M. Gezari, "How to Read Afghanistan," *New York Times*, August 10, 2013, www.nytimes.com/2013/08/11/opinion/sunday/how-to-read-afghanistan.html?pagewanted=all&_r=0.

14. Eva Horn, "Knowing the Enemy: The Epistemology of Secret Intelligence," trans. Sara Ogger, *Grey Room* 11 (2003): 62.

15. Gilles Deleuze and Félix Guattari, *A Thousand Plateaus: Capitalism and Schizophrenia*, trans. Brian Massumi (Minneapolis: University of Minnesota Press, 1987), 353.

16. George W. Bush, "Remarks to a Joint Session of the Philippine Congress in Quezon City, Philippines," Oct. 18, 2003, www.presidency.ucsb.edu/ws/?pid=63501.

17. Alfred W. McCoy, *Policing America's Empire: The United States, the Philippines, and the Rise of the Surveillance State* (Madison: University of Wisconsin Press, 2009), 4, 5. See also Reynaldo Ileto, "Philippine Wars and the Politics of Memory," *positions: asia critique* 13, no. 1 (2005): 215–35.

18. "Basic Rules of the New People's Army," March 29, 1969, in Alfredo B. Saulo, *Communism in the Philippines: An Introduction* (Manila: Ateneo de Manila University Press, 1990), 225. Although the NPA would repudiate the "bourgeois influence in the [prior People's] Army initiated and promoted by the Taruc-Sumulong renegade clique," it positioned itself as a Maoist "rectification, reestablishment and reinvigoration of the Communist Party of the Philippines" and part of a long-standing lineage. See "Constitution and Bylaws of the New People's Army (NPA)," March 29, 1969, in Saulo, 210.

19. Luis Taruc, *Born of the People* (1949; New York: International Publishers, 1953), 65. This memoir was ghostwritten with the American communist and Huk revolutionary William Pomeroy.

20. H. Ford Wilkins, "Outlaws Disturb Philippines; 'Huks' a State within State," *New York Times*, May 20, 1946, 1.

21. See Sison and Rosa, 202.

22. See Stephen R. Shalom, "Philippine Acceptance of the Bell Trade Act of 1946: A Study of Manipulatory Democracy," *Pacific Historical Review* 49, no. 3 (1980): 499–517.

23. See Ahmad, "Revolutionary War and Counter-Insurgency," 18.

24. Jose Maria Sison, "Sympathy for the Victims and Condemnation of Terrorism," Sept. 18, 2001, in Sison and Rosca, 243.

25. "Programme for a People's Democratic Revolution in the Philippines," Dec. 26, 1968, in Saulo, *Communism in the Philippines*, 199.

26. Hernando Abaya, *Betrayal in the Philippines* (New York: A. A. Wyn, 1946), 175.

27. Permanent Peoples' Tribunal, "Statement of the NPA," in *Philippines: Repression and Resistance: Permanent Peoples' Tribunal Session on the Philippines* (Manila: Komite ng Sambayanang, Pilipino, 1981), 213 (emphasis in original).

28. C.L.C. [Central Luzon Command] "Instruction No. 4 for the Rainy Season," June 15, 1947 (translation of captured Huk document in U.S. National Archives), 1135th Counter Intelligence Corps Detachment, Philippines-Ryukyus Command, APO 707, Information Section, National Archives, College Park, MD.

29. Abaya writes, "Paradoxically, the Jap invasion was a blessing to the peasant. The landlord left his hacienda in the hands of the overseer and stayed in Manila where there was 'peace and order' under the Jap bayonet. The peasant stayed behind and worked the fields. He fought the Jap, who tried to grab his produce" (Abaya, 212).

30. Carlos Bulosan, *All the Conspirators* (Seattle: University of Washington Press, 1998), 18.

31. For a discussion of Manuel Roxas's "mailed fist" policy, see Eduardo Lachica, *The Huks: Philippine Agrarian Society in Revolt* (New York: Praeger, 1971), 121–23.

32. See Benedict J. Kerkvliet, *The Huk Rebellion: A Study of the Peasant Revolt in the Philippines* (Berkeley: University of California Press, 1977), 113.

33. Tessa Morris-Suzuki, "Post-War Warriors: Japanese Combatants in the Korean War," *Asia-Pacific Journal* 10, no. 31 (2012): https://apjjf.org/2012/10/31/Tessa-Morris-Suzuki/3803/article.html.

34. See E. San Juan Jr., introduction to *The Cry and the Dedication*, by Carlos Bulosan (Philadelphia: Temple University Press, 1995), xviii.

35. Kim Dong-choon, "Korea's Movement to Settle the Past Issues and Peace in East Asia," *Korea Journal* 50, no. 4 (2010): 160.

36. See Utsumi Aiko, "Korean 'Imperial Soldiers': Remembering Colonialism and Crimes against Allie POWs," trans. Mie Kennedy, in *Perilous Memories: The Asia-Pacific War(s)*, ed. T. Fujitani et al. (Durham, NC: Duke University Press, 2001), 211, 214.

37. Suk-jung Han, "On the Question of Collaboration in South Korea," *Asia-Pacific Journal* 6, no. 7 (2008): http://apjjf.org/-Suk-Jung-Han/2800/article.html.

38. Keith L. Camacho, "The Politics of Indigenous Collaboration," *Journal of Pacific History* 43, no. 2 (2008): 222.

39. See Walter C. Ladwig III, "The Philippine Constabulary and the Hukbalahap Rebellion," in *Policing Insurgencies: Cops as Counterinsurgents*, ed. C. Christine Fair and Sumit Ganguly (Oxford: Oxford University Press, 2014), 21–22.

40. David Jablonsky, "The State of the National Security State," *Parameters* 43, no. 4 (2002–3): 8.

41. George Orwell, "You and the Atomic Bomb," Oct. 19, 1945, *Tribune* (London), http://orwell.ru/library/articles/ABomb/english/e_abomb.

42. Eric Carlton, *Militarism: Rule without Law* (Burlington, VT: Aldershot, 2001).

43. Mark Selden, "Okinawa and American Security Imperialism," in *Remaking Asia: Essays on the American Uses of Power*, ed. Mark Selden (New York: Pantheon, 1974), 279–304.

44. See Arnold C. Brackman, *The Other Nuremberg: The Untold Story of the Tokyo War Crimes Trials* (New York: Morrow, 1987).

45. Kuan-Hsing Chen, *Asia as Method* (Durham, NC: Duke University Press, 2010), 200.

46. Catherine Lutz, "Making War at Home in the United States: Militarization and the Current Crisis," *American Anthropologist* 104, no. 3 (2002): 729.

47. Michael Klare, *Supplying Repression* (New York: Field Foundation, 1977), 10.

48. Permanent Peoples' Tribunal, *Philippines: Repression and Resistance*, 201. For a discussion of the subfascism of U.S. client-states in the Third World, see Noam Chomsky and Edward S. Herman, *The Political Economy of Human Rights: The Washington Connection and Third World Fascism* (Boston: South End, 1979).

49. On the "elite carr[ying] the stigma of having been the historic traitor to the nation," see Ahmad, "Revolutionary War and Counter-Insurgency," 22.

50. Theodor Adorno, "Commitment," trans. Francis McDonagh, in *The Essential Frankfurt School Reader*, ed. Andrew Arato and Eike Gebhardt (Oxford: Blackwell, 1978),

312; Elie Wiesel, "The Holocaust as Literary Inspiration," in E. Wiesel et al., *Dimensions of the Holocaust: Lectures at Northwestern University* (Evanston, IL: Northwestern University Press, 1977), 9.

51. Shoshana Felman, *The Juridical Unconscious: Trials and Traumas in the Twentieth Century* (Cambridge, MA: Harvard University Press, 2002).

52. Aimé Césaire, *Discourse on Colonialism*, trans. Joan Pinkham (1955; New York: Monthly Review, 1972), 35.

53. Wayne Booth, *The Rhetoric of Fiction* (Chicago: University of Chicago Press, 1961), 344.

54. See Horn, "Knowing the Enemy," 64.

55. Caroline S. Hau and Benedict Anderson, introduction to *All the Conspirators* (Seattle: University of Washington Press, 1998), xxi.

56. Sexually enslaved by the Japanese Imperial Army, Maria Rosa Henson, a Huk member, writes: "Among the huk [sic], no one used his or her real name. All the members were known by aliases. They gave me the name Bayang, the nickname for Maria" (28). See Maria Rosa Henson, *Comfort Woman: A Filipina's Story of Prostitution and Slavery under the Japanese Military* (London: Rowman and Littlefield, 1999), 28.

57. At the peak of their wartime anti-Japanese struggle, when they comprised ten thousand full-time guerrillas and one hundred thousand part-time militia, the Huks killed an estimated twenty-five thousand people, of whom 80 percent were "collaborators and 'obstructionists in the class war.'" Ladwig, "The Philippine Constabulary," 21.

58. 1135th Counter Intelligence Corps Detachment, Philippines-Ryukyus Command, APO 707, Information Section, National Archives, College Park, MD.

59. See Stephen R. Shalom, "Counter-Insurgency in the Philippines," *Journal of Contemporary Asia* 7, no. 2 (1977): 163.

60. Shalom, 163–64.

61. Carlos Bulosan, "Terrorism Rides the Philippines," *1952 Yearbook, Local 37*, International Longshoremen's and Warehousemen's Union (Seattle, WA: ILWU, 1952), 27.

62. Carlos Bulosan, "To Whom It May Concern," in *1952 Yearbook, Local 37*, International Longshoremen's and Warehousemen's Union (Seattle, WA: ILWU, 1952), 21.

63. Bruce Cumings, "Boundary Displacement: Area Studies and International Studies during and after the Cold War," *Bulletin of Concerned Asian Scholars* 29, no. 1 (1997): 10. As Cumings further notes: "It is only a bit of an exaggeration to say that for those scholars studying potential enemy countries, either they consulted with the government or they risked being investigated by the FBI" (11).

64. Jodi Melamed, *Represent and Destroy: Rationalizing Violence in the New Racial Capitalism* (Minneapolis: University of Minnesota Press, 2011), xv–xvi.

65. Consider Vicente Diaz's critique of the U.S. "liberation" of Guam: "for what reasons and for whose purposes, did the landing of American forces in Guam on 21 July 1944 get remembered and inscribed—indeed canonized—as an act of liberation, of freedom, particularly when there is overwhelming evidence that America's return had more to do with military strategy than some altruistic desire to free the Chamorros from enemy

occupation?" Vicente Diaz, "Deliberating 'Liberation Day': Identity, History, Memory, and War in Guam," in *Perilous Memories: The Asia Pacific War(s)*, ed. T. Fujitani et al. (Durham, NC: Duke University Press, 2001), 157. Relative to the Philippines, Ronald Edgerton notes that "CIC units were responsible for examining the merits of potential appointees. . . . They usually entered liberated towns even before the PCAU [Philippine Civil Affairs Units] arrived, and in such cases it was their task to establish provisional civil governments. 'The first step . . . was to determine the loyalty of the incumbent mayor, whether a puppet appointee or not. Otherwise, the prewar mayor, if available, was reinstated.' Wherever possible, CIC units maintained close liaison with PCAUs in the clearance of public officials. Between them they left little to chance. In fact, until March 1945, virtually all appointments were made by these units." See Ronald K. Edgerton, "General Douglas MacArthur and the American Military Impact in the Philippines," *Philippine Studies* 25, no. 4 (1977): 433–34.

66. References to *Huklandia* were commonplace in news reports and academic writings on the Huks. Russell Fifield, for example, wrote in 1951, "Inside Huklandia the Huks maintain in many respects a state within a state. They collect taxes called 'dues,' conscript men into the army, have their own courts, perform marriages and grant divorces, and hold their own 'elections.' The national government forces have found buildings labeled 'party school,' 'mess hall,' 'courthouse,' 'hospital,' 'military academy,' and 'auditorium.' Here the principles of Marxism are taught by Huk leaders to their followers." Russell Fifield, "The Hukbalahap Today," *Far Eastern Survey* 20, no. 2 (1951): 17.

67. John Patrick Finnegan and Romana Danysh, *Military Intelligence* (Washington, DC: Center of Military History, United States Army, 1998), 98.

68. John P[atrick] Finnegan, "The Evolution of US Army HUMINT: Intelligence Operations in the Korean War," *Studies in Intelligence* 44, no. 2 (2000): 6.

69. United States Army Counter Intelligence Corps School, *Counter Intelligence Corps History and Mission in World War II* (Fort Holabird, MD: Counter Intelligence Corps School, 1959), 23.

70. See Camacho 221.

71. Daniel B. Schirmer and Stephen R. Shalom, eds., *The Philippines Reader: A History of Colonialism, Neocolonialism, Dictatorship, and Resistance* (Cambridge, MA: South End, 1987), 70 (emphasis mine).

72. It bears noting the continuity of CIA involvement in the figure of Edward Lansdale—often read as inspiration for Alden Pyle—behind the scenes of U.S. Cold War counterinsurgency campaigns in the Philippines and Vietnam. Shalom notes: "A week after Magsaysay's appointment, the CIA's Edward Lansdale arrived in Manila. Lansdale promptly set up a desk in Magsaysay's Defense office and a cot in Magsaysay's private quarters, and the two worked closely together on the problems of counter-insurgency." Shalom, "Counter-Insurgency in the Philippines," 114.

73. 1135th Counter Intelligence Corps Detachment, Philippines-Ryukyus Command, APO 707, Information Section, "Semi-Monthly Activities Report," April 16–20, 1947, National Archives, College Park, MD.

74. Carl von Clausewitz, *On War*, ed. and trans. Michael Howard and Peter Paret (Princeton, NJ: Princeton University Press, 1976), 117 (emphasis in original).

75. David Joel Steinberg, *Philippine Collaboration in World War II* (Ann Arbor: University of Michigan Press, 1967), 132–33.

76. Quoted in Ronald K. Edgerton, "General Douglas MacArthur and the American Military Impact in the Philippines," *Philippine Studies* 25, no. 4 (1977): 428.

77. See also Benedict Anderson, "Cacique Democracy in the Philippines: Origins and Dreams," *New Left Review* 169 (1988): 14.

78. See Rick Baldoz, "'Comrade Carlos Bulosan': U.S. State Surveillance and the Cold War Suppression of Filipino Radicals," *Asia-Pacific Journal* 11, no. 33 (2014): https://apjjf.org/2014/11/33/Rick-Baldoz/4165/article.html.

79. The Philippine police discovered Bulosan's letters to Taruc following their arrest of Philippine Communist Party leader Jesus Lava. See Baldoz.

80. Special Agent in Charge to the Director, Seattle, office memorandum, FBI, July 31, 1950, 2 pp. (partially declassified and released under the Freedom of Information Act).

81. Quoted in Marilyn C. Alquizola and Lane Ryo Hirabayashi, "Carlos Bulosan's Final Defiant Acts: Achievements during the McCarthy Era," *Amerasia Journal* 38, no. 3 (2002): 39.

82. Well into the postwar era, Huks driven underground had advertised prices on their heads "for their killing, capture or surrender." See Department of National Defense, Philippines, "Ranking Huks and Awards for Their Killing, Capture or Surrender," July 31, 1959–March 16, 1970, in Lachica, *The Huks*, 269–82. Taruc surrendered in 1954.

83. Steinberg, 143, 12. MacArthur dubbed postwar Philippines a "citadel of democracy in the East." See "Citadel of Democracy to the East: Gen. MacArthur's Inspiring Message to Filipinos," *The Age*, March 1, 1945, 3. Jonathan Fast comments that U.S. war planners retrieved from "the Philippine counter-insurgency effort of the early 1950s ... a laboratory for later American involvement in Vietnam." See Jonathan Fast, "Imperialism and Bourgeois Dictatorship in the Philippines," *New Left Review* 78 (1973): 85.

Chapter 6. The Enemy at Home

1. Manning Marable, publisher's review of *Freedomways Reader: Prophets in Their Own Country*, ed. Esther C. Jackson (Boulder, CO: Westview, 2000), www.barnesandnoble.com/w/freedomways-reader-esther-cooper-jackson/1127660850. Running from 1961 to 1985, *Freedomways* was subtitled *A Quarterly Review of the Negro Freedom Movement*. For a discussion of vying terminology—"people's tribunal" vs. "international citizens' tribunal"—see Arthur Klinghoffer and Judith Klinghoffer, *International Citizens' Tribunals: Mobilizing Public Opinion to Advance Human Rights* (New York: Palgrave, 2002).

2. Jean-Paul Sartre, "Imperialist Morality," *New Left Review* 41 (1967): 5. Baldwin's essay was anthologized once in 1973 and included in a 2010 volume of his previously uncollected essays. See James Baldwin, "The War Crimes Tribunal," in *Vietnam and Black America: An Anthology of Protest and Resistance*, ed. Clyde Taylor (Garden City, NY: Anchor, 1973), 99–101; and James Baldwin, "The International War Crimes Tribunal,"

in *The Cross of Redemption: Uncollected Writings*, ed. Randall Kenan (New York: Vintage International, 2010), 245–49.

3. James Baldwin, "The War Crimes Tribunal," in *Freedomways* 7, no. 3 (1967): 243. Hereafter "War Crimes Tribunal." Organizers faced serial difficulties in getting countries to host. For an account of delays and difficulties see Kenneth Tynan, "Open Letter to an American Liberal," *Playboy*, March 1968, 137. Tynan poses the question, possibly a rejoinder to Baldwin's critique: "how about setting up a War Crimes Tribunal in the U.S., with a panel of American jurors sitting in judgment on their own political leaders?" (139).

4. See Russell's tribunal description: "We are not judges. We are witnesses. Our task is to make mankind bear witness to these terrible crimes and to unite humanity on the side of justice in Vietnam." See also Noam Chomsky, foreword to *Prevent the Crime of Silence: Reports from the Sessions of the International War Crimes Tribunal, Founded by Bertrand Russell*, ed. Ken Coates et al. (London: Penguin, 1971), 9–27. Baldwin's portrait of the tribunal as a European endeavor is complicated by its non-European membership, including Lazaro Cardenas, former president of Mexico; Stokely Carmichael, Student Non-violent Coordinating Committee chairperson; Amado Hernandez, then-Philippines poet laureate; Melba Hernandez, chairperson of the Cuban Committee for Solidarity with Vietnam; Mahmud Ali Kasuri, Senior Advocate of Pakistan's Supreme Court; Kinju Morikawa, Japan Civil Liberties Union vice-chairperson; and Shoichi Sakata, a Japanese physics professor.

5. Jean-Paul Sartre, "Inaugural Statement," in *Prevent the Crime of Silence: Reports from the Sessions of the International War Crimes Tribunal, Founded by Bertrand Russell*, ed. Ken Coates et al. (London: Penguin, 1971), 66 (emphasis in original).

6. Sartre, "Inaugural Statement," 65. See also Geoffrey Nice, "The Vietnam Informal Transcript," Oct. 2, 2013, lecture delivered at Gresham College, www.gresham.ac.uk/lectures-and-events/the-vietnam-informal-tribunal.

7. Mark Selden, "Okinawa and American Security Imperialism," in *Remaking Asia: Essays on the American Uses of Power*, ed. Mark Selden (New York: Pantheon, 1974), 279–302.

8. Radhabinod Pal, quoted in Ashis Nandy, "The Other Within: The Strange Case of Radhabinod Pal's Judgment on Culpability," *New Literary History* 23, no. 1 (1992): 51. On Pal's singular representation of international legal expertise on the panel of justices see Richard H. Minear, *Victors' Justice: The Tokyo War Crimes Trial* (Princeton, NJ: Princeton University Press, 1971), 86.

9. See Ustinia Dolgopol, "Women's Voices, Women's Pain," *Human Rights Quarterly* 17, no. 1 (1995): 147–48.

10. Randall Williams, *The Divided World: Human Rights and Its Violence* (Minneapolis: University of Minnesota Press, 2010), xiv.

11. See Tynan, "Open Letter," 135. For an account of the legal charges against the United States considered by the Tribunal, see Leon Matarasso, "Outline of the General Introductory Report," in *Prevent the Crime of Silence: Reports from the Sessions of the*

International War Crimes Tribunal, Founded by Bertrand Russell, ed. Ken Coates et al. (London: Penguin, 1971), 68–76.

12. The Vietnam War–era U.S. legal literature that weighed whether the innovative international legal principles established in response to the Holocaust applied to U.S. conduct in Vietnam is vast. See, for example, American Society of International Law, *The Vietnam War and International Law*, ed. Richard Falk, vols. 1 and 2 (Princeton, NJ: Princeton University Press, 1968, 1969); Anthony D'Amato, Harvey Gould, and Larry Woods, "War Crimes and Vietnam: The 'Nuremberg Defense' and the Military Service Resister," *California Law Review* 57, no. 5 (1969): 1055–1111; Erwin Knoll and Judith N. McFadden, eds., *War Crimes and the American Conscience* (New York: Holt, Rinehart and Winston, 1970); Telford Taylor, *Nuremberg and Vietnam: An American Tragedy* (Chicago: Quadrangle, 1970); and Hugo A. Bedau, "Genocide in Vietnam?" *Boston University Law Review* 53, no. 3 (1973): 574–622. For a consideration of this question from the Vietnamese side see Democratic Republic of Vietnam Commission for Investigation on the American Imperialists' War Crimes in Vietnam, *American Crimes in Vietnam* (Vietnam: n.p., 1966).

13. Lelio Basso, "Summing-up of the Second Session," in *Prevent the Crime of Silence: Reports from the Sessions of the International War Crimes Tribunal, Founded by Bertrand Russell*, ed. Ken Coates et al. (London: Penguin, 1971), 335, 326, 327.

14. See Danilo Zolo, *Victor's Justice: From Nuremberg to Baghdad*, trans. M. W. Weir (London: Verso, 2009), 31.

15. Jean-Paul Sartre, "Summary and Verdict of the Stockholm Session," in *Prevent the Crime of Silence: Reports from the Sessions of the International War Crimes Tribunal, Founded by Bertrand Russell*, ed. Ken Coates et al. (London: Penguin, 1971), 180.

16. Jean-Paul Sartre, *On Genocide: And a Summary of the Evidence and the Judgments of the International War Crimes Tribunal*, by Arlette El Kaïm-Sartre (Boston: Beacon, 1968), 64, 82.

17. Ho Chi Minh, "Tenth National Day of the Democratic Republic of Vietnam," in *Against U.S. Aggression for National Salvation* (Hanoi: Foreign Languages Publishing House, 1967), 34; Ho Chi Minh, "Appeal on the Anniversary of the Geneva Agreements," in *Against U.S. Aggression for National Salvation*, 82.

18. Ho Chi Minh, "President Ho Chi Minh's Reply to President Lyndon B. Johnson," in *Against U.S. Aggression for National Salvation* (Hanoi: Foreign Languages Publishing House, 1967), 150. For another translation see "President Ho Chi Minh's Reply to President Johnson's Letter," *Department of State Bulletin* 56, no. 1450 (April 10, 1967): 595–97.

19. Ho Chi Minh, "Message to Lord Bertrand Russell," in *Against U.S. Aggression for National Salvation* (Hanoi: Foreign Languages Publishing House, 1967), 135.

20. Because of the tribunal's evidence-based findings, "the Pentagon was forced to admit that it was . . . using anti-personnel weapons in its attack against North Vietnam (though it could not resist the final lie that the targets were radar stations and anti-aircraft batteries)" (Chomsky, foreword, 10). On the use of antipersonnel weapons in the north see Tariq Ali, "Report from Cambodia and Vietnam," in *Prevent the Crime of Silence:*

Reports from the Sessions of the International War Crimes Tribunal, Founded by Bertrand Russell, ed. Ken Coates et al. (London: Penguin, 1971), 135. In a summary account of the second Copenhagen session Basso states: "the use of ball-bombs was admitted by the Americans only after our Stockholm session had supplied a mass of evidence to prove the fact. Likewise, the use of poison gas was at first denied by them, but later admitted, though they claimed it to be only 'tear gas.' Let us recall that torture was attributed by them to the puppet government: that the concentration camps are called 'new life hamlets.'" See Basso, "Summing-up," 328.

21. Samir Amin, "Whither the United Nations?" trans. Stuart Anthony Stilitz, in *Empire's Law: The American Imperial Project and the "War to Remake the World,"* ed. Amy Bartholomew (Ann Arbor, MI: Pluto, 2006), 364.

22. See Tariq Ali, "Tariq Ali on Political Activism from Pakistan to Vietnam to Iraq," *Democracy Now!* April 14, 2005, www.democracynow.org/2005/4/14/tariq_ali_on_political_activism_from. See also Tariq Ali, *Street Fighting Years: An Autobiography of the Sixties* (London: Verso, 2005).

23. On the PPT as "'people's courts for the dispossessed,' for 'marginalized voices,' which can expose injustices not addressed by governments or the United Nations," see Klinghoffer and Klinghoffer, *International Citizens' Tribunals*, 164, 165.

24. Kenneth Roland A. Guda, "International People's Tribunal to Try Philippines President Aquino and Obama for Crimes against the Filipino People," *Global Research News*, March 17, 2015, www.globalresearch.ca/international-peoples-tribunal-to-try-philippines-president-aquino-and-obama-for-crimes-against-the-filipino-people.

25. According to David Leeming, Baldwin abandoned the Russell experiment because of "other commitments" that made "his presence impossible." See David Leeming, *James Baldwin: A Biography* (New York: Knopf, 1994), 277.

26. Lisa Lowe, *The Intimacies of Four Continents* (Durham, NC: Duke University Press, 2015), 162.

27. William L. Patterson, foreword to *We Charge Genocide: The Historic Petition to the United Nations for Relief from a Crime of the United States Government against the Negro People*, ed. William L. Patterson (New York: Civil Rights Congress, 1951), ix (emphasis added).

28. Malcolm X, "The Ballot or the Bullet," in *Malcolm X Speaks: Selected Speeches and Statements*, ed. George Breitman (New York: Grove Weidenfeld, 1965), 34.

29. See Malcolm X on the hypocritical self-designation of the United States as "Leader of the Free World": "Uncle Sam's hands are dripping with blood, dripping with the blood of the black man in this country. He's the earth's number-one hypocrite. He has the audacity—yes, he has—imagine him posing as the leader of the free world. The free world!—and you over here singing 'We Shall overcome.'" Malcolm X, "The Ballot," 35.

30. For an account of Du Bois's decolonizing interpretation of human rights see Peter Linebaugh, "The Secret History of the Magna Carta," *Boston Review*, June 1, 2003, http://bostonreview.net/books-ideas/peter-linebaugh-secret-history-magna-carta.

31. See Nikhil Pal Singh, *Black Is a Country: Race and the Unfinished Struggle*

for Democracy (Cambridge, MA: Harvard University Press, 2004), 53. In *The Black Panthers Speak* Philip Foner enumerates Cold War "appeal[s] by black Americans to the United Nations," starting with Du Bois et al.'s *An Appeal to the World*, presented by the NAACP to the UN in 1947. Foner also acknowledges exhortations by figures such as novelist John O. Killens, who declared at a June 15, 1964, forum sponsored by the Association of Artists for Freedom at Town Hall "that black Americans had to 'place our case before the United Nations . . . since it is a case of denial of human rights." He also cites Jesse Gray, head of the Harlem Rent strike, who on July 19, 1964, "told the press that he planned to lead a demonstration at United Nations Plaza 'to ask the UN to intervene in the 'police terror in the United States.'" The precise date of Newton and Seale's UN petition is unclear but presumably was drafted in the late 1960s. See Philip S. Foner, ed., *The Black Panthers Speak* (1970; Cambridge, MA: Da Capo, 2002), 281. See also W. E. B. Du Bois et al., *An Appeal to the World: A Statement on the Denial of Human Rights to Minorities in the Case of Citizens of Negro Descent in the United States of America and an Appeal to the United Nations for Redress* (New York: NAACP, 1947); Civil Rights Congress, *We Charge Genocide: The Historic Petition to the United Nations for Relief from a Crime of the United States Government against the Negro People* (New York: Civil Rights Congress, 1951); and Huey Newton and Bobby Seale, "Petition to the United Nations," in Foner, *The Black Panthers Speak*, 254–55. In "The Black Revolution" Malcolm X specifies the charge of "genocide" yet lists subsets of "genocide" as "political murder, economic murder, social murder, and mental murder," thus exceeding the legal definition of "acts committed with the intent to destroy, in whole or in part, a national, ethnical [sic], racial, or religious group, as such": "Take [Uncle Sam] to court and charge him with genocide, the mass murder of millions of black people in this country—political murder, economic murder, social murder, mental murder." *Malcolm X Speaks: Selected Speeches and Statements*, ed. George Breitman (New York: Grove Widenfeld, 1965), 55.

32. Civil Rights Congress, *We Charge Genocide*, 9.

33. Robin D. G. Kelley, *Freedom Dreams: The Black Radical Imagination* (Boston: Beacon, 2002), 114.

34. Frederick Douglass, *My Bondage and My Freedom* (1855; New York: Dover, 1969), 274, 406.

35. See William A. Schabas, *Genocide in International Law: The Crime of Crimes* (Cambridge: Cambridge University Press, 2000), 14. See also Samantha Power, especially her chapter "A Crime without a Name," in *"A Problem from Hell": America and the Age of Genocide* (New York: Basic Books, 2002), 17–29.

36. Janet Lyon, *Manifestoes: Provocations of the Modern* (Ithaca, NY: Cornell University Press, 1999), 14.

37. Susan Zaeske, *Signatures of Citizenship: Petitioning, Antislavery, and Women's Political Identity* (Chapel Hill: University of North Carolina Press, 2003), 12, 5.

38. Malcolm X, "The Black Revolution," in *Malcolm X Speaks: Selected Speeches and Statements*, ed. George Breitman (New York: Grove Weidenfeld, 1965), 56–57.

39. The Russell Tribunal also heard testimony from ordinary rice farmers, teachers, schoolchildren, and medical professionals from north and south of the seventeenth parallel.

40. Malcolm X appears to misconstrue what he calls the "world court"—most likely a reference to the International Court of Justice—as furnishing a permanent forum for the adjudication of grievous state trespasses of human rights. Although Malcolm X exhorts his Cleveland audience to "take Uncle Sam before a world court," proceedings cannot be initiated by individuals. See Malcolm X, "The Ballot," 35.

41. On the UN as "a court of appeal outside the ambit of the nation-state for racially subjected peoples," see Singh, *Black Is a Country*, 53.

42. Hannah Arendt's thesis concerning German colonies in Africa offers a critical prehistory for Nazi atrocities in Europe. See Hannah Arendt, *The Origins of Totalitarianism* (1951; New York: Harcourt Brace, 1975), esp. xix, xx, 185, 186. For a historical analysis of Arendt's hypothesis "that imperialism was one of the chief factors leading to totalitarianism and to its 'final solutions,'" see Isabel V. Hull, "Military Culture and the Production of 'Final Solutions' in the Colonies: The Example of Wilhelminian Germany," in *The Specter of Genocide: Mass Murder in Historical Perspective*, ed. Robert Gellately and Ben Kiernan (Cambridge: Cambridge University Press, 2003), 141–62.

43. Quoted in Carol Anderson, *Eyes Off the Prize: The United Nations and the African American Struggle for Human Rights, 1944–1955* (Cambridge: Cambridge University Press, 2003), 97.

44. Talal Asad, *Formations of the Secular: Christianity, Islam, Modernity* (Stanford, CA: Stanford University Press, 2003), 144.

45. Penny Von Eschen writes, "as their allies in Africa and Asia asserted their independence from the Cold War through a politics of non-alignment, anticolonial activists in the United states were unsuccessful in sustaining an opposition to Cold War orthodoxy." Penny Von Eschen, "Who's the Real Ambassador? Exploding Cold War Racial Ideology," *Cold War Constructions: The Political Culture of United States Imperialism, 1945–1966*, ed. Christian G. Appy (Amherst: University of Massachusetts Press, 2000), 114.

46. James L. Roark, "American Black Leaders: The Response to Colonialism and the Cold War, 1943–1953," *African Historical Studies* 4, no. 2 (1971): 270, 258.

47. Singh, *Black Is a Country*, 222. For a critique of the concept of internal colonialism, see Jodi Byrd, *The Transit of Empire: Indigenous Critiques of Colonialism* (Minneapolis: University of Minnesota Press, 2011), 133.

48. I deeply appreciate Kelley's insight: "too often our standards for evaluating social movements pivot around whether or not they 'succeeded' in realizing their visions rather than on the merits or power of the visions themselves. By such a measure, virtually every radical movement failed because the basic power relations they sought to change remain pretty much intact." Kelley, *Freedom Dreams*, ix.

49. Malcolm X (as told to Alex Haley), *The Autobiography of Malcolm X* (New York: Ballantine, 1964), 108.

50. Stetson Conn et al., *Guarding the United States and Its Outposts* (Washington, DC: Center of Military History, United States Army, 2000), 27.

51. See Robert A. Hill, comp. and ed., *The FBI's RACON: Racial Conditions in the United States during World War II* (Boston: Northeastern University Press, 1995).

52. See Frank Zeidler, as quoted in Peter Galison, "War against the Center," *Grey Room, Inc.* 4 (2001): 23. On the conceptual origins of homeland security in World War II's civil and air defense programs see Jerome H. Kahan, "What's in a Name? The Meaning of Homeland Security," *Journal of Homeland Security Education* 2 (2013): 3.

53. Stephen J. Collier and Andrew Lakoff, "Distributed Preparedness: The Spatial Logic of Domestic Security in the United States," *Environment and Planning D: Society and Space* 26 (2008): 10.

54. *Cointelpro 101*, Freedom Archives (Oakland, CA: Pm Press, 2011), https://vimeo.com/15930463. From December 15, 1956, to February 9, 1965, the FBI generated a 237-page, open-source intelligence file on Malcolm X.

55. On COINTELPRO's "use of the techniques of secret international warfare against domestic targets," see Richard E. Morgan, *Domestic Intelligence: Monitoring Dissent in America* (Austin: University of Texas Press, 1980), 45.

56. Malcolm Little (Malcolm X) FBI HQ file 23, pp. 148–239 (HQ 100-399321-A, sec. 2, March 22, 1964–Feb. 9, 1965), https://vault.fbi.gov/malcolm-little-malcolm-x/malcolm-little-malcolm-x-hq-file-23-of-27/view. Hereafter "FBI HQ file 23, part 2."

57. Malcolm Little (Malcolm X) FBI HQ file 23 of 27, pp. 1–147 (HQ 100-399321-A, sec. 1, Dec. 15, 1956–March 21, 1964), https://vault.fbi.gov/malcolm-little-malcolm-x/malcolm-little-malcolm-x-hq-file-23-of-27/view. Hereafter "FBI HQ file 23, part 1."

58. Martin Luther King Jr., "Declaration of Independence from the War in Vietnam," *Ramparts* 5, no. 11 (1967): 33.

59. Frank Morales, "U.S. Military Civil Disturbance Planning: The War at Home," in *Police State America: U.S. Military "Civil Disturbance" Planning*, ed. Tom Burghardt (Toronto: Arm the Spirit/Solidarity, 2002), 59.

60. Douglas Valentine, "Homeland Insecurity: Phoenix, CHAOS, the Enterprise, and the Politics of Terror in America," in *Police State America: U.S. Military "Civil Disturbance" Planning*, ed. Tom Burghardt (Toronto: Arm the Spirit/Solidarity, 2002), 147.

61. See Valentine, 154. I borrow the term *race-radical* from Jodi Melamed, *Represent and Destroy: Rationalizing Violence in the New Racial Capitalism* (Minneapolis: University of Minnesota Press, 2011), xii.

62. David Wise, *The American Police State: The Government against the People* (New York: Random House, 1976), 311.

63. James Baldwin FBI file, Part 1: 1–559; Part 2: 560–943; Part 3: 944–1844; Federal Bureau of Investigation, (declassified 1998), 846–47, https://archive.org/stream/JamesBaldwinFBIFile/James%20Baldwin%20017_djvu.txt.

64. Wise, *The American Police State*, 402, 400.

65. See Valentine, "Homeland Insecurity," 153.

66. On the illegality of Operation CHAOS see Wise, 408.

67. Jeremy Kuzmarov, *Modernizing Repression: Police Training and Nation-Building in the American Century* (Amherst: University of Massachusetts Press, 2012), 8.

68. Larry Trujillo, review of *Policing America* and *Police in America*, *Crime and Social Justice* 3 (Summer 1975): 72.

69. Tony Platt, "Prospects for a Radical Criminology in the United States," *Crime and Social Justice* 1, no. 1 (1974): 6.

70. Tony Platt et al., *The Iron Fist and the Velvet Glove: An Analysis of the U.S. Police* (Berkeley, CA: Center for Research on Criminal Justice, 1975), 12.

71. See Joshua Bloom and Waldo E. Martin Jr., *Black against Empire: The History and Politics of the Black Panther Party* (Berkeley: University of California Press, 2013), 300.

72. Ruth Wilson Gilmore, "Globalisation and US Prison Growth: from Military Keynesianism to Post-Keynesian Militarism," *Race and Class* 40, no. 2/3 (1998–99): 174.

73. Mark Neocleous, *War Power, Police Power* (Edinburgh: Edinburgh University Press, 2014), 9.

74. "Verdict of the International Tribunal on Political Prisoners and Prisoners of War in the United States," *Yale Journal of Law and Liberation* 4, no. 1 (1991): 47. Hereafter "Verdict of International Tribunal." On the Russell Tribunal as precedent see "Verdict of International Tribunal," 55. On the discursive shift to "terrorism" and "counter-terrorism," Valentine notes counterintelligence programs persisted after their exposure: "Everything was exactly the same as before, including the ultra-secure communications system and restricted filing system, except now it was acceptable because it was done under the aegis of counter-terrorism" (Valentine, "Homeland Insecurity," 158).

75. Tom Burghardt, "'Welcome to the Terrordome': America's Emerging Police State," in *Police State America: U.S. Military "Civil Disturbance" Planning*, ed. Tom Burghardt (Toronto: Arm the Spirit/Solidarity, 2002), 4.

76. On the police as an occupation force "there to contain us, to brutalize us and murder us because they have their orders," see Huey Newton in *Off the Pig* (Richmond, VT: Newsreel Films, 1968), 14 min.

77. See Paul J. Scheips, *The Role of Federal Military Forces in Domestic Disorders, 1945–1992* (Washington, DC: Center for Military History, United States Army, 2012), 172.

78. See Jennifer S. Light, "Urban Security from Warfare to Welfare," *International Journal of Urban and Regional Research* 26, no. 3 (2002): 609.

79. See Adam Yarmolinsky, *The Military Establishment: Its Impacts on American Society* (New York: Twentieth Century Fund, 1971), 163.

80. U.S. Department of the Army, *Civil Disturbance Plan*, or "Garden Plot," Sept. 10, 1968 (Washington, DC: Department of Army), declassified March 10, 1988 (governmentattic.org/2docs/DA-CivilDisturbPlanGardenPlot_1968.pdf), hereafter "Garden Plot"; Ahati N. N. Toure, "Appendix 1," *Jericho Manual*, www.thejerichomovement.com/sites/default/files/resource_file/jericho-manuel-appendix_i_0.pdf.

81. Roger A. Beaumont, "Constabulary or Fire Brigade? The Army National Guard," *Parameters: Journal of the US Army War College* 12, no. 1 (1995): 66.

82. National Advisory Commission on Civil Disorders (Kerner Commission), *Report of the National Advisory Commission on Civil Disorders: Summary Report* (New York: Bantam, 1968), 16, www.eisenhowerfoundation.org/docs/kerner.pdf.

83. See Morales, "U.S. Military," 63.

84. See Platt et al., *The Iron Fist*, 115.

85. See James W. Button, *Black Violence: Political Impact of the 1960s Riots* (Princeton, NJ: Princeton University Press, 1978), 133.

86. On the 519th Military Police Company, more than 25 percent of which was black, see Othello Mahome, "Riot Control Teams: Brothers vs. Brothers," *Liberator* 7, no. 10 (Oct. 1967): 14–15.

87. "Annex B (Intelligence) to Department of the Army Civil Disturbance Plan (U)," in "Garden Plot," 31–39.

88. Harold Black and Marvin J. Labes, "Guerrilla Warfare: An Analogy to Police-Criminal Interaction," *American Journal of Orthopsychiatry* 37, no. 4 (1967): 666–70.

89. Although Baldwin was not the motive force behind the 1969 Dellums Committee, its post–My Lai creation adheres to his earlier suggestions to Russell: "Following the public revelation of the My Lai massacre, members of the Bertrand Russell International War Crimes tribunal proposed that public forums be established within the U.S. (previous tribunals were held in Europe) at which Vietnam veterans could present hundreds of personal accounts of U.S. policy directly to the American people. These forums were to establish that the My Lai massacre was but the logical consequence of strategies and objectives developed by the U.S. command for use in Indochina." The first Citizens' Commissions of Inquiry were held in March of 1970 in Annapolis, Maryland, and repeated in Toronto; Springfield, Massachusetts; New York City; Los Angeles; Boston; Baltimore; Buffalo; Minneapolis; Portland, Oregon; Philadelphia; and finally Washington, DC, in December. See the Citizens Commission of Inquiry, introduction to *The Dellums Committee Hearings on War Crimes in Vietnam: An Inquiry into Command Responsibility in Southeast Asia*, ed. Citizens Commission of Inquiry (New York: Vintage, 1972), viii. These antiwar hearings prompted two further national investigations on U.S. atrocities in Vietnam: the Citizens Commission of Inquiry's National Veterans Inquiry and the Vietnam Veterans against the War's better-known Winter Soldier Investigation.

90. In *The Vietnam War and International Law*, editor Richard Falk, Consultative Council of the Lawyers' Committee on American Policy toward Vietnam chairman, dismissed the Russell hearings as "a juridical farce." Even tribunal member Carl Oglesby regarded the proceedings as anti-American propaganda, liable to be perceived as "a stretched-out and fancified party rally." See Klinghoffer and Klinghoffer, *International Citizens' Tribunals*, 134.

91. James Baldwin, introduction to *The Price of the Ticket: Collected Nonfiction, 1948–1985* (New York: St. Martin's, 1985), xv.

92. Mary Dudziak, *Cold War Civil Rights: Race and the Image of American Democracy* (Princeton, NJ: Princeton University Press, 2000), 242.

93. See Leeming, *James Baldwin*, 277. See also James Campbell, *Talking at the Gates:*

A Life of James Baldwin (Berkeley: University of California Press, 1991), 208. On James Forman's framing of the "desperate plight of the people of African descent . . . [in] the United States" as an issue requiring "full . . . debate . . . in the United Nations as a Human Rights problem," see James Forman, "James Forman of SNCC Addresses the United Nations," *Liberator* 7, no. 12 (Dec. 1967): 8.

94. James Baldwin, "James Baldwin Breaks His Silence," interview by Cep Dergisi, in *Conversations with James Baldwin*, ed. Fred L. Standley and Louis H. Pratt (Jackson: University Press of Mississippi, 1989), 62. See novelist Sam Greenlee's rendering of the same point: "'American white folks got more nerve than anybody; they call them gooks and us niggers, out there in Vietnam and in Korea when I was there. And they don't see any reason why the gooks and niggers shouldn't kill one another for whitey's benefit.'" Sam Greenlee, *The Spook Who Sat by the Door* (1969; Detroit: Wayne State University Press, 1990), 102.

95. Bertrand Russell, *War Crimes in Vietnam* (New York: Monthly Review, 1967), 123.

96. See Klinghoffer and Klinghoffer, *International Citizens' Tribunals*, 109.

97. On the tribunal members stripping Carmichael of the right to vote, see Klinghoffer and Klinghoffer, *International Citizens' Tribunals*, 155.

98. James Baldwin, "Preface to the 1984 Edition," *Notes of a Native Son* (1955; Boston: Beacon, 1984), xv.

99. On the "intellectually empty enterprise" of insisting "on the uniqueness of the Holocaust," including condemning "matter-of-fact references by blacks to their 'ghetto,'" see Peter Novick, *The Holocaust in American Life* (Boston: Mariner, 1999), 9.

100. James Baldwin, "A Television Conversation: James Baldwin, Peregrine Worsthorne, Bryan Magee (Encounter/1972)," in Standley and Pratt, *Conversations with James Baldwin*, 122.

101. Russell, *War Crimes in Vietnam*, 125, 121.

102. James Baldwin, "Conversation: Ida Lewis and James Baldwin," in Standley and Pratt, *Conversations with James Baldwin*, 87–88.

103. James Baldwin, *No Name in the Street* (New York: Delta, 1973), 85.

104. James Baldwin, "Everybody's Protest Novel," in *Notes of a Native Son* (1955; Boston: Beacon, 1984), 15.

105. James Baldwin, "A Report from Occupied Territory," 1966, in *The Price of the Ticket: Collected Nonfiction, 1948–1985* (New York: St. Martin's, 1985), 421.

106. James Baldwin, interview by David Frost, "Are We on the Edge of Civil War?" in Standley and Pratt, *Conversations with James Baldwin*, 94.

107. Bertrand Russell, "Broadcast on National Liberation Front Radio to American Soldiers, May 24, 1966," in *War Crimes in Vietnam*, 108.

108. James Baldwin, "Many Thousands Gone," in *The Price of the Ticket: Collected Nonfiction, 1948–1985* (New York: St. Martin's, 1985), 66.

109. Maurice Merleau-Ponty, *Humanism and Terror: An Essay on the Communist Problem*, trans. John O'Neill (Boston: Beacon, 1969), 34.

110. James Baldwin, interview by Joe Walker, "Exclusive Interview with James Baldwin," in Standley and Pratt, *Conversations with James Baldwin*, 130.

111. James Baldwin, "*The Black Scholar* Interviews James Baldwin," in Standley and Pratt, *Conversations with James Baldwin*, 155.

112. Slavoj Žižek, "Against Human Rights," *New Left Review* 34 (2005): 128.

Chapter 7. Militarized Queerness

1. "Update 12/21/11: Preliminary Media Roundup of Bradley Manning's Pretrial Hearing," *Free Chelsea Manning*, Dec. 21, 2011, www.chelseamanning.org/press/update-122111-brief-pretrial-hearing-media-roundup-more-to-come (site no longer available).

2. Meredith Bennett-Smith, "Lt. Dan Choi, Gay Military Activist on Trial for Protesting DADT Policy, Facing 6 Months in Jail," *Huffington Post*, March 28, 2013, www.huffingtonpost.com/2013/03/28/dan-choi-trial_n_2963990.html.

3. On the perils of military whistleblowing see Chris Hedges, *War Is a Force That Gives Us Meaning* (New York: Anchor, 2003), 14.

4. Steven Estes, *Ask and Tell: Gay and Lesbian Veterans Speak Out* (Chapel Hill: University of North Carolina Press, 2007), 30, 31; Eric Dolan, "Activist Dan Choi: U.S. Is on Trial, Not Bradley Manning," *Raw Story*, Dec. 18, 2011, www.rawstory.com/2011/12/activist-dan-choi-u-s-is-on-trial-not-bradley-manning.

5. Eddie Becker, "Eloquent Support for Bradley Manning," YouTube video, Dec. 18, 2011, www.youtube.com/watch?v=W53OzqrIA-Y.

6. "Iraq Combat Veteran Dan Choi Forcibly Ousted, Barred from Bradley Manning Hearing at Ft. Meade," *Democracy Now!* Dec. 21, 2011, www.democracynow.org/2011/12/21/iraq_combat_veteran_dan_choi_forcibly.

7. During his December 21, 2011, *Democracy Now!* interview, Choi expressed "disappoint[ment] that a lot of the gay groups have not spoken up for Bradley Manning." See also Larry Goldsmith on mainstream LGBT organizations' silence:

> NGLTF, Lambda Legal, and HRC would like to pretend that Bradley Manning's case is not a "gay issue," or worse, remain silent because they know that it is indeed a gay issue, one that threatened to undermine their carefully-crafted plea for admittance to the military. Addressing it as a gay issue would mean looking critically not only at the specific discriminatory policy of the military, but also at the very purpose of the military. It would mean taking a good close look at the patriotic rhetoric of "equal rights" to serve in an "all-volunteer" military, whose purpose is to defend "freedom" and "democracy," where LGBT people can be just as "virile" in carrying out organized killing as their heterosexual counterparts. (Larry Goldsmith, "Rich Man's War, Poor [Gay] Man's Fight," in *Why Are Faggots So Afraid of Faggots? Flaming Challenges to Masculinity, Objectification, and the Desire to Conform*, ed. Mattilda Bernstein Sycamore [Oakland, CA: AK Press, 2012], 183–84)

8. "Merged Manning-Lamo Chat Logs," *Shadowproof*, https://shadowproof.com/merged-manning-lamo-chat-logs.

9. See, e.g., "Collateral Murder," WikiLeaks, April 5, 2010, https://collateralmurder.wikileaks.org.

10. On the "imperialist axiomatics at work behind the advocacy for sexual rights as human rights," see Randall Williams, *The Divided World: Human Rights and Its Violence* (Minneapolis: University of Minnesota Press, 2010), 25.

11. On Manning as a queer contrast to "that butch patriotic homosexual—so central to the gays-in-the-military campaign—who Defends Democracy and Fights Terrorism with a virility indistinguishable from that of his straight buddies," see Goldsmith, "Rich Man's War," 182.

12. See "Does Opposing 'Don't Ask, Don't Tell' Bolster US Militarism? A Debate with Lt. Dan Choi and Queer Activist Mattilda Bernstein Sycamore," *Democracy Now!* Oct. 22, 2010, www.democracynow.org/2010/10/22/does_opposing_dont_ask_dont_tell. See also Lisa Duggan's critique of "the 'gay equality' branch of multi-issue neoliberalism" or "gay tunnel vision," in which "equality" is recoded as "narrow, formal access to a few conservatizing institutions." Lisa Duggan, *The Twilight of Equality? Neoliberalism, Cultural Politics, and the Attack on Democracy* (Boston: Beacon, 2003), 47, 65–66.

13. In the unregulated landscape of the early South Korean adoption industry few safeguards ensured that "orphans" indeed were orphans.

14. Hosu Kim and Grace Cho, "The Kinship of Violence," *Journal of Korean Adoption Studies* 1, no. 3 (2012): 12; see also Ha Jin, *War Trash* (New York: Pantheon, 2004).

15. Leti Volpp, "The Citizen and the Terrorist," *September 11 in History: A Watershed Moment?* ed. Mary L. Dudziak (Durham, NC: Duke University Press, 2003), 151.

16. Kenji Yoshino, *Covering: The Hidden Assault on Our Civil Rights* (New York: Random House, 2007), 27.

17. Quoted in Lee Nichols, *Breakthrough on the Color Front* (New York: Random House, 1954), 171.

18. Chandan Reddy clarifies: "it is not that homosexual military personnel have been made into a race, or made analogous to blacks and Latinos, or to Asian and Middle Eastern enemies. Rather, homosexuality within the military gains its meaning and identity only through an active racial matrix that is . . . central to the production of actual force and its continued disregard for civilian casualties and collateral damage." See Chandan Reddy, *Freedom with Violence: Race, Sexuality, and the US State* (Durham, NC: Duke University Press, 2011), 238, 240.

19. George W. Bush, "Address to a Joint Session of Congress and the American People," Office of the Press Secretary, Sept. 20, 2001, https://georgewbush-whitehouse.archives.gov/news/releases/2001/09/20010920-8.html. We might recall Pat Parker's pithy critique: "The equation is being laid out in front of us. Good American = Support imperialism and war." See Pat Parker, "Revolution: It's Not Neat or Pretty or Quick," in *This Bridge Called My Back: Writings by Radical Women of Color*, ed. Cherrie Moraga and Gloria Anzaldúa (New York: Kitchen Table, 1983), 239.

20. On the "potential for jingoistic blindness" in the post-9/11 "rightward drift" of LGBT politics, with "emphasis on the Americanization of model gay 'heroes' and 'victims'

as a rhetorical boost for demands for inclusion in marriage and the military," see Duggan, *The Twilight of Equality?* 46. Consider, too, Jin Haritaworn's argument on "women's equality" and "gay rights" as emerging bywords of the West's "superior 'modernity' and 'civilisation'": "we find it vital to note that its main basis is not a progress in gender and sexual politics but a regression in racial politics." Jin Haritaworn et al., "Gay Imperialism: Gender and Sexuality Discourse in the 'War on Terror,'" in *Out of Place: Interrogating Silences in Queerness/Raciality*, ed. Adi Kuntsman and Esperanza Miyake (York: Raw Nerve, 2008), 79.

21. Jasbir K. Puar, *Terrorist Assemblages: Homonationalism in Queer Times* (Durham, NC: Duke University Press, 2007), 36.

22. Writing before DADT's repeal, Pamela Lundquist describes Truman's executive order desegregating the U.S. military as precedent for the policy's abolition. See Pamela Lundquist, "Essential to the National Security: An Executive Ban on 'Don't Ask, Don't Tell,'" *Journal of Gender, Social Policy, and the Law* 16, no. 1 (2007): 140, 146. On acute manpower shortages in the Korean theater spurring combat unit desegregation, see Michael Desch, "Does 'Don't Ask, Don't Tell' Preserve Unit Cohesion?" in *Don't Ask, Don't Tell: Debating the Gay Ban in the Military*, ed. Aaron Belkin and Geoffrey Bateman (Boulder, CO: Lynne Rienner, 2003), 89.

23. Barack Obama, "Remarks by the President at 60th Anniversary of the Korean War Armistice," July 27, 2013, Office of the Press Secretary, www.whitehouse.gov/the-press-office/2013/07/27/remarks-president-60th-anniversary-korean-war-armistice.

24. Assistant Secretary of Defense Anna Rosenberg, quoted in Nichols, *Breakthrough*, 179, 53.

25. Nichols, 3. In 1956 James C. Evans, assistant on racial matters to the secretary of the army, stated: "The greatest victory we had in Korea was the integrated use of our manpower. Officers who opposed it before Korea now say they would never go back to segregated units." See "Hit Clark's Jim Crow Stand," *Indianapolis Recorder*, May 12, 1956, 14.

26. Toni Morrison, *Home* (New York: Alfred A. Knopf, 2012), 18.

27. Paul Robeson, *Paul Robeson Speaks: Writings, Speeches, Interviews, 1918–1974*, ed. Philip S. Foner (New York: Citadel, 1978), 253. See also Che Guevara's analysis of South Koreans as "cannon fodder": Che Guevara, "Vietnam Must Not Stand Alone," *New Left Review* 1, no. 43 (1967): 80.

28. Ahn Jung-hyo, "A Double Exposure of the War," in *America's Wars in Asia: A Cultural Approach to History and Memory*, ed. Philip West et al. (Armonk, NY: East Gate, 1998), 168. According to Iraq War veteran Owen West, "the Korean War forced trials by fire—in fact, the units with the highest casualty rates in Korea integrated the fastest—and the Pentagon ultimately acknowledged that recruiting from across America's socio-economic spectrum produced the best force." Owen West, "An About-Face on Gay Troops," *New York Times*, Feb. 9, 2009, www.nytimes.com/2009/02/09/opinion/09west.html.

29. On military labor "as the agent of the state's necropolitical power and as its very potential victim," see Jin-kyung Lee, *Service Economies: Militarism, Sex Work, and Migrant Labor in South Korea* (Minneapolis: University of Minnesota Press, 2010), 38.

30. Tessa Morris-Suzuki, "Lavish Are the Dead: Re-envisioning Japan's Korean War," *Asia-Pacific Journal* 11, no. 52 (2013): www.japanfocus.org/-Tessa-Morris_Suzuki/4054/article.html.

31. Spaceribs, "Korean War Propaganda Targeting Black Soldiers," Feb. 4, 2015, http://imgur.com/gallery/nMpLZ.

32. Robert Williams, *Listen, Brother!* (New York: World View, 1968), 11.

33. Frederick Douglass, "Should the Negro Enlist in the Union Army? [July 6, 1863]," in *Frederick Douglass: Great Abolitionist Leader*, www.marxists.org/history/etol/newspape/fi/vol07/n009/freddoug.htm#s2. See also W. E. B. Du Bois on the black Union soldier: "when he rose and fought and killed, the whole nation with one voice proclaimed him a man and brother. Nothing else made emancipation possible in the United States. Nothing else made Negro citizenship conceivable." W. E. B. Du Bois, *Black Reconstruction, 1860–1880* (New York: Free Press, 1998), 345.

34. See South Korean Vietnam War veteran Ahn Jung-hyo's account: "I saw how the military profession and uniforms could turn ordinary human beings into extraordinary killing beasts. . . . Koreans in Vietnam were famous, and infamous, for bravery and brutality—one and the same quality in the end" (Ahn, 169).

35. Ryan Hediger, "Dogs of War: The Biopolitics of Loving and Leaving the U.S. Canine Forces in Vietnam," *Animal Studies Journal* 2, no. 1 (2013): 59.

36. John C. Burnam, quoted in Hediger, 60.

37. Hediger speculates the "fate of many of the nearly 4,000 American war dogs abandoned in Vietnam was to be eaten" (64).

38. Ewa Płonowska Ziarek, "Bare Life on Strike: Notes on the Biopolitics of Race and Gender," *South Atlantic Quarterly* 107, no. 1 (2008): 91. On the post-9/11 use of dogs as bomb detectors in Iraq, Michael Paterniti points out the U.S. "military bureaucracy regards the working dog as . . . an instrument . . . to master, just as . . . a drone operator had to learn to control a Predator." See Michael Paterniti, "The Dogs of War," *National Geographic*, June 2014, http://ngm.nationalgeographic.com/2014/06/war-dogs/paterniti-text.

39. Erika Cudworth and Steve Hobden, "The Posthuman Way of War," *Security Dialogue* 46, no. 6 (2015): 517.

40. Neel Ahuja, "Abu Zubaydah and the Caterpillar," *Social Text* 29, no. 1 (2001): 145.

41. Walter Simmons, "Kind-Hearted GIs Fall Prey to Korean Urchins," *Los Angeles Times*, August 26, 1951, 30.

42. See, e.g., Eleana Kim, *Adopted Territory: Transnational Adoption and the Politics of Belonging* (Durham, NC: Duke University Press, 2010); Soojin Pate, *From Orphan to Adoptee: U.S. Empire and Genealogies of Korean Adoption* (Minneapolis: University of Minnesota Press, 2014); and Arissa Oh, *To Save the Children of Korea: The Cold War Origins of International Adoption* (Stanford, CA: Stanford University Press, 2015).

43. Andrew Geer, "Red Carpet for Sergeant Reckless," *Saturday Evening Post*, Oct. 22, 1955, 23.

44. Robin Hutton, *Sgt. Reckless: America's War Horse* (Washington, DC: Regnery, 2014), xviii.

45. Hutton, 46. Platoon members vouched that "Reckless has forgotten she's a horse." See Andrew Geer, "Reckless, the Pride of the Marines," *Saturday Evening Post*, April 17, 1954, 185.

46. Consider also the nickname of the unit mascot in Samuel Fuller's *The Steel Helmet* (Lippert Studios, 1951): "Short Round."

47. On the Korean orphan's centrality to American human-interest stories on the war see Pate, *From Orphan to Adoptee*, 78. A 1950 *Stars and Stripes* article, "Korean Orphan Adopted by GIs," for example, highlighted the good fortune of "Skipper," who "was picked up by Cpl. Roosevelt Lewis, Memphis, Tennessee," who "found the boy without clothing and in an acute state of malnutrition." Thanks to his "GI foster fathers," Skipper was in possession of "a bankroll of 225,000 whan [*won*]." See "Korean Orphan Adopted by GIs," *Pacific Stars and Stripes*, Dec. 9, 1950, www.koreanchildren.org/docs/PSS-063-Q.htm.

48. Bernd Hüppauf, "Experiences of Modern Warfare and the Crisis of Representation," *New German Critique* 59 (1993): 46.

49. On the Korean War–era development of area bombing see Sven Lindqvist, *A History of Bombing*, trans. Linda Haverty Rugg (New York: New Press, 2001), 84, 157. On the "manifest contempt for Korean life on the part of the US troops" operating "under a canopy of airborne destruction which created a context of brutalization," see Jon Halliday, "Anti-Communism and the Korean War (1950–1953)," *Socialist Register* 21 (1984): 145.

50. Michael Rougier, "The Little Boy Who Wouldn't Smile," *Life*, July 23, 1951, 92.

51. Christina Klein, *Cold War Orientalism: Asia in the Middlebrow Imagination, 1945–1961* (Berkeley: University of California Press, 2003), 159.

52. C. Richard King, "What Do We Talk about When We Talk about American Indian Imagery in Sports: Thoughts on Mascots and Racialized Masculinity," *Feminist Wire*, March 12, 2013, www.thefeministwire.com/2013/03/what-do-we-talk-about-when-we-talk-about-american-indian-imagery-in-sports-thoughts-on-mascots-and-racialized-masculinity.

53. Philip J. Deloria, "Mascots and Other Public Appropriations of Indians and Indian Culture by Whites," in *Encyclopedia of North American Indians*, ed. Frederick E. Hoxie (Boston: Houghton Mifflin Harcourt, 1996), www.waunakee.k12.wi.us/hs/departments/lmtc/Assignments/McConnellScenarios/mascots4_overview.pdf. Deborah Root also points to the settler colonial implications of redface performance: "In a society where land theft is legitimated by law, and where communities and individuals are repressed to facilitate the colonization of territory, the taking up and popularizing of the culture under siege are not neutral acts." Deborah Root, *Cannibal Culture: Art, Appropriation, and the Commodification of Difference* (Boulder, CO: Westview, 1996), 105.

54. Patrick Wolfe, "Settler Colonialism and the Elimination of the Native," *Journal of Genocide Research* 8, no. 4 (2006): 389.

55. Winona LaDuke, with Sean Aaron Cruz, *The Militarization of Indian Country* (East Lansing: Michigan State University Press, 2013), 9.

56. John Tirman, *The Deaths of Others: The Fate of Civilians in America's Wars* (Oxford: Oxford University Press, 2011), 151.

57. Sharon Patricia Holland, *The Erotic Life of Racism* (Durham, NC: Duke University Press, 2012), 18, 10 (emphasis in original).

58. U.S. Army, *The History of the Counter Intelligence Corps in the United States Army, 1917–1953*, vol. 1 (Fort Holabird: U.S. Army Intelligence Center, 1959), National Archives at College Park, MD, 117.

59. This may partly explain why the Korean War was the last U.S. conflict in which children were allowed to serve as mascots. On Chocoletto's "career as an intelligence man" see Peter Linden, "Chocoletto: A Korean War Orphan Joins the Marines," *Reporter*, April 14, 1958, 28.

60. "7,500 Child Soldiers from Korean War Still Alive," *Chosun Ilbo*, June 21, 2012, http://english.chosun.com/site/data/html_dir/2012/06/21/2012062101193.html. On the efforts of Park Tae-seung, who was recruited in the eighth grade, to have the South Korean government "recognize the contributions of child soldiers," see "Veteran Advocates for Lost Child Soldiers," *Korea Joongang Daily*, June 14, 2014, http://koreajoongangdaily.joins.com/news/article/Article.aspx?aid=2990583. Park clarifies: "Some might say that they answered the country's call, but actually they were forced to. Most of them were from poor families. I've never seen a wealthy child from a powerful family in the army."

61. See Tessa Morris-Suzuki, "Post-War Warriors: Japanese Combatants in the Korean War," *Asia-Pacific Journal* 10, no. 31 (2012): http://apjjf.org/2012/10/31/Tessa-Morris-Suzuki/3803/article.html.

62. Lindqvist, *A History of Bombing*, 141.

63. "2 Tots Become Youngest POWs," *Pacific Stars and Stripes*, August 8, 1950, www.koreanwarorphans.org/the-war-years/9-uncategorised/98.html.

64. David Scott Diffrient, "'Military Enlightenment' for the Masses: Genre and Cultural Intermixing in South Korea's Golden Age War Films," *Cinema Journal* 45, no. 1 (2005): 38. On the naming of Korean War mascots, consider, for example, this story lead: "They found him in Inchon among the rubble of what had been his home. His mother was lying dead and he was crying." "A Navy corpsman," the story continues, "pulled the boy away from the corpse and daubed his cuts with Mercurochrome. After a while the corpsman produced a half-melted candy bar. 'Chocoletto?' he asked. The boy at first refused the candy, but then he took it and ate it hungrily. It was not that he forgot his mother but rather that he had not eaten for two days. So for no greater reason than that, he was called 'Chocoletto.'" See Peter Linden, "Chocoletto: A Korean War Orphan Joins the Marines," *The Reporter*, April 14, 1953.

65. Eleana Kim, "The Origins of Korean Adoption: Cold War Geopolitics and Intimate Diplomacy," *U.S.-Korea Institute at SAIS Working Paper Series* (2009): 7.

66. Morris-Suzuki, "Post-War Warriors."

67. Tony Perucci, *Paul Robeson and the Cold War Performance Complex: Race, Madness, Activism* (Ann Arbor: University of Michigan Press, 2012), 2.

68. Link S. White, *Chesi's Story: One Boy's Long Journey from War to Peace* (Tallahassee, FL: Father and Son, 1995), 81.

69. Mimi Thi Nguyen, "The Hoodie as Sign, Screen, Expectation, and Force," *Signs: Journal of Women in Culture and Society* 40, no. 4 (2015): 792.

70. In a critique of LGBT assimilation, Kenji Yoshino argues that conversion and passing "do not exhaust the forms of assimilation. There is also covering." Although focused on gay conformity to "'straight-acting' norms," this analysis might be applied to the securitization of Korean War mascots: "Outsiders are included, but only if we behave like insiders—that is, only if we cover." See Kenji Yoshino, *Covering: The Hidden Assault on Our Civil Rights* (New York: Random House, 2007), 21, 81, 22.

71. Lee, *Service Economies*, 6. On "militarized multiculturalism" see Melani McAlister, *Epic Encounters: Culture, Media, and U.S. Interests in the Middle East since 1945* (Berkeley: University of California Press, 2001), 259.

72. Bill Hume and John Annarino, *Babysan: A Private Look at the Japanese Occupation* (Tokyo: Kasuga Boeki K. K., 1953), 76.

73. Elizabeth Ramsay, "Feeling across the Color Line: The Gentle Warrior and the Transformative Orphan in Early Cold War U.S. Narratives," *Red Feather Journal* 4, no. 3 (2014): 23.

74. For a fictional account of a girl mascot's rape and murder see Nina Revoyr, *Southland* (New York: Akashic, 2003), 145–46.

75. "Redlegs Adopt Korean Pin-up," *Pacific Stars and Stripes*, Feb. 26, 1951, www.koreanchildren.org/docs/PSS-053-Q.htm.

76. On Bill Hume's Korean War–era cartoons of Babysan, an emblematic Japanese prostitute "created as a local pin-up to help boost the morale of the servicemen in Japan," the major R-and-R site relative to the Korean theater, see Hume and Annarino, *Babysan*, 6.

77. Katharine H. S. Moon, *Sex among Allies: Military Prostitution in U.S.-Korea Relations* (New York: Columbia University Press, 1997), 3. On the term *blanket squad* see Ji-Yeon Yuh, *Beyond the Shadow of Camptown: Korean Military Brides in America* (New York: New York University Press, 2002), 20.

78. The task of creating a "home away from home" inheres in the concept of "hardship duty," which refers to the assignment of U.S. military servicemembers to "locations where living conditions are substantially below those conditions in the continental U.S." "Hardship Duty Pay," Military.com, www.military.com/benefits/military-pay/special-pay/hardship-duty-pay.html.

79. Robert Chester, "'Negroes' Number One Hero': Doris Miller, Pearl Harbor, and Retroactive Multiculturalism in World War II Remembrance," *American Quarterly* 65, no. 1 (2013): 35.

80. Kang Sok-kyong, "Days and Dreams," in *Words of Farewell: Stories by Korean Women Writers*, trans. Bruce and Ju-Chan Fulton (Seattle, WA: Seal, 1989), 22.

81. Heinz Insu Fenkl, *Memories of My Ghost Brother* (New York: Dutton, 1996), 133.

Epilogue

1. "Full Video: Second Presidential Debate," *New York Times*, Oct. 10, 2016, www.nytimes.com/video/us/politics/100000004696519/watch-live-second-presidential-debate

.html. On this point Clinton and Donald Trump essentially agreed. Trump argued during the same debate, "We have to be sure that Muslims come in and report when they see something going on. When they see hatred going on, they have to report it."

2. On Muslim Americans as "conditional citizens" see Laila Lalami, "The Only Way for Muslim Americans to Be Considered Patriotic: Stay Silent," *The Nation*, Sept. 14, 2016, www.thenation.com/article/the-only-way-for-muslim-americans-to-be-considered-patriotic-stay-silent.

3. "Hillary Celebrates American Hero Humayun Khan | Hillary Clinton," Dec. 18, 2015, YouTube video, www.youtube.com/watch?v=dGV29YP_III.

4. See "Gold Star Survivors," U.S. Army website, www.army.mil/goldstar.

5. "Khizr Kahn FULL REMARKS at Democratic National Convention (C-SPAN)," July 28, 2016, YouTube video, www.youtube.com/watch?v=ahr4klZGrOQ; "President George W. Bush's Remarks at Ground Zero September 14, 2001," YouTube video, www.youtube.com/watch?v=9Iw6aDR2a6w.

6. Carson Frame, "As Fewer Americans Serve in the Military, Veterans and Non-veterans Socialize Less," *American Homefront Project*, Jan. 2, 2018, https://americanhomefront.wunc.org/post/fewer-americans-serve-military-veterans-and-non-veterans-socialize-less.

7. See Meghann Myers, "Top Recruiter: Just 136,000 out of 33 Million Young Americans Would Join the Army," *Army Times*, Oct. 12, 2017, www.armytimes.com/news/your-army/2017/10/12/top-recruiter-just-136000-out-of-33-million-young-americans-would-join-the-army. The prime recruiting demographic falls between seventeen and twenty-four years of age.

8. From 1980 to 2015, for example, the number of Latino and Chicano active-duty personnel increased threefold. See Kim Parker et al., "6 Facts about the U.S. Military and Its Changing Demographics," Pew Research Center, April 13, 2017, www.pewresearch.org/fact-tank/2017/04/13/6-facts-about-the-u-s-military-and-its-changing-demographics.

9. Anita U. Hattiangadi et al., *Non-citizens in Today's Military: Final Report* (Alexandria, VA: CNA, 2005), 5.

10. "Military Accessions Vital to National Interest (MAVNI) Recruitment Pilot Program," Department of Defense, https://dod.defense.gov/news/mavni-fact-sheet.pdf.

11. Dianna Cahn, "Deadline Puts Pressure on 'Dreamers' Who Seek to Serve in US Military," *Stars and Stripes*, March 4, 2018, www.stripes.com/news/deadline-puts-pressure-on-dreamers-who-seek-to-serve-in-us-military-1.514985.

12. Tom Vanden Brook, "Army Is Accepting More Low-Quality Recruits, Giving Waivers for Marijuana to Hit Targets," *USA Today*, Oct. 10, 2017, www.usatoday.com/story/news/politics/2017/10/10/army-accepting-more-low-quality-recruits-giving-waivers-marijuana-hit-targets/750844001.

13. Lisa Marie Cacho, *Social Death: Racialized Rightlessness and the Criminalization of the Unprotected* (New York: New York University Press, 2012), 19.

14. From October 1, 2019, to September 30, 2020, U.S. military spending is estimated to reach $989 billion. See Kimberly Amadeo, "U.S. Military Budget, Its Components, Challenges, and Growth," *The Balance*, April 22, 2019, www.thebalance

.com/u-s-military-budget-components-challenges-growth-3306320. On full-spectrum dominance see *Joint Vision 2020: America's Military—Preparing for Tomorrow* (Washington, DC: Institute for National Strategic Studies, 2000), 61.

15. George M. Reynolds and Amanda Shendruk, "Demographics of the U.S. Military," Council on Foreign Relations, April 24, 2018, www.cfr.org/article/demographics-us-military.

16. Melani McAlister, *Epic Encounters: Culture, Media, and U.S. Interests in the Middle East* (Berkeley: University of California Press, 2001), 258.

17. Eric Williams, "The Impact of the International Crisis upon the Negro in the Caribbean," *Journal of Negro Education* 10, no. 3 (1941): 543.

18. See Khan's exceptionalist portrait of the United States, in his DNC speech, as a nation where his three sons "were free to be themselves and follow their dreams." The phrase "peace that is no peace" is George Orwell's. See George Orwell, "You and the Atomic Bomb," *Tribune* (London), Oct. 19, 1945, www.george-orwell.org/You_and_the_Atomic_Bomb/0.html.

19. See "Posthumous Citizenship," *Policy Manual*, vol. 2, *Citizenship and Naturalization* (INA 329A), U.S. Citizenship and Immigration Services, www.uscis.gov/policy-manual/volume-12-part-i-chapter-8.

20. Rob Cuthbert, "Trump's New Targets: Immigrants in the Military," *New York Times*, July 6, 2018, www.nytimes.com/2018/07/06/opinion/trumps-immigrants-military.html.

21. "*Democracy Now!* Confronts Madeleine Albright on the Iraq Sanctions: Was It Worth the Price?" *Democracy Now!* July 30, 2004, www.democracynow.org/2004/7/30/democracy_now_confronts_madeline_albright_on.

22. Madeleine Albright, *Fascism: A Warning* (New York: HarperCollins, 2018), 4–5.

23. Albert L. Lauterbach, *Economics in Uniform: Military Economy and Social Structure* (Princeton, NJ: Princeton University Press, 1943), 139.

24. Arundhati Roy, "The Algebra of Infinite Justice," *The Guardian*, Sept. 29, 2001, www.theguardian.com/world/2001/sep/29/september11.afghanistan. Roy elaborates: "The millions killed in Korea, Vietnam and Cambodia, the 17,500 killed when Israel—backed by the US—invaded Lebanon in 1982, the 200,000 Iraqis killed in Operation Desert Storm, the thousands of Palestinians who have died fighting Israel's occupation of the West Bank. And the millions who died, in Yugoslavia, Somalia, Haiti, Chile, Nicaragua, El Salvador, the Dominican Republic, and Panama."

25. Chalmers Johnson, *Blowback: The Costs and Consequences of American Empire* (New York: Henry Holt, 2000), 8.

26. John S. Brown, "Defending the Homeland: An Historical Perspective," *Joint Force Quarterly*, no. 31(Summer 2002): 11. See also Robert A. Hill, comp. and ed., *The FBI's RACON: Racial Conditions in the United States during World War II* (Boston: Northeastern University Press, 1995).

27. "Mission," U.S. Department of Homeland Security, www.dhs.gov/mission.

28. See George Poste et al., *Protecting the Homeland: Report of the Defense Science*

Board, 2000 Summer Study, Executive Summary, vol. 2 (Washington, DC: Office of the Undersecretary of Defense, 2001).

29. Jean-Paul Sartre, "Genocide," *New Left Review* 1, no. 48 (1969): 14.

30. See George Poste et al., *Protecting the Homeland: Report of the Defense Science Board*, vol. 2 (Washington, DC: Office of the Undersecretary of Defense, 2001), 9.

31. See James S. Allen, "Prologue to the Liberation of the Negro People," *The Communist* 12 (1933): 140.

32. *Islamic Monthly* staff, "TIM Debate—CVE," *Islamic Monthly*, June 27, 2015, www.theislamicmonthly.com/tim-debate-cve.

Index

Abaya, Hernando, 143
abolition, 27, 51, 70, 173
accountability, 84–85, 108, 115, 118–19, 147, 184–85
Adams, Ansel, 87
adoption, 11, 205–6, 279n47
Adorno, Theodor, 21, 149
Adventures of Huckleberry Finn (Twain), 23, 67–74, 243–44n61
Advisory Committee on Human Radiation Experiments (ACHRE), 131
Agent Orange, 18, 170, 204
Agreement in Principle Regarding the Use of Bikini Atoll, 125
Aguon, Julian, 136
Ah Chim Hai, 206. *See also* Reckless
Ahmad, Eqbal, 9, 138, 163
Ahn, Jung-hyo, 278n34
Ahuja, Neel, 205
"Airman Novel" (Ellison), 29–33, 41–42, 233n14
Akutagawa Prize, 59
Albright, Madeleine, 223–24
Ali, Tariq, 169–70
Allen, Ernest, 13
Allied Participation in Vietnam (U.S. Army), 16–17
All the Conspirators (Bulosan), 145, 150–51, 157–58, 162
"America Comes Out as the World's Top in Anything" (Kurihara), 109
American Artists' Congress, 101
American Creed, 33

American exceptionalism, 94, 117, 120, 283n18
American Homefront Project, 221
American Indians, 86, 132, 134
Americanization, 84–91
American Negroes, a Handbook (Embree), 31
Americanness, 91
Amin, Samir, 169
Anderson, Margaret, 89, 252n66
animality, 71, 74, 206–8
animal mascots, 205–6
Anjain, John, 130–31, 134
Anjain, Lekoj, 134
Anjain, Nelson, 131
antiblack racism, 71–72
anticolonialism, 178
anticommunism, 3, 48, 57–58, 140, 146. *See also* communism
antifascism, 10, 27, 29, 31, 34–35, 44, 72–73, 85, 101, 147–49, 162, 168, 183–84, 255; black, 9–10, 21–22, 25, 27–29, 33–38, 41, 45–47, 183–84; Filipino, 143–45, 147–48, 162; Japanese American, 85, 93, 250n45. *See also* fascism
antihumanism, 11, 39, 203
anti-imperialism, 65, 73, 165, 172. *See also* imperialism
antilynching, 173. *See also* lynching
apocalypse, 107, 109, 112, 127
"Appeal to the American Conscience" (Russell), 190

Appeal to the Colored Citizens of the World (Walker), 173
Appeal to the World, An (Du Bois et al.), 171, 176, 268-68n31
Arendt, Hannah, 114
art, 26, 86, 101, 103
Article 9 Association, 74
art of democratization, 20–21, 38–40, 72, 100–105. *See also* democratization; fascist aesthetics
Asahi Shimbun, 61
Asia as Method (Chen), 148
assimilation, 84–85, 87–88, 91, 94, 103, 281n70
asymmetrical war, 5, 54, 197, 201. *See also* interventionist war
Atanasoski, Neda, 11
Atomic Bomb Casualty Commission (ABCC), 107–8, 111, 127, 134
Atomic Bomb Casualty Shop, 107–8
atomic bombing of Japan: depiction of, 20, 62–63, 114–16, 133; generative properties of, 116; justification of, 68, 112, 120–21; legacy of, 3, 55, 107–8; spectacle of, 127; value of, 11, 17–18, 105, 118. *See also* Hiroshima; Nagasaki
Atomic Energy Commission (AEC), 126–27, 130–31
atomic era, 109, 112–13, 117
Auschwitz, 21, 149, 191
authoritarianism, 60
aviation, 41, 45, 54, 59, 75, 77, 153
"Aviation, Geography, and Race" (Lindbergh), 54
Aziz, Sahar, 226

Baby-san (child mascot), 214. *See also* Miss 57th Field Artillery
Babysan (Korean War-era cartoon pinup), 281n76
Bakhtin, Mikhail, 64
Baldoz, Rick, 163
Baldwin, Frank, 231n60
Baldwin, James, 21, 165, 170, 181, 186, 189–91, 193–94

"Ballot or the Bullet, The" (Malcolm X), 174, 177, 179
Balos, Ataji, 135
banality of evil, 90, 114
Bandung Conference, 179
Bandy, Robert, 50
Banerjee, Subhabrata Bobby, 118
Barclay, Robert, 123
Barefoot Gen (Nakazawa), 115–17, 120–22
Barrio United Defense Corps (BUDC), 144–45
Basso, Lelio, 17, 167, 169–70
Beaumont, Roger, 187
Bello, Walden, 15
Beneath the Eagle's Wings (Perry), 61
Bikini Atoll, 122, 125
binary politics, 74, 199
biopolitical excess, 18, 198
biopolitics, 4, 8, 11–12, 96, 138, 203, 213, 216, 226
black airmen, 30, 33, 35–39, 41–44, 59, 62–63, 74, 235n49–235n50, 242n43, 245n69. *See also* Tuskegee airmen
black Americans, 2, 4–5, 7, 9–10, 12–14, 23, 26–27, 37, 40, 42, 44–51, 70, 72, 170–71, 174–79, 181, 186–93, 203, 205, 232n9, 235n54, 236n64, 236n66
black Atlantic, 58–59, 72
black demoralization, 47–48, 179–80
black disposability, 72
black freedom struggle, 8–9, 22, 26, 30, 34, 39, 45, 52, 70, 165, 170–71, 184–85
blacklisting, 139, 144–45, 155, 260n9
Black Lives Matter, 7
black Pacific, 54–59, 72–73
Black Panther Party, 171, 174, 183–84, 194
black POWs, 29–33, 35–37, 42–43, 45, 63–67, 71–74, 233n18, 233n21, 242n43, 245n69
black press, 31–32, 41, 51–52, 234n22. *See also* Pittsburgh Courier
black radical human rights petitions, 20, 170–79, 182

black radicalism, 9–11, 14, 20, 22, 27–28, 33, 170–85, 202, 232n9
Black Reconstruction in America (Du Bois), 56
"Black Revolution, The" (Malcolm X), 174, 177
black surrealism, 234n33
black veterans, 5, 25–26, 135n45, 202–3, 233n18. *See also* veterans
bodies, 111, 118–19, 128
"Bomb and the Opportunity, The" (Stimson), 119
Booth, Wayne, 150
Born of the People (Taruc), 142, 145, 163
Breakthrough on the Color Front (Nichols), 200–201
Brown v. Board of Education, 2–3
Buck, Pearl S., 13, 89
Bulosan, Carlos, 50, 145, 147, 150–52, 157–58, 162
burakumin, 75, 245n68
bureaucracy, 64, 66, 91, 278n38
Bureau of Indian Affairs, 90
Burke, Kenneth, 37
Burning Vision (Clements), 133
Bush, George H. W., 185
Bush, George W., 140–42, 144, 199, 221

Calkins, Deborah, 79, 83
camptown, 214–17
cannon fodder, 20, 198, 203
capitalism, 6, 17–18, 20, 28, 56, 93, 118, 124, 183, 254–55n26
Carmichael, Stokely, 189–90
Castle Bravo, 122, 130, 135, 257n61
censorship, 87, 101, 115, 176
Central Intelligence Agency (CIA), 9, 181–83, 264n72. *See also* Office of Strategic Services (OSS)
Central Luzon, 147, 155
Ceremony (Silko), 132
Césaire, Aimé, 150
Chen, Kuan-Hsing, 64–65, 148
Chicago Tribune, 89, 208
childhood, 65, 69, 206, 208

child mascotry, 205–12, *215–16*
China, 13, 15, 18–19, 129, 136, 146, 153, 161, 203, 208, 222, 242n43
Chinese Civil War, 139
Cho, Grace, 18, 198
Chocoletto (child mascot), 208, 280n59, 280n64
Choi, Dan, 195–96, 199, 212, 275n7
Chomsky, Noam, 266n4
Chow, Rey, 3–4, 113
Churchill, Winston, 172
Citizen 13660 (Okubo), 80–81, 86–91, 95–96, 250n34
citizen-subjects, 84, 93
civil defense, 7, 48, 108, 224
civil-disturbance intelligence program, 181
civilian life, 88
civil rights, 2–3, 5, 10–11, 16, 48, 58, 170–71, 177, 179, 189–90
Civil Rights Congress, 42, 51, 170–71, 176, 203
civil unrest, 187
Civil War, 25, 73
Clark Air Base, 142
Class A trials (of the International Military Tribunal for the Far East). *See* Tokyo Trials
Clements, Marie, 133
client-states, 77, 117, 146, 166
Clinton, Bill, 111
Clinton, Hillary, 219
"Close Ranks" (Du Bois), 236n64
Cobb, Charlie, Jr., 190
Coffey, Cornelius, 235n49
Cohen, Theodore, 55
COINTELPRO, 7, 9, 180–83, 185, 271n55
Cold War: and enmity, 9, 21, 160; and fascism, 28; and homosexuality, 196; hot points in, 16, 162, 176; and human rights, 166, 173; and internationalism, 16; late era of, 184; literature during, 29; and multiculturalism, 11, 48; perceptions

of, 53, 58, 159; postwar era of, 111, 222; and race, 23, 171–72, 177, 198, 212; realpolitik of, 172; start of, 4–5, 11, 42–43, 57, 85, 109, 131, 150, 174; strategies of, 7, 48, 108, 147, 153, 156, 185, 206; and the United States, 110, 117, 140, 146; violence of, 112, 114, 150, 222–23
collaboration, 19, 151, 154, 158; Communist, 160, 163; pro-Japanese, 15, 57, 143–44, 146–50, 156–58, 161–62, 263n57; pro-U.S., 17, 49, 149, 154–56, 230n59
collateral damage, 7, 18, 196, 276n18
collectivism, 34
Collier, John, 85–86, 249n27
Collins, James, 50
colonialism, 17, 31, 177
colorblindness, 25, 58, 200, 207
color line, 9, 12–14, 22, 48–49, 72, 91, 200, 212, 217
comfort women, 166, 213, 263n56. *See also* military sexual slavery
comics, 115–16
Commission on Wartime Relocation and Internment of Civilians (CWIRC), 91, 105–6
Common Ground, 89
communism: and fascism, 14, 28; growth of, 34, 137, 153, 162; opposition to, 48, 57, 76, 149, 178, 206; and race, 44, 51, 72. *See also* anticommunism; *specific parties*
Communist Party of the Philippines (CPP), 137, 139–43
Communist Party of the United States of America (CPUSA), 14, 38, 44, 51, 162, 178
Conard, Robert, 131
concentration camps: closing of, 80, 90, 97; as democratic opportunity, 11, 81, 86, 91, 94, 100; depictions of, 10, 20, 79–80, 83, 85–87, 91–92, 98; in Japan, 76, 92, 94; life in, 67, 79–80, 87, 89, 96, 168, 241n50, 251n52;

of the Nazis, 31, 35, 94, 100–101; terminology of, 105, 247n1. *See also* Japanese mass incarceration; *specific camps*
consumerism, 114
Continental Walk for Disarmament and Social Justice, 116
counterinsurgency, 7, 9, 140, 142, 156, 163, 188
counterintelligence, 6, 52, 151, 156, 161, 179, 208, 225
Counter Intelligence Corps (CIC), 52, 57, 144–46, 155–61, 208
"Counter Intelligence Summary" (CIC), 161–62
crimes against humanity, 167, 169, 172, 175
crimes against the peace, 168. *See also* wars of aggression
criminality, 165–72, 174–77
criminalization, 83, 184
Crisis, The, 50
Cry and the Dedication, The (Bulosan), 147, 150–51, 153, 162–63
Cumings, Bruce, 5, 82–83

Danysh, Romana, 156
Davis, Sasha, 134
Days of Wrath (Malraux), 31, 34–35
deBrum, Tony, 130–31
decolonization, 147–48, 152, 157, 171, 175
Deferred Action for Childhood Arrivals (DACA), 221–22
dehumanization, 33, 80, 203
deimperialization, 148
Deloria, Philip, 207
DeLoughrey, Elizabeth, 110
democracy: discourses of, 3, 68, 142–43; and fascism, 6, 38–45; limits of, 30, 51, 74, 83; potentials of, 8–9, 11, 32, 47, 62, 82, 93, 199, 219; and progress, 16; and the United States, 1, 21–23, 86; vehicles for, 57; and violence, 20, 55, 174

Democracy Now!, 197, 275n6
democratization: aesthetic of, 85; and the Cold War, 58, 226; and concentration camps, 87; discourses of, 20, 39, 98, 101, 103, 142–43; of Japan, 68, 70; and militarism, 17, 149; and the Philippines, 141; potential of, 55, 82; and race, 73. *See also* art of democratization
Dene, 133–34
Department of Defense, 127
Department of the Interior, 8, 110, 125–26
desegregation, 2–5, 10–11, 22, 24, 58, 199–200, 205, 222
deterritorialization, 110, 125–26, 133, 140, 207–8, 214, 217, 220
Dewey Commission, 193
Diné (Navajo), 111, 126, 134
disability, 135
disability rights, 69
discrimination, 45, 75
disposability, 111, 129
dogs of war, 200–205
dojinburaku, 71
Dolgopol, Ustinia, 167
domestic policy, 13, 23, 175
Don't Ask, Don't Tell (DADT) policy, 195, 199–200, 223
double consciousness, 33
Double-V campaign, 29–33, 41–42, 52, 190, 232n13, 238n89
Douglass, Frederick, 172, 203
Dower, John, 13, 104
draft, 47–48, 190, 221
DREAM Act, 221–23
Drinnon, Richard, 90
Du Bois, W. E. B., 12, 33, 56, 70, 73, 171–78, 182, 189, 236n64, 244n65
Dunham, Charles, 131

ecocide, 112
economic modernization, 167
economic recovery, 17–18, 82–83, 120, 140
economy of war, 2–3, 6, 10, 24, 29, 57, 214
Edgerton, Ronald, 155
education, 69, 85, 89, 97, 105, 154, 194, 235n45, 244n61
Eisenbud, Merril, 128
Eisenhower, Dwight, 113
Eisenhower, Milton, 251n52, 252n58
Ellison, Ralph, 6, 10, 14, 20–21, 23–54, 63, 229n33, 231n1, 232n5, 233n18
Ellsberg, Daniel, 195
Embree, Edwin, 31
emergent, 43
empathy, 91, 100
enemy: at home, 21, 49, 51–53, 155, 165–94; Japanese Americans as, 85; nature of, 92; and race, 10, 33; reading of, 151–57
enemy alien, 47, 82, 84, 94, 251n50
enemy-friend distinction, 150, 160, 199
enmity, 111, 159–60, 203, 206–7, 243–44n61
espionage, 47, 49, 51, 95, 144, 179
esprit de corps, 211
evasion sequence, 244n63
Executive Order 8802, 45
Executive Order 9981, 5, 58, 200, 222
extraterritorial expansion, 19, 71, 143, 149

Fabre, Michel, 233n14
Fagen, David, 58
Fahy Committee, 4, 45, 48, 199
Fanon, Frantz, 113
fascism: aesthetics of, 20, 39; and communism, 14, 28; and democracy, 6, 24, 38–45; familiarity of, 36; in Japan, 86, 141; in Nazi Germany, 169; opposition to, 28, 47, 63, 168; and race, 14–15, 38, 53, 183; threat of, 1–2, 42–44, 163; of the United States, 9, 12, 21, 29, 31, 33, 82, 90, 144, 222–23; violence of, 145, 149. *See also* antifascism
fascism (U.S.), 9, 12, 21, 29, 31, 33, 82, 90, 144, 222–23

fascist aesthetics, 20, 39, 101, 226. *See also* art of democratization; mass ornament
fatigues, 210–11
FBI Security Index, 162
Federal Bureau of Investigation (FBI), 7, 9, 51, 162, 180–85, 271n55
Federal Writers' Project (FWP), 10, 26, 46, 229n33, 237n72
Fenkl, Heinz Insu, 217
Finnegan, John, 156
"Flying Home" (Ellison), 25, 41
Foley, Barbara, 232n12, 233n14
Foreign Affairs, 182
foreign policy, 13, 175
Forman, James, 189
Fortune, 79, 81–83, 92, 94–95, 98, 105, 114–15, 251n51
Frank, Waldo, 34
fratricide, 202
Freedom, 25
Freedom of Information Act (FOIA), 51
Freedomways, 165, 170, 181, 190–91
Freud, Sigmund, 34, 234n33
frontier, 244n67
Fujitani, Takashi, 13, 85
Futenma Air Station, 74–75

Garden Plot (U.S. military civil disturbance plan), 7, 188
Genbaku Dome, 107
gender roles, 214
Geneva Agreements, 167
genocide, 21, 42, 168, 172, 175–76, 193, 268–69n31
Genocide Convention, 171–72, 176
geopolitics, 4, 12, 148, 159, 203, 217
Gibson, Truman, 49
Gilmore, Ruth Wilson, 184
Gilroy, Paul, 59
GI photography, 213–14, *215–16*
Global South movements, 165
Goldsmith, Larry, 275n7
Gray, Jesse, 268–69n31
Greene, Graham, 159

Greenpeace, 136
Griffith, Samuel B., 139, 152
"Guerrilla Is like a Poet, The" (Sison), 137–39
guerrillas, 147. *See also* soldiers
guerrilla warfare, 137, 139, 152, 155–56, 161, 163
guilt, 7, 109, 150

Hadashi no Gen (Nakazawa), 115–17, 120–22
Hague Convention, 167
Hamer, Fannie Lou, 190
Han, Suk-jung, 146–47
Hansen, Harry, 89
Hara, Kimie, 18, 125
Harlem, 14, 46, 50, 189–90, 268–69n31
H-bomb, 122
Health and Safety Laboratory (HASL), 128
Hearst, William, 93–94, 106
Hedges, Chris, 196, 198
Hediger, Ryan, 204
Henson, Maria Rosa, 263n56
Herndon, Angelo, 14, 24
Hersh, Seymour, 169
hibakusha, 17–18, 20, 64, 108–9, 112, 115, 120–21
Hill, Robert, 51
Himes, Chester, 10, 47–48
Hirabayashi v. United States, 251n55
Hirohito, 60–62, 242n40, 242n42
Hiroshima, 3, 8, 11, 20, 62, 107, 109–19, 132–33. *See also* atomic bombing of Japan; Nagasaki
Hitler, Adolf, 46–47, 175
Ho Chi Minh, 2, 168–69
Holocaust, 21, 149, 167, 190–91
Home (Morrison), 6, 201, 205
home front, 6, 26, 37, 42, 45–51, 98, 180, 189, 201, 224
homeland security, 220, 224–25, 271n52. *See also* national security
honorary citizenship, 205
Hoover, J. Edgar, 162–63, 185

houseboy, 208, 210, 212
hubris, 77
"Huckleberry Finn and the American Dream" (Oē), 67–68
Huffington Post, 196
Hughes, Langston, 34
Huks, 141–45, 147, 152–53, 155, 157, 161, 163
Humanism and Terror (Merleau-Ponty), 193
humanitarianism, 11, 17, 191, 205–7, 210
humanity, 39, 65, 69, 74, 154
humanization, 105
human rights, 11, 21, 117, 144, 165–66, 170–73, 175, 177, 179–85, 192, 270n40, 276n10; anti-imperialist, 21–22, 165–69, 184–85; black radical, 20, 165, 170–82, 184–85, 189, 268n30, 269n31, 270n40, 274n93; Cold War, 21–22, 173–75, 189; Korean, 189; Marshallese, 110; Okinawan, 75
human solidarity, 34
Hume, Bill, 107, 213, 281n76
Huntington, Samuel, 182
Hüppauf, Bernd, 206
Hutton, Robin, 205–6

"I Become a Nisei" (Noguchi), 86
Ickes, Harold, 5
Ienaga, Saburō, 108
If He Hollers Let Him Go (Himes), 10, 47–48
imaginator, 85, 93, 106, 249n22
Immigration and Nationality Act, 223
imperialism, 12, 14–15, 58, 70–71, 138, 141, 143, 145–51, 173, 175. *See also* anti-imperialism
indigenous land, 8, 71, 111, 124–27, 135, 178
indigenous life, 129, 206–7, 214
indigenous sovereignty, 8, 71, 110–11, 124–27, 135, 178
indistinction, 1, 5, 22, 90, 138
Indo-Pacific Command. *See* Pacific Command

infantilization, 245n72
intelligence, 81, 139, 145–46, 161, 181, 183, 225
Internal Revenue Service (IRS), 182
International Court of Justice, 270n40
internationalism, 179
international law, 17, 167–69, 267n12
International Longshoremen's and Warehousemen's Union, 153
International Military Tribunal for the Far East (IMTFE), 147. *See also* Tokyo Trials
International Movement against All Forms of Discrimination and Racism, 75
international tourism, 114
International Tribunal on Political Prisoners, 166
International War Crimes Tribunal on Vietnam, 17, 165
internment. *See* Japanese mass incarceration
interventionism, 2, 11, 16–17, 166, 170, 196, 222
interventionist war, 2, 7, 9, 11, 16–19, 22, 24, 58, 82–83, 136, 141, 166, 169–70, 176, 180, 191, 196–99, 201, 204, 207, 217, 220, 222–24, 226, 230n57, 240n12. *See also* asymmetrical war; police actions
Invisible Man (Ellison), 23–29, 42–51, 232n12, 233n15
invisible war, 53
Iraq War, 196, 219
Iron First and the Velvet Glove, The, 183
Ishihara, Tsuyoshi, 69
Is Japan the Champion of the Colored Races?, 38, 72
"Issei, Nisei, Kibei," 93–94, 96–99, 104
Iwamatsu, Jun Atsushi, 93

Jackson, Lawrence, 34, 233n14
James, C. L. R., 10–11, 44
Janus-faced regime, 21, 113
Japan: and fascism, 86; as a military-

imperial power, 12, 64–65, 68, 73–75, 77, 146, 161; peripheralization of, 65, 67, 72, 76, 243n50; and the Philippines, 152–53; postwar era of, 57, 60, 64, 146; reconstruction of, 17, 55, 68, 70, 112; social practices of, 71–72; as a symbol of peace, 120; symbols of, 60; and U.S. occupation, 55, 58–59, 61, 115, 146, 240n12; and World War II, 51, 64, 74, 156
Japanese American Citizens League (JACL), 97, 105
Japanese American mass incarceration: depictions of, 10, 79–82, 89; grievances about, 82; opposition to, 90, 97; rationale for, 7, 47, 84–85, 87, 91; redress for, 91, 259n94; representational role of, 94; and settler-colonial themes, 98; terminology of, 95, 105, 247n1. *See also* concentration camps
Japanese American redress movement, 91
Japanese Americans, 72, 88, 90, 100, 103–4, 133–34. *See also* Japanese American mass incarceration
Japanese Communist Party (JCP), 57
Japanese Imperial Army, 76, 129, 167, 246n86
Japaneseness, 103
"Japanese worker and family" (Okubo), *104*
Jim Crow: dismantlement of, 24, 58, 200; on the home front, 201; in Japanese propaganda, 38; legacy of, 58, 74; and the military, 4, 10, 13, 40, 47, 52, 222, 237n76; and the Nazis, 32; practices of, 12; violence of, 6, 177, 189, 205
jingoism, 14, 91, 93, 199–200, 276n20
Johnson, Lyndon, 16, 168, 187
Jones, Claudia, 10, 39, 47
Julius Rosenwald Fund, 29–32, 233n14–233n15, 233n19

Kelley, Robin D. G., 172, 270n48
Kellogg-Briand Pact, 167
Kerner Commission. *See* National Advisory Commission on Civil Defense
Keynesianism, 6
Khan, Ghazala, 220–21
Khan, Humayun, 219–21, 223
Khan-Cullors, Patrisse, 7
Kikkawa, Kiyoshi, 107
kill-chain logic, 64
Killens, John, 25, 268–69n31
Kim, Chi-ha, 64
Kim, Dong-choon, 146
Kim, Eleana, 210
Kim, Hosu, 18, 198
King, Martin Luther, Jr., 2–3, 44, 180, 183
Klein, Christina, 206
Klein, Naomi, 118
Korea International War Crimes Tribunal, 166
Korean theater, 5, 24
Korean War: as an unending war, 200, 212, 217; asymmetry of, 201; and human rights, 205–6; and Japan, 17, 83; legacy of, 29, 176, 198, 202, 218; legality of, 162, 175; and mascots, 195–218; onset of, 48, 175; perceptions of, 2, 23; and race, 4–5, 203; as a total war, 153, 208; and the United States, 15, 68, 76, 223. *See also* police actions
Korean War Memorial, 200
Kuniyoshi, Yasuo, 93
Kurihara, Sadako, 109, 134

labor, 56, 118, 156; affective, 210–15; counterinsurgent, 220; forced, 255n35; indigenous, 126, 213; military, 200, 203, 208, 212, 222, 277n29; necropolitical, 39, 59, 126, 212–13, 277n29; postwar, 57, 98; racial, 13, 39, 56, 59, 70, 98, 203; reproductive, 212–14; sexual, 214,

217; solidarity of, 45, 72; wartime, 2, 12, 200, 208, 212, 234n23, 239n91, 249n28. *See also* reproductive labor
labor rights, 57
labor theory of value, 111
labor unions, 47–48, 57, 153
LaDuke, Winona, 126
Landsberg, Alison, 116
Lange, Dorothea, 87, 101
Lansdale, Edward, 264n72
Law of Land Warfare, The (U.S. Army), 167
League of American Writers, 34
Lee, Chun Jea, 214
Lee, Jin-kyung, 59, 213
Lee, Tanya, 127
LeMay, Curtis, 68
Lester, Julius, 190
Lewis, Roscoe, 46
LGBT military integration, 197, 281n70
Liberal Democratic Party (LDP), 68
liberalism, 4, 11, 53
Liebknecht, Karl, 19, 55
Lifton, Robert, 117
Light, Jennifer, 186
Lim, Deborah, 252n58
Lincoln, Abraham, 31
Lindbergh, Charles, 54
Lindee, M. Susan, 108, 111
Lipsitz, George, 14, 254–55n26
Listen, Brother! (Williams), 203
Little Tokyo, 91–100
Locke, John, 111
Lowe, Lisa, 170
loyalty, 81, 87, 94, 155, 189, 198, 210–11
Luce, Henry, 79, 82–83, 93, 100
Luce, Matthias, 15, 82, 93, 100
Lusane, Clarence, 233n21
Lutz, Norma Jean, 235n49
lynching, 13, 37, 41–42, 46–47, 51, 70, 176, 184, 201, 203–4, 238n85. *See also* antilynching

MacArthur, Douglas, 55–56, 60–61, 76, 105, 143, 161, 242n40
Maclear, Kyo, 115

Maeda, Robert, 86
Malcolm X, 21, 49, 170–71, 173–75, 177, 179, 181, 189, 268–69n31
Malraux, André, 31, 34–35, 234n32
Manning, Chelsea, 195–98, 275n7, 276n11
"Many Thousands Gone" (Baldwin), 193
Maoism, 137
Mao Zedong, 138–39
Marcos regime, 18, 139, 143, 148, 169
marginalization, 17, 75–77, 268n23
Marion, George, 14, 115
Marker, Chris, 5, 114
Marshall Islands: and bearing witness, 112; destruction of, 8, 112, 122, 124, 136; isolation of, 110; lawsuit against the United States, 166; legal status of, 257n71; and radiation experiments, 128, 130–31
Marshall Plan, 17
Maruta project, 129. *See also* Unit 731
Marx, Karl, 34, 118, 234n33
Masaoka, Mike, 97
Masco, Joseph, 114
mascotry, 205–12
mask, 212
mass ornament, 20, 39, 226. *See also* fascist aesthetics
mass suicide, 76
Maus (Spiegelman), 116
McAlister, Melani, 222, 229n37
McCoy, Alfred, 141
McNamara, Robert, 169
McWilliams, Carey, 89, 95, 105
Melal (Barclay), 123
Melamed, Jodi, 90, 154
Memories of My Ghost Brother (Fenkl), 217
Merleau-Ponty, Maurice, 193
MHCHAOS, 9. *See also* Operation CHAOS
Micronesia, 135, 156
militarism: and democracy, 8–9, 17, 19; and everyday life, 110; in Japan, 68; and law, 147; opposition to, 75; and

race, 4, 212; of the United States, 1–2, 6, 21, 55–56, 84, 120, 125, 139, 169, 216
militarization, 11, 87, 113
militarized peace, 62, 113
Military Accessions Vital to the National Interest (MAVNI), 221–23
military draft, 47–48, 190, 221
military-imperialism, 3–4, 8, 11–12, 14–15, 17, 19–21, 29, 58, 64–65, 82, 111, 118, 141, 146, 148, 151, 154, 156, 165, 183, 222, 225
military-industrial complex, 2–3, 12, 15, 24, 77, 110, 183
military integration, 2–3, 5, 10–11, 22, 24, 58, 199–200, 206, 222
military multiculturalism, 13, 48, 212
military sexual slavery, 166. *See also* comfort women
military targets, 4–5, 113, 122–32
military uniforms, 198, 200–202, 212
Miller, Dorie, 58
Miss 57th Field Artillery, 214
Mitchell, Greg, 117
model minority myth, 98, 100, 105
morale, 45, 47–48, 238n89
morale operations, 48, 238n83. *See also* propaganda
Morales, Frank, 187–88
Morrison, Toni, 6, 53, 201, 205
Morris-Suzuki, Tessa, 146, 210, 214
Moscow Trials, 193
Mulroney, Brian, 259n94
multiculturalism, 11, 13, 48, 59, 212, 220, 229n37
Muslim Americans, 219–26
My Bondage and My Freedom (Douglass), 172
Myer, Dillon, 81, 89–90, 97

NAACP, 40, 50, 171, 268–69n31
Nagasaki, 3, 8, 11, 62, 110–12, 118, 132–33. *See also* atomic bombing of Japan; Hiroshima
Nakazawa, Keiji, 115–17, 120–22

napalm, 153, 168, 176, 204
Nathan, John, 60
National Advisory Commission on Civil Defense, 187
National Front for the Liberation of the South (NLF), 174, 189, 193
National Negro Congress, 171
national security, 3, 24, 46, 74–75, 110–11, 118, 129, 147, 154, 182, 225. *See also* homeland security
National Security Act, 222
nation building, 48
Nazis, 14, 21, 31–36, 167, 172, 175, 191, 233n21
necrocapitalism, 118, 123
necropolitics, 3, 55, 59, 72, 112, 129, 213
"Negro and the Second World War, The" (Ellison), 232n5
"Negro and the War, The" (Ellison), 10, 27, 229n3, 232n5
Negro Quarterly, 14, 24, 40, 45, 232n5
Neocleous, Mark, 28, 53, 184
neocolonialism, 15, 150, 169, 210
New Deal, 47
New Left Review, 167
New Masses, 46
New People's Army (NPA), 137, 139, 141–42, 148
New Republic, 5
Newton, Huey, 171, 174
New Yorker, 75
Nguyen, Thi Tho, 174
Nguyen, Van Dong, 174
9/11, 139–40, 142, 199, 220–21, 224–26, 278n38
Nisei, 20, 67, 79–81, 83, 85–86, 90–93, 100, 105, 200–201
Nisei Writers and Artists Mobilization for Democracy, 85
Nishi, Toshio, 61
Nixon doctrine, 17
Nobel Prize, 59, 89, 244n66
Noguchi, Isamu, 85–86, 95, 100
No Gun Ri, 246n87
No Name in the Street (Baldwin), 194

Non-citizens in Today's Military, 221
Non-proliferation Treaty Peace Walk, 135
North Korea, 5, 198, 207–9
NOW, 80
nuclear apocalypse, 107, 109, 112, 127
nuclear fallout, 110, 112, 123, 127–28, 253n11, 257n61
nuclear power, 113, 119
nuclear warfare, 8, 18, 68, 107, 116, 119, 129, 134, 180
nuclear weapons testing, 8, 111, 122–32, 135, 225, 254n13, 258n76
Nuremberg Statute, 167
Nuremberg Trials, 149, 166–67, 171, 189

Obama, Barack, 169, 196, 200, 221, 223
Ochanomizu Shobo, 92
Oē, Kenzaburō, 54–78
Office of Facts and Figures (OFF), 46
Office of Strategic Services (OSS), 48, 238n83. *See also* Central Intelligence Agency (CIA)
Office of War Information (OWI), 33, 46, 238n83
Oguma, Eiji, 77
Okinawa, 15–16, 19, 74–78, 136, 179
Okinawa Citizen's Alliance for Peace, 75
Okinawan Citizens' Alliance for Peace, 75
Okinawa Notes (Oē), 75–76
Okubo, Miné, 79–106
Olbermann, Keith, 195
On Clipped Wings (Hastie), 40
Operation CHAOS, 9, 181–83, 272n66
Operation Crossroads, 126
Operation Mascot, 206
oppositional politics, 29, 43
Organization of Afro-American Unity, 171, 180
orphans, 196, 199, 210, 217, 276n13
Osprey, 74–75, 77–78, 246n91, 247n93–247n95

Pacific Citizen, 105
Pacific Command, 3, 227n8
Pacific Proving Grounds, 8, 254n13

Pacific Stars and Stripes, 210, 214
Pacific theater, 2–3, 12–13, 73, 79, 155
Pacific War. *See* World War II
Pal, Radhabinod, 166
Palmer, Dwight, 199
Park, Gordon, 33
Park Chung-hee, 17, 146–47
Parks, Rosa, 190
Pate, Soojin, 214
patriotism, 4–5, 99, 189
Patterson, Robert, 5
Patterson, William, 21, 42, 170–71, 175–76, 178, 182, 189
Pax Americana, 3, 8–9, 16, 19, 21, 55, 80, 84, 101, 110, 146, 149–50, 157, 162, 226
Pax Japonica, 13, 65
peace: brutality of, 166; discourses of, 120; legacy of peace, 198; and militarization, 62, 113; perceptions of, 2–3; performance of, 62; in the Philippines, 145; symbols of, 120
peaceful violence, 113
Pearl Harbor, 47
Pentagon Papers, 169, 195
People's Anti-Japanese Army. *See* Huks
People's Liberation Armed Forces, 193
Permanent Peoples' Tribunal, 143, 148, 166, 169
Perry, John Curtis, 61
Petersen, William, 100
Petraeus, David, 140
Philippine Air Force, 153
Philippine-American War, 58, 141
Philippine Congress, 140, 144, 147
Philippine Constabulary, 152, 154
Philippines: and Japan, 152–53; and the United States, 18, 54, 140–41, 145, 158
Phoenix Program, 182
Pittsburgh Courier, 32, 71
Platt, Tony, 183
police actions, 6, 9–10, 18, 57, 153, 162, 173, 184, 225, 236n59. *See also* interventionist war; Korean War
police brutality, 186

police power, 1, 8, 12, 18–20, 29, 47, 53, 56, 82, 122, 142, 148, 162, 165, 170, 184–86, 224
police state, 1, 47, 176
Posse Comitatus Act, 183
postcolonialism, 147
posthumanism, 204
"Post Office at the Tanforan WCCA camp" (Okubo), 88
Poston concentration camp, 85
Potsdam, 121
Power of the People, The (Bulosan), 154–55
prisoners of war, 23–54, 59–67, 71, 94, 210, 245n69. *See also* black POWs
Project Gen, 116
propaganda: of the Huks, 152–53; of Japan, 13–14, 38, 51, 86; of North Korea, 198, 202–3; of the United States, 46–47, 81. *See also* morale operations
prosthetic memory, 116
prostitution, 214
proxy governments, 57
Puar, Jasbir, 200
Pueblo, 111, 126, 132, 134
Pyle, Alden, 264n72
Pyongyang, 208

queerness, 195–218, 223
Quiet American, The (Greene), 159

race: and colorblindness, 25, 58, 200, 207; and the color line, 200, 212; and counterintelligence, 7, 51, 179–80, 182; and fascism, 33, 38, 53; and the military, 2–3, 24, 31, 39–45, 129, 198–99; and othering, 14, 30, 46, 67, 90, 95, 97, 158; in the postwar era, 91, 154; and progress, 14, 23–24, 40, 186, 197
race-baiting, 37
race riots, 49, 170, 183, 186, 238n90
race war, 12–13, 85, 193, 225
Rachel Maddow Show, The, 195

racial counterintelligence, 19, 179
racial profiling, 1–2, 7, 49, 68
racial securitization, 207, 211–12
racial soldiering, 19–20, 23–26, 28–30, 58–59, 197–99, 202–3, 222–23. *See also* cannon fodder
racism: and Japan, 61, 71–72, 78; in structural form, 45–46, 89; and United Nations petitions, 42, 75; and the United States, 4, 32, 41, 44, 71–72, 97, 129–30, 143, 175; violence of, 6, 49, 171, 174–75; and war, 4, 8–12, 59, 65, 73, 206–7
"Racism and Fascism" (Morrison), 53
Racketeer Influence and Corrupt Organizations (RICO) Act, 184
RACON (FBI), 7, 51
radiation, 107–8, 111–12, 123, 127, 130
Radiation Exposure Compensation Act, 127
radioactive waste, 124
Ralph Ellison (Rampersad), 233n18
Rampersad, Arnold, 30, 233n14, 233n18
Reader's Digest, 86
Reagan, Ronald, 196, 259n94
realpolitik, 148, 172, 179
Reckless (animal mascot), 205–6
Reconstruction, 27, 56, 61, 70, 232n9, 236n55
red-baiting, 57, 76
Reddy, Chandan, 199
redress movement, 91
"Reflection on the Atomic Bomb" (Stein), 114
refugees, 177; nuclear, 18, 123, 126, 134; war, 210–11, 214
relocation center. *See* concentration camps
reparations: for the atomic bombings of Hiroshima and Nagasaki, 108, 117; for Japanese American mass incarceration, 80, 98; for Japanese war crimes, 146; for slavery and Jim Crow, 172
repatriation, 119

reproductive labor, 212–13. *See also* labor
reverse course, 76
Rhee, Syngman, 208
Riklon, Johnsay, 112
Ringle, K. D., 81
Rivera, Diego, 103
Robeson, Paul, 25, 171, 182, 189, 202
Robinson, John, 235n49
Romero, Ricardo, 180
Rome Statute, 169
Rongelapese, 112, 130, 258n79
Roosevelt, Franklin D., 2, 5, 8, 18, 40, 45, 99, 236n66
Rosie the Riveter, 6
Roxas, Manuel, 161
Roy, Arundhati, 224
rule of law, 21
Runit Island, 124
rural margins, 66
Russell, Bertrand, 165, 169, 190
Russell, John, 71
Russell Tribunal, 76, 165–94

sabotage, 47, 51–52, 95, 180, 224
Sakima, Kiyoko, 77
Sandler, Stanley, 49
Sartre, Jean-Paul, 138, 165–68, 189, 225
Scheips, Paul, 188
Schwenger, Peter, 119, 121
Seale, Bobby, 171, 174, 182
security imperialism, 147, 166
sedition, 47, 49, 180, 224
Selden, Mark, 147
self-determination, 173, 178
"Sergeant Yo-Yo" (Praytor), 211
settler-colonialism, 8, 12, 71, 98–99, 124, 133, 135, 178, 207
Sharp, Grant, 76
Shiiku (Oē), 59–67, 70, 72
Silko, Leslie Marmon, 111, 132
Simbulan, Roland, 18
Simmons, Walter, 208
Sims, Charles, 33
Singh, Nikhil Pal, 178

Sison, Jose Maria, 137–41
slavery, 59, 70–73, 168, 172, 177, 245n68
Socialist Workers Party, 232n13
social services, 98
soldiers: American Indian, 132; Asian, 17; black, 4–5, 10–11, 13, 20, 23–26, 28–33, 37, 41–42, 46, 49–50, 58–59, 63–67, 71, 73–74, 179, 190, 200–204, 212–13, 242n42–242n43, 245n69, 278n33; child, 208–10, 280n60; Japanese, 79, 132; Japanese American, 200; Korean, 16–17, 208, 280n60; Korean American, 195–99; LGBT, 195–200, 211; Muslim American, 219–21; noncitizen, 223; U.S., 7, 56, 69, 94, 188, 195–200, 210–11, 214, 217, 221–22, 252n52. *See also* guerrillas; racial soldiering
solidarity, 12, 14, 22, 32, 34, 45, 72, 111, 136
Son My massacre, 169
Southeast Asia Treaty Organization (S.E.A.T.O.), 168
South Korea, 16–17, 205
South Korea Defense Ministry, 208
sovereignty, 21–22, 28, 82, 110, 125, 143, 146, 151, 168, 178, 181, 185, 216
Soviet Union, 19, 161
Special International Tribunal on the Human Rights Violations, 184–85
spectacle, 63, 108, 117, 127, 206
Spiegelman, Art, 116
Stalinism, 193
Stars and Stripes, 206
Stein, Gertrude, 114
Stern, Bernhard, 44–45, 229n33
Stimson, Henry, 49, 119
Strange Career of Jim Crow, The (Woodward), 5
structural racism, 45–46, 72, 75, 89, 171
Student Nonviolent Coordinating Committee (SNCC), 190
Subic Naval Base, 142, 148
"Submissiveness Is a Japanese Weapon" (Okubo), *84*

subversion, 149, 180, 224, 239n92
Sundquist, Eric, 45, 232n5
Sun Tzu, 140
Supreme Commander for the Allied Powers (SCAP), 60–61
surveillance, 6, 52, 84, 151, 153, 156, 162, 179–80, 182, 187
Survey Graphic, 89, 97, 99
Survey of Racial Conditions in the United States (FBI), 7, 51
Sycamore, Mattilda Bernstein, 197

Tachibana, Reiko, 71
Tajiri, Larry, 80
Tales of My Own People (Bulosan), 154–55
Tanaka, Yuki, 129
Tanforan concentration camp, 85, 87, 88, 95–96, 98
"Tanforan mess hall" (Okubo), 96
targets, 57, 64, 121–32, 138, 211
Taruc, Luis, 142–45, 162–63
terrain of information, 152
territorial geopolitics, 12
terrorism, 140, 142, 149, 184, 192. *See also* war on terror
testimony, 21, 86–87, 89, 115–16, 119, 130, 149
thanotourism, 107
Third World, 22, 148, 173, 178, 194
thyroid cancer, 135, 257n61
Tibbets, Paul, 124
Tokyo Trials, 166, 168. *See also* International Military Tribunal for the Far East (IMTFE)
Topaz concentration camp, 79, 87, 92, 101, 247n3
total war, 1–2, 6–8, 13, 26, 49, 84, 98, 126, 138, 180, 208, 224
Toubaru, Kamerou, 76
Tozier, M. M., 89
translation, 241n32
Trask, Haunani-Kay, 113, 129
Treat, John, 117, 119, 121
Trek, 79, 87, 101, *102*

Trinity test, 126–27
Truman, Harry, 4–5, 24, 58, 107, 200, 222
Trump, Donald, 219, 221, 223
trusteeship, 125
Truth and Reconciliation Commission (South Korea), 146
Tsutsui, Keisuke, 69
Tuskegee airmen, 33, 37, 40–41, 233n19, 233n45, 233n49. *See also* black airmen
Tuskegee Board of Directors, 233n19
Twain, Mark, 23, 54, 67–74, 243–44n61

UN Charter, 167, 171
unending war, 3
uniforms, symbolic power of, 198, 200–202
unilateralism, 18, 28
union busting, 47–48, 57
Union of Radical Criminologists, 183
Unit 731, 129
United Nations, 16, 42, 75, 124, 126, 130, 135, 167, 169, 171–73, 177, 179, 182, 203, 268–69n31
United Nations Human Rights Council (UNHCR), 75
United Nations Trusteeship Council, 124
United States: and accountability, 108, 115, 147; and the Cold War, 110, 140, 147–48; and counterinsurgency doctrine, 140, 142; counterintelligence operations in, 182; and democracy, 82, 86, 93; expansion of, 19, 29, 125–26, 149; fascism in, 9, 12, 21, 29, 31, 33, 82, 90, 222–23; and militarism, 28, 54–56, 75, 139, 216; as a military-imperial power, 5, 15, 29, 39, 71–75, 111, 119, 141–43, 147–48, 156–57, 163–70, 175; and national security, 111, 118, 123, 154; and nuclear power, 123–26, 129–30; and occupation of Japan, 55, 58–59, 61, 115, 240n12; and occupation of the Philippines, 143,

145; perceptions of, 121, 151, 158; as a police state, 1, 141, 176; propaganda of, 46, 81; racism in, 4, 32, 41, 44, 71–72, 129–30, 143, 175–76; society of, 2, 6, 40, 98, 104, 181; symbols of, 54, 58–60, 87, 198; and the United Nations, 16; as a world power, 2, 4, 11, 17–19, 42, 82, 85, 112, 120, 122, 142, 159, 196, 206, 222, 268n29
United States fascism, 9, 12, 21, 29, 31, 33, 82, 90, 222–23
United States military: expansion of, 15, 29, 77, 146, 222; presence of, 16–18, 118; structure of, 76, 88, 148, 200
United States war machine: emergence of, 39, 131, 148; ideology of, 57, 226; perception of, 9–11, 23, 43; and race, 23, 73, 199, 207, 222; violence of, 22, 75, 138, 186, 196, 206
Universal Declaration of Human Rights, 171
uranium mining, 126, 132
urban warfare, 165–94
U.S. Army Forces in the Far East (USAFFE), 156
U.S.-Japan Security Treaty, 62, 68, 75, 120
Utsumi, Aiko, 146

veterans, 5, 25–26, 132, 202–3, 213–14, 233n18, 235n45, 273n89, 277n28, 278n34, 280n60. *See also* black veterans
victim consciousness, 120
Victorious Fatherland Liberation War Museum, 208, *209*
victory, 5, 10, 14–15, 79, 84, 92, 109, 114, 147
Viet Cong, 182, 186, 193
Vietnam War: legality of, 16–17, 166–67, 191, 267n12; perceptions of, 168, 182, 188; and race, 2–3; and South Korea, 17, 83; and U.S. military strategy, 68, 76, 184, 187, 221; and war crimes, 175, 183

virgin targets, 126–27, 129
Virilio, Paul, 138
Vizenor, Gerald, 133
Voice of the Crane, 60
Volpp, Leti, 198
volunteerism, 16
voyeurism, 109, 114, 160–62
Voyles, Traci Brynne, 111

Wada, Fred, 99
Walker, David, 172–73
war: asymmetry of, 5, 54, 197, 201; and culture, 4–5, 26, 81; and democracy, 20; destruction of, 57, 64, 107, 109; and effects on humans, 65, 116; industry of, 2–3, 6, 10, 45, 48; invisibility of, 53; perpetuity of, 3, 27; racism of, 4, 193; strategies of, 68; and total war, 2–3; uncertainty of, 73; and the United States, 8, 81, 121, 163; violence of, 138, 150, 168–69, 205. *See also specific wars*
war crimes, 17, 146–47, 161, 165–94
"War Crimes Tribunal, The" (Baldwin), 186
War Is a Force That Gives Us Meaning (Hedges), 198
war on drugs, 7
war on terror, 140, 199, 219–20, 225–26. *See also* terrorism
war photography, 206
war power, 1, 4, 8–10, 12, 18–20, 26, 28–29, 48, 53–56, 115, 122–24, 126, 130, 142, 148, 151, 153, 163, 165, 170, 175, 184, 217, 220, 222, 224
War Relocation Authority (WRA), 79, 87, 89–90, 94–95, 97, 101
wars of aggression, 9, 11, 16, 60, 163, 167–69, 203. *See also* crimes against the peace
wartime cultural front, 81
war within a war, 38
War without Mercy (Dower), 104
Washington, Booker T., 233n19
"Way It Is, The" (Ellison), 46

We Charge Genocide (Patterson), 51, 170, 176, 203
Weisgall, Jonathan, 128
welfare-warfare state, 2, 6, 28, 40
Western Defense Command, 238n82
whistleblowing, 197
White, Link, 211–13
whiteness, 72, 254n26
white supremacy, 38, 54–55, 65, 71
white terror, 143
white warfare, 111, 132
Widener, Daniel, 5, 24
Wiesel, Elie, 21, 149
Williams, Eric, 222
Williams, Raymond, 43
Williams, Robert, 203
Winant, Howard, 3–4
Winter Soldier Investigation, 273n89
Wise, David, 182
witness, 86–90, 112–13, 116–17, 123, 189
wolf children, 205, 208
Women's International War Crimes Tribunal, 166
Woodward, C. Vann, 5
Works Progress Administration (WPA), 41, 80
World War I, 6
World War II, 91, 171; aftermath of, 150; archives of, 155; death toll of, 64; as a dual front war, 52–53; end of, 1, 30, 60, 74, 110, 146, 167; legacy of, 4, 6, 14, 28, 109, 149, 225; as a peoples' war, 41, 223; postwar era of, 82, 89; as a race war, 12–13, 65; symbols in, 54; as total war, 8, 49, 180; and war crime indictments, 175
Worsthorne, Peregrine, 191
Wright, Richard, 37

Yashima, Taro, 93
yellow peril, 68

zainichi, 64
Zone of the Interior (ZI), 6–8, 48–49, 180, 224

Sarah Brouillette, UNESCO and the Fate of the Literary

Sophie Seita, Provisional Avant-Gardes: Little Magazine Communities from Dada to Digital

Guy Davidson, Categorically Famous: Literary Celebrity and Sexual Liberation in 1960s America

Joseph Jonghyun Jeon, Vicious Circuits: Korea's IMF Cinema and the End of the American Century

Lytle Shaw, Narrowcast: Poetry and Audio Research

Stephen Schryer, Maximum Feasible Participation: American Literature and the War on Poverty

Margaret Ronda, Remainders: American Poetry at Nature's End

Jasper Bernes, The Work of Art in the Age of Deindustrialization

Annie McClanahan, Dead Pledges: Debt, Crisis, and Twenty-First-Century Culture

Amy Hungerford, Making Literature Now

J. D. Connor, The Studios After the Studios: Neoclassical Hollywood (1970–2010)

Michael Trask, Camp Sites: Sex, Politics, and Academic Style in Postwar America

Loren Glass, Counterculture Colophon: Grove Press, the Evergreen Review, and the Incorporation of the Avant-Garde

Michael Szalay, *Hip Figures: A Literary History of the Democratic Party*

Jared Gardner, *Projections: Comics and the History of Twenty-First-Century Storytelling*

Jerome Christensen, *America's Corporate Art: The Studio Authorship of Hollywood Motion Pictures*

The authorized representative in the EU for product safety and compliance is:
Mare Nostrum Group
B.V Doelen 72
4831 GR Breda
The Netherlands

www.ingramcontent.com/pod-product-compliance
Lightning Source LLC
Chambersburg PA
CBHW030608230426
43661CB00053B/1886